# Marketing Research and Information
# 2007–2008

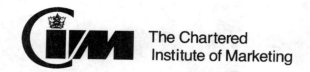
The Chartered
Institute of Marketing

# Marketing Research and Information 2007–2008

Matthew Housden

ELSEVIER

AMSTERDAM • BOSTON • HEIDELBERG • LONDON • NEW YORK • OXFORD
PARIS • SAN DIEGO • SAN FRANCISCO • SINGAPORE • SYDNEY • TOKYO

Butterworth-Heinemann is an imprint of Elsevier

Butterworth-Heinemann is an imprint of Elsevier
Linacre House, Jordan Hill, Oxford OX2 8DP, UK
30 Corporate Drive, Suite 400, Burlington, MA 01803, USA

First edition 2007

**British Library Cataloguing in Publication Data**
A catalogue record for this book is available from the British Library

**Library of Congress Cataloging-in-Publication Data**
A catalogue record for this book is available from the Library of Congress

ISBN: 978-0-7506-8553-5

For information on all Butterworth-Heinemann publications
visit our web site at http://books.elsevier.com

Printed and bound in Italy

07  08  09  10  11     10  9  8  7  6  5  4  3  2  1

Working together to grow
libraries in developing countries

www.elsevier.com | www.bookaid.org | www.sabre.org

ELSEVIER     BOOK AID
             International     Sabre Foundation

# Contents

# Preface
## welcome to the CIM coursebooks

## An introduction from the academic development advisor

The authoring team, Elsevier Butterworth-Heinemann, and I have all aimed to rigorously revise and update the coursebook series to make sure that every title is the best possible study aid and accurately reflects the latest CIM syllabus. This has been further enhanced through independent reviews carried out by CIM.

We have aimed to develop the assessment support to include some additional support for the assignment route as well as the examination, so we hope you will find this helpful.

The authors and Senior Examiners in the series have been commissioned for their CIM course teaching and examining experience, as well as their research into specific curriculum-related areas and their wide general knowledge of the latest thinking in marketing.

We are certain that you will find these coursebooks highly beneficial in terms of the content and assessment opportunities and a study tool that will prepare you for both CIM examinations and continuous/integrative assessment opportunities. They will guide you in a logical and structured way through the details of the syllabus, providing you with the required underpinning knowledge, understanding and application of theory.

The editorial team and authors wish you every success as you embark upon your studies.

*Karen Beamish*
*Academic Development Advisor*

## How to use these coursebooks!

Everyone who has contributed to this series has been careful to structure the books with the exams in mind. Each unit, therefore, covers an essential part of the syllabus. You need to work through the complete coursebook systematically to ensure that you have covered everything you need to know.

This coursebook is divided into units each containing a selection of the following standard elements:

- *Learning objectives* – tell you what you will be expected to know, having read the unit.
- *Syllabus references* – outline what part of the syllabus is covered in the module.
- *Study guides* – tell you how long the unit is and how long its activities take to do.
- *Questions* – are designed to give you practice – they will be similar to those you get in the exam.

- o *Answers* – (at the end of the book) give you a suggested format for answering exam questions. *Remember* there is no such thing as a model answer – you should use these examples only as guidelines.
- o *Activities* – give you a chance to put what you have learned into practice.
- o *Debriefings* – (at the end of the book) shed light on the methodologies involved in the activities.
- o *Hints and tips* – are tips from the senior examiner, examiner or author and are designed to help you avoid common mistakes made by previous candidates and give you guidance on improving your knowledge base.
- o *Insights* – encourage you to contextualize your academic knowledge by reference to real-life experience.
- o *Key definitions* – highlight and explain the key points relevant to that module.
- o *Definitions* – may be used for words you must know to pass the exam.
- o *Summaries* – cover what you should have picked up from reading the unit.
- o *Further study* – provides details of recommended reading in addition to the coursebook.

While you will find that each section of the syllabus has been covered within this text, you might find that the order of some of the topics has been changed. This is because it sometimes makes more sense to put certain topics together when you are studying, even though they might appear in different sections of the syllabus itself. If you are following the reading and other activities, your coverage of the syllabus will be just fine, but do not forget to follow up with trade press reading!

## About MarketingOnline

Elsevier Butterworth-Heinemann offers purchasers of the coursebooks free access to MarketingOnline (www.marketingonline.co.uk), our premier online support engine for the CIM marketing courses. On this site you can benefit from:

- o Fully customizable electronic versions of the coursebooks enabling you to annotate, cut and paste sections of text to create your own tailored learning notes.
- o The capacity to search the coursebook online for instant access to definitions and key concepts.
- o Useful links to e-marketing articles, provided by Dave Chaffey, Director of Marketing Insights Ltd and a leading UK e-marketing consultant, trainer and author.
- o A glossary providing a comprehensive dictionary of marketing terms.
- o A Frequently Asked Questions (FAQs) section providing guidance and advice on common problems or queries.

## Using MarketingOnline

### Logging on

Before you can access MarketingOnline you will first need to get a password. Please go to www.marketingonline.co.uk and click on the registration button where you will then find registration instructions for coursebook purchasers. Once you have got your password, you will need to log on using the onscreen instructions. This will give you access to the various functions of the site.

# unit introduction

The Marketing Research and Information module is an element of stage two of the CIM syllabus and a key part of your study for CIM qualifications including the Post Graduate stage three. The gathering, recording and analysis of information relating to marketing opportunities is a key activity in marketing management. Francis Bacon said, 'Knowledge in itself is power'. Anyone working in business today knows that information lies at the heart of good decision-making; this is especially true in marketing. This module provides you with the knowledge and skill to manage marketing information, and the more specialist knowledge to plan, undertake and present the results from market research.

By the time you have completed this unit you will:

o Understand the role of Marketing Research and Information within the CIM syllabus

o Understand the relation of key skills for marketers and Professional Standards for Marketers (statements of marketing practice) to the CIM syllabus

o Understand the layout of this coursebook and how to use it effectively

o Understand the terms that support your learning through the coursebook

o Be aware of the key supporting texts that you will need to look at as part of your programme of study of stage two of the syllabus

o Understand the role of marketing research and information in business.

## Key definitions

**MRS** – The Market Research Society, the society responsible for professional standards in the market research industry in the United Kingdom.

**ESOMAR** – The European Society of Market Research linked to WAPOR, the World Association of Public and Opinion Research, fulfils a similar role to the MRS.

**Syllabus** – The outline of your course.

1

**Aims and objectives** – The broad educational aims of the course and the more precise learning objectives that deliver the aims.

**Key skills** – Areas of knowledge and competency common to business professionals.

**Professional Marketing Standards (Statements of marketing practice)** – Link aims and objectives to the practice of marketing.

## Study Guide

This unit should take around 3 hours to complete.

# Introduction

The Stage 2 syllabus for the CIM Professional Diploma in Marketing is designed to prepare students for roles in operational marketing management. The syllabus is a crucial document that defines and identifies the areas for your study across all the modules you take for the Diploma.

It also defines key supporting areas for study of the marketing discipline including key skills and Professional Marketing Standards (previously statements of marketing practice). These are covered later in this unit.

The Marketing Research and Information module within stage two of the CIM syllabus has five major components. These are:

1. Information and research for decision-making
2. Customer databases
3. Marketing research in context
4. Research methodologies
5. Presenting and evaluating information to develop business advantage.

A brief insight into each of these components appears below. However, you may find it useful to look at the syllabus in detail in your student handbook or at the CIM website, www.cim.co.uk.

# Information and research for decision-making

## Syllabus elements 1.1–1.4

These elements of the syllabus relate to the role of information in the decision-making process within organizations and the management of marketing. Traditionally, marketers have used the marketing information system (MkIS) and its components to inform the decision-making process. Central to the process was the use of marketing research. Today with the development of customer databases, the marketer has a significant additional weapon in his armoury. We have more information than ever before. And yet companies are still making poor decisions, and still fail to meet their customers' needs effectively and efficiently.

This element of the syllabus explores the background to and the development of information management and the growth of the 'information-based' economy. It links this to the way in which organizations should determine their marketing information requirements and how information users should specify their needs within the organization in order to drive profitable lasting relationships with customers. It also explores formats and components of the technical systems that are available to marketers to manage information and support decision-making.

## Customer databases

### Syllabus elements 2.1–2.5

These elements of the syllabus cover the role of marketing databases in the management of Customer Relationship Management (CRM) systems. They look at the process of developing, maintaining and enhancing the customer database. It explores the role of customer and prospect profiling. In an age in which an ever increasing amount of customer data is captured, the syllabus covers the vital role of data warehousing, data marts and data mining. This allows for actionable intelligence to be distilled from the huge amounts of data to which many organizations have access. Finally, this section of the syllabus explores the key area of the relationship of market research with database marketing. It looks at the way research can enhance data that is captured on customers, and presents the two methods working together to produce actionable intelligence. Clive Humby described this process as the T principle. The database provides broad but shallow data about customers. Market research provides narrow but deep information. Below, Figure 1.1 shows how this can work. The Target Group Index (TGI) is a research service run by BMRB. It provides real insight into customers' behaviour and motivation in many markets (more about TGI later). In this example, TGI is run against the internal database and these are linked by common characteristics. This process enhances the data that is held on the database whilst keeping TGI responses anonymous.

Match customer database to 3 years of TGI respondents

*Figure 1.1* The first T process TGI and the database
*Source*: Clive Humby BMRB

Market research and the database can together work incredibly effectively in generating advantage for organizations. The use of data from the club card scheme has propelled Tesco into leadership of the highly competitive UK grocery retailing sector. But this has been done not just using data, but through careful analysis of that data and the input from research.

3

## Case history

### Tesco

Tesco is an excellent example of a company that is successfully utilizing the tools of marketing research and transactional data to improve its customer focus. The device that Tesco uses to capture transactional data on its customers is Clubcard. Clubcard was set up in 1995 and today over 80 per cent of all transactions are captured. As you can imagine, this is a huge amount of data. In fact over 50 gigabytes of data is captured, including 250 million sales items for 10 million customers in 2365 stores. Tesco now accounts for just over 12 per cent of all retail high street sales by value and turn over was £34 billion in 2005 from 51.8 million square feet of retail selling space. Tesco's data analysis company is DunnHumby and it is their job to make sense of the data. In 1995 the data was used to create simple market segmentation models. Today, with enhancement through a range of market research methodologies, Tesco is producing mailings to its Clubcard customers with over 6 million variations. We'll look at Tesco again later.

*Source*: DunnHumby.

### Experian and marketing research

Experian runs the Mosaic profiling system. They are now investing in the development of marketing research services to their clients, providing them with breadth of information through Mosaic and depth through bespoke or panel based surveys.

## Marketing research in context

### Syllabus elements 3.1–3.6

These syllabus elements cover the nature, size and scope of the industry that supports the provision and management of the marketing research process. This includes the suppliers of research services in their diverse forms as well as the providers of database and other information services.

The industry has changed dramatically over the last decade, and research companies have internationalized and expanded their activities to include the full range of online services and techniques. In many ways, the research industry is always at the leading edge of what is contemporary in business, as companies seek to test new ideas and new technologies in the market place through the research process.

The syllabus covers the stages of a research programme and the procedures and briefing of external agencies. The ability to brief, motivate and get the best out of suppliers is a key part of the marketing manager's job and this remains true in market research. The ability to communicate a research problem and inspire the agency to produce a thoughtful, well-structured research plan is crucial to the process of marketing decision-making.

It also outlines the ethical and social responsibilities of the researcher as laid down within the codes of conduct and legislation. More and more data is being captured on customers and research shows that there is a high degree of distrust in the use of data. The recent problem for the industry over the use of the electoral register testifies to this. The responsibility for the careful custodianship of customers' data is laid down in law through the 1998 Data Protection Act and through a number of codes of conduct that relate to data protection and the responsibilities of companies to individuals. Failure to comply with these codes of conduct and self-regulation has serious implications for the future of data-driven marketing. Failure to comply with legislation is of course even more serious!

## Research methodologies

### Syllabus elements 4.1–4.6

These elements of the syllabus deal with the marketing research task and the methods that support the research process. They cover the range of methods and techniques that underpin good research design. The design of marketing research methodologies is a complex task and it draws on techniques that have been tested in other subject areas; in psychology and the social sciences and particularly in statistics. Many students are worried about the numeracy skills required to complete this course. You do need to be numerate – after all, figures are the raw material of the business world. However, the key thing in marketing research is to know the right questions to ask and to understand what the statistics do to data. Statistics enable decisions to be made that reduce the risk to the business and are an invaluable tool in the process of effective marketing.

The syllabus also looks at the role of secondary or desk research in research both on- and off-line. Secondary data is data that has been published elsewhere. Current techniques draw heavily on the Internet and this has changed this aspect of research beyond recognition. We still need to be able to distinguish good from poor data and the workbook gives a range of techniques that you can use to determine this.

The syllabus distinguishes between and defines both qualitative and quantitative research and the range of techniques that are used to gather this information. Finally, the syllabus explores the fascinating area of questionnaire and topic guide design and delivery, and the statistical techniques that support research design and analysis.

## Presenting and evaluating information to develop business advantage

### Syllabus elements 5.1–5.3

These final syllabus elements cover the evaluation and presentation of research data and conclusions. The syllabus covers the statistical basis of the analysis of quantitative research data. It also covers the range of techniques that are used in the analysis of qualitative data. Finally, the syllabus covers the production of written research reports and oral presentations of the results.

## Understanding aims and objectives of marketing research and information, and achieving your learning outcomes

Having reviewed the CIM syllabus for this module, you can see that the syllabus is broken down into six levels.

1. Aims and objectives
2. Related Professional Marketing Standards (statements of marketing practice)
3. Knowledge and skills requirements
4. Related skills for marketers

5. Assessment
6. Support materials.

It is important to understand the role of each of these in informing your learning on the module. As a student on CIM courses, you are, of course, learning to be a marketing professional and also to study more effectively. As the marketer has a range of tools at his disposal to deliver effective marketing, the learner has a range of tools to help him study more effectively. Understanding the syllabus and the terms that marketing educators use will help you use this manual more effectively, and help your progress towards success on CIM courses.

## Aims and objectives

The aims and objectives are the broad objectives for the module as a whole. They explain clearly what the module is designed to achieve and, most important, give you a clear idea of the broad areas of study and what you will be learning.

You can see that the key aims and objectives of the marketing research and information module are to 'provide participants with both the knowledge and skills to manage marketing information, and the more specialist knowledge and skills required to plan, undertake and present results from market research' (CIM, 2003).

## Related professional marketing standards (statements of marketing practice)

- o These standards link the syllabus to the tasks of the marketing professional. They link with other statements that are included in the design of other modules within stages two and three of the syllabus. By the time you complete the syllabus, you will have shown that you possess the skills that sustain the marketing manager in today's business environment. The standards have been developed by the CIM in consultation with senior marketers. The standards cover six marketing roles, business competencies within those roles and the expected level of engagement with those roles at four levels: support, practitioner, manager and senior. The Professional Diploma sets its standard at manager level, the standards for this level are laid out below and you can see that some are more relevant to the Marketing Research and Information course than others for example: The evaluation of information requirements, the management of research projects and the marketing information system.
- o The evaluation and presentation of information for business advantage.
- o The ability to contribute information and ideas to the strategy process.

However, these standards must be set in the context of the range of skills the marketing manager is expected to possess and some of these are delivered more obviously by the other courses that will be taken by you.

## Professional marketing standards professional diploma in marketing

### Research and analysis

#### Understand markets
- o Obtain information about markets
- o Analyse information

- Identify information requirements and manage research projects and the MkIS
- Evaluate and present information for business advantage.

## Strategy and planning

### Develop strategy and marketing plans
- Influence strategy formulation
- Produce marketing plans
- Contribute information and ideas to the strategy process
- Create competitive operational marketing plans.

## Brands

### Develop and manage brands and reputation
- Create effective brands
- Manage brands and brand reputation
- Create and build competitive brands
- Manage competitive brands and coordinate brand support activities.

## Implementing marketing programmes

### Communicate with stakeholders
- Develop effective communications
- Deliver effective communications
- Create effective communications plans
- Manage communications activities.

### Manage products and services
- Develop competitive products and services
- Manage competitive products and services
- Prepare business case for a product/service and progress it to market
- Manage and maintain competitive products/services or portfolio.

### Manage and set price
- Develop competitive pricing policies
- Implement pricing policies
- Create competitive and sustainable pricing strategies
- Manage implementation and monitor the effectiveness of pricing strategies.

### Manage channels
- Develop effective channels to market
- Provide support to channel members
- Establish and develop effective support for channels to market
- Manage and monitor support to channel members.

### Manage customer relationships
- Maintain and improve customer relationships
- Deliver effective customer service
- Establish and monitor activities and information for delivering effective customer relationships
- Manage and monitor provision of effective customer service.

### Manage programmes and projects

o Plan and prepare projects
o Manage the running of programmes and projects
o Plan marketing projects and prepare budgets
o Manage and report on delivery against plan and objectives.

## Measure effectiveness

### Monitor and evaluate the effectiveness of marketing

o Measure the effectiveness of marketing activities
o Explain the success or failure of marketing activities
o Define measurements appropriate to the plan or business case and ensure they are undertaken
o Evaluate activities and identify improvements using measurement data.

## Managing people

### Managing marketing teams

o Develop teams and individuals to enhance marketing performance
o Manage a marketing team
o Work with other functions and disciplines
o Maintain relationships with other functions and disciplines within the organization
o Enhance own performance
o Encourage and help others to develop their competencies relevant to a marketing role
o Manage change
o Embrace change and influence others to modify behaviours and attitudes.

## Learning outcomes and knowledge and skills requirements

Learning outcomes are developed to narrow and focus the aims of the programme around specific subject areas. They are interesting for you as the assessment is designed against the outcomes. If you understand the learning outcomes of the module then you have a clear idea of what the examiners will be looking for in your assessment. They are also linked to the knowledge and skills requirements, which describe the main content of the course. Some learning outcomes are delivered through the same knowledge and skills requirements (Table 1.1).

*Table 1.1* Learning outcomes and knowledge and skills requirements

| Learning outcomes | Knowledge and skills requirements |
|---|---|
| Identify appropriate marketing information and market research requirements for business decision-making | 1.1 Demonstrate a broad appreciation of the need for information in marketing and its role in the overall marketing process |
| | 1.2 Explain the concept of knowledge management and its importance in the knowledge-based economy |
| | 1.3 Explain how organizations determine their marketing information requirements and the key elements of user specifications for information |
| | 1.4 Demonstrate an understanding of marketing management support systems and their different formats and components |

| | | |
|---|---|---|
| Plan for and manage the acquisition, storage, retrieval and reporting of information on the organization's market and customers | 2.1 | Demonstrate an understanding of the application, the role in CRM and the benefits of customer databases |
| | 2.2 | Describe the process for setting up a marketing database |
| | 2.3 | Explain how organizations profile customers and prospects |
| | 2.4 | Explain the principles of data warehouses, data marts and data mining |
| | 2.5 | Explain the relationship between database marketing and marketing research |
| Explain the process involved in purchasing market research and the development of effective client–supplier relationships | 3.1 | Describe the nature and structure of the market research |
| | 3.2 | Explain the stages of the market research process industry |
| | 3.3 | Describe the procedures for selecting a market research supplier |
| | 3.4 | Explain the ethical and social responsibilities inherent in the market research task |
| Write a research brief to meet the requirements of an organization to support a specific plan or business decision | 3.5 | Identify information requirements to support a specific business decision in an organization and develop a research brief to meet the requirements |
| Develop a research proposal to fulfil a given research brief | 3.6 | Develop a research proposal to fulfil a given research brief |
| Evaluate the appropriateness of different qualitative and quantitative research methodologies to meet different research situations | 4.1 | Explain the uses, benefits and limitations of secondary |
| | 4.2 | Recognize the key sources of primary and secondary data |
| | 4.3 | Describe and compare the various procedures for observing behaviour |
| Design and plan a research programme | 4.4 | Describe and compare the various methods for collecting qualitative and quantitative data |
| | 4.5 | Explain the theory and processes involved in sampling |
| Design a questionnaire and topic guide | 4.6 | Design a questionnaire and discussion guide to meet a project's research objectives |
| Interpret quantitative and qualitative data, and present coherent and appropriate recommendations that lead to effective marketing and business decisions | 5.1 | Demonstrate an ability to use techniques for analysing qualitative and quantitative data |
| | 5.2 | Write a research report aimed at supporting marketing decisions |
| | 5.3 | Plan and design an oral presentation of market research reports. Critically evaluate the outcomes and quality of a research project |
| | 5.4 | Plan and design an oral presentation of market research reports |

*Source*: CIM module two syllabus

# Key skills for marketers

Key skills relate to the broader areas of learning and knowledge required by professional marketing managers, they are defined in the syllabus document as:

'Key skills for marketers are areas of knowledge and competency common to business professionals. They fall outside the CIM's syllabus, providing underpinning knowledge and skills. As such they will be treated as systemic to all marketing activities, rather than subjects treated independently in their turn...The key skills for marketers have been identified from research carried out in organizations where marketers are working. They are closely related to key skills and graduate skills defined as part of the national framework by the UK government. They are relevant to marketers in all organizations since they encompass the knowledge and skills concerned with identifying, solving and delivering solutions to problems in organizations. Definitions of the national key skills are available as downloadable PDF files on the QCA website (see www.qca.org.uk/6507). (CIM, 2004)

For marketers these key skills cover the following areas:

## Using ICT and the Internet

Planning and using different sources to search for and select information; explore, develop and exchange information and derive new information; and present information including text, numbers and images.

## Using financial information and metrics
Planning and interpreting information from different sources; carrying out calculations; and presenting and justifying findings.

## Presenting information
Contributing to discussions; making a presentation; reading and synthesizing information and writing different types of document.

## Improving own learning and performance
Agreeing targets and planning how these will be met; using plans to meet targets; and reviewing progress.

## Working with others
Planning work and agreeing objectives, responsibilities and working arrangements; seeking to establish and maintain cooperative working relationships; and reviewing work and agreeing ways of future collaborative work.

## Problem-solving
Exploring problems, comparing different ways of solving them and selecting options; planning and implementing options; and applying agreed methods for checking problems have been solved.

## Applying business law
Identifying, applying and checking compliance with relevant law when undertaking marketing activities.

Not all of these will apply directly to the Marketing research and Information module but by the end of your studies on the CIM your learning will have covered them.

## Assessment

There are two types of assessment that you may encounter. The first is the traditional written exam and the second is a work-based project. Whatever you choose, the content of the assessment will reflect the content of the learning outcomes, and knowledge and skills requirement. It is really important that when you revise for the exams that you cover the entire syllabus. Questions may relate to detailed elements of the curriculum but the entire syllabus will be used to inform the examination. It is important that you also include a range of well-worked examples that allow you to illustrate your answers and bring them to life. Remember the CIM course is giving you a licence to practise marketing, and the use of examples in the right context shows that you understand how the theory can be applied in a business context.

The exam will be practical in nature. Questions will ask you to solve a problem or prepare a briefing document, write a plan or evaluate between different techniques. It will ask you to use the theory to deliver solutions to particular situations and show that you understand how to apply the theory in a variety of business contexts.

Preparation for the exam is really important and the CIM will support you in this task. www.cim.co.uk provides a range of exam guidelines, tips and examples. You should practise writing against the clock. It is really hard work to write freehand for any length of time, particularly as most of us now rarely write freehand.

## Recommended resource materials

These are listed in the syllabus and in the curriculum information section of this text. They will form the background reading for the course as a whole. This workbook reflects the resources that are recommended, and adds to them with other books, websites, examples and case studies. The secret is to read widely and keep careful notes.

 **Activity 1.1**

The use of a portfolio of cases derived from your reading of the trade press and other materials is recommended. This is a valuable practice throughout your career. Your reading of the trade press is vital to keep up to speed with current practice. As a minimum for this module you should include Marketing and Marketing week, Campaign, Precision Marketing and Direct Response and Research, the magazine of the Market Research Society. It should go without saying that you also keep up to date with the general business press including the *Financial Times*, *The Economist* and the *Wall Street Journal*. It is important that you keep a file of a range of material that relates to marketing research, database marketing and CRM, at home and in international markets.

You may choose to access these resources online at www.mad.co.uk, www.ft.com, www.economist.com and www.wsj.com.

A range of websites reporting on the marketing research and information sector is listed in the curriculum information section.

## Summary

This unit introduced the programme of study you are about to embark on. We looked in detail at the CIM curriculum and saw the importance of understanding the contents of the curriculum and its objectives and assessment policies. This will guide and focus your study on key elements of the course.

We looked at each section of the book in detail and introduced the broad concepts that will be explored in more detail in the rest of the coursebook.

## Further study

Go to the CIM website at www.cim.co.uk and familiarize yourself with the material that is available to you.

## Hints and tips

Take a look at the following sites www.mrs.org and www.esomar.org. They are packed with useful material.

## Bibliography

CIM (2003) *Syllabus for Stage Two*, CIM, p. 19.

CIM (2004) CIM Professional Diploma Syllabus.

# unit 2 information in the knowledge economy

By the end of this unit you will be able to

- Outline the development of the information industry

- Explain the integration of marketing research and database marketing

- Identify the key drivers behind the growth of the knowledge economy

- Be able to define key terms including database marketing, marketing research, data mining and data warehousing, Marketing Information Systems (MkIS) and Decision Support Systems (DSS)

- Understand the nature and extent of the marketing information industry

- Identify the key organizations involved in the information industry

- Understand and analyse the role of marketing research and information in decision-making in organizations

- Place marketing research and database marketing within the context of the MKIS and DSS

- Understand the broad ethical dimensions of research and database marketing

- Understand the principles underpinning legislation and codes of conduct that relate to data protection

- Be able to outline the 8 principles of the 1998 Data Protection Act

- Identify the sources for the MRS, ICC/ESOMAR and DMA codes of Practice

- Cover syllabus elements 1.1, 1.2, 1.3, 2.5, 3.1, 3.6, 5.4. See the table below.

| Learning outcomes | Knowledge and skills requirements |
|---|---|
| Identify appropriate marketing information and market research requirements for business decision-making | 1.1 Demonstrate a broad appreciation of the need for information in marketing and its role in the overall marketing process<br><br>1.2 Explain the concept of knowledge management and its importance in the knowledge-based economy<br><br>1.3 Explain how organizations determine their marketing information requirements and the key elements of user specifications for information<br><br>1.4 Demonstrate an understanding of marketing management support systems and their different formats and components<br><br>2.5 Explain the relationship between database marketing and marketing research<br><br>3.1 Describe the nature and structure of the market research industry<br><br>3.6 Develop a research proposal to fulfil a given research brief<br><br>5.4 Plan and design an oral presentation of market research reports |

## Key definitions

**Marketing** – Marketing is the management process responsible for identifying, anticipating and satisfying customer requirements profitably (CIM, 2003).

**Knowledge** – A fluid mix of framed experience, values, contextual information and expert insight that provides a framework for evaluating and incorporating new experience and information. It originates and is applied in the minds of knowers. In organizations, it often becomes embedded not only in documents or repositories, but also in organizational routines, processes, practices and norms (Davenport and Prusak, 1998).

**Knowledge management** – Embodies organizational processes that seek synergistic combination of data and information processing capacity of information technologies, and the creative and innovative capacity of human beings (Malhotra, 1998).

**Marketing research** – The collection, analysis and communication of information undertaken to assist decision-making in marketing (Wilson, 2003).

**The marketing database** – A manual or computerized source of data relevant to marketing decision-making about an organization's customers (Wilson, 2003).

**Data mining** – The process of extracting hidden and actionable information from large databases.

**Data warehouse** – A database whose records contain information aggregated from multiple locations on a customer basis.

> **Data mart** – A cut-down version of a data warehouse, containing only that data deemed useful for analysis and reporting purposes.
>
> **Data capture** – The process and system for gathering and recording data on customers.
>
> **ESOMAR** – European Society for Opinion and Market Research.

## Study Guide

This unit should take you around 3 hours to complete. You should supplement your reading of the unit with at least 3 hours' activity around the unit including reading relevant sections of the recommended texts and reviewing the trade press to begin your case study and clippings portfolio.

## Introduction

As we have already heard from Francis Bacon (1597), 'Knowledge itself is power'. Bacon was referring to power in a political context and was writing at a time when knowledge was an exclusive product. We all know, however, the value of good information in our day-to-day lives. Today the problem is not accessing information but analysing this to produce intelligence upon which we can act. We also know the value of information in our business lives; the information that allows you to pre-empt a competitor's sales promotion campaign; the customer insight that allows for a direct mail piece to land on the doorstep just as the consumer is deciding whether or not to buy, or the research that allows your website to have greater impact. Peter Chisnall (2004) takes Bacon's idea and applies it in a business context. In his classic text on marketing research, he described good information as 'the raw material used by management in deciding a company's policy and day to day operations'.

He is right. Without pertinent, reliable, accurate and timely information, decision-making would be impossible. Management decisions would be made in a vacuum. Without information and intelligent analysis of the data, the organization is disconnected from its markets, suppliers, people, customers and future.

## One more time, what is marketing?

The starting point for this coursebook has to be the definition of marketing. Can you remember it?

 **Activity 2.1**

See if you can remember the CIM definition of marketing. If you can't remember the whole thing, try to write a paraphrased version. You may be able to remember other definitions. What are the differences? What are the similarities? You may need to visit your notes for the planning module.

Let us have a look at the CIM definition in detail.

*Marketing is a management process.* We will not dwell too long on this. It is enough to say that marketing is about getting things done through and with people. We need to work with a range of colleagues, suppliers and intermediaries to deliver satisfaction to our customers.

'Customers' is an interesting word. They are the only reason businesses exist. It is easy to say marketing is about customers but even this simple word has multiple meaning in the marketing context. Are we talking about current customers, lapsed customers, future customers, profitable customers, best customers or key account customers? The list is as long as the number of segmentation variables we can use.

Of equal interest to us are the next few words.

*Marketing is about identifying customer needs.* This sounds straightforward. Let us think about this in more detail.

 ## Activity 2.2

I buy mineral water. What need am I fulfilling?

Write down as many as you can think of.

It may help you to think about the context in which a person may buy water. Think hard, you should have at least 6 points.

*The next part of the definition is concerned with the anticipation of customer needs.* This task is even harder. Forecasting has been described as trying to tell someone where to steer a car by looking through the rear window. Think about the pace of development of new technology. Gordon Moore of Intel Corporation, the computer chip manufacturer, has said that the processing power of computers will double every 18 months and the price will halve. This has become known as Moore's Law. He was right and wrong. The pace of change has been faster. Those companies that are at the forefront of the IT revolution have found it very hard to anticipate customer needs as the customers themselves have found it hard to understand the pace of change and how this might affect their buying patterns.

## The IT revolution and the airlines

In the mid-1990s, airlines were re-specifying their fleets. The lead-time for commissioning and delivery of new planes is significant. Airlines asked their business customers what changes they would like to see. Some said more legroom, some said better food and more choice of films. Some said that they would like to telephone from the plane. Only a few mentioned at-seat power jacks for their laptops. This meant that many of the new planes that came on line in the late 1990s and early 2000 did not allow business executives to run laptops other than on the laptop's battery.

It is not always enough simply to ask your customers what they want. The questions have to be asked in the right way. We will look at this in detail later on.

Some markets change quickly, others evolve but they always change. As Hugh Davidson (1997) says 'tomorrow's standards are always higher'. The information strategy of the organization must be set up to ensure that these changes can be anticipated, monitored and acted upon. Risk can never be eliminated from business decision-making. The key thing is to manage and, where possible, reduce the levels of risk to which the organization is subject to within acceptable levels relative to required return on shareholders' investments.

*The next part of the definition is concerned with customer satisfaction.* This has been an area of growth in marketing over the last 10 years as concepts of relationship marketing and Customer Relationship Management (CRM) have become popularized and applied in businesses. The measurement of lifetime value and work on loyalty (notably by Frederick Reichheld (2001) in his book *The Loyalty Effect*) has shifted the emphasis from one of sales and new business to customer retention and repeat business. A corollary of this has been a focus on customer satisfaction. The idea is that satisfied customers stay loyal, and loyal customers are more profitable. Well again research shows that this is not always the case. Customers may be satisfied but still leave. They may be enticed away by better offers or products or may no longer have a need for our products or services. They may seek variety or new experiences. Jones and Sasser's (1995) work published in the Harvard Business Review confirms that satisfied customers do defect.

So establishing levels of satisfaction is not enough. The organization must ensure that the underlying attitudes and behaviours are revealed. If customers do defect, then the organization needs to ensure that the reasons for leaving are established and changes are made if appropriate.

*Finally, the definition talks about profit.* The reason we are in business. Simple – well not really. The development of the marketing database that captures data on the buying behaviour of customers means that we can begin to see that some customers are more profitable than others. We can see that the Pareto Effect which states that 20 per cent of customers account for around 80 per cent of profit is generally true. Indeed in many businesses less than 20 per cent of customers account for more than 80 per cent of profits. So if under Henry Ford all customers were created equal, we now can prove that some customers are more equal than others.

## P and O and Elsie Mader

P and O ran a competition to establish who had been on P and O cruises the longest. The winner was Elsie Mader. She had been cruising with P and O so many times that her total time aboard came to more than 10 years.

*Source:* IDM Course Material.

Companies are using this information to work out which customers they need to retain, and by profiling existing highly profitable customers they can more easily identify the type of customer they wish to recruit. For P and O this would be more Elsie Maders! More controversially some companies are using this transactional data to deselect or 'sack' customers who are unprofitable.

Another aspect of profit is deciding when to take profit. Companies using direct response techniques know that many customers are acquired at a loss. The relationship with customers only makes sense from a business perspective over time.

## Direct insurance

The average cost of acquiring a customer in the insurance market has been estimated as £120. If the premium is £200, it is clear that this does not allow for very much profit to be made on a one-off transaction. This is why as soon as you buy insurance products you will receive mailings for extended cover, other insurance products or other financial services products.

So the definition of marketing is not as straightforward as perhaps it first appeared. At the centre of all the elements of the definition is the need for information and research, analysis and insight that allow for a depth of understanding and marketing decisions made at reduced risk.

This applies to all organizations whether they be in business-to-consumer (b2c) markets, in business-to-business (b2b) markets, in fund-raising or in government or not-for-profit markets. At the heart of all successful enterprises is managed information. This may come from marketing research or from the customer database but, as Alan Wilson points out in the module's core text, it is integration that is important.

> *Integrated information is critical to effective decision-making. Marketing information sources can be thought of as separate jigsaw pieces; only when they are connected does the whole picture become clear. Taking decisions by looking at each of the pieces individually is not only inefficient but is likely to result in wrong assumptions and decisions being made.* (Wilson, 2003)

The role of knowledge management within organizations has become central to the delivery of the above definition of marketing orientation. Tom Peters and Robert Waterman (1995) in their influential book *In Search Of Excellence* attempted to identify the characteristics of successful companies. Published in 1995, at the beginning of the information revolution, the book identified customer focus and knowledge acquired largely through the use of marketing research as central to the success of the companies they researched. Since 1995 many of the companies they researched have gone out of business or no longer exist in the same structure! However, the point that they made is still valid. In the FT on 18 November 2003 Charlie Dawson wrote:

> *The way to make a difference is to get managers to see the world from the customers' perspective ... with the right set up guided by formal research it can change their world ... (however) the customer never makes it beyond the research chart or the mission statement. Given this context market research is bound to fail. It is the market researchers who connect with customers but then have to turn their learning into meeting fodder.*

What we see here is that advantage in the market place does not simply come from carrying out research, it is about identifying, collating, understanding, analysing and acting upon the many diverse sources of knowledge within an organization. Wal-Mart is one organization that manages this very well.

## Case study

### Wal-Mart knows its business

Hurricane Frances was on its way, barreling across the Caribbean, threatening a direct hit on Florida's Atlantic coast. Residents made for higher ground, but far away, in Bentonville, Ark., executives at Wal-Mart Stores decided that the situation offered a great opportunity for one of their newest data-driven weapons, something that the company calls predictive technology. A week ahead of the storm's landfall, Linda M. Dillman, Wal-Mart's chief information officer, pressed her staff to come up with forecasts based on what had happened when Hurricane Charley struck several weeks earlier. Backed by the trillions of bytes' worth of shopper history that is stored in Wal-Mart's computer network, she felt that the company could 'start predicting what's going to happen, instead of waiting for it to happen', as she put it. The experts mined the data and found that the stores would indeed need certain products – and not just the usual flashlights. 'We didn't know in the past that strawberry Pop-Tarts increased in sales, like seven times their normal sales rate, ahead of a hurricane', Ms. Dillman said in a recent interview. 'And the pre-hurricane top-selling item was beer.'

Thanks to those insights, trucks filled with toaster pastries and six-packs were soon speeding down Interstate 95 toward Wal-Mart in the path of Frances. Most of the products that were stocked for the storm sold quickly, the company said. Such knowledge, Wal-Mart has learned, is not only power. It is profit, too.

Plenty of retailers collect data about their stores and their shoppers, and many use the information to try to improve sales. Target Stores, for example, introduced a branded Visa card in 2001 and has used it, along with an arsenal of gadgetry, to gather data ever since. But Wal-Mart amasses more data about the products it sells and its shoppers' buying habits than anyone else, so much so that some privacy advocates worry about potential for abuse.

With 3600 stores in the United States and roughly 100 million customers walking through the doors each week, Wal-Mart has access to information about a broad slice of America – from individual Social Security and driver's license numbers to geographic proclivities for Mallomars, or lipsticks, or jugs of antifreeze. The data are gathered item by item at the checkout aisle, then recorded, mapped and updated by store, by state, by region.

By its own count, Wal-Mart has 460 terabytes of data stored on Teradata mainframes, made by NCR, at its Bentonville headquarters. To put that in perspective, the Internet has less than half as much data, according to experts. Information about products, and often about customers, is most often obtained at checkout scanners. Wireless hand-held units, operated by clerks and managers, gather more inventory data. In most cases, such detail is stored for indefinite lengths of time. Sometimes it is divided into categories or mapped across computer models, and it is increasingly being used to answer discount retailing's rabbinical questions, like how many cashiers are needed during certain hours at a particular store.

All of the data are precious to Wal-Mart. The information forms the basis of the sales meetings the company holds every Saturday, and it is shot across desktops throughout its headquarters and into the places where it does business around the world. Wal-Mart shares some information with its suppliers – a company like Kraft, for example, can tap into a private extranet, called Retail Link, to see how well its products are selling.

*New York Times*, November 2004.

...anizations, however, are still not geared up to manage this process effectively. What ...d is a significant cultural and internal organizational change. However, many compa- ...this change very difficult to manage. Baker and Mouncey (2003) describe this as a ...faced by many businesses locked, as they say, in a 'cultural prison'.

> *We have been struck by how repetitive some of the messages have been and found ourselves asking why so little change has followed. We would offer the view that the industry has not moved quickly enough and appears to have been struck by a level of inertia characteristic of 'cultural prisoners' – those who find themselves doing things the way they've always been done simply because that's the way they've always been done. Are there any 'cultural architects' within the industry in a position to move now to build a brighter future?* (Baker and Mouncey, 2003)

What these organizations find is that they are unable to gear up the knowledge capital that has been established within their business.

Customer information may exist in silos that are not connected, leading to vital gaps in under- standing and failure to provide basic service standards. As we will see later, when customers give us information they expect us to use it responsibly and to improve levels of service to them (Figure 2.1).

*Figure 2.1* Multiple sources of data
*Source*: Teradata

A single view of the truth provides greater knowledge and insight (Figure 2.2).

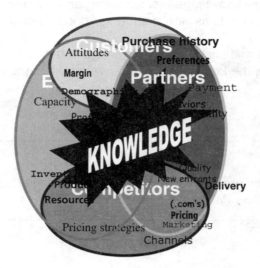

*Figure 2.2* The aim of knowledge management
*Source*: Teradata

These organizations may find that knowledge rests with individuals or departments within the company and that these political assets are fiercely protected. For example, sales people or key account managers may see the introduction of a marketing database as a serious threat to their position rather than a means by which their efficiency and effectiveness (and their commissions) may be improved. These multiple systems, for example, separate sales, accounts and fulfilment databases operating under different protocols and on different plat-forms cost money to run and maintain and lead to duplication and wastefulness, disillusioned staff and very often, the research tells us, unhappy and poorly served customers. Equally the lack of systems for capturing and storing information means that when key personnel leave an organization they take their knowledge assets with them.

The aim of knowledge management is to integrate systems and individuals to enable and encourage knowledge transfer between employees and other stakeholders. For example, knowledge management systems may work between retailers and their suppliers to ensure 'Just in Time' delivery of new stock, to plan and implement sales promotion campaigns and to jointly manage the marketing research that underpins new product development. In the United States, Wal-Mart is an excellent example of a company that gears up its knowledge assets to produce value for itself, its stakeholders and its customers. Knowledge is often defined as distinct from information. Whilst much of this is semantics the key distinguishing factor is that knowledge is not data. Data are facts; knowledge involves interpreting, analysing and under-standing facts to produce actionable intelligence. Knowledge within organizations can take many forms; these are usefully identified by Yahya and Goh (2002):

o *Individual knowledge* – Resides in the mind of an individual.
o *Organizational knowledge* – Is knowledge gained through the interactions between technologies, techniques and people?
o *Explicit knowledge* – Can be documented and shared through IT, it is 'structured, fixed and externalized and conscious'. Marketing research data is a good example of this type of knowledge.
o *Tacit knowledge* – Is hard to codify and document. It lies in human behaviour and perception and is personal, cognitive and context sensitive. It may be important in interpersonal relationships within a business and may be important in creating and sustaining the culture of knowledge transfer within the system.

**21**

The aim of Knowledge Management is to:

o Identify where knowledge resides within an organization
o Develop mechanisms for capturing, documenting, enhancing or augmenting this knowledge
o Transferring and sharing this knowledge and
o Finally using the knowledge to improve marketing and business performance.

 **Activity 2.3**

You are the insight manager for a large food manufacturer. Outline the sources of knowledge that might feed a knowledge management system.

## Marketing management support systems – The marketing information system (MkIS)

The 'MkIS' is a term that has largely fallen out of favour in the marketing world. It has been replaced by a whole tranche of new descriptors, the most common amongst these being CRM systems and Database marketing. What we are looking at in this section is the range of tools that exists to help the marketing manager handle the vast amount of information that he or she has access to today.

The MkIS is the system that organizations use to put information at the heart of the decision-making process.

The MkIS defined by Kotler 'consists of people, equipment and procedures to gather, sort, analyse, evaluate and distribute timely and accurate information to marketing decision makers' (Kotler *et al.*, 1999).

The typical MkIS consists of four elements:

1. *The marketing research system* – This is the backbone of the marketing information system. However, the MkIS also contains other elements. These are:
2. *The marketing intelligence system* – This refers to the published data existing in the market place. It may include published research reports, government statistics or the national or trade press. We will look at this in detail when we examine secondary research.
3. *The decision-support system* – The decision-support system contains the tools needed to make sense of data; it may include statistical packages and the Intranet with a range of tools and information designed to help marketers make decisions.
4. *Internal records* – These include sales records, accounts records, details on past communications and the results of previously commissioned marketing research.

These last elements are often now consolidated within the marketing database. Let us look at the two mainstays of the MkIS in turn, starting with marketing research.

# What is marketing research?

Let us start with a few definitions. Alan Wilson (2003) in the course text defines marketing research as, 'The collection, analysis and communication of information undertaken to assist decision-making in marketing'. This picks-up on the essential characteristics of marketing research, that is, the gathering and analysis of information to inform decisions. This decision-making aspect is important. Marketing research should enable decision-making. Some authors would argue that a decision MUST result from the marketing research process, and in practice this is most often the case, even if the decision is to do nothing!

 ## Activity 2.4

On page 4 of Wilson's book he identifies four characteristics of marketing research. Go to page 4 and write them down in your notes. These will underpin your study of the discipline.

There are a number of other definitions and we need to look at these. Perhaps the most important from the UK perspective is that of the Market Research Society (MRS). The MRS is the professional body overseeing professional standards in the Marketing Research industry in the United Kingdom (more about them later).

Marketing research is defined by the MRS (1999) as 'the collection and analysis of data from a sample of individuals or organizations relating to their characteristics, behaviour, attitudes, opinions or possessions. It includes all forms of marketing and social research such as consumer and industrial surveys, psychological investigations, observational and panel studies'.

As you can see and as you might expect, it is much more technical. It covers techniques and sector applications. Do not worry now if you do not understand terms like 'sample', or 'observational and panel studies'. You will by the time you finish the coursebook!

The American Marketing Association's early definition sounds like Alan Wilson's.

In the past, the American Marketing Association (1961) defined research as the 'Systematic gathering, recording and analysing of data relating to problems in the marketing of goods and services'. They changed this definition. Why do you think they did?

The word 'problems' causes some difficulties. Marketing research is also about identifying opportunities for growth in business. They changed this to the following definition; notice they included opportunities this time.

'Marketing research is the function that links the consumer, customer and public to the marketer through information – information used to identify and define marketing opportunities and problems; generate, refine and evaluate marketing actions; monitor marketing performance; and improve understanding of marketing as a process. Marketing research specifies the information required to address these issues, designs the method for collecting information, manages and implements the data collection process, analyses the results, and communicates the findings and their implications' (American Marketing Association, 2005).

How about the CIM? They too have their own definitions. This is taken from the website www.cim.co.uk, which has a useful glossary of Marketing terms. You should add this to your 'Favourites' list.

The CIM (2005) defines marketing research as 'The gathering and analysis of data relating to market places or customers; any research which leads to more market knowledge and better-informed decision-making'.

You may have noticed by now that the definitions refer to marketing and market research almost interchangeably. The distinction is not important. Market research has come to be seen as a subset of marketing research. Market research refers to research on markets whereas marketing research covers the broad scope of marketing activity.

## The database

The other elements of the MkIS are often incorporated within the marketing database. Alan Wilson (2003) defines the marketing database as 'A manual or computerized source of data relevant to marketing decision-making about an organization's customers'.

There are a few things about this definition that need to be explained.

The database does not have to be computer-based. It can be kept on hard copy. However, access to database technology is very easy and cheap. Even the cheapest and simplest software is capable of storing a significant number of records. Microsoft Access is perfectly serviceable for many businesses.

While the definition limits itself to 'customers' other definitions spell out the fact that the database will collect data about past and potential customers as well as current customers. De Tienne and Thompson use the following definition of database marketing:

> *The process of systematically collecting in electronic or optical form data about past, current and/or potential customers, maintaining the integrity of the data by continually monitoring customer purchases and/or by inquiring about changing status and using the data to formulate marketing strategy and foster personalized relationships with customers.* (De Tienne and Thompson, 1996)

The IDM defines the marketing database as 'a comprehensive collection of inter-related customer and/or prospect data that allows the timely accurate retrieval, use or manipulation of that data to support the marketing objectives of the enterprise' (Downer, 2002).

Wilson says that the database differs from an accounting system in that the data must be relevant to marketing decision-making. This is a subtle but important difference. Clearly the accounting system may reveal very interesting information to the marketer. It may contain details of what the customer has bought and when, and the frequency of purchase. We will see later that this information is important to successful database marketing. However, it is important that the data fed into the marketing database is relevant to marketing decisions now and in the future. It costs money to store and process data and in this information age it is easy to have too much data.

Wilson (2003) suggests that marketers develop customer databases for four reasons:

1. To personalize marketing communications
2. To improve customer service
3. To understand customer behaviour
4. To assess the effectiveness of the organization's marketing and service activities.

The motivation for setting up databases is quite broad. Let us look in detail at the uses of marketing information.

## Information and the scope of marketing research

So what is marketing information used for? The clue is in the definitions in the section above. But let us try and be more specific.

### Activity 2.5

Think about the marketing planning process. How does marketing information help this process? Write as many things as you can. Use your textbooks when you run out of ideas. We'll resolve this question in the debriefing activity.

## The marketing research and database industry

The information industry has changed dramatically over the last 20 years in line with changes in business generally. The business has internationalized, and the major organizations that supply research and database services to the market are amongst the largest organizations in marketing services.

The industry has embraced new technology and whilst it is still possible to carry out research without the use of a computer, much of the drudgery has been taken out of the process. The emergence of the Internet as a major channel and communications medium has meant that online research and research about online marketing is perhaps the fastest growing area. In 2001 according to ESOMAR, US$15.9 billion was spent on marketing research worldwide; of this, US$1.7 billion was spent in the United Kingdom (Table 2.1). By 2004 this had risen to $21.5 billion with $2.3 billion spent in the United Kingdom.

*Table 2.1* World market research turnover and growth rates by region 2004

| Region | Turnover in million US$ | Turnover in million US$* | Turnover in million US$ | Growth rate % (unadj. for inflation)** | Real growth rate % (adj. for inflation)** |
|---|---|---|---|---|---|
| | 2002 | 2003 | 2004 | 2003/04 | 2003/04 |
| EU15 | 6327 | 7590 | 8827 | 5.2 | 3.0 |
| New member states | 191 | 249 | 299 | 10.5 | 6.0 |
| Other Europe | 368 | 454 | 534 | 10.7 | 6.1 |
| Total Europe | 6885 | 8293 | 9660 | 5.6 | 3.2 |
| North America | 6707 | 7137 | 7853 | 9.5 | 6.7 |
| Central and South America | 632 | 720 | 830 | 14.8 | 8.2 |
| Asia Pacific | 239 | 2526 | 2863 | 6.5 | 5.2 |
| Middle East & Africa | 205 | 251 | 294 | 8.6 | 6.3 |
| Total World | 16 668 | 18 928 | 21 501 | 7.5 | 5.0 |

\* Some 2003 figures revised since 2003 Industry Report published last year
\*\* Growth rates are based on turnover in local currencies for 2003 and 2004 converted into dollars using 2004 exchange rate; real growth adjusted using the local inflation rate for 2004 (*Source*: IMF).
*Source*: ESOMAR Market Research Industry Survey 2004

We estimate the worldwide market research market grew by a healthy 7.5 per cent in 2004. After adjusting for inflation, the real growth rate is 5 per cent which is higher than for 2003. Unadjusted growth rose from 5.1 per cent in 2003 to 7.5 per cent in 2004 and adjusted growth from 2.7 per cent to 5 per cent. 2003 was the first year where the effects of fluctuating exchange rates were eliminated when calculating growth. For this reason, there are no comparable figures for the years before 2003.

More information and to purchase a full report containing this data and much more: www.esomar.org

## Who carries out research?

Research and database information can be produced internally or externally and the management task can be carried out in-house or externally.

Alan Wilson (2003) identifies the types of organizations that exist to provide information and research services to the companies. These include:

*List brokers* – These are suppliers of lists of contacts for marketing purposes. They may include names and addresses, telephone numbers and e-mail addresses. Details of list owners and types are held by the DMA in the United Kingdom. You can see these at www.dma.org.uk.

*Full service agencies* – These are agencies that provide a full range of research services, for example TN Sofres.

*Table 2.2* Leading UK research companies by turnover 2004

| | 2004 (in £'000) | 2004 vs. 2003 (in %) | Total ranking | Domestic ranking | International ranking |
|---|---|---|---|---|---|
| **COMPANY** | | | | | |
| TNS plc | 161.4 | 1.2 | 1 | 1 | 1 |
| NOP World | 80.3 | 5.1 | 2 | 2 | 3 |
| Synovate | 51.9 | 11.5 | 3 | 6 | 2 |
| Ipsos (UK) Ltd | 49.4 | 5.1 | 4 | 4 | 5 |
| MORI (Market & Opinion Research International) | 44.2 | 12.2 | 5 | 3 | 11 |
| Information Resources | 35.2 | 4.6 | 6 | 5 | 15 |
| HI Europe | 23.5 | 6.8 | 7 | 8 | 4 |
| Incepta Marketing Intelligence | 20.0 | 2.0 | 8 | 7 | 7 |
| GfK Martin Hamblin | 15.5 | −10.9 | 9 | 13 | 6 |
| ORC International | 12.5 | 0.1 | 10 | 9 | 12 |
| Marketing Sciences | 7.7 | 5.1 | 11 | 14 | 13 |
| Total | 1288.00 | 5.4 | | | |

*Source*: BMRB

*Specialist service agencies* – These are those that specialize in certain types of research, for example international research or online research.

*Field agencies* – Specialize in the delivery of fieldwork and the administration of questionnaires.

*Data analysis companies* – As the name suggests these specialize in the analysis of data.

*Consultants* – These are independent consultants who may offer a range of services.

Other suppliers into the industry include database bureaux who may host an external database for a company (Table 2.3).

*Table 2.3* Leading global research companies 2003

| Rank 2003 | Rank 2002 | Organization | Parent country | Revenue US$ millions | % Change |
|---|---|---|---|---|---|
| 1 | 1 | VNU N.V. | Netherlands | 3048.3 | −7.5 |
| 2 | – | Taylor Nelson Sofres Plc. | UK | 1585.1 | 2.8 |
| 3 | 4 | *Taylor Nelson Sofres* | UK | 1050.5 | 3.4 |
| – | 8 | *NFO WorldGroup Inc.* | UK | 514.6 | 1.5 |
| 3 | 2 | IMS Health Inc. | USA | 1381.8 | 13.3 |
| 4 | 3 | The Kantar Group | UK | 1002.1* | 6.7* |
| 5 | 6 | GfK Group | Germany | 873.6 | 3.7 |
| 6 | 7 | Ipsos Group S.A. | France | 644.6 | −0.8 |
| 7 | 5 | Information Resources Inc. | USA | 554.3 | −0.1 |
| 8 | 9 | Westat Inc. | USA | 381.6 | 11.6 |
| 9 | 11 | Synovate | UK | 357.7 | 0.9 |
| 10 | 10 | NOP World | UK | 335.6 | −4.6 |
| 11 | 12 | Arbtron Inc. | USA | 273.6 | 9.5 |
| 12 | 13 | Martz Research | USA | 188.8 | 3.0 |
| 13 | 14 | Video Research Ltd.** | Japan | 166.7 | 1.6 |
| 14 | 16 | J.D. Power and Associates | USA | 144.8 | 9.6 |
| 15 | 17 | Harris Interactive Inc. | USA | 137.01 | 3.3 |
| 16 | 15 | Opinion Research Corp. | USA | 131.2 | −1.1 |
| 17 | 18 | INTAGE Inc.** | Japan | 122.3 | 7.5 |
| 18 | 19 | The NPD Group Inc. | USA | 117.6 | 19.2 |
| 19 | 21 | AGB Group | Italy | 81.6 | 2.6 |
| 20 | 23 | Market & Opinion Research Int* | UK | 64.4 | 8.5 |
| 21 | 25 | Lieberman Research Worldwide | USA | 63.2 | 19.9 |
| 22 | 20 | Denlsu Research Inc. | Japan | 57.0 | −14.9 |
| 23 | 23 | Abt Associates Inc. | USA | 54.0 | 0.4 |
| 24 | – | Nikkei Research Inc. | Japan | 52.1 | 9.0 |
| 25 | 22 | Wirthlin Worldwide | USA | 52.0 | −5.8 |
| | | | | 11 651.0 | 1.4 |

* Estimated

** For fiscal year ending March 2003

*Note:*

(a) The total revenue that includes non-research activities for some companies are significantly higher.

(b) The rate of growth (from 2002 to 2003) has been adjusted so as not to include revenue gains or losses from acquisitions or divestitures.

(c) The rate of growth is based on home country currency and includes currency exchange effects.

*Source*: ESOMAR 2004, Honomichl Global 25 annual report on the global research industry, AMA's Marketing News, 15 August 2004. I

Total growth of the Top 25 was 10.5 per cent in 2003, much of it coming from 17 acquisitions around the world as well as higher growth firms replacing those with lower growth. At the time of their acquisition, these firms had revenues of $675 million, most of it due to Taylor Nelson Sofres which bought NFO WorldGroup with annual revenues of $515 million. By contrast, while the Top 25 made 37 acquisitions in 2002, the revenues of those acquisitions were $265 million, over 40 per cent less.

Once again VNU heads the list by virtue of its ownership of ACNielsen, Nielsen Media Research and other research firms, such as National Research Group and half of Scarborough Research.

VNU now controls 26 per cent of Top 25 revenues, and is expected to control more in the future as it sheds its directory business, providing funds for future research company acquisitions.

By virtue of NFO's acquisition, TNS moved up to the second largest in the world, overtaking both IMS Health, and The Kantar Group.

These three account for 34 per cent of Top 25 revenues, and together the top four firms now control 60 per cent of the Top 25 marketplace and 34 per cent of total world spend.

Just ten of Top 25 firms had revenue declines in 2003 or did not grow enough to cover estimated world inflation rate of 2.0 per cent. Last year it was thirteen. Biggest gains were achieved by IMS, Westat, Harris Interactive and Lieberman Research Worldwide, all higher than 11 per cent growth and all US-based.

The number of public research firms on the list declined further this year with the sale of Information Resources. Only one firm – Nikkei Research – is new to the Top 25 vs. four last year. Nikkei replaced NFO.

Top 25 firms employed 85 471 full-time in market research operations worldwide in 2003, an increase of 2 per cent over the last year but down 4 per cent from the year before.

Among the Top 25 in 2003, 12 are US owned, and these account for 30 per cent of Top 25 revenues, up from 25 per cent last year when NFO was owned buy the media conglomerate Interpublic. Four are British, accounting for nearly 29 per cent of total revenues. Just one, VNU in The Netherlands, alone accounted for 26 per cent of Top 25 total. France, home to Ipsos, accounting for 5.5 per cent of total. Germany, home of GfK, accounted for 5.8 per cent. Four of Top 25 are based in Japan, accounting for 3.4 per cent. AGB, based in Italy, accounted for under 1 per cent. This data is provided by ESOMAR they promote their mission as:

> *ESOMAR's mission is to promote the use of Opinion and Market Research for improving decision-making in business and society worldwide. Founded in 1948, ESOMAR unites 4000 members in 100 countries, both clients and providers of opinion and marketing research. Members can also be found in advertising and media agencies, universities and business schools, as well as in public authorities and institutions.*

These companies are carrying out a variety of research techniques (Table 2.4). The table below shows the split between techniques. 2002 is the latest date for which data is available. The BMRA are about to repeat this survey in 2006. Do not worry if you do not understand all the terms – you will by the end of this book!

*Table 2.4* Per cent research turnover by method 2002

| Type of research | % |
|---|---|
| Face-to-face interviews | 32.9 |
| Telephone interviews | 19.5 |
| Discussion groups | 8.8 |
| Consumer panels | 8.3 |
| Postal/self-completion | 8.0 |
| Hall/central location test | 7.7 |
| Retail audits | 4.5 |
| In-depth interviews | 3.6 |
| Street interviews | 2.0 |
| Observation | 0.3 |
| Web/Internet interview | 0.2 |

*Source*: BMRA (2002)

## Professional bodies and Institutes

There are a range of professional bodies that support the profession in the United Kingdom. These are divided between the Professional Institutes and the Professional Associations. The main difference is that the institutes support the individuals in the industry while the association supports the industry in the economy.

In the United Kingdom, the Institutes that support the market researcher and information professional include:

The CIM – www.cim.co.uk
The MRS – www.mrs.org.uk
The IDM – www.theidm.com.

The associations that support marketing research and information industry include:

The British Market Research Organization (BMRA) – www.bmra.org.uk
The Direct Marketing Association (DMA) – www.dma.org.uk.

These national institutes and associations are linked to regional and world representative bodies. For example, the MRS is linked to ESOMAR or the World Association of Opinion and Marketing Research Professionals (WAPOR). The origins of ESOMAR were in Europe. It was founded in 1948 as the European Society for Opinion and Marketing Research. Its links with WAPOR mean it represents over 4000 members in 100 countries.

ESOMAR can be found at www.esomar.org and WAPOR at www.unl.edu/WAPOR. Both sites are well worth visiting. The DMA is linked to FEDMA, the Federation of European Direct Marketing. FEDMA can be found at www.fedma.org

Most of the national bodies have a links page through to their international counterparts.

**Activity 2.6**

Go to the MRS website www.mrs.org.uk and look at The Research Buyer's Guide. This will give you a clear picture of the types of services that its members provide.

Do the same at the Direct Marketing Association's site at www.dma.org.uk.

## Ethics, regulation and codes of practice in market research

The 'data' industry has grown rapidly as the technology that is available to capture, store, analyse and exchange data has improved. The amount of data held on individuals is incredible and this raises many issues. The data has value. It has personal and possibly material value to the individual, and commercial value to the company that has acquired the data. It also has a range of costs that are associated with its capture and storage. It is therefore important that companies manage the data effectively and do not betray the trust placed in them by individuals who may have given up very sensitive information. The amount of data captured will only increase. 3G mobile phones can capture location information of users and this can be used to target customers with messages for local retail stores.

Wilson (2003) points out that ethics in market research are the moral guidelines that govern the conduct of behaviour in the marketing research industry. He says that the industry is dependent on:

- *Goodwill of respondents* – They have to be willing to carry out research and give up information.
- *Trust* – Underpins all relationships in the industry. Respondents have to trust researchers to handle their data in an ethical manner; clients trust researchers to carry out research properly.
- *Professionalism* – Data must be used in a professional manner.
- *Confidentiality* – Data must be kept confidential and anonymous, and not disclosed to third parties.

The right to privacy is enshrined in the Human Rights Act.

## Data protection and freedom of information

The United Kingdom has had data protection legislation since 1984. The current Data Protection Act which was passed in 1998 and came into force in 2000 was introduced in response to the 1995 European Union Directive on Data Protection. The Act regulates 'processing' of data; this covers data on any living person and there are separate rules for sensitive data, for example health, sexuality, religion, disabilities and so on. If you collect data on Halal meals then your data falls in this separate, more sensitive category. The Freedom of Information Act (2000) came into force on 1 January 2005. The Act regulates access to information held by public authorities.

The guiding principles of transparency and consent in the Data Protection Act are most relevant for Marketing Research Professionals. Individuals must have a clear understanding of why their data is being captured and what it will be used for, and they must consent to its use and be given the opportunity to opt out of any later use of this data.

Opt-out is the standard at the moment. However, this is changing, and the latest rules seem to be asking people to actively opt in to future use of their data. This is almost certain to become the standard and it is good practice now to ask individuals to actively opt in to the future use of their data.

There are three key terms to understand in the Act:

1. *Data controller* – Is the collector of data.
2. *Data processor* – Is the processor of the data. For example, Sainsbury is the collector of Nectar card data and Loyalty Marketing Group is the processor.
3. *The data subject* – Is the individual on whom information is collected.

Every UK business that processes data must register with the Information Commissioner's offices; this can be done online at www.informationcommissioner.gov.uk/. It costs £35 per year, as part of the process you must identify all uses to which the data will be put.

The current Act has eight key principles:

*1st Principle* – Where a company/organization processes data it must be done fairly and lawfully. Overarching principle means that information about the organization gathering information must be given and consent from data subjects must be obtained. Information must be given about the identity of the processor, the use to which the information will be put and all else that is relevant.

Exemptions do exist, for example, when data is collected and used in pursuit of a contract. For example, Amazon could use your name and address to send you a book. Other exemptions refer to data that is needed to ensure the well-being of the subject, for example health records may be accessed in accidents and emergency situations. It is always best to check with legal counsel to understand these exemptions in detail.

*2nd Principle* – Data must be obtained only for specific and lawful purposes, and shall not be further processed in a manner incompatible with that purpose.

*3rd Principle* – Personal data must be adequate, relevant and not excessive in relation to the purposes for which it is processed.

*4th Principle* – Personal data must be accurate and where necessary up to date, with every reasonable step taken to ensure this.

*5th Principle* – Personal data should not be kept for longer than is necessary.

*6th Principle* – Personal data shall be processed in accordance with the data subjects' rights. These include:

- Right to access – if an individual pays £10 within 30 days, a copy of the data held should be provided.
- Right to prevent data being used for direct marketing – direct marketing is communication by any means of advertising or marketing material communicated to particular individuals. Individuals can write and materials must not be sent.
- Right to prevent decisions being made on automated processing, for example automated decision on credit.
- Right to prevent processing that may cause damage or distress.

*7th Principle* – The data must be kept secure against accidental loss, destruction or damage. The data controller, that is, the collector of the data must have a written contract with the data processor who may process data on behalf of the controller guaranteeing security. There must be appropriate technical and organizational procedures to ensure this and preventing any unauthorized or unlawful processing of data.

*8th Principle* – Overseas transfer of data, should not be outside the European Economic Area (EEA), EU plus Norway, Iceland and Liechtenstein, unless consent is given. If data is exported, it must be to countries approved by the information commissioner. Hungary, Switzerland, New Zealand and Canada are the only ones that qualify at present. The United States has set up a system called safe harbour [*sic*]. Under the safe harbour system US companies can self-certify as complying with EEA data rule. In the United States, 175 companies have signed up.

Penalties for non-compliance or contravention of the Act are fines of £5000 or more and damages.

Exemptions also exist for data processed for marketing research. Personal data for research can be reprocessed and data relating to longitudinal studies may be kept. Once data is anonymized, it can be kept indefinitely, and once personal identifiers are removed, subjects do not have the right to access data.

The advice is to take advice; enormous damage may be done through the negative publicity surrounding breaches of the Data Protection Act.

There are a number of other relevant Acts but the Data Protection Act is the most onerous. You may need to consider the Telecommunications (Data Protection and Privacy) Regulations 1999 replaced on 11 December 2003 by the Privacy and Electronic Communications (EC Directive) Regulations 2003, which stipulate that it is unlawful to make unsolicited direct marketing calls to individuals who have indicated that they do not want to receive such calls via the Telephone Preference Service (TPS).

There is now also a Corporate TPS, to quote the TPS.

'The Corporate Telephone Preference Service (CTPS) is the central opt out register whereby corporate subscribers ... can register their wish not to receive unsolicited sales and marketing telephone calls to either all their organization's telephone numbers, or to certain numbers. It is a legal requirement that companies do not make such calls to numbers registered on the CTPS.

It takes 28 days for the registration to become fully effective.

If you register any of your telephone numbers you need to be aware that you may not receive unsolicited telephone calls from other organizations which you and your colleagues may find useful and would be interested in receiving.

For information on the Regulations which dictate this new legal requirement please visit Privacy and Electronic Communications (EC Directive) (Amendment) Regulations 2004 at www.hmso.-gov.uk/si/si2004/20041039.htm (tpsonline.org 2006)'.

It also covers opt-out via the Fax Preference Service (FPS). These are the responsibility of the Director General of Telecommunications. There are codes of practice that relate to list and database practice; these amongst many other things say that lists should be run against the latest Mail Preference Service (MPS) or baby MPS suppression files. They should comply with the Data Protection Act. They should not use selections from a database that is more than 6 months old. If data is to be used for a significantly different purpose than originally intended, then consumers must be informed.

# Codes of practice and guidelines

These are self-regulatory codes developed by the professional bodies responsible for the regulation of the industry. These are not legally binding but do represent good practice, and members of the professional bodies must comply with the code of conduct. The MRS Code was updated in 2005 and is presented below. The full document is available at www.mrs.org.uk/standards/downloads/code2005.doc

The ESOMAR code of conduct can be viewed at http://www.esomar.org/web/show/id=43240. The MRS also publishes a range of guidelines on aspects of marketing research. The current list is as follows:

- Market research guidelines
- Best practice in Mystery Customer Research (also see new revised draft)
- Free Prize Draws Guidance Note
- Guidance Note: How to Apply the MRS Code of Conduct in Employee Research
- Guidelines for Research Among Children and Young People
- Internet Research Interim Guidance Note
- Qualitative Research Guidelines (also see new revised draft)
- Quantitative Data Collection Guidelines
- Questionnaire Design Guidelines
- The Responsibilities of Interviewers
- Legislative guidelines

## A basic guide to the Data Protection Act 1998

The Data Protection Act 1998 and Market Research: Guidance for MRS Members

- Market Research Processes and the Data Protection Act (DPA) 1998
- Draft guidelines
- Code of practice for conducting Market Research in town centres
- Draft Business to Business Guidelines

Draft Guidelines for collecting data for mixed or non-market research purposes

- Draft Mystery Shopping Guidelines
- Draft Observational Research Guidelines
- Draft Public Opinion Research Guidelines
- Draft Qualitative Research Guidelines

*Source*: MRS

The Guidelines are currently being rewritten and should be reviewed at the MRS website. An important addition is the guideline on Internet research.

# The DMA code of practice

The DMA code of conduct is available at www.dma.org.uk. There are a range of codes that relate, for example, to SMS marketing and marketing to children. You should review these as part of your study at www.dma.org.uk/content/Pro-Code.asp.

## The preference services

Preference services are suppression lists that enable consumers to stop receiving marketing communications via various media. Consumers register on the service, and companies must run and deduplicate their files against the suppression list. Information on these is available from the DMA at www.dma.org.uk (Figure 2.3). The e-mail preference service is a new service that is run out of DMA in the United States.

Preference services cover Telephone, Mail (there is a separate category for households expecting a baby), Fax and e-mail.

 The Mailing Preference Service allows you to register your wish not to receive unsolicited direct mail.

 Baby MPS is a service which allows parents who have suffered a miscarriage or bereavement of a baby in the first weeks of life to register their wish not to receive baby-related mailings.

 The Telephone Preference Services allows you to register your home phone number not to receive unsolicited sales and marketing calls.

 The Fax Preference Service allows you to register your home or business fax number not to receive unsolicited sales and marketing faxes.

 The e-mail Preference Service is a global service managed by the DMA in the States which allows you to register your e-mail address so as not to receive unsolicited sales and marketing e-mail messages.

*Figure 2.3* DMA Services
*Source:* www.dma.org.uk

### Direct Marketing Authority

The Direct Marketing Authority acts as the final arbiter on complaints referred to it by the DMA governance secretariat.

### List Warranty Register

The List Warranty Register (LWR) was set up in June 1994. This initiative, inspired by the DMA Data Council, is designed to make compliance with the industry codes of practice easier for both DMA and non-DMA members alike. It is a free service paid for by the industry.

The LWR is a central database of list owner and user warranties. It helps to eliminate paperwork within the industry by negating the requirement for list owners and users to supply separate warranties every time a list is rented. It promotes best practice within the list industry and helps to raise standards for the benefit of the industry and the consumer. The warranty is an assurance that the data has been collected lawfully, is up to date and complies with relevant Codes of Practice. It should not be taken as a guarantee of responsiveness.

If you would like to check whether a list owner or list user has a current warranty, e-mail your query to lwr@dma.org.uk.

MPS www.mpsonline.org.uk or call 020 7291 3327
TPS www.tpsonline.org.uk or call 020 7291 3326
FPS www.fpsonline.org.uk or call 020 7291 3326
Baby MPS www.mpsonline.org.uk or call 020 7291 3327
Emps www.e-mps.org

*Source*: DMA

## Deceased suppressions

There are a range of services that enable companies to remove the names of the deceased from their lists. These include the Bereavement Register, the Deceased Register, Death Screen and Mortascreen.

Information on these is available at www.dma.org.uk.

## Summary

This unit has introduced the concepts of marketing and the information that is needed to enable effective management of the marketing function in all organizations. The definition of marketing as the management process responsible for identifying, anticipating and satisfying customer needs profitably means that timely, accurate and pertinent information underpins marketing orientation. We looked at the MkIS as the mechanism for delivering this information, and in detail explored Marketing Research and the Database as the key components of this system. We looked at a number of different definitions of marketing research and database marketing. Marketing research was defined as 'the collection and analysis of data from a sample of individuals or organizations relating to their characteristics, behaviour, attitudes, opinions or possessions. It includes all forms of marketing and social research such as consumer and industrial surveys, psychological investigations, observational and panel studies' (MRS,

2005). We looked at this definition in detail and outlined the scope of marketing research within the organization, centring on the planning process.

The database was defined as 'A manual or computerized source of data relevant to marketing decision-making about an organization's customers' (Wilson, 2003). We saw that the database can be enhanced by other data, including geo-demographic and lifestyle data.

We went on to look in detail at the legislative and self-regulatory environment within which the industry works. We looked at the eight principles of the Data Protection Act, the Freedom of Information Act and the MRS and ICC/ESOMAR codes of practice. We also looked at the codes of practice of the DMA and the preference services. The suppression of deceased names was also covered.

We also looked at the structure of the industry and the nature of the organizations that support the industry in the United Kingdom and overseas.

## Further study

### Question 2.1

You are the marketing manager for a major supplier of computer hardware, mainly to the consumer market. The company has a database of 350 000 active customers. The company wishes to enter the small office/home office sector. You have been given the job of researching and contributing to the development of the marketing plan for this new venture. The board feels that their investment on the database should be adequate to inform the development process.

Write a report to the board outlining the following:

o How the database and marketing research will work together to help the marketing planning process?
o In order to convince the board, illustrate your report with examples from other industries.

### Question 2.2

#### Splash Ltd

The Spanish-based cosmetics company Splash Ltd has built an international retail chain that is in a strong expansion phase. Its fresh, hand-made soaps and cosmetics are available in 240 stores world-wide. The emphasis is on making and selling products without animal ingredients made from only fresh fruit and vegetables, finest essential oils and safe synthetics. It controls the whole process of getting its products to the consumer, including design, manufacturing and retail.

The retail stores look like a cross between a cheese shop and a market stall, with slabs of soap and other fresh products stacked ready for cutting and bagging. The retail environment is dominated by an aroma of soaps and perfumes. The company is now planning to open its first UK store in the centre of London.

Prior to designing the outlet, determining the product range and potential promotions, the company is keen to undertake a programme of market research with potential customers, to examine the buying behaviour and attitudes of British consumers of high quality soap and cosmetic products.

The company hopes that answers to such questions will help in the successful launch of their first UK store.

The company is willing to spend up to £50 000 on the research project.

*Note*: The above data has been based on a fictitious situation drawing on a variety of events and does not reflect the management practices of any particular organization.

## Part B – Answer TWO questions only

## Question 2

As a recent graduate recruited to the marketing department of Splash Ltd, you have received an enquiry from the marketing director asking for a report which addresses the following:

(a)  The descriptive, comparative, diagnostic and predictive roles that marketing information can provide

**(8 marks)**

(b)  Why are some marketing research departments in large organizations widening their remit beyond marketing research?

**(10 marks)**

(c)  What ethical issues are raised by such a change being made?

**(7 marks)**
**(Total 25 marks)**

## Bibliography

American Marketing Association (1961) Report of the definitions committee, Chicago: AMA. (Quoted in Chisnall, P. (2004) *Marketing Research*, 7th edition, McGraw-Hill).

American Marketing Association (2003) www.marketingpower.com/live/content.php? Item_ID 1/ 44620.

Bacon, F. (1597) 'Of Heresies', *Religious Meditations*.

Baker, S., Mouncey, P (2003) 'The market researcher's manifesto', *International Journal of Market Research*, **45**.

Bennett, P. (1995) *Dictionary of Marketing Terms*, 2nd edition, American Marketing Association.

Chisnall, P. (2004) *Marketing Research*, 7th edition, McGraw-Hill.

CIM (2005) www.cim.co.uk

Crouch, S., Housden, M. (2003) *Marketing Research for Managers*, 3rd edition, Butterworth-Heinemann.

Davidson, H. (1997) *Even More Offensive Marketing*, Penguin.

Davenport, T., Prusak, L. (1998) *Working Knowledge How Organisations Manage What They Know*, Harvard Business School Press (Quoted in Yahya, S. and Goh, W. (2002) 'Managing human resources for knowledge management', *Journal of Knowledge Management*, **6**(5).

Dawson, C. (2003) *Creative Business, Financial Times*, 18 November 2003.

De Tienne, K., Thompson, J. (1996) 'Database marketing and organizational learning theory: Towards and research agenda', *Journal of Consumer Marketing*, **13**(5).

www.dma.org

Downer, G. (2002) *The interactive and Direct Marketing Guide* The IDM. Experian (2003) www.micromarketing-online.com.

www.Esomar.org

Jones, T., Sasser, W. (1995) *Why Satisfied Customers Defect*, Harvard Business Review.

Kotler, P. *et al.* (1999) *Principles of Marketing*, 2nd European edition, Prentice Hall Europe.

Malhotra, Y. (1998) 'Deciphering the knowledge management hype', *Journal for Quality and Participation*, **21**. (Quoted in Yahya, S. and Goh, W. (2002) 'Managing human resources towards achieving knowledge management', *Journal of Knowledge Management*, **6**(5).

MRS (2005) *Code of Conduct*, MRS.

Peters, T., Waterman, R. (1995) *In Search of Excellence*, Profile Business.

Reichheld, F. (2001) *The Loyalty Effect: The Hidden Force Behind Growth Profits and Lasting Value*, Harvard Business School Press.

Wilson, A. (2003) *Marketing Research, An Integrated Approach*, FT Prentice Hall.

Yahya, S., Goh, W. (2002) 'Managing human resources for knowledge management', *Journal of Knowledge Management*, **6**(5).

# unit 3 the marketing database

| Learning outcomes | Knowledge and skills requirements |
|---|---|
| Plan for and manage the acquisition, storage, retrieval and reporting of information on the organization's market and customers | 2.1 Demonstrate an understanding of the application, the role in CRM and the benefits of customer databases |
| | 2.2 Describe the process for setting up a marketing database |
| | 2.3 Explain how organizations profile customers and prospects |
| | 2.4 Explain the principles of data warehouses, data marts and data mining |
| | 2.5 Explain the relationship between database marketing and marketing research |

## Key definitions

**Behavioural data** – Data that is derived directly from the behaviour of the customer.

**Volunteered data** – Data that is given up by the customer through, for example, registering on a website.

**Profile data** – Data that is obtained by linking the database with other sources of information.

**Attributed data** – Data that is extrapolated from the results of market research.

**Golden fields** – The key information elements of the database that must be completed and maintained for good database marketing.

**Lifestyle data** – Lifestyle companies collect information on customers' lifestyles. The data is assembled from various sources; guarantee cards filled in, in return for an extended warranty; questionnaires inserted in magazines or mailed to previous respondents; competition entry forms and so on (Thomas and Housden, 2003).

**Geo-demographics** – Companies supply a system of categorizing the country into a number of different demographic types. Each postcode in the country is assigned one of these types. This means that each customer on your database can be matched to a demographic type. When this is done across all of your customer records, a demographic profile emerges (Thomas and Housden, 2003).

**Data capture** – Information taken on to a computer system.

**Deduplication** – System of removing names and addresses which appear in a list more than once.

**OLAP** – Online Analytical Processing.

Customer relationship management – CRM is an integrated approach to identifying, acquiring and retaining customers. By enabling organizations to manage and coordinate customer interactions across multiple channels, departments, lines of business and geographies, CRM helps organizations maximize the value of every customer interaction and drive superior corporate performance (Siebel, 2003).

## Study Guide

This unit should take you around 3 hours. You should add another 3 hours for supplementary reading and case studies.

## Customer relationship management (CRM)

CRM has been one of *the* business buzzwords of the last 5 years. It reflects the fact that marketing orientation must run through the entire enterprise. As organizations have come to recognize this, it has become clear that marketing is too important just to be the responsibility of the marketing 'department'; all parts of the business throughout the value chain, from suppliers to accounts and HR to our marketing intermediaries, have a role in promoting the organization and its products and services. CRM attempts to reflect the reality of the customer experience.

It is an old marketing chestnut, but it is nonetheless true that customers do not recognize the output of organizations as 'sales promotion' or 'advertising' or 'sales force' activity. All they see is an organization dealing with them as customers, potential customers (prospects) or lapsed customers, better or worse than another company.

## Touching BMW

Research done for BMW by its award-winning below-the-line agency Archibald Ingall Stretton identified over 240 different ways in which a customer or prospect could come into contact with the BMW brand. Some of these are managed through communications planning, some can be controlled, perhaps through PR, some cannot be managed, for example word of mouth and day-to-day contact of customers with BMW drivers. The key output of this research was to provide BMW with a network analysis and allow them the opportunity to explore further the intensity and relevancy of these 'touchpoints' for customers.

Customer Relationship Management attempts to integrate an approach to customers that uses information about them gleaned from multiple contact points to develop appropriate strategies to manage the customer experience to deliver a consistent customer experience that maximizes mutual value from the relationship.

Gamble, Stone and Woodcock (2001) define CRM as 'CRM is an enterprise wide commitment to identify your named individual customers and create a relationship between your company and these customers so long as that relationship is mutually beneficial'.

It is important to realize that for many organizations the word 'CRM' is inevitably attached to 'systems'. However, as you can see from the above definition it is not necessary for CRM to be IT based and indeed the design of CRM programmes, as with all strategic decisions in business, should involve the matching of resources to opportunities. That is, the system design should be appropriate to the resource base of the organization and its planned future growth.

It is the IT systems that tend to cause most dissatisfaction. A survey by Gartner recently found that over 55 per cent of managers were dissatisfied with the results of the implementation of CRM systems in their business.

There is much debate about why this should be and at present it is fair to say that CRM's star is waning.

This is unfortunate as there is no doubt that the principles of CRM are absolutely worth striving for. The main problems with CRM implementation can be summarized simply:

Too often CRM is seen as a means to take costs out of the business.

The United Kingdom's largest ISP recently sent VAT-registered subscribers a letter saying that having listened to their customers in order to improve customer service they would no longer be mailing VAT receipts but would be e-mailing them to customers. The customer concerned was certainly not asked and now has the inconvenience and cost of logging on to a rarely used e-mail account and downloading and printing a receipt that previously was sent free of charge. This company has upset a customer worth at least £300 per year, has created negative word of mouth and equally has closed down an opportunity to communicate through a more intimate channel with an existing customer.

As Admap (2001) puts it 'Companies seem to see CRM as a means by which the consumer herself can handle their own service issues. From this standpoint, customer contact is an inconvenience to be minimized, rather than an opportunity to be maximized – as is demonstrated by the many companies that brief their call centres to minimize call lengths to reduce costs'.

The idea should be that CRM aligns the business more effectively with customers' needs and wants and promotes solutions to customers more effectively and as a result more efficiently. Too often we seem to focus on efficiency without recognizing the impact that this has on effectiveness. If we raise expectations then we MUST deliver against these expectations.

In its optimum form, CRM integrates information sources, learns from this information and delivers a consistent targeted offer through multiple contact points; Figure 3.1 presents this clearly.

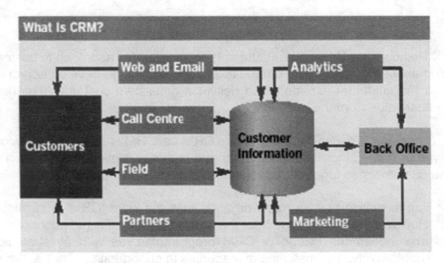

*Figure 3.1* CRM structure
*Source*: Siebel

Customer information sits at the heart of this and will include data from the following

- o Websites
- o Dealers
- o Sales force
- o Accounts
- o Operation
- o Fulfilment and response handling
- o Call centres
- o Partners
- o Transaction data
- o Marketing database.

Teradata, a leading supplier of data warehousing systems, show a slightly different structure (Figure 3.2).

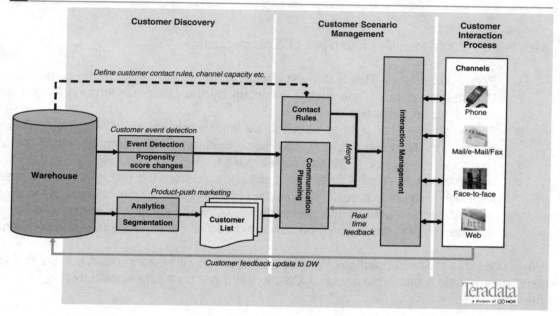

## Teradata CRM Process Flow

*Figure 3.2* CRM and data warehousing
*Source*: Teradata

# The marketing database

We defined the marketing database in Unit 1. Can you remember any of the definitions?

We had three. The course textbook by Alan Wilson (2003) defines the database as 'A manual or computerized source of data relevant to marketing decision-making about an organization's customers'.

De Tienne and Thompson use the following definition of database marketing:

> *The process of systematically collecting in electronic or optical form data about past, current and/or potential customers, maintaining the integrity of the data by continually monitoring customer purchases and/or by inquiring about changing status and using the data to formulate marketing strategy and foster personalized relationships with customers.* (De Tienne and Thompson, 1996)

The IDM defines the marketing database as 'a comprehensive collection of inter-related customer and/or prospect data that allows the timely, accurate, retrieval, use or manipulation of that data to support the marketing objectives of the enterprise' (Downer, 2002).

## Activity 3.1

We have three definitions. What are the common characteristics that link them?

Alan Wilson (2003) identifies four types of customer data:

1.  *Behavioural data* – This is derived directly from the behaviour of the customer.
2.  *Volunteered data* – Data that is given up by the customer through – for example, registering on a website.
3.  *Profile data* – This data is obtained by linking our database with other sources of information. They are linked by commonly held data – for example, name, address or postcode. For example, Mosaic (see below).
4.  *Attributed data* – This is data that is extrapolated from the results of market research. Although held anonymously, the results of research on a small sample of the database can be flagged against the entire database. For example, a survey that looked at attitudes by age group could be used to group all customers into a relevant segment.

What does this mean in practice? We have all heard of information overload. So in that case what data should a database contain? Clearly there will be a difference between b2c and b2b markets.

## Activity 3.2

The list below presents six categories of data that might be collected. Try to flesh out the list. Under each heading write as many types of information that you may need to inform marketing decisions. What are the implications for B2B markets?

o   Identification data
o   Demographic data
o   Financial data
o   Lifestyle data
o   Transactional data
o   Other data.

Complete the debrief before proceeding.

## Geo-demographic and lifestyle profiling

Geo-demographic and lifestyle profiling is a useful addition to the marketers' armoury. Once we have data in the 'Golden' fields, they can be enhanced through overlaying bought in data. Data can be bought from, for example, Experian who runs the Mosaic system, CACI who runs ACORN and Acxiom runs a number of different data products.

Dunn and Bradstreet offers profiling and other services in the b2b market.

**Activity 3.3**

Visit the following websites:

- www.experian.com
- www.acxiom.co.uk
- www.caci.co.uk
- www.dnb.com.

Review the services that these companies offer and add them to your favourites list.

Lifestyle classification works normally on researched lists. Acxiom, for example, collects data from the warranty registration cards for domestic appliances filled in by new customers. Geodemographics works on the idea that 'birds of a feather flock together' and that customers who share postcodes will share behavioural characteristics.

You can see this with the Mosaic classifications at group level below. Mosaic divides households in the country into 11 groups and 61 types. The Mosaic classification is based in large part on census data but also includes other data sources. According to MOSAIC 54 per cent of the data used to build Mosaic is sourced from the 2001 Census. The remaining 46 per cent is derived from their Consumer Segmentation Database, which provides coverage of all of the United Kingdom's 46 million adult residents and 23 million households. It includes:

- The edited Electoral Roll
- Experian Lifestyle Survey information, and Consumer Credit Activity
- The Post Office Address File
- Shareholders Register
- House Price and Council Tax information
- ONS local area statistics.

*Source*: www.business-strategies.co.uk/

The Mosaic system's 11 groups are as follows:

---

Symbols of Success
Happy Families
Suburban Comfort
Ties of Community
Urban Intelligence
Welfare Borderline
Municipal Dependency
Blue Collar Enterprise
Twilight Subsistence
Grey Perspectives
Rural Isolation

---

The census happens every 10 years in the United Kingdom. In the past, census data was gathered from what are called Enumeration Districts of about 150 households and then translated into postcode areas. The 2001 data is presented in what are called output areas and is postcode based. It is this data that the Mosaic system now uses. Other geo-demographic systems work in a similar way. For example, ACORN is shown in Figure 3.3.

## THE ACORN CONSUMER CLASSIFICATION

| CATEGORY | | % UK POP | GROUP | | % UK POP |
|---|---|---|---|---|---|
| 1 | WEALTHY ACHIEVERS | 25.1 | A | WEALTHY EXECUTIVES | 8.6 |
| | | | B | AFFLUENT GREYS | 7.7 |
| | | | C | FLOURISHING FAMILIES | 8.8 |
| 2 | URBAN PROSPERITY | 10.7 | D | PROSPEROUS PROFESSIONALS | 2.2 |
| | | | E | EDUCATED URBANITES | 4.6 |
| | | | F | ASPIRING SINGLES | 3.9 |
| 3 | COMFORTABLY OFF | 26.6 | G | STARTING OUT | 2.5 |
| | | | H | SECURE FAMILIES | 15.5 |
| | | | I | SETTLED SUBURBIA | 6 |
| | | | J | PRUDENT PENSIONERS | 2.6 |
| 4 | MODERATE MEANS | 14.5 | K | ASIAN COMMUNITIES | 2.5 |
| | | | L | POST-INDUSTRIAL FAMILIES | 15.5 |
| | | | M | BLUE-COLLAR ROOTS | 6 |
| 5 | HARD-PRESSED | 22.4 | N | STRUGGLING FAMILIES | 14.1 |
| | | | O | BURDENED SINGLES | 4.5 |
| | | | P | HIGH-RISE HARDSHIP | 1.6 |
| | | | Q | INNER CITY ADVERSITY | 2.1 |
| | | | U | UNCLASSIFIED | 0.3 |

| GROUP | TYPE | | % UK POP |
|-------|------|--|----------|
| A | 1<br>2<br>3<br>4 | Wealthy mature professionals, large houses<br>Wealthy working families with mortgages<br>Villages with wealthy commuters<br>Well-off managers, larger houses | 1.7<br>1.5<br>2.7<br>2.6 |
| B | 5<br>6<br>7<br>8 | Older affluent professionals<br>Farming communities<br>Old people, detached homes<br>Mature couples, smaller detached homes | 1.8<br>2.0<br>1.9<br>2.0 |
| C | 9<br>10<br>11<br>12 | Older families, prosperous suburbs<br>Well-off working families with mortgages<br>Well-off managers, detached houses<br>Large families and houses in rural areas | 2.1<br>2.3<br>3.7<br>0.6 |
| D | 13<br>14 | Well-off professionals, larger houses and converted flats<br>Older professionals in suburban houses and apartments | 0.9<br>1.4 |
| E | 15<br>16<br>17<br>18<br>19 | Affluent urban professionals, flats<br>Prosperous young professionals, flats<br>Young educated workers, flats<br>Multi-ethnic young, converted flats<br>Suburban privately renting professionals | 1.1<br>0.9<br>0.6<br>1.1<br>0.9 |
| F | 20<br>21<br>22<br>23 | Student flats and cosmopolitan sharers<br>Singles and sharers, multi-ethnic areas<br>Low income singles, small rented flats<br>Student terraces | 0.6<br>1.6<br>1.2<br>0.4 |
| G | 24<br>25 | Young couples, flats and terraces<br>White-collar singles/sharers, terraces | 1.0<br>1.4 |
| H | 26<br>27<br>28<br>29<br>30<br>31 | Young white-collar couples with mortgages<br>Middle income, home owning areas<br>Working families with mortgages<br>Mature families in suburban semis<br>Established home owning workers<br>Home owning Asian family areas | 1.9<br>2.9<br>2.6<br>3.3<br>3.6<br>1.1 |
| I | 32<br>33<br>34 | Retired home owners<br>Middle income, older couples<br>Lower incomes, older people, semis | 0.9<br>3.0<br>2.1 |
| J | 35<br>36 | Elderly singles, purpose built flats<br>Older people, flats | 0.7<br>1.9 |
| K | 37<br>38 | Crowded Asian terraces<br>Low income Asian families | 0.5<br>1.1 |
| L | 39<br>40 | Skilled older families, terraces<br>Young working families | 2.8<br>2.1 |
| M | 41<br>42<br>43 | Skilled workers, semis and terraces<br>Home owning families, terraces<br>Older people, rented terraces | 3.3<br>2.8<br>1.8 |
| N | 44<br>45<br>46<br>47<br>48<br>49 | Low income larger families, semis<br>Low income, older people, smaller semis<br>Low income, routine jobs, terraces and flats<br>Low income families, terraced estates<br>Families and single parents, semis and terraces<br>Large families and single parents, many children | 3.3<br>3.0<br>1.4<br>2.6<br>2.1<br>1.7 |
| O | 50<br>51<br>52 | Single elderly people, council flats<br>Single parents and pensioners, council terraces<br>Families and single parents, council flats | 1.8<br>1.9<br>0.8 |
| P | 53<br>54 | Old people, many high-rise flats<br>Singles and single parents, high-rise estates | 0.8<br>0.9 |
| Q | 55<br>56 | Multi-ethnic purpose built estates<br>Multi-ethnic, crowded flats | 1.1<br>1.1 |
| U | 57 | Mainly communal population | 0.3 |

*Figure 3.3* The ACORN consumer classifications
*Source:* ACORN 2005

Variations of the ACORN system have been introduced to serve the classification needs of specific markets. These include:

- o Investor ACORN
- o Scottish ACORN
- o Financial ACORN.

Examples of one of the Mosaic classifications can be seen below. Whilst there are some weaknesses in the approach, you can see that in certain markets the use of this data would be very helpful.

## Group A: Symbols of Success

### Type A06: High Technologists

### Sociology and environment

#### Summary

*High Technologists* are found in areas of modern, high specification family housing, mostly in outer metropolitan areas, which attract well-paid executives working in large corporations.

#### Demography

This Type contains many areas of new wealth where larger corporations, many of which are based in the high technology sector, recruit highly paid executives to manufacture products or services with a high value added content. Many of these corporations are based along the M3/M4 corridors and have generated a demand for highly paid labour that could not have been satisfied without planning policies that allowed developers to build large numbers of very high specification estates on the edge of existing settlements. These developments, many of which took place during the 1980s, were designed for people on good salaries who wanted a smart and modern environment in which to raise their families within reasonable commuting distance of their offices. In many of these areas the demand for houses in pretty country villages way exceeds the supply and these modern estates, however much character they may lack, present an easy option in a market of very limited choice. The populations who now live in these estates have now begun to age. Children who were of nursery school age are now less common than children of secondary school age and the parents, who in earlier times may have been in their thirties, are now very often moving across the cusp into later middle age. In these well-organized homes people are more likely to be married than co-habiting, and young singles and old-age pensioners are noticeably absent. Wives as well as husbands are well qualified and many go out to work in challenging professional jobs. In these outer metropolitan areas the population is almost entirely white and many residents will have migrated from more distant areas of the country. Almost all the homes are owner occupied and most residents are still some way from completing their mortgage repayments. Situated on the outskirts of older towns, most people commute considerable distances to get to work and are often poorly integrated into the local community. These are very much car-based cultures. Public transport is infrequent and offers access to limited destinations and most of the national multiples have set up positions in out-of-town centres which are impossible to reach other than by car. The culture of these areas is strongly child and family centred and though lives are busy and individuals have to go their own way, many family decisions are made collectively. It is common for leisure activities, including shopping, to be undertaken by the family as a unit.

#### Environment

Neighbourhoods of High Technologists tend to consist of quite large detached houses, mostly of modern design, laid out in quiet cul-de-sacs and in relatively small developments. Houses are typically arranged in an irregular manner and many of the designs, though they use common components, look as though they are one off. These tend mostly to be open plan estates and many residents have difficulty fitting their cars into the private space available. Most houses have garages but few will accommodate two cars and it is quite common to find boats, caravans and children's cycles also parked outside on expensive brick-laid driveways which present an air of greater opulence than the concrete hard standing that would be put down in older developments. In the gardens, plants tend to be trimmed rather than allowed to ramble and whilst some residents seem to have a natural ability for the management of their small estates, for many others this task appears to be a responsibility rather than a pleasure. Beyond the houses it is seldom far to the open countryside except where even newer estates have been recently built. Trips to schools and to shops often require more than a few minutes drive and the general absence of local convenience shops encourages petrol stations to diversify into the sales of convenience items, which is particularly helpful for the dual income families who work on office parks which offer poor opportunities for lunchtime shopping.

### Economy

Neighbourhoods of High Technologists are scattered throughout the country but occur in largest numbers in the triangle between Newbury, Basingstoke and Windsor within the commuter hinterland of Oracle and Microsoft. Whilst by no means all the residents work in high-tech industries, these are very much areas where corporate executives work in a high-technology office environment and need to be confident in coping with automation. Experience in the use of these technologies at work leads many to make more extensive use of them at home not just for entertainment but also for product information and online ordering. The use by adults of these technologies encourages children to appreciate the wider uses to which these technologies can be put and introduces a virtuous circle creating an ever more IT literate workforce. Despite high costs and low unemployment in these regions, IT companies continue to concentrate in them providing plentiful alternatives to their current employers for those eager for further career advancement.

### Consumer values

High Technologists typically approach consumer decisions from a rational perspective and value brands that offer high levels of flexibility and personalization and convey an image of innovation and high performance. These people are well informed on the relative merits of different brands and are keen to try new products. There is a tendency for these people to be more focused on material possessions, and on equipment in particular, than on experiences. Votes at election time tend to assist Conservative candidates.

### Consumption patterns

*High Technologists* have high levels of disposable incomes, not least as a result of the benefits such as company cars and pension and insurance schemes to which many of them are entitled. These are good markets for home furnishings, for new kitchens, bathrooms, conservatories and extensions and for electronic equipment particularly relating to home entertainment and information technology. Significant amounts of money are also spent on sports and outdoor equipment and many residents prefer climbing mountains and sailing boats to visiting theatres or art galleries. Much leisure equipment is purchased for children. Visits to supermarkets are infrequent but expensive and shopping trolleys are likely to be loaded with multi-pack offers and ready-made meals.

### Change

The age profile of *High Technologists* areas will continue to age, though once residents get to retirement age it is likely that many of them will move to more rural locations.

(Experian, 2005).

Mosaic also works at a European level and has a number of other targeting tools that the marketer can use.

## Case study

### Bang & Olufsen and Micromarketing

Bang & Olufsen is one of the world's leading premium audiovisual and telecoms product retailers. Operating throughout most major international markets, the company's innovative products place great emphasis on design, originality and sound quality. It is essential, however, for an organization like Bang & Olufsen to continually seek effective methods of refining its marketing and store-planning activities in order to maintain a clear competitive lead. These marketing requirements led the company to conceive an international development project that used the latest micromarketing analysis tools to establish two main levels of intelligence:

o A greater understanding of target customer profiles
o Improved intelligence on the relative value and potential of existing and prospective store locations.

As the first stage in this international project, Experian was asked to undertake a test exercise in the United Kingdom, covering a number of key stages. An in-depth analysis of the existing customer base identified dominant target customer types using *MOSAIC* and defined catchment areas. Areas of high likely demand were identified, along with an appraisal of catchment overlaps, providing an understanding of the best areas in which to site new stores. Catchment areas, customer data and demand models were input into Experian's *Micromarketer* software along with *Site Quality Indicators (SQI's)*. SQI's are derived from data about each specific retail site, including the quality of its location within a retail centre, the proximity of major attractors such as department stores, as well as transport, access and parking factors. This meant that each potential Bang & Olufsen store site could be evaluated with a new level of precision.

Key differences are already evident between the different country markets. For instance, the longer distances which the UK customers are prepared to travel to a Bang & Olufsen store vary little between a concession in a major city centre store and a destination store in a small market town. In other words, these stores operate uninfluenced by the normal shopper flow. In contrast, however, some French and Spanish city centre outlets have been revealed to attract as much as 50 per cent of their customers from a mere 1 kilometre radius. Finally, further enhancements are also taking place in the United Kingdom. Now that refined key target profiles have been established centrally, Experian's CD-based electoral roll selection tool, *Prospect Locator*, is now being used to target local mailings around each store, combining these profiles with the additional strength of local knowledge and market intelligence (Experian, 2003).

Thomas (Thomas and Housden, 2003) suggests a general rule as to the hierarchy of data held on the database:

1. *Your own customer data* – most powerful as it relates to your customers and their existing relationship with you.
2. *Lifestyle data* – as it relates to individuals by name and address.
3. *Demographic data* – dealing as it does with the characteristics of neighbourhoods rather than households.

## The process of setting up a marketing database

The process of setting up a database is complex and demanding. A staged planning approach is outlined below.

- ○ Business review
- ○ Data audit
- ○ Data strategy, specification and verification
- ○ Data verification
- ○ Hardware/software
- ○ Data capture, maintenance and enhancement
- ○ Management issues – should the database be run in-house/out-of-house?
- ○ Applications
- ○ Review.

We will look at each of these stages in turn (Figure 3.4).

*Figure 3.4* The database development process

### Business review

It is important that the overall mission and objectives are reviewed in order to inform the process of establishing the database. It could be that a database is not required to fulfill the mission of the business or that the cost of a particular database design or hardware is too great. All business decisions should begin with an understanding of the strategic direction of the business. The database decision is no exception. We must ask:

- ○ How will data help the business achieve its business and marketing objectives?
- ○ Where will the business be in 10 years' time?
- ○ What media, information and technology changes will need to be built into the system?
- ○ What segments will the data support now and in the future?

o What business processes will the database support?
o How will the database be accessed?
o Is the database open to customers through the Internet?

## The data audit

Carrying out an in-depth data audit is the next stage of the process. We need to establish the following:

o What information requirements does the organization have now and in the future?
o Where is this information held currently?
o What unnecessary information is currently held?
o How is this information currently used?
o How will it be used in future?
o Which departments and individuals need access to this information?
o If information is not available, where does it come from?
o Who will enter the data and ensure that is accurate and complete?
o What applications will this information support?
o How does the proposed system integrate with existing information management systems?
o Data strategy, specification and verification.

The review of strategy and the data audit should result in a long-term strategy for data within the organization. This should be capable of evolution and development over time as the markets served by the organization and the organization itself changes.

The strategy should specify the information that is required by the organization outlining where the information is available and what additional data is to be acquired and managed.

It should determine the following:

o Who and what departments are able to use and update data held on the database?
o How will the data be kept up to date and who is responsible for this?
o What data verification rules will be put in place to ensure quality and completeness?
o What analysis systems will the database support?

 **Activity 3.4**

> Where will this data come from? Think about the ways that your company or a company of your choice may capture data on its customers. Write down as many data sources as you can.

Data needs to be kept up to date. This is a legal obligation under the 1998 Data Protection Act but is also vital for good practice in database marketing. Information has a life. It is estimated that professional marketers change their job every 18 months to 3 years. The lapse rates for trade press titles such as *Marketing* and *Marketing Week* are around 25–30 per cent. In the consumer market, data expires almost as quickly.

- ○ People move house. About 10 per cent of households move house each year. The Royal Mail keeps a list of movers called the National Change of Address File (NCOA). The Postal Address File (PAF) will also help. This is a list of all 26.5 million addresses in the United Kingdom and is regularly updated.
- ○ They die. It is dreadful to send mailings to dead people; it is ethically unacceptable and causes distress for families that have recently suffered bereavement. There are a number of services that help the marketer avoid this, for example The Bereavement Register and Mortascreen. These services allow companies to remove the deceased from their lists. The Deceased Register is a service based on cards completed at the Register Office and is supported by the Information Commissioner and Local Government. For further details, go to the DMA website or the Royal Mail website.
- ○ They are enticed away by the competition, by better, more relevant or cheaper offers.
- ○ They leave due to poor marketing.
- ○ They move out of the market; Club 18–30 has a clear target market!
- ○ Their lifestyle changes, they marry or have children, or simply stop drinking or smoking or go on a diet.
- ○ Their financial circumstances change, they trade up or trade down.

## Telegraphing your renewal date

If you have taken out a subscription deal with the *Daily Telegraph,* you will have to decide at the end of your subscription period whether you wish to continue with the arrangement. The Telegraph knows from its database records when this decision will have to be made and they will mail you beforehand.

They will remind you what a great newspaper you read and restate the benefits of taking out a further subscription. The marketing database enables them to time these communications so that they are highly relevant to the individual recipients.

The Telegraph will not stop at simply sending you a simple reminder. They will also carry out anti-attrition studies. This is an important area – having gone to the considerable time and expense of recruiting a customer, one does not want to lose them through lack of understanding of their needs. Many companies fail to carry on these simple procedures. Research from the Swedish Post Office shows that 65 per cent of customers leave because of a lack of contact from the company. This has been confirmed in another study by McGraw-Hill (Thomas and Housden, 2003).

# Kimberly Clark

# Nappy talk

Kimberly Clark market the Huggies brand of nappies. Kimberly Clark has around two and a half years to sell the estimated 4500 nappies that the average child uses in this time. They try to ensure that every nappy used is a Huggies nappy. This involves a range of broad-scale communications and a series of data-driven targeted direct marketing communications. The Huggies Mother and Baby Club recruits members through the Bounty list, a list of expecting mothers that is compiled through responses to take ones and other media distributed to pregnant women. The women sign up for a range of free samples including Huggies nappies that are delivered after the delivery of the child. A series of targeted communications is also delivered to the family covering the period from the date of birth to potty training. Amongst these is a series of publications that provide information on care and other elements of child rearing. These include free samples and coupons. The publications are seen as valuable in themselves. They cover the following:

Step 1    Pregnancy
Step 2    Birth and early days
Step 3    Reaching out to the world
Step 4    Sitting up
Step 5    Crawling everywhere
Step 6    First steps
Step 7    Toddler days.

The publications deepen and strengthen the relationship between customers and the brand at a crucial time of life and the trust developed during this time sustains other brands in the Kimberly Clark family.

## *Data verification*

Data verification is important. A regular review of the data is important. Data fields should be reviewed to check that they are up to date and that they hold the data they are supposed to hold. We need to check if the data is usable and if not determine what we have to do to make use of the data? We also need to check that we do not hold duplicate data.

## *Deduplication*

Deduplication is an important part of the process of verifying data. Duplication of records may occur for a number of reasons, including keystroke error or other data entry problems, or simply the fact that volunteered information is not provided in a consistent way.

We may have two addresses with slightly different names:

for example, Lewis K 128 Greene St SL6 8TY 12/8/62

or Lewes Keith 128 Greene Ave SL6 8PY 12/8/62.

These may be different people or the same person. Deduplication ensures that we do not send multiple mailings or make repeat contacts in other ways. There are a number of software solutions that allow for deduplication of records. These packages can be set to different degrees of sensitivity and may be based on the number of matched characters and/or numbers or a string of digits or may allocate a weighting depending on the character of the data that is being assessed.

The two types of system are deterministic decision tables or probabilistic linking.

Deterministic decision tables evaluate data fields for degree of match and a letter grade is assigned, the grades form a match pattern which is looked up in a table to determine if a pair matches or not.

| Lewis | K | 128 | Greene | St | SL6 8TY | 12/8/62 |
|-------|---|-----|--------|-----|---------|---------|
| Lewes | Keith | 128 | Greene | Ave | SL6 8PY | 12/8/62 |
| B | B | A | B | D | B | A = BBABDBA |
| +5 | +2 | +3 | +4 | −1 | +7 | +9 □ = □ +29 |

Probabilistic linkages evaluate fields for degree of match and a weight is assigned that represents the informational content contributed by those values. The weights are summed to derive a total score that measures the reliability of the match.

The deduplication strategy will be determined by the cost of holding duplicate data and the cost of deduplicating this data and can be set for under or over kill.

Reference tables may be used to help the verification of data. Wilson (2003) gives examples of reference tables for titles, job description, brands, models of car and so on. These are crucial for the maintenance of data quality as they reduce errors.

Formatting will be used to ensure that data is entered consistently, that it fits the fields and is presented in consistent style. International databases have a range of issues around salutations, titles, address and postcode formats.

## Hardware and software

There are a range of vendors in the market. There are dozens of questions that need to be asked. The key questions are:

- o Mainframe or PC
- o Cost and time
- o Integration with existing systems
- o Scalability
- o Do we have in-house expertise?
- o Support offered
- o Analysis systems support
- o Maintenance costs
- o Data capture, maintenance and enhancement
- o Management issues – should the database be run in-house/out-of-house?

### In-house or out-of-house
Database bureaux will host your database for your organization.

In-house operation has advantages and disadvantages:

## Advantages

- o  Strategic orientation of the business should be assured.
- o  Integration and access is manageable.
- o  Greater control and ownership.
- o  Cost may be lower.

## Disadvantages

- o  Cost of hardware and consultancy may be significant.
- o  Speed of development can be slow.
- o  Service standards may be lower than those from an out-of-house provider.
- o  Skills in IT and strategy may be weak.
- o  Specialist processing skills may not be readily available.

## Database bureaux have the following advantages

- o  Skills and systems are developed and tested.
- o  No fixed costs. You pay for what you get.
- o  Speed. Resources can be allocated to ensure prompt delivery and penalty clauses can be built in.
- o  Performance guarantees can be built into the contract.

Often there is migration from the bureau into the organization. This means that learning can take place at lower risk. The usual approach is outlined below:

- o  Set-up at the bureau
- o  Sort out data issues
- o  Set-up updates and enhancements
- o  Develop internally
- o  Run the two in parallel
- o  Import.

## Applications

As we saw with the Tesco example, a huge amount of data may be captured by organizations. The key thing is to be able to analyse the data.

# How it all works

Thomas and Housden (2003) put it simply in their book *Direct Marketing in Practice*:

Remember the marketing database is a series of tables. These can cover a huge range of data:

- A list of names and addresses
- A list of transactions
- A list of suppliers/delivery methods and so on
- A list of promotion codes
- A list of customers who have been mailed, and their responses or any logical collection of data.

For instance, it would not be logical to store details of every transaction against every customer in the same table. Some customers may have dozens of transactions, others only one. To avoid large areas of wasted space, transactions are stored in a separate table, with a link between the customer's name and address and the transaction.

Having assembled the data, records have to be selected for a particular mailing campaign. This is done by a process of raising queries. For instance, if we wished to mail customers who had spent more than £500 in the past 6 months we would:

- Tell the computer to identify all transactions of £500 or more between the dates XX and YY
- Link these transactions to the name and address table
- Get a count of how many names and addresses have been identified
- If and when required, extract the related names and addresses for use in the promotion.

Using queries in this way enables us to model campaigns and identify whether our selection parameters have been appropriate. If the count shows we have only 50 customers who fit the category (spent £500 within the last 6 months), we may wish to broaden the parameters.

We could extend the period to 12 months and/or reduce the qualifying total to £250. This would produce a larger number of prospects. The exact process used depends on the software being used. PC software is generally more user-friendly and allows the marketer to access the data directly. This makes modelling campaigns easier and quicker than was the case with mainframes and IT departments.

## Using the database to profile your customers

Profiling is something that the database allows us to do quite easily. Because of the range of information that we capture on our customers we can create quite sophisticated profiles of our customers. By linking our database to services like Mosaic and Acxiom's products we can extend this profile significantly. For example, a Mosaic code based on a customers' postcode will also unlock information collected by BMRB through a service called the Target Group Index (TGI) (see below). This means that we can effectively link our base with TGI data based on over 25 000 customer interviews.

Simple profiling might be used to identify the best value customers according to certain demographic or lifestyle indicators. This would be based on the value of past purchases, how often they purchased, and when they last purchased. This is known as recency, frequency and value analysis or RFV analysis. You may also see it written as FRAC (Frequency Recency

Amount and Category) analysis. By matching this to other data, for example, income, family status and postcode, we can identify similar people in the market who do not transact with us and target them for acquisition. Of course the process of identifying these top customers allows us to begin the process of retaining them. It is believed that it costs between three and thirty times more to acquire a customer than it does to retain a customer. Reichheld's book *The Loyalty Effect* goes into this in far more detail (Reichheld, 2001).

Academic research shows that the use of modelling and profiling via the database is a far more reliable and profitable approach to decision-making in marketing.

## Profiling the car buyer

A leading car manufacturer profiled its existing customer base and matched this to a rented list.

It produced a mailing to 2000 people on this list and sold 20 cars.

The mailing cost £1500, it produced £500 000 revenue.

### The data warehouse and data marts

There is a narrow but important difference between the database, data marts and data warehouses. In many ways they are different levels of the same thing – the range of data held on customers and marketing and other activity within an organization. A data mart is a collection of databases that may serve a particular purpose (Figure 3.5). These tend to be expensive to maintain as they duplicate information. Data warehouses are created to form a single view of the truth for the organization as a whole and consolidate data marts (Figure 3.6).

The creation of data warehousing may involve a complex reorganization of business processes. For example, one major manufacturing company had several different product codes for each component. The rationalization of these product codes was vital to enable sensible queries to be made of the data.

*Figure 3.5* Data marts
*Source*: Teradata

*Figure 3.6* Data warehouses combine data marts
*Source*: Teradata

The development of the data warehouse may be an expensive task especially around the integration of different systems and platforms. However, the advantages are clear and the enabling of complex decisions, not just at the marketing level, is one clear benefit. As the warehouse becomes more established, the level of decision-making its supports becomes higher (Figure 3.7).

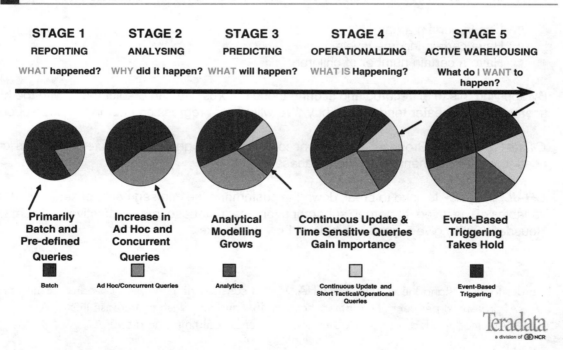

*Figure 3.7* Information evolution in data warehousing
*Source*: Teradata

## Activity 3.5

Visit the following websites, browse the sites to identify the range and nature of the claims for CRM and supporting systems. Bookmark these sites.

www.ibm.com
www.ncr.com

### Data mining

Data mining is the process of analysing the database or the data warehouse to extract meaningful and actionable information. Antinou (1997) defines it as 'the process of extracting hidden and actionable information for large databases'. Data mining software can help this process. The process of analysis includes the process of statistical analysis of data or simple counts. It also includes a range of tools to help analyse the database. These are known as online analytical processing or OLAP.

Online analytical processing tools establish an analysis universe and allow for queries to be made of data, for example counts of the number of people of a certain age who bought a particular product. These tools allow us to drill into the database to analyse sub-samples in detail. This sample may be removed from the database and analysed offline.

### Other analysis techniques

Regression identifies the nature of a relationship. Regression analysis scores individuals according to their characteristics.

For example, buyers of a certain product may have certain other characteristics. They may:

- ○ Live in certain areas
- ○ Have certain income levels
- ○ Have a certain number of children.

By applying this to all records and scoring those records, we can predict those with the highest scores have a greater tendency to buy. We will look at regression later in the coursebook.

*Cluster analysis* – Groups customers according to their general characteristics. This can be used to create segments from the database.

*CHAID analysis*– Is used to break down the customer base into segments based on certain key variables. It is used to target subgroups on the database more effectively. Thomas and Housden (2003) give a good example of how this works.

In order to understand the workings of CHAID let us consider an example of a bank wishing to sell ISAs. At present, 8 per cent of customers have an ISA and they wish to increase this to 10 per cent. The CHAID model is fed, say 30 000 customer records containing data on:

- ○ Number of ISAs
- ○ Household income
- ○ Size of mortgage
- ○ Years as a customer and so on.

The CHAID software considers all of the given variables and determines which is the most important in this case.

Let us say it establishes that the most significant factor is 'years as a customer'. It further subdivides this factor into, say: less than 1 year with the bank; 1 to 5 years as a customer; more than 5 years. It may then identify something like the following:

o Less than 1 year as a customer – only 3 per cent have an ISA
o 1 to 5 years – 8 per cent have an ISA
o More than 5 years – 12 per cent have an ISA.

The CHAID model then moves on to the next stage which is to take each of these three segments and considers the next most significant variable in each instance.

It may ascertain that in the most loyal customer segment (more than 5 years with the bank) the next best discriminator is mortgage size. People in this segment with mortgages of more than £100 000 may have a 14 per cent take-up of ISAs.

By breaking down each segment into its significant variables, a number of potentially good sub-segments may emerge.

Figure 3.8 An example of CHAID analysis in fundraising
Source: © The IDM (2005)

The analysis shows that the number of previous gifts would have been the best variable: 36 per cent who sent 2 or more donations account for 65 per cent of the money.

This model shows 88.5 per cent of the cash could have been raised from just 60 per cent of the mailing list.

10.5% Yields    12.5% cash

26.0% Yields    33% cash

10.0% Yields    32% cash

13.5% Yields    11% cash

60% Volume = 88.5% cash

## How can the data be used?

The data can be used in a number of ways. The case below presents an outline of how the database works in financial services.

## The database and financial services

The financial services sector is a heavy-user of database analysis. Amongst others, a major bank has used their database in the following ways:

1. To manage the branch network

   (a) Identifying the most profitable branches
   (b) Staff appraisal, monitoring, reward and recognition
   (c) To identify staff training needs
   (d) To manage branch location.

2. To acquire new customers

   (a) Through profiling of good, existing customers and using this
   (b) To plan for the acquisition of new customers.

3. To increase profitability of existing customers

   (a) Reducing the cost of marketing
   (b) Improved targeting
   (c) Personalizing marketing communications
   (d) Reduce attrition.

4. Developing new products
5. Developing new market segments.

*Planning* – Defining objectives, segmentation studies, targeting, campaign management analysis costs and return on investment.

*Contacting customers* – Which medium or combination of media is the most effective and efficient, at what time?

*Data processing* – Counts and reports to aid planning.

*Production* – Production of lists and labels for address management; producing lists for follow-up activities; merging letter copy and addresses.

*Response handling* – Recording responses to promotional mailings via unique tracking codes.

*Lead processing* – Tracking enquiries through 'to sale' and 'after sales'.

*Campaign management* – Customer paperwork and reports to help manage promotions.

*Customer research* – Information from questionnaires may be added to records to make the future planning process more effective.

*Analysis* – Pre-determined reports and other analysis.

Marketing applications of the database can be summed up as:

- Finding
- Acquiring
- Keeping
- Cross-selling additional products
- Up-selling higher value products
- Prevent inactivity
- Renewing.

Customers!!

## Marketing research and the database

The MRS code of conduct that we shall look at in detail later specifically prohibits the use of market research to build databases. Data collected by market research techniques must be aggregated and anonymous. The research industry went to some lengths to ensure that it was exempt from the provision of the 1998 Data Protection Act that would have severely compromised its role in social and economic research. We will look later at the way that anonymous research data can be used to enhance our understanding of the customers on our database.

Despite this it is clear that the use of databases can enhance the information that we hold on our prospects, and current and lapsed customers. The database can provide a sample frame of customers and marketing research can use this provided that the research design indicates that this is appropriate and free of bias. Very often, however, the database does not adequately support pure marketing research simply because the sample that is available is only of existing customers, responders to past communications or lapsed customers. It does probably not include those who might be interested in a new product but have never responded or transacted with the company before. Given this the uses of the database in helping the research function are limited.

Conversely the use of marketing research data overlaid on the database is becoming more common. Anonymous data can be linked at postcode level or other consumer characteristic to provide texture depth of understanding to information held on the database. Together the quality of management information is significantly enhanced.

## Summary

We started this unit by exploring the concept of CRM and the systems that support it. We looked particularly at the database and the range of applications it can support.

We have explored the processes involved in setting up a database looking at the management issues and the process of capturing, verifying and enhancing data.

We saw that there were several types of data and that the data gathered varies from consumer to b2b markets. We looked at the process of gathering data on international customers and saw that this raises issues of consistency due to name and address formats.

Data types include:

- Identification data
- Demographic data
- Financial data
- Lifestyle data
- Transactional data.

These fit into four categories:

- Behavioural data
- Volunteered data
- Profile data
- Attributed data.

We looked in detail at the process of setting up a database exploring each of the phases in turn. These were:

- Business review
- Data audit
- Data strategy, specification and verification
- Data verification
- Hardware/software
- Data capture, maintenance and enhancement
- Management issues: should the database be run in-house/out-of-house?
- Applications
- Review.

We looked at data enhancement through lifestyle and geo-demographic systems.

We looked at the process of maintaining data and explored methods of deduplication.

We looked at analysis techniques including the use of OLAP tools, cluster regression and CHAID analysis.

Finally, we looked at the applications that the database can support. We saw that they could be described as:

- Planning
- Contacting customers
- Data processing
- Production

- Response handling
- Lead processing
- Campaign management
- Customer research
- Analysis.

The marketing applications of the database were summed as:

- Find
- Acquire
- Keep
- Cross-sell
- Up-sell
- Prevent inactivity
- Renew.

# Further study

## Question 3.1

You have been appointed as marketing manager for the Drama Factory, a small regional arts and entertainments venue. You want to develop a marketing database to facilitate the marketing of the centre, but need to convince the trustees of the centre of its value in order to receive funding.

Write a report for the trustees outlining the process involved in establishing a database for marketing.

- How will external suppliers help this process?
- What applications will the database facilitate?

## Question 3.2

CIM Professional Series Stage Two: Marketing Research and Information

### Jack Ltd

Jack Ltd is a leading international speciality retailer offering clothing, accessories and personal care products for men, women, children and babies under the Jack brand name. In the United Kingdom, Jack Ltd operates more than 150 stores nationwide. Each of the stores employs sales associates and other store personnel that are trained to answer customers' questions about fabric, fit and fashion and to help them select merchandise that's perfect for them. However, even with this training, around 85 per cent of all potential customers that enter a Jack store (measured using electronic counters in the doorways of each store) leave without buying anything. Senior management are keen to reduce this percentage, however, they are unclear as to the reasons why people leave their stores empty-handed. It may be due to the product range, store layout, service quality, pricing or any range of factors. Marketing research is therefore needed to explore the reasons why such a large percentage of potential customers fail to make a purchase.

The company hopes that answers to such questions will help to identify ways to increase sales amongst these customers.

The company is willing to spend up to £40 000 on the research project.

## Part B Question 2

As a recent graduate recruited to the marketing department of Jack Ltd, you have received an enquiry from the marketing director asking for a report which sets out:

(a)  The differences between a marketing decision support system and a customer database.
**(8 marks)**

(b)  The issues involved in using the respondent details from the marketing research project to create a customer database.
**(8 marks)**

(c)  The benefits of building a customer database through the creation of a loyalty card scheme.
**(9 marks)**


## Question 3.3

### Donaldson Builders Merchants

Donaldson Builders Merchants is a small chain of builders merchants located in the central belt of Scotland. The company has four outlets located around the edge of the major conurbations of Edinburgh and Glasgow. These supply small builders, plumbers, roofers and similar tradesmen as well as some members of the public (i.e. those more skilled in major do-it-yourself, renovations and house improvements). Customers may collect items direct from the trade counter at the warehouse or have the items delivered direct to the building site or house by the company's fleet of 14 lorries. The lorries are equipped with hoists for handling the larger items.

Donaldson supplies:

o  Timber and timber products.
o  Bricks and paving.
o  Sand and aggregates.
o  Roofing materials.
o  Plumbing and heating supplies.
o  A small range of hand tools.

The company provides credit to the majority of its trade customers. As a result it has a computerized database with details on most of its trade customers relating to name, address, trading address, telephone number, type of business, and purchasing patterns. There are approximately 1100 customers on the database, which probably represents 85 per cent of the company's customers. For the other 15 per cent of customers (the public and trade customers who do not have a credit account), the database holds no record, with the exception of a delivery address if a delivery is required

The market in which Donaldson operates is becoming more competitive, with the company losing shares to national chains such as Jewson and a number of recently opened B&Q trade depots. Tom Donaldson, the Managing Director, feels that the company's personal service and flexibility is far superior to these competitors, and is therefore keen to build on this and find ways in which to compete other than on price. The company has never undertaken research before but is keen to find out more from its customers about:

o  Their existing and future purchasing behaviour.
o  Their attitudes towards Donaldson Builders Merchants (such as product range, service, flexibility of delivery, etc.).
o  Their suggestions about improvements required in Donaldson's offering.
o  They are willing to spend up to £50000 on the research project.

## Part B Question 2

Tom Donaldson is keen to make more use of his company's database and turn it into a customer database for marketing intelligence and customer relationship purposes. He has asked you as a newly qualified Marketing Executive within the firm to produce a report which sets out:

(a) The benefits and weaknesses of database information to a company such as Donaldson Builders Merchants.

**(7 marks)**

(b) The manner in which data should be stored and processed for it to be of most use in the provision of marketing intelligence and customer relationship activity.

**(9 marks)**

(c) The need for the distinction between marketing research and the creation of databases for direct marketing purposes.

**(9 marks)**
**Total marks = 25**

## Question 3.4

Davidson Hotels operate in a group of seven hotels in the United Kingdom. The hotels are all rated at the three- or four-star level, with four of them having swimming pools and leisure centres. They tend to be located close to tourist/leisure type areas of outstanding natural beauty and local heritage sites. Their customer mix has traditionally consisted of 50 per cent business travellers, 30 per cent coach parties, and 20 per cent leisure travellers/leisure breaks. However, with the growth in budget hotels offering standard rooms and limited additional services, the number of business travellers has dropped by more than 38 per cent over the past 12 months. The coach party market is relatively static, so therefore the company's main opportunity for growth is seen by management as being in the leisure travel market, with the swimming pools being used to promote all-weather/all-year leisure destinations.

The company is therefore keen to understand more about the leisure travel sector, in particular:

o The trends in the market
o The criteria used by leisure travellers when selecting their accommodation in areas with outstanding natural beauty or heritage sites
o The reasons why existing leisure customers use Davidson Hotels and their likelihood of returning to the same hotel or another hotel in the Davidson Hotel chain.

They are willing to spend up to £50 000 on the research project.

Note: The above material has been based on a fictitious company for assessment purposes.

## Part B Question 2

Tom Davidson in Question 1 is of the opinion that his hotels' management should know much more about the characteristics of their guests. This would reduce the need for research and would also be useful for future direct marketing activity, building loyalty, and obtaining repeat business. Currently, basic name and address information is stored on the hotels' reservations systems. However, this is only used for operational and billing purposes. He has asked you as a new recruit to the company to produce a report that sets out:

(a) the types of information that could be collected on a database about hotel guests and the manner in which the information could be collected.

**(9 marks)**

(b) the benefits that would result from holding such information.

**(7 marks)**

(c) the issues involved in attempting to merge the information from the marketing research study with the databases.

**(9 marks)**
**(25 marks in total)**

## Question 3.5

### SeaLux Cruises

SeaLux Cruises is a new cruise operator consisting of two ships sailing out of the port of Southampton in Southern England. It has been established for just over one year and provides cruise-based vacations using its 1400 berth ship, Med Blue, around the Mediterranean, and cruises around Scandinavia and the Baltic States on its 1250 berth ship, Northern Blue. The focus is on offering relaxing vacations with an emphasis on 'luxurious discovery' through a wide range of dining, entertainment and excursion choices. A 12-day Mediterranean cruise on the Med Blue with stops in Venice, Barcelona, Rome and five other cities, starts at around £2000.

Although the first year has gone well with very satisfied passengers and no technical problems, the cruises have been running at below optimum capacity. The level of bookings for the sixteen cruises scheduled for the next 12 months is also around 35 per cent below target. This is causing the company some concern, particularly when industry sources and the performance of competitors clearly suggest that the UK cruise market is going through a period of tremendous growth. There is a view among the senior management of the company that the product offering is correct for the target market but the promotion and sales activity is failing to raise awareness and attract or convert potential passengers. Unlike other cruise lines that use travel agents to sell their cruises, SeaLux undertakes direct advertising in national newspapers and magazines leading to customers booking direct with SeaLux through their internet site or telephone hotline.

The senior management is now concerned that low sales may reflect an unwillingness of the target market (the over 40 age group) to book cruises on a direct basis, as they may require the advice and reassurance of a travel agent. Alternatively, the poor sales may simply reflect a low awareness of the advertising and the company's offerings.

SeaLux is therefore keen to undertake a programme of research to examine the effectiveness of the advertising and the attitudes of the target market towards the preferred methods and channels for the booking of cruise-based holidays. The company is willing to spend up to £70 000 on the research project.

The above data has been based on a fictitious situation drawing on a variety of events and does not reflect the management practices of any particular organization.

## Part B Question Two

The senior management of SeaLux is of the opinion that the company should know much more about the characteristics of their passengers. This would be useful in customer profiling, building loyalty and obtaining repeat business. Currently, basic name, address and billing information are stored on the company's computers. You have been asked as a new recruit to the Marketing Department to produce a report which sets out:

(a) the types of information that could be collected on a database about passengers and the approaches that could be adopted to collect such information

**(9 marks)**

(b) the potential benefits that would result from holding such information

**(7 marks)**

(c) the issues involved in attempting to merge the information from the database with the customer satisfaction surveys undertaken at the end of each cruise.

**(9 marks)**
**(Total 25 marks)**

Go to www.CIM.co.uk for specimen answers to this question

## Hints and tips

Thomas and Housden's book Direct Marketing in Practice contains a very useful and accessible chapter on database and its applications.

## Bibliography

Admap (2001) *Who is Killing CRM*, Admap.

Antinou, T. (1997) 'Drilling or mining? Handling and analysis of data between now and the year 2000', *Marketing and Research Today*, 115–120.

Experian (2003) *Experian Company Case Studies*.

Experian (2005) www.experian.com.

Gamble, P., Stone, M., Woodcock, N. (2001) *Up Close and Personal*, Kogan Page.

Reichheld, F. (2001) *The Loyalty Effect*, HBSP.

Siebel (2003) www.siebel.com.

Thomas, B., Housden, M. (2003) *Direct Marketing in Practice*, Butterworth-Heinemann.

Wilson, A. (2003) *Marketing Research: An Integrated Approach*, FT Prentice Hall.

# unit 4 the marketing research process

## Learning objectives

After completing this unit you will

- Be able to identify the stages of a marketing research plan

- Identify and brief a range of marketing research suppliers

- Be able to construct a proposal document in response to a marketing research brief

- Have covered syllabus elements 3.2, 3.3, 3.4, 3.5, 3.6.

Explain the process involved in purchasing market research and the development of effective client–supplier relationships

3.2 Explain the stages of the market research process

3.3 Describe the procedures for selecting a market research supplier

3.4 Explain the ethical and social responsibilities inherent in the market research task

Write a research brief to meet the requirements of an organization to support a specific plan or business decision

3.5 Identify information requirements to support a specific business decision in an organization and develop a research brief to meet the requirements

Develop a research proposal to fulfil a given research brief

3.6 Develop a research proposal to fulfil a given research brief

**Key definitions**

**The marketing research brief** – Description of a research problem used to inform potential suppliers of solutions.

**The proposal** – A written and often an oral response to the research brief.

**Qualitative research** – An unstructured research approach using a small number of selected individuals to produce non-quantifiable insights into attitudes, behaviour, emotions and motivations.

**Quantitative research** – A structured research approach using a sample of the population designed to produce quantifiable data.

**Primary research** – Is research carried out to meet a specific objective. It is new to the research world.

**Secondary research** – Published research or research carried out for some other purpose.

**Desk research** – The collation of existing research results and data from published secondary sources for a different purpose (MRS, 2005).

**Experimental research** – Research measuring causality or the changing of one variable to observe the effect on another whilst other extraneous variables are kept constant.

**Coding** – The process of allocating codes to responses collected during fieldwork facilitating analysis of data (MRS, 2005).

**Editing** – Checking raw data for consistency, coherence and completeness before coding.

**Exploratory research** – Research intended to develop initial ideas or insights and to provide direction for any further research (Wilson, 2003).

**Fieldwork** – The collection of primary data from external sources by means of surveys, observation and experiment (MRS, 2005).

**Group discussions/focus groups** – A number of respondents gathered together to generate ideas through the discussion of, and reaction to, specific stimuli. Under the steerage of a moderator, focus groups are often used in exploratory work or when the subject matter involves social activities, habits and status (MRS, 2005).

**Pilot** – The pre-testing of a research design on a small scale prior to full roll out.

**Longitudinal research** – Data collection over time to examine trends.

**Causal research** – Research that examines whether one variable causes or determines the value of another variable (Wilson, 2003).

**Descriptive research** – Research studies that describe what is happening in a market without potentially explaining why it is happening (Wilson, 2003).

**Observation research** – A non-verbal means of obtaining primary data as an alternative or complement to questioning (MRS, 2005).

## Study Guide

This unit should take around 3 hours to complete.

## Introduction

We now move on to the discipline of marketing research. In this unit we explore the process of planning research and briefing researchers to carry out the process. This will be an important part of your course. The senior examiner in a recent briefing to tutors told them to focus on the process of developing research briefs, responding to those briefs through the presentation of the proposal and then presenting the final report. This activity represents the day-to-day management of the research function in business and you may expect it to form an important part of your assessment in this module.

The brief is very important. Even if the research is to be carried out in-house, a briefing document is required. It provides a fixed reference that all parties involved should sign off. For the commissioner of the research, it provides 'bullet proof' evidence that a certain date or budget was agreed on. In complex research studies, it keeps all parties on track and can help the process of project management.

In this unit we will also look at the research planning process in detail. This will be important for you as it provides the framework for the next few sections of the workbook. We will introduce concepts here that will be explored in more detail in later units.

The planning process is one of the frameworks you will need to learn for the exam. Other structures that will be covered in this unit are the briefing document – this too will be useful to learn.

## The marketing research plan

The planning process for marketing is important (Figure 4.1). Research costs money and takes time, and a planned approach to the process can save both.

1. Review the business situation
2. Define the marketing issue or problem
3. Carryout exploratory research
4. Previous research
5. Internal research
6. Redefine the problem
7. Brief issued
8. Agency selected
9. Research design
10. Desk research
11. Primary research
    a. Qualitative
    b. Quantitative
12. Pilot
13. Fieldwork
14. Data input coding and editing
15. Data analysis
16. Results
17. Findings and recommendations
18. Report/presentation
19. Decision.

Figure 4.1 The marketing research plan

The process may appear complicated but the degree of complexity is dependent on the nature of the research task. Research problems may be solved at the exploratory or internal research phase and a decision may result from a simple database enquiry. For example, 'how many of our customers were repeat buyers last year?' Other problems may demand more complex solutions and may involve the use of multiple external partners to deliver. Let us look at each stage of the process.

## Review the business situation

We start the process with a review of the current business position. Restating the values and mission of the business, and identifying markets served and our unique selling proposition help to focus the research process on the broader goals of the business. It may help to state the marketing objectives of the business and summarize the current marketing plan, which should provide the underpinning for all activity.

Marketing decisions need to be made in response to a constantly changing business environment and research may be needed to inform these decisions.

## Activity 4.1

You are a marketing manager for a major whisky manufacturer. Whisky sales are stagnant and you are looking at the success of spirits-based drinks like Reef and Breezer. You have been asked to look at the development of a whisky-based drink to target a younger market. What information would you need to carry out this project?

The review of the business environment is an ongoing process and research requirements may reflect the dynamic nature of this environment – for example, customers' reaction to a competitor's new product. Or, it may reflect the planned development of the business as expressed in the marketing plan – for example, the international launch of a product range. The process of environmental scanning may be the responsibility of the research department and the issue of sector or competitive briefings either face to face or through a corporate Intranet may be part of this process. The vital thing is that the key decision-makers are kept informed of changes and are able to make intelligent decisions. The business case needs to be established as resources within the marketing function are always under pressure. We need to ensure that the research proposed is fully informed by the business situation and that the relative costs and benefits are weighed up before going ahead.

## Defining the issues or problem

Defining the problem, despite appearances, is not easy. Problems can generally be solved in many ways. The problem definition needs to reflect the organization's resources, or be expressed in a way that clearly identifies the opportunity that is being looked at.

Sometimes, a view of the problem for a pressured executive may not actually be the real issue. The research company that is asked to review marketing communications activity may find that there are particular political issues with the current agency or that the brand is poorly managed or that the pricing strategy is wrong. Very often we have to carry out informal or exploratory research to identify and define the research question we are trying to answer. Poor research questions or problem definition can lead to expensive and unnecessary work being carried out.

## Research problems

Being able to define a problem in an appropriate way is very important. Often managers appear to want the answer to the meaning of life by 5.00 p.m. Understanding the business to be able to isolate and define a problem is a skill that comes with experience. For example, the ill-informed manager may say 'why are our sales falling?' while the experienced manager might say 'what are the perceptions of our service standards against our key competitors?' He has already limited the research to a narrow problem area and researchers have a much clearer idea of the purpose to which the research will be put. It may be that the researcher has to carry out this refining and defining process but it can be helped by good communication and understanding at this stage.

## Carry out exploratory research

This stage, as outlined above, is designed to clarify the research problem. It is largely informal and may involve a range of techniques. It should involve discussions with those who are involved with the problem and its solution. It may involve a review of the trade press and simple scanning of internal documents and resources. The aim is to inform the process and to become 'immersed' in the problem and its potential solutions. Even at this stage the researcher may be thinking ahead about methods that could be used to deliver the information required. The key thing is to uncover the real purpose of the research and, possibly, the constraints in terms of time and budget that may affect the process.

We also need, at this stage, to think about the value of the research. There is little point in spending more on research than the profit to be gained by making a right decision, or the cost of making a wrong decision. Remember research will not eliminate risk entirely but may reduce it to acceptable levels. An understanding of the commercial constraints of carrying out research may be gained through intuition or experience but it can also be worked out more scientifically.

If research is required to justify packaging redesign, then we can estimate the improved sales of such a move and offset the cost of research against this. This objective-and-task approach to setting research budgets is the best way of managing research budgets. However, it is not always possible to carry out this process accurately.

If the cost of a research project to determine between two product flavours was £25000, and the research-based launch generated incremental profits of £40000, then clearly, the research is worthwhile. It should always be possible to estimate the likely impact on a project if it is done with or without research and this can help in determining whether the research should be done and the extent of that research.

## Previous research

As part of this process, previously carried out research should be reviewed to see if the problem has been dealt with elsewhere. It may be that the solution lies in work that has been done in other departments. For example, work to improve the navigation of the website may have been done in the IT department. Access to previously commissioned work may be through the Intranet or through the company library. Or it may be that individual managers have commissioned research which has not been distributed widely through the organizations.

Visiting a major Belgian food manufacturer, a market research executive noticed the same research report on the bookshelves of three separate senior managers. This report cost US$10 000 and the company had effectively wasted US$20 000.

## Internal research

Internal research will involve the use of the MkIS and the database. It may be that the problem, as we said, can be solved at this stage. Whatever, it is worth spending time now on internal records to, maybe, solve the problem or help to define it.

For example, a problem that involves finding out the average age of a company's existing customers may be solved through a simple interrogation of the customer database.

## Redefine the problem

The output of this stage is a clear statement of the research problem that is agreed by all parties. After this, a brief can be written.

## The marketing research brief, short listing and proposal

These sections are covered in more detail below. However, a brief should be written for all projects even if the research is to be carried out in-house. The proposal written to the brief will become the contract for the research when it is accepted, and is equally important.

## Research design

In this part of the process, we start thinking about the type of research methods we might employ to solve the particular problem we have identified. At this stage, we will introduce the terms. Later we will drill down into more detail.

Wilson identifies three types of marketing research. These are:

1. Exploratory
2. Conclusive – descriptive research
3. Conclusive – causal research.

Whilst Wilson tells us that these are not mutually exclusive, they represent a research continuum from purely descriptive to purely causal.

**Activity 4.2**

Using your textbooks write down definitions for the three types of research.

## Desk research

Desk or secondary research is information that has already been gathered for some other purpose. It may be held within the organization or by other organizations. It is called desk research because it is usually accessible from a desk via the Intranet or online or in hard copy. This is dealt with in detail in the next section. In the research plan, desk research is carried out before primary research. This is because it is generally cheaper. It may solve the problem without any need for expensive primary work.

## Primary research

Primary research is research carried out to meet a specific objective. It is 'new to the world research'. Primary research is the common currency of marketing research. It is what most of us have come across either through telephone research, or face-to-face interviews or increasingly through online research.

Primary research may be based on observation, may be qualitative or quantitative.

Observation research is data gathered by observing behaviour. No questions are asked of participants.

The MRS (2005) defines observational research as:

 **Definition**

A non-verbal means of obtaining primary data as an alternative or complement to questioning.

Qualitative research describes research that cannot be quantified or subjected to quantitative analysis. It typically uses small sample sizes and is designed to produce a depth of understanding, context and insight. It helps to uncover the motivation behind the behaviour rather than to identify the behaviour itself. It seeks to get under the skin of respondents, uncovering their deeper feelings. It is essentially subjective but it is a highly developed and important research methodology.

The MRS (2005) defines qualitative research as:

 **Definition**

A body of research techniques which seeks insights through loosely structured, mainly verbal data rather than measurements. Analysis is interpretative, subjective, impressionistic and diagnostic.

## Quantitative research

Quantitative is the opposite of qualitative in that it is statistically verifiable. It provides answers to the questions 'who' and 'how many' rather than the depth of insight as to why. It uses a structured approach to problem-solving using a sample of the population to make statistically based assumptions about the behaviour of the population as a whole.

The MRS (2005) defines quantitative research as:

 **Definition**

> Research which seeks to make measurements as distinct from qualitative research.

## Questionnaire design

Both qualitative and quantitative work require some form of data collection. In qualitative work, this usually involves the creation of a topic guide, which helps the researcher to ensure that all the areas intended to be covered have been dealt with. The data capture mechanism is usually an electronic recording either digitally or via an audio or videotape.

Quantitative research is usually gathered and recorded via a questionnaire. This can be delivered via a number of different media including face-to-face, telephone, mail or online.

## The pilot

All primary research should be piloted or tested to see that the data collection methods are sound. This may be difficult with some forms of qualitative work but a basic run-through is very important. Pilots will help with the structure and sequencing of questions and may identify areas of questioning that have not been considered. It ensures that the data collection device is effective and efficient.

## Fieldwork

Fieldwork is the generic term given to the collection of primary data. It may cover the collection of observational, quantitative and qualitative data. The administration of a major quantitative study may involve serious logistical considerations whilst qualitative work may involve highly qualified and skilled researchers. The management of fieldwork is often given to specialist field managers or fieldwork agencies. The process is very important as the failure to adhere to methodology at this stage may compromise the entire project.

## Data input, coding and editing

Data that is gathered from respondents must be recorded and edited to produce a data set that is capable of being analysed. In qualitative work, this may mean producing a transcript of the interview. In quantitative work, it means creating a data set that the computer can work with. This is covered in detail in Unit 2 where questions have been asked that allow for a number of different answers (open questions). All potential responses must be given a different code to enable analysis. Data is checked for completeness and consistency, and if there are significant problems the respondent may be called back to check details. Often today, data is input straight into the computer via systems known as CATI, CAPI and CAWI.

These are:

- ○ CATI – Computer-aided telephone interviewing
- ○ CAPI – Computer-aided personal interviewing
- ○ CAWI – Computer-aided web interviewing.

## Data analysis

Data is analysed via the computer to produce a range of results. This process is covered in detail in Unit 2.

## Results, findings and recommendations

A marketing decision should result from the results of the research. Results should be presented clearly in a way that focuses on the problem to be solved. It is easy with today's statistical packages to produce hundreds of tables to a high degree of statistical sophistication. Results must be presented in a way that is accessible to the audience and that presents clearly the solution to the problem posed.

## Report/presentation

Presentation of the results will usually be in the form of a written report and this may be supported by an oral presentation. The data will need to be presented but this should be in the appendices. The body of the report remains solutions-focused.

## Decision

The output should be marketing decisions that are made at reduced risk and a feedback loop should exist to the business situation.

## The marketing research brief

We will now look more in detail at the marketing research brief. The briefing document is perhaps the most important stage of the research process. As the old aphorism states 'be careful what you ask for, you may get it'. A tight brief is vital to the management of the marketing research process. It provides a focus for discussion and a guiding hand through the project. Many companies see the briefing process as part of an almost gladiatorial trial of strength where a brief is issued, limited information is given, and the resulting proposals are torn to bits in the arena of the pitch. The justification is that ideas are tested in the heat of the moment and that if an agency cannot justify an approach under fire, they are unlikely to be effective. The lack of detail is seen as allowing the agency to interpret and explore ideas. Some research briefs are given on one side of a page of A4. This may be sufficient but is almost certainly inadequate for complex multifaceted research tasks. Equally some companies go the other way, even specifying the colour and weight of paper for the final presentation. This maybe overkill.

On the other side, some agencies receive a brief as Drayton Bird (2003) says 'rather like a baby bird waiting to be fed by its mother, passively, humbly and gratefully'.

Both approaches are wrong. The best marketing solutions come through cooperation and active involvement. Agencies need the right information in order to be able to produce a suitable proposal. If there are issues over confidentiality, then, confidentiality agreements can be signed before the brief is issued. Members of the MRS are obliged to comply with the code of conduct that ensures client confidentiality. But the agency needs the tools to do the job – in this case, information.

The development of the brief should be a team activity. The structure is outlined below:

o *Identification details* – These should include the title, date, contact names and details.
o *Current business position* – This should detail the nature and scope of the business, key markets served, key competitors and future direction.
o *Marketing and business objectives* – Should be laid down and distinguished between.
o *Research objectives* – Will almost certainly differ from marketing objectives but are informed by them. For example, the marketing objectives may be to enter a new market while the research objectives may be to identify the product attributes that appeal most to potential customers.
o *How the results will be used* – The overall purpose and context for the research needs to be specified. How will the research be used and what other decisions might it inform in the future?
o *Outline methodology* – This is a difficult area but in discussing the problem, research methods may have been discussed. Certainly, where there is expertise in the briefing team the research methodology may have been discussed in detail. There is no danger in allowing the proposing agency to have access to these views. Certainly the brief should include details on whether a qualitative or quantitative approach is required. Also outline question areas could be given.
o *Sample details* – The details of the group of interest should be indicated. If the sample is to include businesses over a certain size, then the agency should be told to avoid them wasting their time.
o *Previous research* – Previously commissioned work that is relevant to the current study may be outlined or made available to the agency pitching for the business.
o *Timings* – It is important that a detailed timetable of activity is included. This should cover time for questions, and details of the formal date and time for the presentation to take place if this is required.
o *Budget* – A tricky area but generally it is advisable to give some indication of the budget that is available for the project.
o *Deliverables* – How will the results be presented and when? Will there be a formal debriefing presentation? How many copies of reports will be needed?
o *Terms and conditions* – Confidentiality and so on.
o *Key personnel names* – And details of all key staff involved in the project.

## Briefing (*Note:* This is a cut-down brief presented to ensure client confidentiality)

Usage and attitudes in the ambient ready meals market (ARMs)

Purpose of the research to establish usage and attitudes to the consumption of ambient ready meals in the domestic UK market

*Background to the company*

Description of the company

Ownership, turnover, brands, ambient ready meal brands

Market's size and market share data, trend's volume and value's competition

*Background to the problem*

Falling retail share, seek to stabilize market share through refined mix

*Research objectives*

Why are ARMs bought?

When are they used?

Who prepares them?

On what occasions?

Perception of quality relative to other RM categories

To competitors

Attitudes to price

Attitudes to advertising

Methods

**Qualitative**

Focus groups in key target audiences

**Quantitative**

Around 1500 housewives, representative of UK households. Quota sample

Question areas built out of the qualitative study

Brands bought, brands recognized, consumption occasion, attitudes to ARMs and other RM categories

We would like your advice on this aspect of research design and implementation

*Timing*

Proposal: 2 April

Presentation: Week commencing 12 April

Commission: 4 May

Report: Early July

*Budget*

In the region of £15 000

*Report to*

Brand manager

Marketing research manager

Marketing director.

## Short listing

Once the brief is written and agreed, it should be sent to a short list of agencies. The short list generally should be no longer than four. Occasionally, more than four agencies are asked to pitch. It is courteous to let the agencies know how many other companies they are up against. It is unlikely if they value their work that they will refuse to pitch. Generally four agencies should be adequate. The MRS code recommends that four agencies are used. It also covers the issue of ownership of the work, which can be significant, put into the proposal. The relevant part of the code is highlighted below (MRS 2005).

### D. The Mutual Rights and Responsibilities of Researchers and Clients

16. These rights and responsibilities will normally be governed by a written Contract between the Researcher and the Client. The parties may amend the provisions of Rules 19–23 below if they have agreed to this in writing beforehand; but the other requirements of this Code may not be altered in this way. Marketing research must also always be conducted according to the principles of fair competition, as generally understood and accepted.

17. The Researcher must inform the Client if the work to be carried out for that Client is to be combined or syndicated in the same project with work for other Clients but must not disclose the identity of such Clients.

18. The Researcher must inform the Client as soon as possible in advance when any part of the work for that Client is to be subcontracted outside the Researcher's own organization (including the use of any outside consultants). On request the Client must be told the identity of any such subcontractor.

19. The Client does not have the right, without prior agreement between the parties involved, to exclusive use of the Researcher's services or those of his organization, whether in whole or in part. In carrying out work for different Clients, however, the Researcher must endeavour to avoid possible clashes of interest between the services provided to those Clients.

20. The following Records remain the property of the Client and must not be disclosed by the Researcher to any third party without the Client's permission:

    (a) Marketing research briefs, specifications and other information provided by the Client.

    (b) The research data and findings from a marketing research project (except in the case of syndicated or multi-client projects or services where the same data are available to more than one Client).

The Client has however no right to know the names or addresses of Respondents unless the latter's explicit permission for this has first been obtained by the Researcher (this particular requirement cannot be altered under Rule 16).

21. Unless it is specifically agreed to the contrary, the following Records remain the property of the Researcher:

    (a) Marketing research proposals and cost quotations (unless these have been paid for by the Client). They must not be disclosed by the Client to any third party, other than to a consultant working for the Client on that project (with the exception of any consultant working also for a competitor of the Researcher). In particular, they must not be used by the Client to influence research proposals or cost quotations from other Researchers.

    (b) The contents of a report in the case of syndicated and/or multi-client projects or services where the same data are available to more than one Client and where it is clearly understood that the resulting reports are available for general purchase or subscription. The Client may not disclose the findings of such research to any third party (other than to his own consultants and advisors for use in connection with his business) without the permission of the Researcher.

    (c) All other research Records prepared by the Researcher (with the exception in the case of non-syndicated projects of the report to the Client, and also the research design and questionnaire where the costs of developing these are covered by the charges paid by the Client).

22. The Researcher must conform to currently agreed professional practice relating to the keeping of such Records for an appropriate period of time after the end of the project. On request the Researcher must supply the Client with duplicate copies of such Records provided that such duplicates do not breach anonymity and confidentiality requirements (Rule 4); that the request is made within the agreed time limit for keeping the Records; and that the Client pays the reasonable costs of providing the duplicates.

23. The Researcher must not disclose the identity of the Client (provided there is no legal obligation to do so), or any confidential information about the latter's business, to any third party without the Client's permission.

24. The Researcher must on request allow the Client to arrange for checks on the quality of fieldwork and data preparation provided that the Client pays any additional costs involved in this. Any such checks must conform to the requirements of Rule 4.

25. The Researcher must provide the Client with all appropriate technical details of any research project carried out for that Client.

26.  When reporting on the results of a marketing research project the Researcher must make a clear distinction between the findings as such, the Researcher's interpretation of these and any recommendations based on them.
27.  Where any of the findings of a research project are published by the Client the latter has a responsibility to ensure that these are not misleading. The Researcher must be consulted and agree in advance the form and content of publication, and must take action to correct any misleading statements about the research and its findings.
28.  Researchers must not allow their names to be used in connection with any research project as an assurance that the latter has been carried out in conformity with this Code unless they are confident that the project has in all respects met the Code's requirements.
29.  Researchers must ensure that Clients are aware of the existence of this Code and of the need to comply with its requirements.

The short list can be drawn up in a number of ways.

 ## Activity 4.3

How would you go about choosing a research agency? With your fellow CIM delegates or on your own brainstorm the methods of selecting an agency.

## The proposal

The proposal should be presented in a written format and on time. A formal presentation may accompany the proposal. The proposal should be seen before any formal face-to-face presentation in order for it to be assessed and questions framed (Figure 4.2). These questions may be sent to the agency before the formal meeting. A proposal may form the final contract for a project and as such can include contract details and terms and conditions as an appendix. The proposal is a marketing tool for the research agency and the use of client testimonials and relevant past contracts is normal. It goes without saying that presentation, spelling and grammar should be faultless.

*Identification data*
> Key contact details, title and date.

*Situation analysis*
> An outline of the current business position.

*Research objectives*
> A clear statement of the purposes of the research.

*Methodology and rationale*
> Crouch and Housden (2003) suggest that the following
> questions should be answered:
> - Why use the sample selection procedure indicated?
> - Why use the size of sample indicated?
> - Why the personal interview technique rather than group discussion?
> - Why a 20-minute questionnaire and not a 30-minute questionnaire?
> - Why are open-ended questions requiring expensive coding and analysis being
>   included in a large-scale quantitative survey?
> - Why is a written report or verbal presentation included, or why not?
> - Why the timetable indicated?
> - Why is the cost indicated?

*Sample*
> A precise definition of the sample to be selected and a justification of this.

*Fieldwork*
> What data collection methods are proposed?

*Questionnaire/topic guide*
> It is unreasonable to expect a final questionnaire but an indication of what the agency
> expects to see in the questionnaire should be provided.

*Data handling and processing*
> How will data be captured, edited, coded and analysed? What tables will be provided?
> How will the data be presented?

*Reporting*
> What is included in the cost?

*Timetable*
> A full detailed timetable of research activity and key milestones.

*Costs*
> What is included? Is VAT included? How long is the quote valid? Terms of business and
> payment schedule.

*CVs of key staff*
> Are the people who are presenting, the people you will be dealing with? What is their
> experience? What professional memberships do they have?

*Supporting evidence*
> Is the agency a member of professional bodies? Are references provided?
> Contract details: the proposal will generally form the contract on acceptance.

Figure 4.2 The proposal: an outline structure

## Selecting the agency

So how do we finally select the agency?

Wilson (2003) identifies a checklist of seven points:

1. The agency's ability to understand the brief and translate it into a comprehensive proposal.
2. The compatibility of agency and client teams. Can we work with them?
3. The evidence of innovation in the proposal. Has the agency added value?
4. Evidence of understanding of the market and the problem facing the organization.
5. Sound methodology.
6. Meeting budget and time scales.
7. Relevant experience.

To this we can add relevant professional body memberships.

## Managing the agency relationship

In a recent article, Baker and Mouncey wrote the following about the problems that research companies have in adding real value to the relationship with their clients. Baker and Mouncey (2003) describe this as an issue faced by many research businesses locked as they say in a 'cultural prison'.

> *We have been struck by how repetitive some of the messages have been and found ourselves asking why so little change has followed. We would offer the view that the industry has not moved quickly enough and appears to have been struck by a level of inertia characteristic of 'cultural prisoners' – those who find themselves doing things the way they've always been done simply because that's the way they've always been done. Are there any 'cultural architects' within the industry in a position to move now to build a brighter future?* (Baker and Mouncey, 2003)

They go on to say that good researchers should follow the following rules to enhance the relationship with their clients:

o Get very involved with the marketing team and understand their problems.
o Anticipate research opportunities.
o Constantly develop research tools which relate to the commercial issues your company and its clients face.
o Deliver your research more effectively and more efficiently.
o Investigate opportunities to deliver research 'online', especially continuous research.
o Encourage informal contact with users.
o Take all opportunities to 'educate' senior management on the actual and potential value of research to the business.
o Be intellectually attuned to your key clients' needs.
o Be sensitive to broad user needs, including the political aspect of commissioning of research and applications in decision-making.
o Create a trusting and open relationship with users.
o Be self-critical, reflective but value your contribution.

It goes without saying that this is the type of relationship that clients should be looking for in a research company. The recruitment of any agency needs to be based on sound relationships at both the business and personal level. Mutual respect, concern and understanding are the cornerstones of good agency–client relations and the best people will go out of their way to ensure that the job is done to the clients' specifications. Relationships based solely on power games or solely on price and the budget are unlikely to live for a long time. Remember both parties in any deal have to make money.

Recruiting international agencies is today straightforward, but there are a range of additional complexities involved.

Proctor (2005) suggests four different approaches to carry out international research.

1. Using own staff or importing agents.

    (a) Problems here may be due to lack of impartiality and lack of skills.

2. Using overseas agencies.

    (a) Selection may be difficult but they should possess knowledge of their home markets.

3. Using a UK-based firm supported by locally based researchers.

    (a) This offers few advantages over 2.

4. Using a consortium of agencies.

    (a) Problems here include variability between agencies.

Most major companies in the United Kingdom have overseas offices or a network of associate agencies operating overseas. In selecting one of these companies the problems of international research are managed as the agency will need to manage an appropriate methodology to meet the objectives of the study.

They will need to ensure that language and cultural differences are recognized and built into research design. The use of back translation of questionnaires and careful piloting is crucial to ensuring comparability in these areas.

They will need to ensure that the research covers similar product use and definition. For example, candied fruits are classified as confectionery products in parts of SE Asia.

They also need to ensure that proposed methodologies are appropriate for each market. For example, online research in some regions is easier than in others.

## In-house or out-of-house
In-house has a range of advantages:

- Control of the research process rests with those who commissioned the work.
- Awareness of the market or sector dynamics.

o  Knowledge of both methodology and results resides within the organization of the cumulative knowledge.
o  Costs – it may be cheaper to manage the tasks in-house.
o  Timing – it may be quicker to produce results.

Disadvantages include:

o  Lack of skills or methodological expertise.
o  Inability to provide true national or international coverage.
o  Bias in terms of interpreting the result from a predetermined point of view.

Advantages of using an agency include:

o  Tighter cost control may be possible.
o  Penalty clauses in contracts can protect the commissioning party.
o  MRS code of conduct or other industry quality control standards will ensure the integrity of data.
o  There is no political element to the research.

Disadvantages:

o  Conflict of interest with other clients.
o  Lack of industry expertise.
o  Allocation of junior staff to smaller projects.

## Evaluating other research reports

It will often be the case that a manager is presented with a research report and asked to apply its findings when he or she was not personally responsible for commissioning the research programme. In this case, the research must be assessed for its quality before its findings can be used with confidence. The following checklist can be used to judge research quality when only the report is available for assessment (Figure 4.3).

# Evaluating existing research

**A scheme for judging research quality**

**1. What were the objectives of the research?**

Are they appropriate to the problem to which the findings are now to be applied?

**2. What method was used to collect the information?**

Is it appropriate to the information needed?

**3. Who was asked the questions?**

Is the sample definition appropriate?

**4. How many people were asked?**

Is the sample size adequate?

**5. What were the actual questions?**

Check the copy of the questionnaire in the technical appendix. Do they seem to be good questions – well framed and appropriate to the objectives?

**6. Who did the fieldwork?**

Is there a basis for judging the quality of the fieldwork? Were professional interviewers used? What checking procedures were used?

**7. When was the fieldwork carried out?**

Was the timing sufficiently recent for the results still to hold? Was the time of year/time of day appropriate?

**8. Are the tabulations comprehensible?**

Are they legible, with clear headings, and indexed?

**9. Would further cross-tabulations produce useful information?**

Are these possible?

**10. Is the report in a logical order and readable?**

Does it make sense?

**11. Is there a meaningful summary?**

Is it easy to grasp the main points being made?

**12. Are there conclusions? (if appropriate)**

Are they supported by the data?

**13. Did the research meet its objectives, and if not, why not?**

Does this invalidate the research?

*Figure 4.3* A Scheme for judging research quality
*Source*: Crouch and Housden (2003)

# Summary

In this unit we looked at the research planning process. We saw that the definition of the research problem is enabled through internal and exploratory research. The use of research should be justified where possible by the cost of making a poor marketing decision or the profit to be made from a better marketing decision.

We saw that the efficient solution of problems through research means that we should start with the cheapest sources of information, that is secondary or desk research. If this does not produce the required information, then we move to primary work. We outlined the different types of marketing research and looked at qualitative and quantitative work. We saw that qualitative work should precede and inform the development of quantitative methodology. We looked in detail at the difference between qualitative and quantitative work.

We went on to look in detail at the briefing process and looked at each stage in turn.

- Identification details
- Current business position
- Marketing and business objectives should be laid down and distinguished between
- Research objectives
- How the results will be used?
- Outline methodology
- Sample details
- Previous research
- Timings
- Budget
- Deliverables
- Terms and conditions
- Key personnel.

We saw that the brief was an important document and that the proposal which is delivered by the short-listed agencies, ultimately, will become the contract for the research programme. We looked at the process of producing a proposal and how we should select the agency.

- Identification data
- Situation analysis
- Research objectives
- Methodology and rationale
- Sample
- Fieldwork
- Questionnaire/topic guide
- Data handling and processing
- Reporting
- Timetable
- Costs
- CVs of key staff
- Supporting evidence
- Contract details.

Finally, we looked at the process of evaluating published work.

# Further study

## Question 4.1

You are the marketing manager for a company marketing china collectibles. You wish to establish an online service for your products. You wish to recruit a research agency to evaluate the potential of this market. Write a briefing document for the project. Explain how you would choose a short list of agencies to pitch for your business and how you would go about selecting the company to do the work.

## Question 4.2

CIM Professional Series Stage Two: Marketing Research and Information

## Donaldson Builders Merchants

Donaldson Builders Merchants is a small chain of builders merchants located in the central belt of Scotland. The company has four outlets located around the edge of the major conurbations of Edinburgh and Glasgow. These supply small builders, plumbers, roofers and similar tradesmen as well as some members of the public (i.e. those more skilled in major do-it-yourself renovations and house improvements). Customers may collect items direct from the trade counter at the warehouse or have the items delivered direct to the building site or house by the company's fleet of 14 lorries. The lorries are equipped with hoists for handling the larger items.

Donaldson supplies:

- Timber and timber products
- Bricks and paving
- Sand and aggregates
- Roofing materials
- Plumbing and heating supplies
- A small range of hand tools.

The company provides credit to the majority of its trade customers. As a result it has a computerized database with details on most of its trade customers relating to name, address, trading address, telephone number, type of business, and purchasing patterns. There are approximately 1100 customers on the database, which probably represents 85 per cent of the company's customers. For the other 15 per cent of customers (the public and trade customers who do not have a credit account), the database holds no record, with the exception of a delivery address if a delivery is required.

The market in which Donaldson operates is becoming more competitive, with the company losing share to national chains such as Jewson and a number of recently opened B&Q trade depots. Tom Donaldson, the Managing Director, feels that the company's personal service and flexibility is far superior to these competitors, and is therefore keen to build on this and find ways in which to compete other than on price. The company has never undertaken research before but is keen to find out more from its customers about:

- Their existing and future purchasing behaviour.
- Their attitudes towards Donaldson Builders Merchants (such as product range, service, flexibility of delivery, etc.).
- Their suggestions about improvements required in Donaldson's offering.

They are willing to spend up to £50 000 on the research project.

## Part A Question 1

You are a director of a market research agency and have been asked to:

(a) Identify any further information that you would require from Donaldson prior to writing a proposal.

**(10 marks)**

(b) Having made reasonable assumptions regarding the answers to the information required in Question 1a, produce a short 3- to 5-page proposal to address the needs of Tom Donaldson. (For the purpose of this question your proposal should exclude the sections relating to Personal CVs, Related Experience and References and Contract Details.)

**(40 marks)**

## CIM Professional Series Stage Two

## Part B Question 4

As Mr Donaldson has never undertaken research before, he needs guidance in the selection of an agency to undertake the research. He has received proposals from three agencies and he has asked you as an old friend who has used agencies in the past to provide a report on:

(a) The selection criteria to use in determining the successful agency.
(b) The elements of the professional codes of market and social research practice that relate to the relationships between researchers and clients.

## Question 4.3

CIM Professional Series Stage Two: Marketing Research and Information

Davidson Hotels operate in a group of seven hotels in the United Kingdom. The hotels are all rated at the three- or four-star level, with four of them having swimming pools and leisure centres. They tend to be located close to tourist/leisure type areas of outstanding natural beauty and local heritage sites. Their customer mix has traditionally consisted of 50 per cent business travellers, 30 per cent coach parties and 20 per cent leisure travellers/leisure breaks. However, with the growth in budget hotels offering standard rooms and limited additional services, the number of business travellers has dropped by more than 38 per cent over the past 12 months. The coach party market is relatively static, therefore the company's main opportunity for growth is seen by management as being in the leisure travel market, with the swimming pools being used to promote all-weather/all-year leisure destinations.

The company is therefore keen to understand more about the leisure travel sector, in particular:

o The trends in the market
o The criteria used by leisure travellers when selecting their accommodation in areas with outstanding natural beauty or heritage sites
o The reasons why existing leisure customers use Davidson Hotels and their likelihood of returning to the same hotel or another hotel in the Davidson Hotel chain.

They are willing to spend up to £50 000 on the research project.

*Note*: The above material has been based on a fictitious company for assessment purposes.

## Part A Question 1

You are a manager of a market research agency and have been asked to:

(a)  identify any further information that you would require from Tom Davidson, the chief executive of the company, prior to writing a marketing research proposal.

**(10 marks)**

(b)  using the information in Question 1a and making reasonable assumptions, you are required to produce a short 3- to 5-page proposal to address the needs of Tom Davidson. (For the purpose of this question, your proposal should exclude the sections relating to personal CVs, related experience and references and contract details.)

**(40 marks)**

## Question 4.4

### Professional Diploma in Marketing: Marketing Research and Information

### Splash Ltd

The Spanish-based cosmetics company Splash Ltd has built an international retail chain that is in a strong expansion phase. Its fresh, hand-made soaps and cosmetics are available in 240 stores worldwide. The emphasis is on making and selling products without animal ingredients made from only fresh fruit and vegetables, finest essential oils and safe synthetics. It controls the whole process of getting its products to the consumer, including design, manufacturing and retail.

The retail stores look like a cross between a cheese shop and a market stall, with slabs of soap and other fresh products stacked ready for cutting and bagging. The retail environment is dominated by an aroma of soaps and perfumes. The company is now planning to open its first UK store in the centre of London.

Prior to designing the outlet, determining the product range and potential promotions, the company is keen to undertake a programme of market research with potential customers, to examine the buying behaviour and attitudes of British consumers of high quality soap and cosmetic products.

The company hopes that answers to such questions will help in the successful launch of their first UK store.

The company is willing to spend up to £50 000 on the research project.

*Note*: The above data has been based on a fictitious situation drawing on a variety of events and does not reflect the management practices of any particular organization.

### Part A – Compulsory

### Question 1

You are a research executive in a market research agency and have been asked to:

(a)  Identify appropriate further information that you would require from the company, prior to writing a proposal.

**(10 marks)**

(b)  Having made reasonable assumptions regarding the answers to the information required in part 1a, produce a proposal to address the research needs of the company1

**(40 marks)**

For the purpose of this question, your proposal should exclude the sections relating to personal CVs, related experience and references and contract details.

**(Total 50 marks)**

## Question 4.5

### Professional Diploma in Marketing: Marketing Research and Information

### Jack Ltd

Jack Ltd is a leading international speciality retailer offering clothing, accessories and personal care products for men, women, children and babies under the Jack brand name. In the United Kingdom, Jack Ltd operates more than 150 stores nationwide. Each of the stores employs sales associates and other store personnel that are trained to answer customers' questions about fabric, fit and fashion and to help them select merchandise that's perfect for them. However, even with this training, around 85 per cent of all potential customers that enter a Jack store (measured using electronic counters in the doorways of each store) leave without buying anything. Senior management are keen to reduce this percentage, however, they are unclear as to the reasons why people leave their stores empty-handed. It may be due to the product range, store layout, service quality, pricing or any range of factors. Marketing research is therefore needed to explore the reasons why such a large percentage of potential customers fail to make a purchase.

The company hopes that answers to such questions will help to identify ways to increase sales amongst these customers.

The company is willing to spend up to £40 000 on the research project.

### Part A – Compulsory

### Question 1

You are a research executive in a market research agency and have been asked to:

(a) Identify any further information that you would require from the company, prior to writing a proposal.

**(10 marks)**

(b) Having made reasonable assumptions regarding the answers to the information required in part 1a, produce a proposal to address the research needs of the company. (For the purpose of this question, your proposal should exclude the sections relating to personal CVs, related experience and references and contract details.)

**(40 Marks)**
**(Total 50 Marks)**

## Question 4.6

### PART A

### SeaLux Cruises

SeaLux Cruises is a new cruise operator consisting of two ships sailing out of the port of Southampton in Southern England. It has been established for just over one year and provides cruise-based vacations using its 1400 berth ship, Med Blue, around the Mediterranean, and cruises around Scandinavia and the Baltic States on its 1250 berth ship, Northern Blue. The focus is on offering relaxing vacations with an emphasis on 'luxurious discovery' through a wide range of dining, entertainment and excursion choices. A 12-day Mediterranean cruise on the Med Blue with stops in Venice, Barcelona, Rome and five other cities, starts at around £2000.

Although the first year has gone well with very satisfied passengers and no technical problems, the cruises have been running at below optimum capacity. The level of bookings for the 16 cruises scheduled for the next 12 months is also around 35 per cent below target. This is causing the company some concern, particularly when industry sources and the performance of competitors clearly suggest that the UK cruise market is going through a period of tremendous growth. There is a view among the senior management of the company that the product offering is correct for the target market but the promotion and sales activity is failing to raise awareness and attract or convert potential passengers. Unlike other cruise lines that use travel agents to sell their cruises, SeaLux undertakes direct advertising in national newspapers and magazines leading to customers booking direct with SeaLux through their internet site or telephone hotline.

The senior management is now concerned that low sales may reflect an unwillingness of the target market (the over 40 age group) to book cruises on a direct basis, as they may require the advice and reassurance of a travel agent. Alternatively, the poor sales may simply reflect a low awareness of the advertising and the company's offerings. SeaLux is therefore keen to undertake a programme of research to examine the effectiveness of the advertising and the attitudes of the target market towards the preferred methods and channels for the booking of cruise-based holidays. The company is willing to spend up to £70 000 on the research project.

The above data has been based on a fictitious situation drawing on a variety of events and does not reflect the management practices of any particular organization.

### PART A – Compulsory

### Question One

You are a Research Executive in a market research agency and have been asked to:

(a) identify appropriate further information that you would require from SeaLux, prior to writing a proposal.

**(10 marks)**

Having made reasonable assumptions regarding the answers to the information required in part 1a, produce a proposal to:

(b) address the research needs of the company.

**(40 marks)**
**(Total 50 marks)**

For the purpose of this question, your proposal should exclude the sections relating to personal CVs, related experience and references and contract details.

Go to www.CIM.co.uk for specimen answers to this question.

# Bibliography

Baker, S., Mouncey, P. (2003) 'The market researcher's manifesto', *International Journal of Marketing Research*, **45**(4).

Crouch, S. and Housden, M. (2003) *Marketing Research for Managers*, 3rd edition, Butterworth-Heinemann.

Drayton Bird (2003) www.draytonbird.com.

MRS (2005) www.mrs.org.uk.

Proctor, T. (2005) *Essentials of Marketing Research*, 4th edition, FT Prentice Hall.

Wilson, A. (2003) *Marketing Research: An Integrated Approach*, FT Prentice Hall.

# unit 5 using secondary research

## Learning objectives

On completing this unit you will be able to

- Define secondary marketing research

- Explain types of secondary data

- Understand where to find secondary data

- Understand the limitations and strengths of secondary research

- Look for data online

- Understand the applications of secondary research

- Complete syllabus elements 4.1, 4.2.

| | |
|---|---|
| Evaluate the appropriateness of different qualitative and quantitative research methodologies to meet different research situations | 4.1 Explain the uses, benefits and limitations of secondary data<br>4.2 Recognize the key sources of primary and secondary data |

## Key definitions

**External data** – Data that is held by external organizations.

**Internet** – A network of computers.

**World Wide Web** – An Internet protocol supervised by the worldwide web consortium at www.w3.org.

**Intranet** – A closed private company network based on web technology.

96

**Extranet** – A process that shares information from internal source with selected external organizations.

**Search engines** – Internet-based tools for searching for Uniform Resource Location (URL) or web addresses.

**Newsgroups** – Web-based notice board services.

**Chat rooms** – Locations on the Internet enabling web-based text or video-based real time interaction.

**ISP** – Internet service provider.

## Study Guide

This unit should take you around 3 hours to complete. You will need to explore online services, so make sure that you have access to the Internet. You should allow another 2 hours to complete the tasks set for you.

## Introduction

Secondary desk research is an important part of the researcher's armoury. In the last unit, we saw that the key goal of marketing research is to provide effective solutions efficiently. The use of desk research can ensure this. In the planning process, it precedes primary work. This is because it generally can be acquired at lower cost and can be obtained far more quickly. The key thing for the researcher is knowing where and how to look, and how to judge the quality of this work. In the IT age, there are a vast range of sources available to the researcher; some are more reliable than others.

## What is secondary or desk research?

The MRS (2005) defines desk research as 'The collation of existing research results and data from published secondary sources for a specific, often unrelated, project'.

Crouch and Housden (2003) define secondary desk research as 'data that has already been published by someone else, at some other time period, usually for some other reason than the present researcher has in mind. The researcher is therefore a secondary user of already existing data which can be obtained and worked on at a desk'.

Alan Wilson (2003) defines secondary data as 'Information that has previously been gathered for some purpose other than the current research project. The data is available either free or at a cost and can be delivered electronically by computer or in printed hard copy format'.

There are two broad classifications of secondary data – internal and external.

We dealt with internal data in Unit 2 on the database. In this unit we will explore external data.

The definitions raise issues about the nature of secondary data.

## Activity 5.1

Reflect on the definitions of secondary research. What problems do you think the researcher may experience in using secondary data?

## The strengths and weaknesses of secondary data

### Strengths

- It is cheap or free of charge. Costs vary but very often a full report on markets or market sectors can be put together very quickly and cheaply.
- It may provide an answer to the problem – this will save enormous time and effort.
- It can guide or provide direction for primary work.
- It can suggest methodologies for data collection.
- It can indicate problems with particular methodologies.
- It can provide historic or comparative data to enable longitudinal studies.

### Weaknesses

- It is not related to the research question and the temptation may be to force the data to fit the question.
- It may not be directly comparable. This is particularly the case in international markets where markets may be defined differently. For example, data on the low-alcohol drinks market varies from market to market as definitions of 'low' alcohol change.
- Data may be incomplete. For example, the cross channel trade in drinks and tobacco is significant but not included in official statistics. Data may relate to certain markets – for example, data on food markets may relate to the retail trade rather than to the retail and catering markets, or vice versa. Pan-national studies will certainly find this. In many countries, a significant amount of the retail trade is made through street markets. This is very hard to quantify. In this case it may be possible to weight data or use other techniques to complete the data set.
- It may not be available. It may be that there are certain markets that are not adequately covered – for example, in Europe, data on the Belgian or Dutch market is often hard to obtain as these are relatively small markets within the European Union.
- The data may have been gathered for a particular purpose. Production statistics in certain markets are unreliable. Data may be presented to portray a company or government in a more favourable light. We see this in the United Kingdom with the ongoing debate of how unemployment figures should be presented. Information that is reviewed without access to the methodology should be viewed with suspicion and other data sources should be brought in to confirm the data under review.
- Data for international markets may be more expensive and unreliable. Secondary data in certain markets may not be up to date. It may be collated at a different level. For example, your client may be interested in chocolate-coated biscuits but data only covers the total market for baked goods. A common problem is data that has been gathered at manufacturing selling price and researchers take this value as the retail value of the market. You need to be quite clear at what point in the value chain data has been captured. Is it retail or ex-factory?
- Data for international markets may be in a foreign language. Translating costs in business markets are very expensive.
- Time series data may be interrupted by definition changes, for example the recent announcement by the British government about changes to the way inflation is calculated.

## Monitor your Euro market

A major research company was commissioned by a leading American food manufacturer to research the market for its products in the European Union. The starting point of the research design was to buy secondary research from Euromonitor. The report provided market data on all 15 EU countries, including market size, trends, market segmentation data, brand shares, brief profiles of the leading players in the sector retail and distribution analysis, and some basic consumer research. At around £7500 the report gave executives very good background data and a short cut through the research problem.

## Evaluating secondary data

When looking at published research reports, the user should ask the following questions:

- Who published the study? Was it a national government? Was it a trade association? What is the nature of the organization? Is the publisher of the data the same as the organization that collected the data?
- For what purpose? Is the study designed to sell a service? Is it designed to counter negative publicity? Is it designed to generate publicity?
- When was the data gathered? Is it relevant?
- How was the data collected? Was the data capture mechanism reliable? Was it a self-selecting sample?
- Who collected the data? Are they independent? Are they trained? Are they members of a professional body? What sample was used?
- How reliable is the data?
- Is raw data presented?
- Can I replicate the study? Is the methodology included? Can I test the data for accuracy?
- Is the data comparable?

## Sources of secondary data

There is a vast range of sources of secondary data, and the emergence of the Internet as a key information consolidator and provider has increased the availability of information to the desk researcher. It has increased access to previously remote information, for example data held in libraries overseas, and it has increased the ability to distribute this information. We will look later at online sources and methodology.

Data on markets and organizations can be obtained from many different sources. An able researcher will be flexible and innovative in their approach to information searches, and the most unlikely sources can reveal important information. For example, the publications of the HR department in a certain company told a researcher about the staffing levels at particular factories in India which had been classified as confidential by the corporate affairs and marketing departments.

## List of sources

One of the best aids to secondary researchers are lists of sources. The specialists in this area are Euromonitor and Croners.

Euromonitor publishes a range of information directories.

These include the following:

### *Companies*

Global Market Share Planner: 7 Volume Set

Major Market Share Companies: Americas

Major Market Share Companies: Asia-Pacific

Major Market Share Companies: Eastern Europe, Middle East And Africa

Major Performance Rankings

Market Share Tracker

World Leading Global Brand Owners

### *Countries*

Asian Marketing Data And Statistics 2003

European Marketing Data And Statistics 2006

International Marketing Data And Statistics 2006

Latin American Marketing Data & Statistics 2004

The Enlarged European Union: A Statistical Handbook

World Consumer Lifestyles on The Internet

World Economic Factbook 2005/2006

World Economic Prospects 2003

World Health Databook New

World Marketing Data And Statistics on the Internet

### *Business information sources*

Asia-Pacific Marketing Information Sourcebook

World Retail Directory And Sourcebook

Try looking at the Euromonitor website at www.euromonitor.com.

Other research directory services are available from www.marketresearch.com. Other companies providing this type of service include:

- o Market Search Directory is a list of market research reports from 700 research companies. Worldwide details at www.marketsearch-dir.com
- o Croners Executive Companion and Croners Office Companion includes a list of business information services. The service is available on- and off-line. Details are at www.croner.co.uk
- o www.europa.eu./index_en.htm: A listing of information sources in the European Union.

## Governments

Governments publish vast quantities of data about the economy and society. Much of this data forms the basis of commercial services, provided at some cost by research firms. For example, the geo-demographic profiling services draw heavily on census data. These publications are very cheap and it is always worth checking to see what is available. Certain governments are making this data available online. The US government is exceptional and the UK government's e-government initiative is slowly opening up data sources to online enquiry. A good example of this is the tradepartners' website which can be found at the following address:

www.tradepartners.gov.uk

Other sources can be identified through the following sites:

www.direct.gov.uk

www.statistics.gov.uk

UK online is a general guide to government online services whilst www.statistics.gov.uk is the website of National Statistics, the statistical service of the UK government.

There is also a statistical service for the European Union and this provides comparative data across all member countries.

These can be found at

http://unstats.un.org/

Other national governments have their own statistical services and these can normally be accessed online.

The UN statistical service offers links through to these sites at

http://unstats.un.org/unsd/methods/inter-natlinks/sd_natstat.htm

National and international data sources and links are available also via the Euromonitor website or by searching on Google or other search engines.

The US census also provides excellent international data at http://www.census.gov/ipc/www/idbnew.html.

## Activity 5.2

Visit www.statistics.gov.uk and spend 30 minutes surfing through the site. Add it to your favourites. Try to identify publications that may be useful for your business.

## Trade organizations

Trade organizations is a broad category of information providers that include

- Trade associations
- The trade press
- Professional institutes
- Chambers of commerce
- Regulatory bodies and pressure groups.

### Trade associations

These exist for almost every industrial sector. Some publish amazing details on their members' activities. Associations such as the BMRA publish annual reviews of the Market Research industry for its members. A directory of trade associations is published by CBD and this identifies trade associations with contact details and details of activities. These can be found at www.cbdresearch.com.

### Trade press

Trade press is invaluable as a source of up-to-date information on markets and companies. Almost every trade is represented, and titles like Pig Farmer Weekly, Tunnels and Tunnelling, Wood Based Panelling International, The Grocer, Advertising Age and Off Licence News give an indication of the range of sources that are available. The journalists quickly become experts in their field and they too are worth contacting. Details of trade titles can be found in the advertisers' annual.

Web address: www.hollis-pr.co.uk.

For international press, Willings Press Guide is an alternative source both on- and off-line. Online they are at www.willingspress.com.

### Professional institutes

These institutes generally represent individuals within the profession and some provide excellent data on their industries.

The CIM is a good example. It has a wide range of information on its website and supports members through its knowledge centre and library in Cookham. Hopefully, you have already used the website. It is at www.cim.co.uk.

### Chambers of commerce

These can be very helpful for organizations, particularly in overseas markets, where commitment to the Chambers' mission is sometimes greater than in the United Kingdom.

The British Chambers of Commerce website is at www.britishchambers.org.uk. The world organization is the World Chambers Federation and their web address is at www.iccwbo.org.

## Regulatory bodies and pressure groups

The activities of organizations like the Financial Services Authority, the Advertising Standards Authority and Oftel generate information on the sectors they cover.

Look at the Advertising Standards Authority website at www.asa.org.uk.

Pressure groups like Greenpeace or Action on Smoking and Health (ASH) can provide data on the industries they monitor and causes they represent. www.ash.org.uk. has a statistical report on smoking and smoking behaviour.

Trade unions and other member organizations can provide useful data. For example, the Salmon and Trout Association covers the market for fly fishing through its activities aimed at preserving habitat and stocks.

## Financial data

The activities of investment houses and stockbrokers produce regular reports on the activities of their target companies. The briefings that inform these reports often contain useful market and strategic data that can be extremely revealing.

## The press

The *Financial Times* and *Wall Street Journal* are required reading for marketing professionals, and their services include online archives. Other national and local press can be accessed for relevant data.

The FT and *Wall Street Journal* are at

www.ft.com

www.wsj.com

# Specialist services

## Information about companies

The best source of information in the United Kingdom is Companies House; all companies over a certain size are obliged by law to lodge financial and other information at Companies House. The companies house website also has a range of links to international disclosure of company data.

Companies House is found online at www.companies-house.gov.uk.

Other organizations provide information on companies. Services such as Dunn and Bradstreet and Kompass are excellent commercial sources of company information.

## Information on markets

There are hundreds of companies providing secondary or published data on markets.

A full list can be accessed at the MRS website: www.mrs.org.

Some of the more important providers include

## *ACNielsen*

Nielsen provides data on media and advertising spend and a range of data to industry.

www.acnielsen.co.uk

**BMRB**

It is a leading UK research agency that provides the Target Group Index (TGI) which is a valuable resource to marketers and allows customer data to be enhanced in a number of ways. It also provides a useful insight into diverse markets.

## Activity 5.3

Go to www.bmrb-tgi.co.uk. Follow the links and find out as much as you can about TGI. After your session, you should be able to answer the following questions:

- What is TGI?
- What sample is used?
- How is data captured?
- What implications does this have for my business?

Many companies exist to provide services to industry in the area of secondary research.

### Syndicated research services

Companies like Mintel, Euromonitor, and Frost and Sullivan provide what are known as syndicated or multi-client studies on a huge range of markets. These are published market research studies that are available to anybody who wishes to buy them. Prices range from a few hundred to many thousands of pounds depending on the complexity of the report and number of markets covered.

Typically, reports will cover

- Market size, structure and trends
- Import, export and production data
- Key players' competitive profiles including financial data
- Market share data
- Advertising and marketing communications spend.

Details can be found at the following websites:

- www.mintel.com
- www.euromonitor.com
- www.frost.com.

### Online aggregators

The development of the Internet and its diverse capabilities has lead to the emergence of a new breed of information providers who aggregate or bring together information from diverse sources and allow access on a subscription basis or for a one-off payment.

Examples include general services like Hoovers, Profound and Lexis Nexis, and specialist services like the World Advertising Research Centre (WARC) or MAD which covers the UK marketing press. These may contain translations from a range of international publications. Details can be found at the following websites:

www.mad.co.uk

www.profound.com

www.hoovers.com

www.lexisnexis.com

www.warc.com.

## Information on online markets

There is a great deal of information on the Internet on online markets. Not all of it is reliable. The government, as indicated above, is often the most reliable source and there are more reputable suppliers in the market. The best sources for online research are often based in the United States, but there are a range of other useful suppliers.

## Activity 5.4

Look at some or all of the following websites. They have been shown to be useful sources of research or data on the online sector.

- o www.clickz.com/stats
- o www.intersperience.com
- o www.forrester.com
- o www.oracle.com
- o www.ncr.com
- o www.gartner.com
- o www.broadvision.com
- o www.accenture.com
- o www.pwc.com
- o www.bcg.com
- o www.idc.com
- o www.bitpipe.com
- o www.iabuk.net
- o www.ovum.com

Evaluate them against the following criteria:

- o Name of company
- o Business sector
- o Research company, hardware supplier, software supplier, consultancy, trade association
- o Quality of data
- o Range of data
- o Credibility
- o Recency
- o Geographic scope
- o Sector coverage
- o Cost
- o Data collection method.

Follow the links and add them to your favourites list.

Other sources include

- o CRM technology companies
- o Management consultancy
- o IT consultants.

## Searching online

Online research is the fastest growing area of research today and the area of secondary research is no different. The problem is that with such a huge array of sources available, where do we start looking.

If you know the URL or web address, then you can go online via your Internet service provider (ISP) and go directly to the site. From this site a series of links may be followed or 'surfed' and this process can yield useful information. If you do not know the URL or your search is more general, then the starting point is the use of search engines or directories.

 **Definition**

**Search engines** – Search engines use 'spiders' or 'robots' to go out and search the web and create a database of sites which is then matched against the search terms or keywords entered by the browser in the search engine.

Some examples of search engines include

- o Alta Vista www.altavista.com
- o Google www.google.com
- o www.lycos.com
- o Northern Light www.northernlight.com.

 **Activity 5.5**

Try searching for marketing research using at least two different search engines. What are the differences? Try using the advanced search options to narrow the search to qualitative research.

 **Definition**

**Directories** – Directories are compiled lists or indexes of websites that are reviewed and often rated by compilers. This can remove the randomness of searches through engines which may be an advantage in the early stages of exploratory research. It is possible to pay web directory compilers to ensure that a site occurs early in the list of sites presented as the result of a search. *Source*: Crouch and Housden (2003).

Examples of subject directories include

- o LookSmart www.looksmart.com
- o Lycos www.lycos.com
- o Yahoo www.yahoo.com.

**Activity 5.6**

Try exercise five using the directories. What differences do you notice?

## Searching online

Successful online searching will be achieved if the search terms are carefully defined. We saw how this process works in Unit 3. Careful phrasing of the search term and creative use of Boolean operators can help.

Boolean operators are usually found in the advance search section in the search engine or directory.

Boolean logic operators help the browser search the web.

The simplest of these are the words 'and' or '+', 'not' or '–' and 'or'. Others may allow the use of what are known as proximity operators, such as 'followed by' or 'near'. These can help refine search terms and produce more relevant results.

For example, MRS 'and' UK 'not' USA would refine search terms on this term.

Other engines may have advanced search facilities which employ Boolean operators in a more user-friendly format.

The use of Google's advance search feature can reduce the number of results for any search term to far more manageable and relevant numbers.

There are directories of search engines at www.searchability.com and www.virtualfreesites.com.

### Newsgroups, blogs and discussion forums

Newsgroups exist for almost every topic under the sun, including marketing research. Newsgroups can be useful sources of information and also for establishing opinions on products and services. Some companies monitor newsgroups for research purposes and some seed newsgroups with product information and recommendations. This is a dubious practice if it is not done transparently and if uncovered can lead to the user being barred from the service.

Most search engines allow groups to be searched for. Try www.groups.google.com.

Blogs can be very useful sources of information and there are significant resources available on research and marketing. Search via http://blogsearch.google.com, to find relevant content.

# Summary

In this unit we looked at definitions of secondary research, and looked at the strengths and limitations of research. These were

## Strengths

o   It is cheap or free of charge.
o   It may provide an answer to the problem; this will save enormous time and effort.
o   It can guide or provide direction for primary work.
o   It can suggest methodologies for data collection.
o   It can indicate problems with particular methodologies.
o   It can provide historic or comparative data to enable longitudinal studies.

## Weaknesses

o   It is not related to the research question and the temptation may be to force the data to fit the question.
o   It may not be directly comparable.
o   Data may be incomplete.
o   It may not be available.
o   The data may have been gathered for a particular purpose.

We looked at the range of sources that are available to the researcher.

These included

o   Government data
o   Trade associations
o   Professional institutes
o   Pressure groups
o   Regulatory bodies
o   Financial institutions
o   Company data
o   Online aggregators
o   Directories
o   The trade press
o   National press
o   Specialist companies
o   Syndicated services.

We saw that almost anything published on or by companies is capable of yielding useful data on companies, industries and markets.

We also explored secondary data relating to companies' markets and online markets. We explored how search engines and directories work and the use of Boolean operators in helping searches on the Internet.

Finally, we looked at the online market and explored ways of maximizing the effectiveness of searching online.

# Further study

## Question 5.1

You are working for a small Midlands-based manufacturer of components for the motor industry. Your sales manager has identified a potential new market in the Czech Republic. The company cannot afford to carry out marketing research without establishing the nature of the demand for the product.

You have been asked to produce a preliminary market report from secondary data. There is no syndicated study available. What are the advantages and disadvantages of this approach? How can the disadvantages be overcome?

# Hints and tips

Both Wilson (2003) and Crouch and Housden (2003) have significant resources outlined in the relevant chapters. You should scan these chapters and add relevant websites to your list of favourites.

# Bibliography

Crouch, S., Housden, M. (2003) *Marketing Research for Managers*, 3rd edition, Butterworth-Heinemann.

MRS (2005) www.mrs.org.

National Statistics (2005) www.statistics.gov.uk.

Wilson, A. (2003) *Marketing Research: An Integrated Approach*, FT Prentice Hall.

# unit 6 observation research

Evaluate the appropriateness of different qualitative and quantitative research methodologies to meet different research situations

4.3 Describe and compare the various procedures for observing behaviour

## Key definitions

**Observation** – A non-verbal means of obtaining primary data as an alternative or complement to questioning (MRS, 2005).

**Panels** – A permanent representative sample maintained by a market research agency from which information is obtained on more than one occasion either for continuous research or for ad hoc projects (MRS, 2005).

**Audit** – The measurement of product volume and value through the distribution network. Audit may be wholesale, retail or consumer.

**Mystery shopping** – The collection of information from retail outlets, showrooms and so on, by people trained to observe, experience, record and measure the customer service process posing as ordinary members of the public (MRS, 2005).

**Peoplemeter** – The mechanical device used by BARB to collect data on TV audiences in the United Kingdom.

**EPOS** – Electronic Point Of Sale equipment.

**Cookies** – A file stored on your hard drive used to identify your computer and other information including preferences to another remote computer.

**Ethnographic research** – Observation involving total immersion in the life of the subject.

## Study Guide

This unit should take you around 3 hours to complete.

## Introduction

Observation research is one of the fastest growing areas of marketing research. Techniques such as mystery shopping and audits are growing in popularity as the need to ensure customer satisfaction is growing and the technical ability to monitor individuals' behaviour expands. Our online behaviour can be tracked even to the extent of being able to trace the search terms used to access a particular website. The use of CCTV and video means that the average UK consumer is caught on camera many times a day. This of course raises ethical considerations that we discussed earlier. Observation is however a tried and tested technique in marketing research.

## Definitions of observation research

The MRS (2005) defines observation as 'A non-verbal means of obtaining primary data as an alternative or complement to questioning'.

Wilson defines (2003) it as 'a data gathering approach where information on the behaviour of people, objects and organizations is collected without any questions being asked of the participant'.

## Observation strengths

Observation has several strengths:

- o It is not dependent on the respondents' memory. It records exactly what has happened, not what the respondent believes has happened.

## Smoke and mirrors

In surveys of smoking behaviour, respondents have been shown to under-report the number of cigarettes they smoke by up to 100 per cent. The same applies to alcohol units. Very often GPs will write cigarettes smoked as 10/20; 10 being the reported number, 20 the more likely figure.

- o The potential for bias in research is reduced as the researcher is the witness of behaviour rather than actively asking for information – the way an interviewer asks for information can influence responses.
- o Mechanical recording of observed behaviour may reduce the incidence of reporting errors.
- o Observation does not rely on the verbal skills of a respondent to describe the behaviour.
- o Observation measures what has happened, not what respondents say that they will do in a certain situation.
- o Observation can counter the high refusal rates in some markets.
- o Observation can be used to monitor behaviour preceding an action. For example, picking up and looking at competing products before making a final decision.
- o Observation does not interfere with the respondents' day-to-day life. It is their activity that is of interest. They do not have to fill in diaries or complete questionnaires.

## Disadvantages of observation techniques

There are some disadvantages:

- o Observation does not measure the reasons for certain behaviour. It cannot uncover motivation or attitudes
- o Observation cannot measure the likelihood of repeat behaviour
- o Only public behaviour can be assessed. Private behaviour is very difficult to research in this way although efforts have been made to manage this process.

## Categories of observation research

Wilson (2003) identifies five different categories of observation research. These are as follows:

1. Natural versus contrived
2. Visible versus hidden
3. Structured versus unstructured
4. Mechanized versus human
5. Participant versus non-participant.

| Natural | Contrived |
|---|---|
| Rather like David Attenborough and mountain gorillas, customers are observed in their natural state | The researcher sets up an observation situation |
| Respondents may be observed going around a supermarket, browsing a website and so on | This may be a supermarket fixture set up in a room or children playing with new toys with the researcher present |
| They are not aware that they are being observed | Customers are aware that they are being observed |
| **Visible** | **Hidden** |
| Customers are aware that observation is taking place because they can see the recording equipment | Respondents know that they are being observed but cannot see the observer or recording equipment |
| **Structured** | **Unstructured** |
| Observers keep a tally or count of certain behaviours | Observers record or make notes on all aspects of the observed behaviour |
| **Mechanical** | **Human** |
| The installation of equipment to measure behaviour | More appropriate for complex behaviour involving multiple interactions |
| **Participant** | **Non-participant** |
| The observer participates in the observed behaviour, for example, in mystery shopping | The behaviour is observed remotely |

## Telephone man

Observational research by Abbott Meade Vickers for British Telecommunications informed an advertising strategy that aimed to get men spending more time using the telephone. Observation found that men spent less time on the telephone, generally stood whilst talking on the phone and passed the phone to their partner when family or social events were being discussed.

The campaign that was developed from this involved a student ringing home, the phone was answered by her father who said 'I'll fetch your mother'. The student said 'I phoned to talk to you'. A surprised father then enjoys his chat with his daughter. The strap line 'it's good to talk' followed.

## Observation methodologies

There are a range of observational techniques that are used throughout the research industry. Many of these take advantage of new technology.

## Audits and scanner-based observation

An audit measures product movement and consumption through the value chain.

There are three types of audit – wholesale, retail and home.

The use of EPOS and hand-held scanning devices has changed this sector of the market significantly over the last 10 years.

Audits have been in place for some time, but the process of carrying them out was far more time-consuming than it is today. Researchers used to do stock counts looking at stock delivered into retail stores, stock out and stock remaining. This would give a clear idea of retail sales in the period under consideration. Companies still carry out this work in smaller stores to verify wastage and stock loss through theft, but the use of EPOS technology has significantly reduced the amount of time taken to produce results. Companies like ACNielsen and TN Sofres are significant players in this market.

## Activity 6.1

Visit www.acnielsen.co.uk/products/cps.shtml and www.superpanel.tns-global.com/. Review the information that is available on the services that ACNielsen and TN Sofres offer to the market. At the ACNielsen site you should review the retail measurement services and consumer panel services, particularly Homescan.

In the past, home audit methodology has included the keeping of written diary records. Respondents keep a diary of behaviour. These are still used in markets or by companies where scanning technology is not available, and to measure behaviour that is not capable of being scanned, for example meal times and number of people eating together.

Home audits can also involve waste bin audits. Though not a pleasant task, this allows researchers to evaluate product consumption or usage rate in the home.

The use of observation equipment in stores can produce data on other areas of the shopper's behaviour, for example the route around the store, or the way that a consumer browses a retail fixture.

Audit data can produce a huge range of analysis, and the services of ACNielsen and TN Sofres provide the raw material for the marketing management of the retail and grocery marketing sector.

These data include

- ○ Market share
- ○ Brand share
- ○ Brand loyalty
- ○ Category loyalty
- ○ Retail sector analysis
- ○ Retail share
- ○ Retail price checks
- ○ Average basket
- ○ Sales promotion responses and so on.

The services are available internationally and most European markets are covered. Some European markets remain harder to audit through traditional means, and statistical weightings are used to produce a full picture of retail sales. Other markets can be audited but the use of scanning technology may mean that more low-tech solutions are needed to carry out the task.

For example, in Indonesia sales of cigarettes are made from kiosks that may sell 1–2 cigarettes from a pack at a time. This is hard to measure!

## Media measurement

The measurement of media is a key element of observation research. The most important of these in the United Kingdom is the Broadcaster's Audience Research Board (BARB). It provides the measurement service for television viewing in the United Kingdom. In early 2003 the contract for TV-viewing measurement was changed. This new contract is due to run for 5–8 years. The old panel which was set up in 1991 was replaced with a new panel recruited from scratch over the last 2 years. The main change is to increase the size of the panel from 4300 homes to 5100 homes and covers 11 500 viewers. This reflects the changes in the media landscape in the United Kingdom. In 1983 there were only three TV channels in the United Kingdom; today there are hundreds. The old sample was not large enough to ensure robust data on smaller TV audiences.

Other changes to the panel design were reported by BARB to include

- Removal of demographic disproportionality. The undersampling of downmarket audiences has ended and the entire panel is now proportionate to the population.
- Improved geographic representation. Regional panels will be represented more closely to their proportion of the UK population. London, for example, has 20 per cent of the UK population, but under the old BARB system had only 12 per cent of panel homes. Under the new system it will have 17 per cent of panel homes.
- Revised panel controls (the aspects against which the panel is recruited to ensure it is representative – such as age, social class and so on). Multi-channel television homes will be recruited with a greater level of panel controls than on the previous system.
- A more detailed weighting scheme to introduce a greater level of representativeness to the reporting sample.
- An increased annual Establishment Survey (the source of population estimates and penetration figures on which panel controls are based) of 50 000 interviews to provide more robust estimates, particularly by platform.
- Updated metering equipment that is non-intrusive, upgradeable and therefore future-proofed.

*Source*: BARB.

# BARB: Watching you watching them

Television measurement service

The measurement service provides television audience data on a minute-by-minute basis for channels received within the United Kingdom. These data are available for reporting nationally as well as at the ITV and BBC at the regional level.

Viewing estimates are obtained from panels of television owning households representing the viewing behaviour of the 24+ million households within the United Kingdom. The panels are selected to be representative of each ITV and BBC region. Panel homes are selected via a multi-stage stratified and unclustered sample design. This ensures that the panel is fully representative of households across the whole of the United Kingdom. Each panel is maintained against a range of individual and household characteristics (panel controls). As the estimates for the large majority of the panel controls are not available from Census data, it is necessary to conduct surveys (Establishment Survey) to obtain this information.

The Establishment Survey is a random probability survey carried out on a continuous basis involving some 50 000 interviews per year. The nature of this survey ensures that any changes within the characteristics of the population can be identified. Panel controls can therefore be updated and panel household representation, adjusted to ensure representativeness, is maintained. In addition to being the prime source of television population information, the Establishment Survey also generates a pool of potential recruits from which panel member homes are recruited. Each of the panel member households have all their television receiving equipment (sets, video cassette recorders, set-top box decoders, etc.) electronically monitored by a 'peoplemeter' monitoring system. This system automatically identifies and records the channel to which each television set is tuned when switched on and all viewing involving a VCR (recording, playback, viewing through the VCR, etc.). In addition, the metering system incorporates the capability to 'fingerprint' videotapes during recording sessions and to subsequently identify such recorded material when played back (time-shifted viewing).

All permanent household residents and guests declare their presence in a room whilst a television set is on by pressing an allocated button on a handset. The metering system monitors all registrations made by each individual.

Throughout each day, the meter system stores all the viewing undertaken by the entire household. Each night the panel household is contacted by the processing centre by telephone to collect the stored data. This procedure is carried out on every home each day to produce 'overnight' television viewing data.

*Source:* www.barb.co.uk.

Other media are audited in different ways – some are based on observation, some on other research methods.

In the United Kingdom, the measurement of poster sites is carried out though observation. Video cameras are used to measure the number of full faces looking at a poster. This data is used to help the media sales people.

A really useful site that discusses the full range of media research services is www.zenithoptimedia.com or www.marketersportal.com/. The A to Z listing covers the full range of research services for media.

**Activity 6.2**

Go to www.zenithoptimedia.com or www.marketersportal.com/and find out the following:

1. What is the name of the poster research organization in the United Kingdom?
2. List three Internet audience research businesses.
3. What is the NRS?
4. What is the ABC?

# Other observation techniques

## Ethnography

Ethnography is a research technique that has been used in the social sciences for some time and is increasingly used in marketing. Ethnographic research involves total immersion in the life of the subject and researchers may spend a considerable amount of time with the subject of the research. Results may be recorded or written down post-experience. The research may look at family interaction with a product or brand and may be looking for depth of insight to inform market positioning.

## Football crazy – who ate all the pies?

Ethnographic research has been used by researchers looking at the problem of football hooliganism in the United Kingdom. Researchers travel with known hooligans and later record their experiences. As you might imagine, other research techniques would be impossible to use to research this behaviour.

This research has informed government policy and policing tactics.

Researchers at the Football Research Unit at Liverpool John Moore's University have joked that there is no football hooligan problem in the United Kingdom. It is, in fact, completely made up of ethnographic researchers posing as hooligans.

## Mechanical observation

A range of mechanical observation techniques are used in observation research which include:

### Psychogalvanometers

This measures the respondents' reaction to a message. It uses the same techniques as a lie detector, measuring the electrical resistance of the skin. The amount of sweat on the skin increases during arousal and it is this that is measured. It is most often used for pre-testing advertising and copy.

## Pupilmeters

Pupilmeters measure the same responses through a measurement of pupil dilation.

## Eye cameras

Eye cameras are used to track the movement of the eye around an object, maybe a piece of creative or a retail fixture. This method has been used on websites' research to explore the navigation of sites and may be combined with a mechanical record of key strokes or mouse movement.

## Tachistoscopes

Reveal the test material in microsecond bursts. The respondents' ability to recall detail is measured. It is believed to predict advertising effectiveness amongst other uses.

# Mystery shopping

Mystery shopping is defined by the MRS (2005) as 'The collection of information from retail outlets, showrooms and so on by people trained to observe, experience, record and measure the customer service process posing as ordinary members of the public.'

This may be done by companies assessing the activities of competitors in the market or by companies assessing the performance of their own sales staff.

Wilson (2003) identifies three main purposes for mystery shopping:

1. To act as a diagnostic tool identifying failings and weak points in service delivery
2. To encourage and reward staff
3. To assess competitors.

Mystery shoppers should present facts rather than opinions and these may include the shopping environment as well as interactions between the researcher and staff. This is designed to reduce researcher bias. There needs to be careful recruitment of mystery shoppers as staff may become familiar with them, and age, gender and appearance of shoppers may affect the experience. Also, the shopper needs to fall within the target market. The shopper needs to be natural and to make the experience as close to life as possible. Some mystery shopping has involved the use of hidden cameras. Training is also very important and data capture and recording needs to be carefully considered. Analysis of the data can be highly subjective and a formal structure for analysis might be needed to ensure the valid comparison of results between retail outlets – the use of some form of recording equipment may help this task.

## This dealer bites

Mystery shopping is used extensively in the car market. The brand advertising of the leading car companies is ultimately reinforced or compromised by the sales people staffing the room. One mystery shopper described the experience of entering the sales show room as like 'being thrown into a shark-filled pool'.

## Online observation

We have already mentioned the use of observation techniques in designing websites. However, the characteristics of the Internet allow for a lot of data to be captured through remote observation. The use of cookies allows the website owner to identify repeat visits.

A cookie is a text file placed on the browser's computer that allows the browser's computer to be identified on subsequent visits. A cookie may contain the computer's address or the details of a customer registration. This means that when the customer logs on, a personalized greeting can be made or passwords provided. Cookies cannot extract information.

Most online retailers use this system, for example Amazon will drive content to particular customers based on their previous behaviour. Browser behaviour through the site can also be captured and used. This has been used to tailor-make print brochures based on customers' browsing behaviour through the site. We can track where browsers have come from and where they go to after leaving the site.

## Ethics in observation research

There are clearly significant ethical considerations in the use of observation research. The basic rule is that if observation is to take place in a situation in which behaviour could not usually be observed, then permission should be asked. The MRS code of conduct has specific sections on Mystery Shopping. This includes the liaison with employees who are the subject of mystery shopping communicating the fact that the technique being used covers the organization from any data protection issue and may be motivating in itself.

## Zipping Zapping and Lewd behaviour

Recently the London Business School used cameras filming viewers of TV commercials to try to identify behaviour during advertisement breaks. As media-buying is based on audiences for programmes, LBS tried to categorize behaviour during commercial breaks to see whether companies were truly buying the number of TV rating points they believed.

The cameras were left in place for sometime and whilst in the early stages viewers were clearly aware of the cameras, after a while they clearly had forgotten that they were there and resumed their normal Friday night behaviour.

*Source*: FT/LBS Feb 2003.

## How is observation research used?

 ## Activity 6.3

Reflecting on the various approaches to observation research, think about the potential applications for observation research. Brainstorm as many ideas as you can and then go to the textbooks to fill in the gaps.

## International issues

The use of observation is appropriate in all markets. Indeed, in some international markets it may be the preferred method.

In addition to the usual international caveats of cost, comparability and availability of resources, for example CCTV, we have to add the problem of interpretation. The interpretation of body language, signs (semiotics) and non-verbal behaviour is culturally determined.

For example, in certain African countries it is not unusual for men to hold hands as they are walking together.

In other markets, colours may mean something very different from the United Kingdom. In China, red means good luck while in other countries it means danger.

In some other markets, green is the colour for danger.

In the United Kingdom, white is the colour representing purity and is worn by brides at their weddings. In Japan, white is the colour of mourning, and in Brazil, purple is the colour of mourning.

International marketing is fraught with these difficulties but they are certainly not insurmountable.

One way to manage this is to use James Lee's idea of self-reference criteria (Lewis and Housden, 1999). The researcher should interpret the behaviour in response to his own domestic culture, identify the factors affected by his cultural bias, isolate them and interpret the observation through an understanding of this bias.

Otherwise, it is important to use local agencies who can interpret the behaviour observed from their own cultural perspective. One person's aggressive argument might be a lively discussion between friends in other markets.

## Summary

In this unit we looked at observation research. We looked at the types of research.

These are as follows:

1. Natural versus contrived
2. Visible versus hidden
3. Structured versus unstructured
4. Mechanized versus human
5. Participant versus non-participant.

In particular, we looked at the audit process. We looked at the key suppliers of audit data in the United Kingdom – ACNielsen and TN Sofres.

We looked in depth at the role of mystery shopping in observation research and at the ethical constraints on its use. We saw that its main function was to

o  Act as a diagnostic tool identifying failings and weak points in service delivery
o  Encourage and reward staff
o  Assess competitors.

We saw that other purposes of observational research were to

o Improve customer service
o Improve store layout
o Improve staffing levels to ensure reduced waiting time at call centres or at service points
o Generate information to inform reward and recognition schemes
o Monitor time spent on any activity, for example TV consumption
o Measure the amount of product consumed
o Look at product combinations
o Explore alternative product uses
o Explore product interaction.

International observation research was covered, and the use of self-reference criteria in the interpretation of results was advised.

We looked at the mechanical devices used for capturing data both on- and off-line.

A range of mechanical observation techniques are used in observation research. These include

o Psychogalvanometers
o Eye cameras
o Tachistoscopes.

Finally, we looked at issues to do with online observation including the use of cookies.

## Further study

### Question 6.1

You work as a marketing manager for a major car dealership. The dealership has 150 sites throughout the United Kingdom. Your Customer Satisfaction Scores have been falling recently. You have been to an MRS training course on Mystery Shopping and feel that this technique might help identify the causes for the fall in satisfaction.

Write a report to your director outlining why you feel that this might help.

Discuss the role of mystery shopping in delivering service quality.

What are the benefits and limitations of this technique?

### Question 6.2

Davidson Hotels operate in a group of seven hotels in the United Kingdom. The hotels are all rated at the three- or four-star level, with four of them having swimming pools and leisure centres. They tend to be located close to tourist/leisure-type areas of outstanding natural beauty and local heritage sites. Their customer mix has traditionally consisted of 50 per cent business travellers, 30 per cent coach parties and 20 per cent leisure travellers/leisure breaks. However, with the growth in budget hotels offering standard rooms and limited additional services, the number of business travellers has dropped by more than 38 per cent over the past 12 months. The coach party market is relatively static, therefore the company's main opportunity for growth is seen by the management as being in the leisure travel market, with the swimming pools being used to promote all-weather/all-year leisure destinations.

The company is therefore keen to understand more about the leisure travel sector, in particular:

- ○ The trends in the market.
- ○ The criteria used by leisure travellers when selecting their accommodation in areas with outstanding natural beauty or heritage sites.
- ○ The reasons why existing leisure customers use Davidson Hotels and their likelihood of returning to the same hotel or another hotel in the Davidson Hotel chain.

They are willing to spend up to £50 000 on the research project.

*Note*: The above material has been based on a fictitious company for assessment purposes.

## Part B – Answer TWO questions only

## Question 4

Tom Davidson in Question 1 has heard about other hotels using mystery shopping techniques to monitor the quality of their services. He has asked you to produce a report explaining:

(a) the advantages and disadvantages of using mystery shopping.

**(10 marks)**

(b) the issues to consider when establishing and implementing a mystery shopping programme.

**(15 marks)**
**(25 marks in total)**

## Question 6.3

Professional Diploma in Marketing: Marketing Research and Information

## Jack Ltd

Jack Ltd is a leading international speciality retailer offering clothing, accessories and personal care products for men, women, children and babies under the Jack brand name. In the United Kingdom, Jack Ltd operates more than 150 stores nationwide. Each of the stores employs sales associates and other store personnel that are trained to answer customers' questions about fabric, fit and fashion and to help them select merchandise that's perfect for them. However, even with this training, around 85 per cent of all potential customers that enter a Jack store (measured using electronic counters in the doorways of each store) leave without buying anything. Senior management are keen to reduce this percentage, however, they are unclear as to the reasons why people leave their stores empty-handed. It may be due to the product range, store layout, service quality, pricing or any range of factors. Marketing research is therefore needed to explore the reasons why such a large percentage of potential customers fail to make a purchase.

The company hopes that answers to such questions will help to identify ways to increase sales amongst these customers.

## Part A Question 4

The senior executives of Jack Ltd have been examining their long-term marketing research requirements. In order to better understand customer and staff behaviour, they would like to make more use of observation techniques. However, their knowledge of these techniques is limited and they have asked you to write a paper clarifying:

(a) The approaches available for observing customer behaviour in a retail environment and the issues involved in using them.

**(15 marks)**

(b) The nature of mystery shopping and the issues involved in running an effective mystery shopping programme.

**(10 marks)**
**(Total 25 Marks)**

## Bibliography

Lewis, K., Housden, M. (1999) *International Marketing*, Kogan Page.

MRS (2005) www.mrs.org.uk.

Wilson, A. (2003) *Marketing Research: An Integrated Approach*, FT Prentice Hall.

# unit 7 qualitative research

## Learning objectives

After completing this unit you will be able to

- Define qualitative data

- Identify and apply methods for collecting qualitative data

- Understand the process of analysing qualitative data

- Understand the techniques of online qualitative research

- Understand how to use qualitative research to inform marketing decision-making

- Complete syllabus elements 4.4, 4.5, 4.6.

---

Evaluate the appropriateness of different qualitative and quantitative research methodologies to meet different research situations

Design and plan a research programme

Design a questionnaire and topic guide

4.4 Describe and compare the various methods for collecting qualitative and quantitative data

4.5 Explain the theory and processes involved in sampling

4.6 Design a questionnaire and discussion guide to meet a project's research objectives

---

**Key definitions**

**Projective techniques** – A form of disguised questioning that encourages participants to attribute their feelings, beliefs or motivations to another person, object or situation. Examples of projective techniques are word association, sentence completion and thematic apperception tests (ESOMAR, 2005).

**Focus groups** – A number of respondents gathered together to generate ideas through the discussion of, and reaction to, specific stimuli. Under the steerage of a moderator, focus groups are often used in exploratory work or when the subject matter involves social activities, habits and status (MRS, 2005).

**Moderator** – An individual who facilitates but does not influence a group discussion.

**One-way window** – A device used to allow researchers to view respondents without themselves being seen.

**Depth interviews** – A variety of data collection techniques, mainly for qualitative research undertaken with individual respondents rather than groups (MRS, 2005).

**Topic or discussion guide** – An outline of the structure, themes and timing of a focus group or depth interview.

**Content analysis software** – Computer software that helps with the textual analysis of qualitative research.

**Respondents** – An individual or organization from whom information is sought, directly or indirectly, which could, in whole or in part, form the results of a research project (MRS, 2005).

**Brand personality tests** – Asks respondents to describe a brand as a person.

## Study Guide

This unit should take you around 3 hours to complete. You should set aside another 3 hours to complete the activities outlined throughout the unit.

## Introduction

Qualitative research accounts for between 10 and 15 per cent of total research expenditure in the United Kingdom. It is growing in importance as marketing professionals recognize its vital role in providing depth of understanding about customers and their behaviour. This unit will introduce you to the methods used in qualitative research and the major applications supported by this methodology.

## Qualitative research defined

So how can qualitative research be defined? The MRS (2005) defines qualitative research as 'A body of research techniques which seeks insights through loosely structured, mainly verbal data rather than measurements. Analysis is interpretative, subjective, impressionistic and diagnostic'.

Crouch and Housden's (2003) definition is 'Qualitative research is so called because its emphasis lies in producing data which is rich in insight, understanding, explanation and depth of information, but which cannot be justified statistically'.

Alan Wilson (2003) in the course text defines qualitative research as 'Research that is undertaken using an unstructured research approach with a small number of carefully selected individuals to produced non quantifiable insights into behaviour motivations and attitudes'.

## What are the essential characteristics of qualitative research?

- o It is unquantifiable and is not representative of larger populations.
- o Data collection techniques are unstructured.
- o It involves small samples of individuals or groups of people.
- o It seeks to reveal opinions, motivations and attitudes.
- o It is about insight and depth of understanding.
- o It is subject to a high degree of interpretation by skilled researchers.
- o It often precedes quantitative work but can be independent of it (Figure 7.1).
- o It can inform the nature of quantitative research.

| Comparative element | Qualitative research | Quantitative research |
| --- | --- | --- |
| Type of questions | Probing | Non-probing |
| Sample size | Small | Large |
| Information per respondent | Much | Varies |
| Management | Special skills | Fewer skills |
| Type of analysis | Subjective | Statistical |
| Ease of replication | Difficult | Easy |
| Type of research | Exploratory | Descriptive or causal |
| Research training needed | Psychology | Statistics |
| | Sociology | Decision models |
| | Consumer Behaviour | Computer programming |
| | Marketing | Marketing |
| Hardware needed | Tape recorders | Computers |
| | Projection devices | PDA |

*Figure 7.1* Key differences between qualitative and quantitative work
*Source*: AMR (2003)

# Data collection techniques in qualitative research

## Focus groups or group discussions

○ Wilson (2003) defines group discussions as 'depth interviews with a group of people; they differ in that they involve interaction between respondents'.

○ The MRS (2005) defines group discussions or focus groups as 'A number of respondents gathered together to generate ideas through the discussion of, and reaction to, specific stimuli. Under the steerage of a moderator, focus groups are often used in exploratory work or when the subject matter involves social activities, habits and status'.

○ Focus groups are generally made up of around 6–12 respondents. The most common number is 8. A lower number may be used when a particularly specialist topic is being discussed. The higher number would be used for a wide-ranging discussion. This design aspect is determined by the need to reflect the range of views held on a subject by the target market or concerned population.

○ They are run and managed by an interviewer, usually called a moderator. The moderator maybe the same researcher who produced the research proposal, maybe a specialist consultant or maybe employed from a fieldwork agency. The moderator will control the group keeping the discussion on track and probing for further information when needed. The moderator will introduce other tasks that may occur within the group. The main aim of the group is to ensure that the group members discuss the topic amongst themselves; the moderator's touch should be as light as possible. However, the skilled moderator will use a range of techniques to control the input of particularly vociferous members and to encourage quieter members of the group to make their contribution. Groups will normally last between 45 minutes and 2 hours. Discussions are generally tape recorded or videoed.

○ Groups usually occur at the beginning of a research project as they can provide very useful information to explore through other methods. The groups may be observed remotely and agencies offer clients the chance to view groups set up in special rooms, where the client can observe the group through a one-way window. The moderator can be linked by a concealed or a discrete microphone to the observers so that a particularly interesting line of discussion can be probed further.

## What makes a moderator?

Sally is an open and friendly woman aged 40. She is a freelance qualitative researcher and has moved into this career after a successful period in advertising planning, where she worked at a senior level on a range of accounts.

She has a degree in Psychology and holds both the CIM and MRS diplomas. She is from London but it is hard to discern any accent. She dresses conservatively.

She is a good listener but can be assertive when required.

**127**

...ators should be

- Highly qualified and experienced in research and, possibly, psychology.
- Business-and-marketing aware. They need to be able to translate respondents' feelings into business advantage for their clients.
- Strong communicators, able to relate to a range of people.
- Hard to place regionally in terms of socio-economic class.
- Socially able, relaxed and friendly, but strong enough to control a room of animated, or conversely, disinterested respondents.
- Flexible and quick thinking, with the ability to respond to the unexpected.

## Focus group discussion guide – Bedford

- Intros – ensure everyone understands nature of the focus group and the objectives and so on, as well as that it is an independent study ... allow everyone to introduce each other! [5 mins]. As part of this – who do you work for – Franchise or brand owner?
- What brands would you consider to be successful brands? [5 mins]
- Why do you think these brands are so successful? [5 mins]
- What is your perception of our brand [for this you will create some visual ideas]? We will base this on the following:

    - If the brand was a famous personality, who would it be – Popstar or Politician? [10 mins]
    - If it were a place, where would it be? What would the weather be like? [10 mins]

- What do you feel our customers see as important? [10 mins]
- How do you think you can make a difference to what is important? [7.5 mins]
- If you were the boss, what would you do to change the image/brand, if anything? [7.5 mins]
- Close.

Thanks and incentives.

## Stimulus material

Stimulus material may include a range of physical objects which respondents can use to reflect upon or use to express their views non-verbally.

These may include

- Creative samples: Proofs, animated outlines of TV commercials, concept or story-boards, mail copy or print advertisements
- Mocked-up product packs
- Product samples
- Materials for projective work.

## Recruitment of respondents

The recruitment of respondents is an important part of the process. Participants may be recruited in a number of ways:

- o Through screening interviews at home or in the street
- o Through professional recruitment services identified in the research buyer's guide, or the MRS website.

The use of recruiters may save time and money but can have the drawback of recruiting 'professional' group respondents who are not typical of an audience. Screening questions should ensure that respondents fit the overall profile of the population under consideration.

For example,

- o male
- o over 50
- o who has a home computer
- o who has bought via the Internet in the last month
- o who has no connection with the computer or research industry.

Generally, respondents' attendance is incentivized through a cash payment or gift. Refreshments are usually provided. It is advisable to invite more respondents to attend than the minimum required to complete the group, as non-attendance can be an issue.

Typically, four groups would be carried out but more may be required if looking at sub-sectors or regional variations.

Group interviews cost between £1500 and £4500 depending on the type of group (e.g., professional groups are more expensive), complexity and the moderator. Group moderation is a highly skilled job, and good moderators are usually highly trained and commercially astute.

## The topic or discussion guide

### Creating the discussion guide

It is important to realize that a discussion guide is NOT a questionnaire. It is designed almost as an aide memoire to guide the moderator through the relatively lengthy and complex task of moderating a group of animated people.

The guide may contain outline timings and broad areas for questioning, or it may be more specific depending on the nature of the task.

The key point is that moderators should not be referring constantly to the discussion guide as this will disrupt the dynamics of the group. Positive body language and the use of eye contact are essential to the positive control of the group.

Moderators should be totally familiar with the guide before the group takes place; it should be used as a backstop to ensure that all areas have been covered and probed adequately.

The structure of a discussion guide will simply follow introduction, main body and summary but within the main body there may well be staging posts and breakout activity that need careful management.

To summarize: The discussion guide is a route map for the group interview. It outlines a timetable of activity and highlights key stages in the process. It is not a list of questions. It covers key themes that should be covered within the group discussion and allows the moderator to mentally or physically cross off areas that have been covered.

Wilson suggests that the guide breaks the group into three distinct phases:

1. Introduction

    (a) Objectives
    (b) Personal introductions
    (c) Agenda.

2. Discussive phase

    (a) Topic areas
    (b) Stimulus material.

3. Summarizing phase

    (a) Summarizing discussion
    (b) Closing
    (c) Administration.

 **Activity 7.1**

Using Wilson's template, write a discussion guide for a car dealership client who has asked you to research new customers' experience of the sales experience. Remember to try to focus on themes rather than questions. Produce an outline timetable for a group lasting one and a half hours.

## Focus groups have a number of advantages

- They replicate the dynamic social interactions that occur in the market place and may allow reluctant responders to contribute effectively.
- They provide rich and detailed knowledge of a subject, they are excellent for uncovering hidden motivations and in generating new ideas and insight.
- They are more efficient in terms of time. One focus group can be done in a day while 14 depth interviews might take at least 2 weeks to complete. They also allow for a range of opinions to be elicited in one group.
- They are cheaper per interviewee than depth interviews.
- They can be viewed remotely in real time and recorded for later analysis.
- Remote viewers can communicate additional questions or discussion points to moderators via a radio-linked earpiece.
- They allow interaction with physical stimuli, for example products.
- They can involve multiple techniques within the framework of the focus group.

Disadvantages include the following:

- They can be hard to control.
- They take skill to analyse.
- They can intimidate reluctant responders although the skill of the moderator is to bring out reluctant contributors.
- They can be derailed by vociferous respondents. Again the moderator should manage this.

# Depth interviews

The MRS (2005) defines 'depth interviews' as a term used to 'describe a variety of data collection techniques, but mainly for qualitative research undertaken with individual respondents rather than groups'.

Usually in a study that involves depth interviews, 10–14 interviews will be carried out depending on the nature of the sample. Depth interviews cost between £400 and £700 per interview.

Depth interviews have several advantages:

- They are conducted face to face, and body language can be interpreted.
- Proximity may encourage respondents to reveal more than they might in a remote interview.
- The respondent is the centre of attention and can be probed at length to explore issues that the researcher feels are important. This is the 'annoying child' syndrome with the researcher asking 'why' (but more subtly) until the issue is explored adequately.
- Group dynamics may prevent individuals expressing themselves particularly over areas that are sensitive, like income.
- Recruitment tends to be easier.
- The logistics are easier, no special rooms are needed.
- They reveal depth of understanding.
- They are flexible. The line of questioning may evolve within the interview and between interviews.
- They can involve a range of techniques.

Generally depth interviews last between 45 minutes and 2 hours. The interviews are tape recorded or videoed to enable the researcher to concentrate on the discussion and its implications rather than writing down notes. As for group discussion, the researcher does not have a list of questions but rather a topic guide as a route map through the interview. The location of the interview may be in the office or in the home. The main thing is that the respondent feels comfortable and relaxed. Interviews generally take place with an individual but interviews may involve more than one respondent if the research question is dealing with a subject in which the respondents may affect each other's decision, for example high involvement purchases like pensions or cars.

## Example of topic guide

Questions/discussion guide for in-depth interviews at the strategic level.

Part One

1. *Introduction to topic* – this research is focused on looking at how relationships can add value. The subject of the research is: Does employee behaviour at the retailer level have an impact on brand values?
2. *Objectives of the interview* – I am looking to understand your thoughts, opinions and feelings at a strategic level to gauge your perception of the brand and the impact of people's behaviour upon its value.

Part Two

1. What factors do you consider important in the creation of a successful brand?
2. What is your current perception of the brand?
3. What is it about the brand that you believe is important to customers?
4. In your opinion, what is your staff's perception of the brand?
5. How do you feel the retailer impacts on brand value?
6. What role do you think the retail staff play in creating a positive brand image?
7. If you had a blank sheet of paper, what would your vision be of the future for the brand?

The interviewer needs to have the same or similar skills as the group moderator. The respondent must feel at ease, and techniques such as positive reinforcement and mirroring of body posture can be used. The interviewer must be skilled in managing depth interviews, and in b2b interviewing the interviewer may need a considerable amount of industry knowledge in order to ask the right questions and know when and how to probe for more information.

## What are we like?

Depth interviews are used a great deal to uncover perceptions held by key audiences in a market. This may be used to establish organizational values and mission. It ensures that the current perception of an organization is known. In recent studies, depth interviews were carried out with the following type of people:

- Key suppliers
- A range of competitors
- Journalists in the national and trade press
- Trade association representatives
- Key account customers
- Trade unions
- Employee representative groups.

## What do they like?

Group interviews were used by a Japanese entrant into the UK food market.

The research objectives were broad and this research was part of an exploratory phase that looked at market potential for their range of instant meals.

Researchers were asked to explore various potential brand names and to taste-test the existing Japanese product range.

The research provided the basis for a successful European launch.

### Projective techniques

Projective techniques are designed to allow respondents to 'attribute their feelings, beliefs or motivations to another person, object or situation' (ESOMAR, 2005). They are usually very interesting to administer and reveal some fascinating insight into the research problem. They free respondents from the bonds of language and allow them to express feelings they may find hard to describe in words.

They have several other advantages:

o They are engaging for respondents, are usually fun to do and get respondents motivated.
o They provide richer insight than conventional questioning: in the right hands the analysis can be extremely revealing.
o They can create excellent ideas for further exploration.

The disadvantage is that they are hard to interpret.

### Sentence completion

This technique involves (as the term describes) simply asking respondents to complete sentences or fill in a missing word or words from a sentence. For example:

'I think that McDonald's food is . . . . . . . . . . . . . . . . . . . . . . . . . . . . . . . . . . . . . . . . ,'

'People who buy Dell computers are . . . . . . . . . . . . . . . . . . . . . . . . . . . . . . . . . . . ,'

'CIM workbooks are . . . . . . . . . . . . . . . . . . . . . . . . . . . . . . . . . . . ,'

### Story completion

A set of events is related to a respondent who is asked to complete the story or say what he would have done in a similar situation. The respondent may also be asked to explain the behaviour described.

### Word association

This technique has been used in psychoanalysis for many years.

It simply asks respondents to state the first word that comes into their head after a cue word is given. Reponses may be spoken or written down.

Researchers may chain responses together to go deeper into the association or probe the reason for the association.

For example, 'Skoda' and 'cheap' reveals something about the Skoda brand but respondents may be thinking about value for money and this would need to be probed further.

## Cartoon completion

This involves showing the respondent a cartoon drawing. These may be single images or paired images in which one individual is talking to another. In single images, speech bubbles are left blank, or in paired drawings the second speech bubble is left blank for the respondent to complete.

## Mood boards

Mood boards are collages of images that are cut from magazines and assembled together either glued or pinned on a board. This technique can reveal the associations with other products' images and colours that may not come out in conventional research. The same objective lies behind asking respondents to model images relating to a brand in plasticine or clay or to draw them on paper.

## Brand personality or brand CVs

Brand personality asks respondents to describe a brand as a person. Another term is the 'brand CV' in which respondents write a mock curriculum vitae for the brand under consideration. This can be very useful in determining the accuracy of positioning in the market.

## Activity 7.2

Try the brand CV task with brands of your choice. Try it with friends or colleagues. Are there any differences? Try it with Volvo.

Association can also be made with objects or known people or celebrities, the reason for the association is the most important thing here. So if a car brand is described as 'Roger Moore' the researcher needs to probe to uncover the meaning of the association. Unfortunately for the brand and Roger Moore, the association in this piece of work was due to the fact that 'he was once glamorous but now past it'.

### Brand mapping

It is an extension of the brand personality test that involves multiple brands. Respondents are asked to identify key attributes or dimensions of a product sector and then position brands against those relative to the competition. This can be useful in identifying positioning and segmentation criteria and is very useful in identifying gaps in the market place. The alcopops sector was developed from this type of work. Consumers identify the fact that as children they drink fizzy, sweet, non-alcoholic drinks and as adults they drink flat, bitter or dry, alcoholic drinks. Alcopops filled the gap for sweet fizzy alcoholic drinks (Figure 7.2).

These are also known as perceptual maps and in the right hands can be very revealing. Many people, however, simply choose to use standard dimensions to build the maps; most often price and quality.

*Figure 7.2* Category mapping in the drinks market

In the past, this was adequate to differentiate products in markets. Jacobs Creek, for example, entered the UK wine market as a reasonably priced, reasonably good wine. This was a sustainable position in an undifferentiated market, in which wine choices were often Blue or Black (Blue Nun or Black Tower) and luxury was a bottle of Mateus Rose. Today, wines labelled Tastes Great with Chicken and Tastes Great with Beef are available. New differentiated positions in this market are hard to imagine. Maybe Tastes Great with Chicken Wings!!

In most of today's competitive markets, price and quality are inadequate dimensions to make a difference or to differentiate one product from another. The dimensions can usefully be developed from research or the perceptual maps can be used to assess alternative positions in the market. For example, Lucozade was effectively repositioned as an adult fitness drink through understanding that the brand's values of adding recovery from illness could be translated into a more positive and contemporary positioning: enabling recovery from exercise and today allowing you to exercise longer (Figure 7.3).

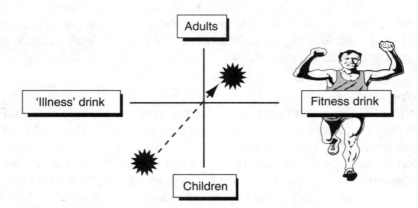

*Figure 7.3* Lucozade brand repositioning

### Thematic apperception tests or TAT tests
Images are shown to the respondents and they are asked to place the image in a story context. Or respondents are asked to describe what is happening and what will happen next.

### Photo sorts
Images of different people are presented and classified as to the brands they would and would not use.

### Role play
Respondents are asked to act out a scene. If used in groups, it is important that the group is well-motivated and prepared to participate fully.

## Role play is a pain

In a well-known example, respondents were asked to play the victim of a headache, the pain and the pain relief. Some described the pain as sharp, aggressive and violent; others described it as dull, nagging and annoying. The pain relief was either aggressive or gentle. This research led to the development of a positioning for over-the-counter pain relief.

### Online qualitative research

The web is increasingly being used for a range of research activities and this applies equally to qualitative research. This includes depth interviews and focus groups.

Focus groups use chat room technology to manage the interaction. People interact using their computers to talk to each other (Figure 7.4). Newsgroup technology is also used. Online noticeboards are used to post messages and a group of people exchange information about a specific topic (Figure 7.5).

Respondents are often recruited by e-mail and agree to participate at a certain time, at a certain URL. Each member is able to read the responses of other members and respond to their comments as if in a group situation.

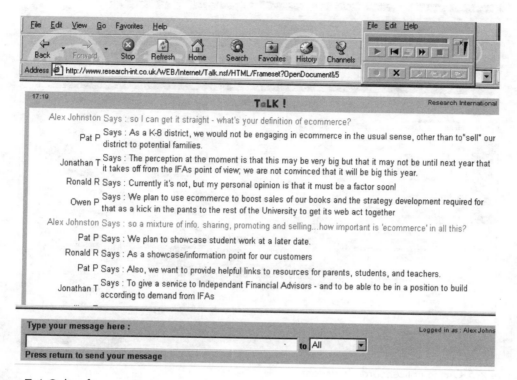

*Figure 7.4* Online focus groups
*Source*: Research international/Crouch and Housden (2003)

Depth interviewees are recruited in the same way but the communication takes place simply between the respondent and the interviewer.

The Web is not the ideal medium to deliver this type of research.

- It is often hard to recruit suitable respondents.
- Technical knowledge is required to participate and a common technical platform is required. There are issues over the reliability of the Internet connection, and diverse browsers and so on. Respondents may view screens at different speeds, in different frame sizes and so on.
- Interaction is limited and body language cannot be seen although the use of web cams may help this.
- It is hard to interpret sarcastic comments other than through the use of emoticons, icons that express emotion, for example :–) or :–(.
- It is hard to maintain attention for long periods.
- It is a less creative environment for respondents.
- It is hard to moderate the contribution of all respondents.
- It is hard to establish who exactly is sitting at the terminal.

Advantages include the following:

- o Bringing geographically dispersed samples together.
- o It may be appropriate for b2b markets.
- o It may be useful for e-commerce businesses.

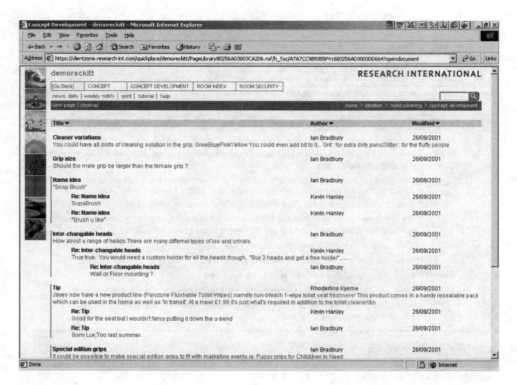

*Figure 7.5* Online noticeboard discussions
*Source*: Research international/Crouch and Housden (2003)

Online depth interviews have similar disadvantages but depth interviews online are hard to sustain for more than 10 minutes.

There are some advantages especially in b2b markets where the use of online techniques may fit more easily with the respondents' work practices.

## Analysis of qualitative data

The analysis of qualitative data is a skilled job and vital to get maximum value from the research.

It is usual for the moderator or interviewer to carry out the analysis. The starting point is to organize the data, which is contained on tape. These tapes should always be kept. It may be that a written transcript of the tapes has to be made and this can take a significant amount of time, but is nearly always needed to enable effective analysis.

The analysis should enable the broad themes discussed during the research to be explored. We are looking for areas of agreement and disagreement, looking to reflect the range of views held and whether these views were strongly held. We may be trying to report on underlying behaviour and attitudes. Where stimuli have been used, these should be presented in the report and the output analysed.

## Organizing the data

Wilson (2003) suggests four methods for data organization:

1. *Tabular* – In which data is organized according to certain characteristics or themes. The content from the groups or interviews is then divided into these areas. This can be done on spreadsheets or within word processing packages.
2. *Cut and paste* – Material is physically cut from transcript and pasted into separate thematic sections.
3. *Spider diagrams or mind maps* – Places the material at the centre of a diagram with responses emanating from the centre.
4. *Annotation* – The researcher colour codes or annotates the transcript to bring together common themes.

## Computer-based analysis

There are a number of computer systems that help the qualitative researcher in his task. Content analysis software counts the number of time a word or phrase appears in a transcript. This can help in initial analysis but tends to be a bit flat and gives a feel for the data but little more.

Text analysis or theory building software is more advanced in that it attaches codes to categories of statements and groups them together. This can help significantly in organizing data but still does not help in its interpretation, in which the skills of analysis and contextualization are combined with instinct and gut feel and these remain paramount.

The leading suppliers of qualitative data analysis software are QSR. They supply three packages – Nvivo, N6, the updated version of NUD*IST, and N4 for Mac operators. Nvivo 7 is to be launched in 2006.

Look at their website at www.qsrinternational.com.

## Activity 7.3

Write down a list of the applications of qualitative research. Use your textbooks when you run out of ideas.

# Summary

In this unit we looked at the area of qualitative research. We saw that among other definitions, qualitative research can be defined as 'Research that is undertaken using an unstructured research approach with a small number of carefully selected individuals to produce non-quantifiable insights into behaviour motivations and attitudes' (Wilson, 2003).

We saw that the essential characteristics of qualitative research are as follows:

- It is unquantifiable and it is not representative of larger populations.
- Data collection techniques are unstructured.
- It involves small samples of individuals or groups of people.
- It seeks to reveal opinions, motivations and attitudes.

We looked at the various data collection methods that are used in this area including focus groups, depth interviews and projective techniques. We looked at the advantages and disadvantages of each technique.

We looked in detail at the skills required of the moderator or interviewer.

Moderators should be

- Highly qualified and experienced in research and, possibly, psychology.
- Business and marketing aware. They need to be able to translate respondents' feelings into business advantage for their clients.
- Strong communicators, able to relate to a range of people.
- Hard to place regionally in terms of socio-economic class.
- Socially able, relaxed and friendly, but strong enough to control a room of animated, or conversely, disinterested respondents.
- Flexible and quick thinking, with the ability to respond to the unexpected.

We saw that the topic guide is a route map and timetable for both group and depth interviews and that the guide should break the interview into three distinct phases:

1. The introduction phase
2. The discussive phase
3. The summarizing phase.

We looked at the advantages of focus groups:

- They replicate the dynamic social interactions that occur in the market place.
- They provide rich and detailed knowledge of a subject.
- They are more efficient in terms of time. One focus group can be done in a day. Fourteen depth interviews might take at least 2 weeks to complete.
- They are cheaper per interviewee than depth interviews.
- They allow interaction with physical stimuli, for example products.
- They can involve multiple techniques within the framework of the focus group.

And depth interviews:

- They are conducted face to face, and body language can be interpreted.
- Proximity may encourage respondents to reveal more than they might in a remote interview.

- The respondent is the centre of attention and can be probed at length to explore issues that the researcher feels are important. This is the annoying child syndrome with the researcher asking 'why?' (but more subtly) until the issue is explored adequately.
- Group dynamics may prevent individuals expressing themselves particularly over areas that are sensitive, like income.
- Recruitment tends to be easier.
- The logistics are easier, no special rooms are needed.
- They reveal depth of understanding.
- They are flexible. The line of questioning may evolve within the interview and between interviews.
- They can involve a range of techniques.

We explored the use of projective techniques and saw that these techniques can be revealing and interesting to administer. Techniques included

- Sentence completion
- Story completion
- Word association
- Cartoon completion
- Mood boards
- Brand personality or brand CVs
- Brand mapping
- Thematic apperception tests or TAT tests
- Photo sorts
- Role play.

We explored the online applications of qualitative research. We saw that there are problems in carrying out qualitative work online. These included

- It is often hard to recruit suitable respondents.
- Technical knowledge is required to participate, and a common technical platform is required.
- Interaction is limited and body language cannot be seen.
- It is hard to interpret the meaning of words without the tone of voice and body language.
- It is hard to maintain attention for long periods.
- It is a less creative environment for respondents.
- It is hard to moderate the contribution of all respondents.
- It is hard to establish who exactly is sitting at the terminal.

Finally we looked at the techniques for analysing the data, both offline and using the computer packages that are available. We saw that there are several ways of organizing qualitative data:

- *Tabular* – In which data is organized according to certain characteristics or themes.
- *Cut and paste* – Material is physically cut from transcript and pasted into separate thematic sections.
- *Spider diagrams or mind maps* – Places the material at the centre of a diagram with responses emanating from the centre.
- *Annotation* – The researcher colour codes or annotates the transcript to bring together common themes.

Finally, an exercise brought together the various applications discussed in the unit.

# Further study

## Question 7.1

As the marketing research executive of a leading confectionery company, you have been asked to commission qualitative research into the positioning of your leading brand in the market place. You have to select a moderator to facilitate the groups.

What is the role of the moderator in managing focus groups?

Describe the key skills required by a moderator of focus groups?

How would you make your final decision?

## Question 7.2

### Davidson Hotels

Davidson Hotels operate in a group of seven hotels in the United Kingdom. The hotels are all rated at the three- or four-star level, with four of them having swimming pools and leisure centres. They tend to be located close to tourist/leisure type areas of outstanding natural beauty and local heritage sites. Their customer mix has traditionally consisted of 50 per cent business travellers, 30 per cent coach parties, and 20 per cent leisure travellers/leisure breaks. However, with the growth in budget hotels offering standard rooms and limited additional services, the number of business travellers has dropped by more than 38 per cent over the past 12 months. The coach party market is relatively static, therefore the company's main opportunity for growth is seen by management as being in the leisure travel market, with the swimming pools being used to promote all-weather/all-year leisure destinations.

The company is therefore keen to understand more about the leisure travel sector, in particular:

- o The trends in the market.
- o The criteria used by leisure travellers when selecting their accommodation in areas with outstanding natural beauty or heritage sites.
- o The reasons why existing leisure customers use Davidson Hotels and their likelihood of returning to the same hotel or another hotel in the Davidson Hotel chain.

They are willing to spend up to £50 000 on the research project.

*Note*: The above material has been based on a fictitious company for assessment purposes.

## Part B – answer TWO questions only

## Question 3

Assuming that qualitative research could be used to meet some of the research objectives of the project set out in Question 1, design a discussion guide involving appropriate projective techniques to address theses specific objectives.

**(25 marks)**

## Question 7.3

### Splash Ltd

The Spanish-based cosmetics company Splash Ltd has built an international retail chain that is in a strong expansion phase. Its fresh, hand-made soaps and cosmetics are available in 240 stores worldwide. The emphasis is on making and selling products without animal ingredients made from only fresh fruit and vegetables, finest essential oils and safe synthetics. It controls the whole process of getting its products to the consumer, including design, manufacturing and retail.

The retail stores look like a cross between a cheese shop and a market stall, with slabs of soap and other fresh products stacked ready for cutting and bagging. The retail environment is dominated by an aroma of soaps and perfumes.

The company is now planning to open its first UK store in the centre of London.

Prior to designing the outlet, determining the product range and potential promotions, the company is keen to undertake a programme of market research with potential customers, to examine the buying behaviour and attitudes of British consumers of high-quality soap and cosmetic products.

The company hopes that answers to such questions will help in the successful launch of their first UK store.

The company is willing to spend up to £50 000 on the research project.

*Note*: The above data has been based on a fictitious situation drawing on a variety of events and does not reflect the management practices of any particular organization.

## Part B Question 3

Design a discussion guide and appropriate projective techniques, for use in a series of group discussions, to address the research objectives of the mini case set out in Question 1

**(25 Marks)**

## Question 7.4

### Jack Ltd

Ltd is a leading international speciality retailer offering clothing, accessories and personal care products for men, women, children and babies under the Jack brand name. In the United Kingdom, Jack Ltd operates more than 150 stores nationwide. Each of the stores employs sales associates and other store personnel that are trained to answer customers' questions about fabric, fit and fashion and to help them select merchandise that's perfect for them. However, even with this training, around 85 per cent of all potential customers that enter a Jack store (measured using electronic counters in the doorways of each store) leave without buying anything. Senior management are keen to reduce this percentage, however, they are unclear as to the reasons why people leave their stores empty-handed. It may be due to the product range, store layout, service quality, pricing or any range of factors. Marketing research is therefore needed to explore the reasons why such a large percentage of potential customers fail to make a purchase.

The company hopes that answers to such questions will help to identify ways to increase sales amongst these customers.

The company is willing to spend up to £40 000 on the research project.

## Part B Question 3

Design a discussion guide involving appropriate projective techniques for use in a series of group discussions to address the research objectives of the project set out in Question 1

**(Total 25 Marks)**

## Question 7.5

### SeaLux Cruises

SeaLux Cruises is a new cruise operator consisting of two ships sailing out of the port of Southampton in Southern England. It has been established for just over one year and provides cruise-based vacations using its 1400 berth ship, Med Blue, around the Mediterranean, and cruises around Scandinavia and the Baltic States on its 1250 berth ship, Northern Blue. The focus is on offering relaxing vacations with an emphasis on 'luxurious discovery' through a wide range of dining, entertainment and excursion choices. A 12-day Mediterranean cruise on the Med Blue with stops in Venice, Barcelona, Rome and five other cities, starts at around £2000.

Although the first year has gone well with very satisfied passengers and no technical problems, the cruises have been running at below optimum capacity. The level of bookings for the 16 cruises scheduled for the next 12 months is also around 35 per cent below target. This is causing the company some concern, particularly when industry sources and the performance of competitors clearly suggest that the UK cruise market is going through a period of tremendous growth. There is a view among the senior management of the company that the product offering is correct for the target market but the promotion and sales activity is failing to raise awareness and attract or convert potential passengers. Unlike other cruise lines that use travel agents to sell their cruises, SeaLux undertakes direct advertising in national newspapers and magazines leading to customers booking direct with SeaLux through their internet site or telephone hotline.

The senior management is now concerned that low sales may reflect an unwillingness of the target market (the over 40 age group) to book cruises on a direct basis, as they may require the advice and reassurance of a travel agent. Alternatively, the poor sales may simply reflect a low awareness of the advertising and the company's offerings. SeaLux is therefore keen to undertake a programme of research to examine the effectiveness of the advertising and the attitudes of the target market towards the preferred methods and channels for the booking of cruise-based holidays. The company is willing to spend up to £70 000 on the research project.

The above data has been based on a fictitious situation drawing on a variety of events and does not reflect the management practices of any particular organization.

## PART B – Question Three

(a) Design a discussion guide for use in a series of group discussions to address the research objectives of the project set out in answer to Question 1.

**(15 marks)**

(b) Provide a detailed description of **TWO** projective techniques that could also be used within the group discussions, alongside the discussion guide, to help address the research objectives.

**(10 marks)**
**(Total 25 marks)**

Go to www.CIM.co.uk for specimen answers to this question.

# Bibliography

Crouch, S., Housden, M. (2003) *Marketing Research for Managers*, Butterworth-Heinemann, 3rd edition.

ESOMAR (2005) www.esomar.org.

MRS (2005) www.mrs.org.uk.

Wilson, A. (2003) *Marketing Research: An Integrated Approach*, FT Prentice Hall.

# unit 8 quantitative data

Evaluate the appropriateness of different qualitative and quantitative research methodologies to meet different research situations

Design and plan a research programme

Design a questionnaire and topic guide

4.4 Describe and compare the various methods for collecting qualitative and quantitative data
4.5 Explain the theory and processes involved in sampling
4.6 Design a questionnaire and discussion guide to meet a project's research objectives

## Key definitions

**Quantitative data** – Research which seeks to make measurements as distinct from qualitative research (MRS, 2005).

**CAPI** – Computer Aided Personal Interviewing.

**CAWI** – Computer Aided Web Interviewing.

**CATI** – Computer Aided Telephone Interviewing.

**Surveys** – 'The systematic collection, analysis and interpretation of information about some aspect of study. In market research the term is applied particularly to the collection of information by means of sampling and interviews with the selected individuals' (MRS, 2005).

**Omnibus surveys** – 'A survey covering a number of topics, usually for different clients. The samples tend to be nationally representative and composed of types of people for which there is a general demand. Clients are charged by the market research agency on the basis of the questionnaire space or the number of questions required' (MRS, 2003).

**Postal surveys** – Self-administered surveys are delivered to the respondents who then complete the questionnaire and return it.

**Telephone interviewing** – Interviews carried out using the telephone.

**Face-to-face interviews** – These are interviews that are carried out with respondents in face-to-face contact with the interviewer. Results are recorded on paper or digitally on a Personal Digital Assistant, palmtop or laptop computer.

## Study Guide

This unit should take around 3 hours to complete.

## Introduction

Quantitative data is the best known currency of marketing research. It is quantitative data that gives us the state of the opinion polls or allows companies to claim that nine out of ten customers prefer their product. It is quantifiable because data is collected in a way that allows generalizations to be made about a general population from taking a sample of that population. We will deal with this later. In this unit we are going to look at how data is collected, exploring the principal methods of data collection and their application.

## What is quantitative data?

The MRS (2005) defines quantitative data as 'Research which seeks to make measurements as distinct from qualitative research'.

Wilson (2003) defines quantitative research as 'research that is undertaken using a structured research approach with a sample of the population to produce quantifiable insights into behaviour motivations and attitudes'.

Wilson identifies five key characteristics of quantitative data:

1. Data gathering is more structured.
2. Research involves larger samples than qualitative research.
3. The data gathered can provide answers that will quantify the incidence of particular behaviour motivations and attitudes in the population under consideration.
4. Studies can be more easily replicated and direct comparisons can be made between studies.
5. Analysis is statistical in nature and will usually be done with the help of computer software.

**147**

# Survey methods

Surveys are defined by the MRS (2005) as 'The systematic collection, analysis and interpretation of information about some aspect of study. In market research, the term is applied particularly to the collection of information by means of sampling and interviews with the selected individuals.'

In this unit we are looking at the first element of this definition, that is the collection of data. There are many ways of gathering research data in a structured way and almost every medium is capable of delivering research questions. These media have a range of capabilities and strengths and weaknesses relating to them. As a CIM delegate, you will need to understand the range of data collection methods used and the relative strengths and weaknesses of these methodologies.

The two broadest categories are self-completion and interviewer-administered surveys.

We will start with interviewer-administered surveys.

## Face-to-face interviews

These are interviews that are carried out with respondents in face-to-face contact with the interviewer; results are recorded on paper or digitally on a Personal Digital Assistant, palmtop or laptop computer. These can be distinguished from interviewer-administered surveys that are carried out remotely via the telephone or a 'help me' button on a Web page.

## Marks for Marks

Marks and Spencer use face-to-face interviewing for evaluating consumer reaction to the store experience.

Interviewers can approach respondents as they leave the store when the experience of the store is fresh in their minds.

This allows for immediate reactions to be assessed without the respondents relying on their memory. The interviewer can interpret body language and probe to elicit real understanding.

Face-to-face interviewing also allows for a range of prompts to be used. These may be pack shots or lists of brands to stimulate customer responses.

The advantages of face-to-face contact methods are many:

o There is greater acceptance of the validity of the research if an interviewer can introduce the reasons for the research and show professional membership cards.
o The interview process is more efficient as non-eligible respondents can be screened out more effectively.
o They improve response rates as the interviewer can answer questions or help with any difficulty in completing the questionnaire.
o Personal contact creates a sense of obligation and this can be useful with long surveys. This can reduce the incidence of incomplete or unfinished interviews.

- Complexity can be introduced into the survey – for example, the use of show cards or other stimuli material is more easily managed.
- Empathy and encouragement can enable deeper consideration of the questions and ensure accuracy of some claims – for example, gender and age.

There are some disadvantages:

- Costs particularly in b2b research may be high, but this must be offset against a higher response rate.
- It can take a considerable amount of time to complete a survey.
- Interviewers may be demotivated and may take short cuts to ensure that their quota of completed surveys is made.
- Interview bias is a problem. Bias may affect:

  - Who is interviewed – interviewers may select those people who want to be interviewed. An Australian researcher used to do all his interviews on the beach at Bondi.
  - The way questions are asked – with a negative inflection or a preceding ad-libbed comment 'I know this sounds stupid but . . .'
  - The way an interviewer responds verbally and visually to an answer – a raised eyebrow or an expression of shock is not required!
  - The way an answer is recorded, the interpretation of a response may be biased.

- Safety of interviewing staff may be an issue in some areas.
- The training and control of field staff is important and adds to costs.
- A dispersed sample geographically, for example regional store managers, is clearly difficult to administer in this way and other data collection methods might need to be considered.

## The Interviewer Quality Control Scheme

The Market Research Society operates a scheme to ensure the quality of fieldwork. The Interviewer Quality Control Scheme aims to institute and maintain quality fieldwork. In 2005, 64 companies were members of the scheme.

The scheme covers:

1. Consumer, social and qualitative research
2. Consumer and retail panels, and audits
3. Hall tests
4. Telephone research.

The scheme lays down minimum standards for recruitment, office procedures, supervision, training, quality control (IQCS standards are in line with BS 5750) and survey administration.

Each member company is visited annually by an independent inspector, and required to produce documentation and other evidence that it conforms to or exceeds the minimum standards.

Inspection can be made with a minimum of 24 hours' notice. If accepted as a member of the scheme, this is shown in the Market Research Society listing of organizations and providing market research services, in the Research Buyer's Guide. Members of the IQCS are also listed in its own annual handbook,

'IQCS Minimum Service Standards for Market Research Data Collection'.

That booklet and full details of the IQCS standards will be sent on request by IQCS. E-mail: gwareing@lineone.net. Or you can visit the website at www.iqcs.org/

## In-home or doorstep interviews

These are interviews carried out at the home of the respondent. These may be important if the sample is determined by postcode or type of dwelling. They have the advantage of putting the respondent at their ease but are generally hard to manage; and with the number of women in paid employment outside the home, their value in terms of ensuring access is reduced.

## Street interviews

These are perhaps the most visible forms of marketing research. Respondents describe their mixed feelings on seeing the smiling face of the interviewer approaching them. However, street interviewing has a number of advantages:

- o They are less expensive than home interviews.
- o They allow respondents who conform to quota specifications to be identified and approached – for example, women with children or older men.

Disadvantages include:

- o Some shopping centres charge a fee or do not allow researchers to interview customers.
- o Respondents are unlikely to stop in the open air if it is raining.
- o Interviews need to be as short as possible.
- o There are many distractions to the respondent – for example, children or friends who are impatient.

## Executive interviewing

This involves interviewing business people at their place of work. It is expensive and time-consuming. As for depth interviews, researchers must be knowledgeable and access may be difficult over a dispersed sample. Generally for b2b interviews alternative data collection methods are more appropriate.

## Others

Other types of face-to-face interviewing do exist. These may take place in other public places, for example in galleries or on buses and trains.

## What makes a good interviewer?

From the above, it is clear that the weak point in the collection of survey data is often the interviewer.

## Activity 8.1

What do you think makes a good market research interviewer? Write your list and compare it with the list in the debrief.

## Computer Assisted Personal Interviewing (CAPI)

The CAPI, defined by the MRS as 'Computer Assisted Personal Interviewing, is conducted face to face, usually employing laptop computers. The interviewer is prompted with the question by the computer and the appropriate response codes are keyed-in directly according to the respondent's answers. Routing procedures use these codes to determine which question appears next. Since the data is entered directly into the computer, analyses can be produced quickly' (MRS, 2005).

The MRS definition is a little out of date as technology changes mean that personal interviews can now be administered using Personal Digital Assistants (PDAs) and if these are connected to a mobile telephone network, results can be uploaded immediately. It has a number of advantages:

- Data entry is much simpler.
- There is no print production, so it is cheaper.
- The computer can check for inconsistent replies – for example, if a respondent has said that he is a non-smoker and later tells an interviewer that he smokes three cigarettes a week on average.

## The costs of face-to-face interviewing

Costs will vary according to the sector and method of data collection. Face-to-face interviews range between £20 and £50. According to the BMRA, about 40 per cent of quantitative data is captured using face-to-face methods.

## Ensuring the quality of data

Interviewers, as we have said, can be the weak link in the chain. Membership of the IQCS should help ensure data quality but other factors need to be considered.

## Good interviewer briefing

We talked about the importance of the briefing document in research design. Briefing sessions for interviews should introduce the object of the research, introduce the questionnaire, allow the interviewers to practise using the questionnaire and ask any questions.

## Monitoring in the field
Field force managers should observe interviewers and ensure that standards are maintained.

## Back checking
The IQCS insists that a sample of completed interviews is checked by phone or face to face.

## Careful editing
Ensuring that the data is consistent and complete.

## Good research design
The questionnaire must be easy to use and efficient.

When employing a fieldwork agency, Crouch and Housden (2003) present the following check-list that may be used to ask the right questions:

o Is there a fieldwork manager?
o How many interviewers you have?
o How many supervisors are there?
o Do the supervisors work exclusively for this agency?
o What is the agency's supervisory structure, that is how many supervisors and how many interviewers per supervisor?
o How are interviewers selected?
o How are interviewers trained?
o On average, how long do interviewers stay with your organization?
o How many interviewers work exclusively for your agency?
o What quality control procedures are used?

## Telephone interviewing

Telephone research involves interviewing respondents over the telephone. This may be done at home but more usually is managed via a call or contact centre. The use of the telephone in market research is growing. This is due to a number of factors:

o Changing environment. There is far greater acceptance of the telephone as a means of communication. Younger people are very comfortable on the telephone. It is common to see people using their mobile phones to talk to each other even when they are only 30 metres away from each other.
o Telephone research mirrors many business processes and distribution networks. Business is changing. People are used to transacting over the telephone.
o Over 30 per cent of Motor Insurance policies are sold over the telephone.
o Two per cent of the entire UK workforce is employed in the 'call centre' industry. This is more than mining, fishing and agriculture combined.
o The United Kingdom is the largest user of call centres in Europe employing 39 per cent of the total agents in Europe.
o The United Kingdom has 5000–16 000 call centres depending on the definition used.

- o Legislation and de-regulation, the market for telephone services has opened up and cost of calls has fallen.
- o Mobile phones and mobile Internet mean that research can use a range of methods to reach and stimulate respondents.
- o Technology enables very efficient calling procedures. These include Computer Telephony Integration (CTI) linking the call centre to the marketing database, CATI systems, bespoke systems for the management of telephone research and Interactive Voice Recognition (IVR) that enables calls to be made automatically.

Telephone interviewing has a number of advantages and disadvantages.

Advantages:

- o The cost at around £10–20 per interview is lower than face-to-face interviewing. Larger surveys can be administered via a call centre far cheaper than this at around £5 per call. The use of automated research is more common in the United States but it is possible to run a research programme using voice recognition software.
- o Control is much easier. The latest call centre software allows for call and interviews to be recorded or monitored by research managers.
- o Bias due to non-verbal influence is removed and verbal influence can be controlled through the monitoring process.
- o It is very good for international or other geographically dispersed samples. These can be accessed through the telephone without the need for the interviewer to travel. This saves time and money.
- o It is fast. We can see this during the election process. The research companies can produce statistically valid data within hours of a particular issue emerging.
- o It is convenient for the interviewer and the respondent. Calls may be made that allow the interviewer to call back at a convenient time to deliver the interview.
- o Third-generation mobile phones, mobile Internet and SMS text messaging have extended the capability of the phone as a medium for data capture.

Disadvantages:

- o Generally the telephone has lower response rates than face-to-face interviews.

  - Respondents find it easier to say 'no' on the telephone.
  - They may screen their calls.
  - They may be ex-directory.
  - They may not engage fully with the interview process and fail to complete the questionnaire.

- o Research design is restricted. The use of stimuli is limited even if the interview is carried out via mobile Internet. The length of the interview has to be shorter than face-to-face interviews in order to maintain the interest of the respondent.
- o Some social classes have a greater preponderance of ex-directory numbers.
- o Access to mobile telephone numbers may be difficult to obtain.
- o As the use of the telephone becomes ubiquitous, negative reaction to the use of the telephone becomes more common. The telephone is intrusive and the use of cold-calling by certain market sectors has created a problem for market researchers.
- o In certain international markets, issues of telephone access might be a concern.
- o Attitudes to the use of telephone in market research may be less positive than in the United Kingdom.

## The Telephone Preference Services (TPS)

The Telephone Preference Service (TPS) is run by the Direct Marketing Association in the United Kingdom. They describe the services as follows:

The Telephone Preference Service helps you to make sure your telephone number is no longer available to organizations who may telephone you with offers and information you do not wish to receive.

Under Government legislation it is unlawful to make unsolicited direct marketing calls to individuals who have indicated that they do not want to receive such calls.

You can either do this by contacting companies directly and asking them not to phone you or you can register with a central service (TPS) to stop all such calls.

The term 'individual' includes consumers at their residential address, sole traders and, except in Scotland, partnerships.

It is free to register with the service.

For more information go to www.tpsonline.org.uk.

## Computer Assisted Telephone Interviewing (CATI)

It is defined by the MRS as 'Computer Assisted Interviewing, over the telephone' (MRS, 2003).

- It can facilitate the design administration and analysis of telephone interviewing.
- Questionnaires can be customized and verbal comments can be recorded.
- Inconsistencies can be highlighted and the researcher can probe to correct the inconsistency.
- Automated dialling allows for efficient management of the interviewer.
- It is more possible and may be used to capture simple research data, for example customer satisfaction data.

### Web-based interviews

Whilst not strictly interview administered, the use of 'call me' or 'help me' buttons on Web-administered questionnaires allows a degree of interviewer assistance to take place. 'Help me' buttons allow a pop-up dialogue screen in which questions can be asked and answered. 'Phone me' allows the respondent to be contacted by telephone and helped through the questionnaire. In some instances, it is possible for a contact centre to see the respondent's screen. Use of CAWI is helping this process.

### Self-administered surveys

Self-administered surveys are delivered to the respondents who then complete the questionnaire and return it.

There are several types of self-completion surveys. They are:

- Postal
- Fax
- Hand delivered
- E-mail or Web based.

## Postal surveys

Postal surveys are used significantly within the research industry. They are mailed to respondents with a covering letter, a response device, usually a Business Reply Envelope, and a questionnaire. Postal research is used in the direct marketing industry where the mechanism reflects the medium used to communicate to customers but it is popular throughout industry sectors. It has several advantages:

o  The main advantage is that it is cheap; the cost can be as low as £5 per interview.
o  It is useful for geographically dispersed and larger samples.
o  It reduces interview bias.
o  Questionnaires can be piloted and revisions made. On large-scale samples, testing can lead to careful measurement of expected response rates.
o  It is very convenient for interviewees as the questionnaire can be completed at any time.
o  The research design is limited but longer questionnaires can be delivered and completed effectively in this way.
o  The use of self-completion allows respondents to confer and this may be desirable when researching high-involvement purchases.

There are disadvantages:

o  Response rates *may* be low, sometimes as low as 1–2 per cent. They can be increased through time-limited incentives and appeals to a sense of duty – rates can be as high as 50–60 per cent and sometimes even higher.
o  Research design is limited.
o  They may take time to complete and this can lead to low response.
o  The availability of lists to form a sample frame may be limited in certain markets. The DMA can help in this area.
o  There is limited control over the respondent and a higher incidence of incomplete questionnaires or inconsistent answers may be expected. This can be alleviated through good questionnaire design and careful piloting.
o  There is potential for bias in responders as those who respond may be those who feel strongly about an issue.

## Activity 8.2

How would you go about increasing response to a postal survey? Write down as many points as you can; then go to your text books to complete the list.

## Hand-delivered surveys

Questionnaires can be handed out or left for collection; for example, flight surveys or surveys left in hotel bedrooms or given to diners in restaurants. These can achieve high response rate, are cheap to administer but generally are hard to control and should be used carefully with support from other methods.

## Fax surveys

Share similar strengths and weaknesses to postal surveys. A few years ago these were very popular, today they are less so. The development of e-mail and the Internet has superseded this technology that was used largely in b2b research.

### E-mail and web surveys

A growing area for research in both B2B and consumer markets, the range of methods using e-mail and the Internet is expanding very quickly.

E-mail surveys and Web surveys are difficult to separate out as e-mail surveys may contain a link through to a website survey or they may include the questionnaire as an attachment to the e-mail or within the e-mail itself.

Online methods have a number of advantages:

- They are cheap to administer, design, deliver and analyse.
- They are flexible in content and can include image and sound files.
- They are fast to administer and to report on.
- They have immediate and low-cost global reach.
- They can replicate customer behaviour in both consumer and business markets.
- They can be used automatically as pop up, as a browser scrolls over a certain part of the site. Dell use this system on their website – a service designed by Opinionlabs (www.opinionlabs.com).
- They are easy to control.
- They can be completed at the respondents' convenience.

There are several disadvantages:

- Technology is varied and the use of attachments or HTML e-mails may not be supported by all computers.
- The amount of unsolicited e-mails or spam may affect perception of the questionnaire.
- Samples might be difficult to construct as e-mail lists are not very reliable and there is limited access to the Internet and e-mail – especially in the lower socio-economic groups and in certain international markets.
- It may be hard to validate who has responded as anybody could be using the computer.
- People remain suspicious of the Internet and confidentiality needs to be ensured.
- There may be a cost to the respondent especially if the questionnaire takes time to download.
- The ease of use in some organizations has led to very poor 'research' being carried out on an ad hoc basis.

## Omnibus surveys

Omnibus surveys are defined by the MRS (2005) as 'A survey covering a number of topics, usually for different clients. The samples tend to be nationally representative and composed of types of people for which there is a general demand. Clients are charged by the market research agency on the basis of the questionnaire space or the number of questions required.'

Wilson (2003) defines omnibus surveys as a 'Data collection approach that is undertaken at regular intervals for a changing group of clients who share the costs involved in the survey's set up sampling and interviewing.'

Crouch and Housden (2003) define Omnibus research as 'Research surveys which are under-taken with a stated frequency and a decided method, using a set number of respondents and sampling points.'

Omnibus surveys represent a halfway house between secondary and primary research. For the user, it gives access to low cost primary data that is representative and fast to report on. The user pays only for the questions asked, but has no control over question order or sequencing.

Omnibus surveys have a number of advantages:

- They are cheap.
- Quantified analysis can be accessed extremely quickly.
- Representative of a market and statistically valid.
- Gives access to 'hard to research' markets – for example, directors or small business owners.

Disadvantages:

- The sample cannot be changed.
- Questions must be phrased simply.
- Not suitable for opinions or attitudes.
- Question order may affect responses.

The Research Buyer's Guide identifies suppliers of Omnibus surveys and there is a useful section on this in Marketing Research for Managers, one of your course texts.

There are two types of Omnibus research. General Omnibus surveys represent the entire adult population and specialist surveys cover sectors, for example motorist or gardeners. According to Wilson (2003), when choosing an omnibus supplier you should consider the following aspects:

- The population covered
- Data collection methods
- Frequency of fieldwork
- Reputation of the supplier
- Speed of reporting
- Sample size and composition.

 **Activity 8.3**

Go to www.mrs.org.uk and use the Research Buyer's Guide to identify Omnibus surveys for your business or a sector in which you are interested.

International students can try the same at www.esomar.org.

## Hall tests

Hall tests are defined by the MRS as 'A group of respondents are recruited to attend a fixed location, often a large room or hall, where they respond – usually as individuals – to a set of stimuli'.

Hall tests can be used to evaluate new products, designs and creative propositions. These stimuli can be tested on their own, known as monadic tests, or in comparison with others, known as multiple tests.

Hall tests are usually carried out in a number of locations and typically 100–400 respondents will be interviewed.

## Placement tests

This involves placing products in the home. Respondents use the product and then complete a questionnaire on it. Two or more products may be compared at the same time or different products may be compared sequentially.

## Simulated test markets

Simulated test markets have, to some extent, replaced traditional test marketing.

The process is as follows:

- Participants are recruited who are representative of the target market.
- They are exposed to marketing stimuli in the sector including the new product.
- Participants are given the opportunity to buy from a range of products in a catalogue held by the researcher, using their own money.
- Rebuy must be from the researcher.
- This data is then modelled to produce a picture of the roll-out of the new product.

## Panels

Panels are defined by the MRS (2005) as 'A permanent representative sample maintained by a market research agency from which information is obtained on more than one occasion either for continuous research or for ad hoc projects.'

Panels cover a range of market sectors and can be identified via the MRS website and the Research Buyer's Guide.

Panels can be used to ensure that data can be gathered quickly or on a continuous basis. We looked at panels in Unit 5 on observation.

The key requirements for setting up panels are:

- Recruitment
- Retention
- Replacement.

Panels exist in a range of sectors and include online shoppers, media behaviour and consumption patterns in a range of markets.

 **Activity 8.4**

Go to www.mrs.org.uk and find examples of suppliers of panel data using the Research Buyer's Guide.

International readers can do the same for their markets at www.esomar.org.

# Summary

In this unit we looked at the methods of collecting survey data for quantitative research.

Quantitative research was defined as 'research that is undertaken using a structured research approach with a sample of the population to produce quantifiable insights into behaviour motivations and attitudes' (Wilson, 2003).

We saw that data gathering is more structured, and is made from larger samples. This enables quantitative analysis and comparable studies to be carried out.

We looked in detail at data collection methods. These included interviewer-administered questionnaires and self-completion questionnaires.

Interviewer-administered methods included face-to-face, telephone- and Web-based questionnaires. Self-completion included postal, fax, e-mail and web questionnaires.

We saw that face-to-face data collection had a number of advantages:

o There is greater acceptance of the validity of the research if an interviewer can introduce the reasons for the research and show professional membership cards.
o The interview process is more efficient as non-eligible respondents can be screened out more effectively.
o They improve response rates as the interviewer can answer questions or help with any difficulty in completing the questionnaire.
o Personal contact creates a sense of obligation and this can be useful with long surveys. This can reduce the incidence of incomplete or unfinished interviews.
o Complexity can be introduced into the survey – for example, the use of show cards or other stimuli material is more easily managed.
o Empathy and encouragement can enable deeper consideration of the questions and ensure accuracy of some claims – for example, gender and age.

There were also some disadvantages:

o Costs particularly in B2B research may be high, but this must be offset against a higher response rate.
o It can take a considerable amount of time to complete a survey.
o Interviewers may be demotivated and may take short cuts to ensure that their quota of completed surveys is made.
o Interview bias is a problem. Bias may affect:

  – Who is interviewed
  – The way questions are asked
  – The way an interviewer responds verbally and visually to an answer
  – The way an answer is recorded.

o Safety of interviewing staff may be an issue in some areas.
o The training and control of field staff is important and adds to costs.
o A dispersed sample geographically, for example regional store mangers, is clearly difficult to administer in this way and other data collection methods might need to be considered.

Face-to-face interviews may be carried out:

- In the home
- In the street
- In the office (executive interviews)
- In other public places.

We looked at the personal qualities of good interviewers and at the IQCS as a means for ensuring quality of fieldwork.

We went on to look at CAPI and its advantages:

- Data entry is much simpler.
- There is no print production, so it is cheaper.
- The computer can check for inconsistent replies – for example, a respondent has said that he is a non-smoker and later tells an interviewer he smokes on average three cigarettes a week.

Telephone is one of the fastest growing media to collect data. We looked at the reasons for this:

- Changing environment.
- Telephone research mirrors many business processes and distribution networks.
- Mobile phones and mobile Internet means that research can use a range of methods to reach and stimulate respondents.
- Technology enables very efficient calling procedures.

We looked at the advantages and disadvantages of using the telephone.

Advantages:

- The cost
- Control
- It is very good for international or other geographically dispersed samples
- It is fast
- It is convenient
- Third-generation mobile phones, mobile Internet and SMS text messaging have extended the capability of the phone as a medium for data capture.

Disadvantages:

- Lower response rates.

  - Respondents find it easier to say 'no' on the telephone.
  - They may screen their calls.
  - They may be ex-directory.
  - They may not engage fully with the interview process and fail to complete the questionnaire.

- Research design is restricted.
- Some social classes have a greater preponderance of ex-directory numbers.
- Access to mobile telephone numbers may be difficult to obtain.
- It is intrusive and may be irritating.
- In certain cases international access might be a concern.
- Attitudes to the use of telephone in market research may be less positive than in the United Kingdom.

We examined CATI and its advantages. These were:

- CATI can facilitate the design administration and analysis of telephone interviewing.
- Questionnaires can be customized and verbal comments can be recorded.
- Inconsistencies can be highlighted and the researcher can probe to correct the inconsistency.
- Automated dialling allows for efficient management of the interviewer.
- Completely automated telephone interviews are more possible and may be used to capture simple research data, for example customer satisfaction data.

We saw that Web-based interviews could be interviewer-aided and that the use of CAWI is helping this process.

Self-administered surveys are surveys that are delivered to the respondents who then complete the questionnaire and return them, and covered postal, hand-delivered, fax and e-mail or web questionnaires.

We looked at each in turn discussing the advantages of each.

Postal surveys were seen to have several advantages:

- Cheap.
- It is useful for geographically dispersed and larger samples.
- It reduces interview bias.
- Questionnaires can be piloted and revisions made.
- It is very convenient.
- Longer questionnaires can be delivered and completed effectively.
- They allow respondents to confer and this may be desirable when researching high involvement purchases.

The disadvantages:

- Response rate may be low.
- Research design is limited.
- They may take time to complete and this can lead to low response.
- The availability of lists to form sample frames.
- There is limited control over the respondent.
- A high incidence of incomplete questionnaires or inconsistent answers may be expected.
- There is potential for bias in responders as those who respond may be those who feel strongly about an issue.

We looked briefly at fax and hand-delivered surveys, and in more depth at online surveys.

Online methods were seen to have a number of advantages:

- They are cheap to administer, design, deliver and analyse.
- They are flexible in content.
- They are fast to administer and to report on.
- They have immediate and low-cost global reach.
- They can replicate customer behaviour in both consumer and business markets.
- They can be used automatically.
- They are easy to control.
- They can be completed at the respondents' convenience.

There are several disadvantages:

- Technology may not be supported by all computers.
- The amount of unsolicited e-mails or spam may affect perception of the questionnaire.
- Samples might be difficult to construct.
- It may be hard to validate who has responded.
- People remain suspicious of the Internet and confidentiality needs to be ensured.
- There may be a cost to the respondent especially if the questionnaire takes time to download.
- The ease of use in some organizations has led to very poor 'research' being carried out on an ad hoc basis.

Finally, we looked at Omnibus surveys, hall tests and reviewed the use of panel data.

Omnibus surveys were seen to have the following advantages:

- Cheap
- Fast
- Representative
- Flexible.

Disadvantages:

- The sample cannot be changed.
- Questions must be phrased simply.
- Not suitable for opinions or attitudes.
- Question order may affect responses.

Finally, we looked at hall tests, simulated test markets, placement and panel data.

## Further study

### Question 8.1

As an executive of a leading research agency, you are pitching to persuade a client to extend the qualitative work they have carried out on their brands to include quantitative work, using face-to-face interviews.

Write a report to the client outlining the advantages and disadvantages of quantitative research.

What are the advantages and disadvantages of face-to-face interviewing?

How can the disadvantages be countered?

## Question 8.2

### Splash Ltd

The Spanish-based cosmetics company Splash Ltd has built an international retail chain that is in a strong expansion phase. Its fresh, hand-made soaps and cosmetics are available in 240 stores worldwide. The emphasis is on making and selling products without animal ingredients made from only fresh fruit and vegetables, finest essential oils and safe synthetics. It controls the whole process of getting its products to the consumer, including design, manufacturing and retail.

The retail stores look like a cross between a cheese shop and a market stall, with slabs of soap and other fresh products stacked ready for cutting and bagging. The retail environment is dominated by an aroma of soaps and perfumes.

The company is now planning to open its first UK store in the centre of London.

Prior to designing the outlet, determining the product range and potential promotions, the company is keen to undertake a programme of market research with potential customers, to examine the buying behaviour and attitudes of British consumers of high quality soap and cosmetic products.

The company hopes that answers to such questions will help in the successful launch of their first UK store.

The company is willing to spend up to £50 000 on the research project.

*Note*: The above data has been based on a fictitious situation drawing on a variety of events and does not reflect the management practices of any particular organization.

## Question 4

The senior executives of Splash Ltd have been examining their future marketing research requirements for testing new products. However, their knowledge of product testing techniques is limited and they have asked you to write a paper that:

(a) Describes the workings of hall tests and placement tests in the context of cosmetics and soaps.

**(15 marks)**

(b) The circumstances when one of these techniques should be used in preference to the other.

**(10 marks)**
**(Total 25 marks)**

## Question 5 June 2006

### Question Five

'Postal surveys take too long and response rates are typically low. Therefore, it is not usually a worthwhile approach'.

(a) Is there any future for marketing research using postal surveys? Give reasons for your viewpoint.

**(8 marks)**

(b) Suggest ways in which you might overcome the disadvantages usually associated with postal surveys. Illustrate your answer with examples.

**(9 marks)**

(c) What advantages and disadvantages would e-mail based surveys offer in comparison with postal surveys?

**(8 marks)**
**(Total 25 marks)**

Go to www.CIM.co.uk for specimen answers to this question

# Bibliography

Crouch, S., Housden, M. (2003) *Marketing Research for Managers*, 3rd edition, Butterworth-Heinemann.

MRS, (2005) www.mrs.org.uk.

Wilson, A. (2003) *Marketing Research: An Integrated Approach*, FT Prentice Hall.

# unit 9
# questionnaire design

| Design and plan a research programme | 4.4 | Describe and compare the various methods for collecting qualitative and quantitative data |
| | 4.5 | Explain the theory and processes involved in sampling |

**Key definitions**

**Questionnaire** – A structured data collection mechanism involving a range of question formats and completed orally or in print. Questionnaires may be administered by interviewers or self-completed by the respondent.

**Coding** – Turning responses into a form that enables analysis usually by allocating a unique number to each response.

**Semantic differential** – A scaling question that asks respondents to indicate the strength of their views on normally a 5- or 7-point scale between bipolar adjectives and statements.

**Open questions** – Questions that ask for the respondent's own response.

**Dichotomous questions** – Questions for which there are two possible replies.

**Multiple choice questions** – Questions with a number of predetermined answers.

**Closed questions** – Questions to which there are a limited number of predetermined responses.

**Forced scale** – A scaling question that does not allow for a neutral response.

**Likert scales** – A scaling approach that asks respondents to indicate their strength of agreement or disagreement with a range of statements on a 5-point scale.

**Scaling questions** – Questions assigning numerical values to subjective concepts.

**Skip questions** – Questions that take respondents to other questions determined by the answer.

**Biased question** – A question that is phrased so that it influences the respondent's answer.

**Pilot study** – A small-scale test of a completed questionnaire.

## Study Guide

This unit should take about 3 hours to complete.

## Introduction

A questionnaire is a structured data-collection mechanism involving a range of question formats and completed orally or in print. This is distinct from a discussion guide or topic guide created for qualitative research in focus groups or depth interview that we looked at in detail in Unit 7.

As we have seen, questionnaires may be administered by interviewers or self-completed by the respondent. The design of the questionnaire is a key task in the research and proves that good design can make the difference between a successful project and a failure.

The questionnaire has four main purposes. It is designed to

    (a)   Collect relevant data
    (b)   Remove bias
    (c)   Make data comparable
    (d)   Motivate the respondent.

This unit will outline the process of developing a good questionnaire.

## The questionnaire design process

Wilson (2003) identifies a process for questionnaire development.

    a.   Develop question topics
    b.   Select question and response formats
    c.   Determine sequence
    d.   Design layout and appearance
    e.   Pilot test
    f.   Undertake the survey.

## Developing question topics

This process will draw on the results of any exploratory, desk or qualitative research carried out already. The research objectives laid down in the research brief and proposal will also be drawn on to inform the process. The idea is to make the questionnaire as efficient as possible. The questionnaire should produce the maximum amount of required information at minimum time.

The characteristics of the respondents should also be considered:

    o   Do they have the information we are asking for?
    o   Will they be able to remember the information?
    o   Are they likely to tell us the information we are asking for? Is it particularly sensitive data, for example income, sexual practices and so on?
    o   How literate and numerate are they? Will they be able to articulate the information?
    o   Will they understand the questions?
    o   Will they be interested in the survey?

## Question and response formats

What does a questionnaire contain?

There are three parts to any questionnaire:

    (a)   Identification data
    (b)   Classification data
    (c)   Subject data.

*Identification data* – It is usually completed by the interviewer. It contains identification of the respondent, maybe name, address and a contact number. It also includes the time, date and place of the interview and the name of the interviewer. This data is required to allow check backs to be made. It is important to note that the MRS code of conduct aims to ensure the anonymity of the respondent. These questions may be kept to the end of the questionnaire to allow sufficient rapport to be built-up between the interviewer and the respondent.

*Classification data* – It is the data that is required to classify respondents. It may include

- o Age
- o Gender
- o Income
- o Job title
- o Marital status.

This allows the information to be analysed effectively and also to help the interviewer ensure that the respondent has the characteristics of the sample that is required to be interviewed.

*Subject data* – It refers to the nature of the information that is being gathered to meet the survey objectives. This may be laid down in a flow diagram which allows us to begin to plan the question sequence.

This flow chart is a route map through the questionnaire to be created in outline and allows the designer to introduce what are known as 'skip' or 'filter' questions to take the respondent through the questionnaire.

For example:

Do you drink wine?

If YES go to Q.2

If NO go to Q.9

Care needs to be taken in the use of skip questions; too many can be confusing to a respondent who is self-completing or to an inexperienced interviewer. The use of CATI and CAPI systems can help here as the computer will go to the appropriate question automatically, given the response to the skip question.

## What type of questions can be asked?

There are four main question types. These are:

1. Closed questions

   (a) Dichotomous
   (b) Multiple Choice

2. Open ended
3. Rating scales.

## Closed questions – dichotomous

Simply these are questions to which there are only two possible answers, for example yes and no. This sounds simple but the question asked must fit into this answer structure. A question that asks:

'Do you intend to go on holiday in the next 12 months?' may be answered

'It depends'.

For completeness a 'don't know' option is usually offered. For example:

Do you bank online?

| | Code |
|---|---|
| Yes | 1 |
| No | 2 |
| Don't know | 3 |

Each of these is given a code number for analysis.

## Closed questions – multiple choice

These appear straightforward but are quite difficult to construct as the designer needs to know all possible answers. This is known as being 'collectively exhaustive'. This can be achieved by piloting the questionnaire to ensure that all possible answers are offered.

To avoid this, the 'other' response is often used and this usually leaves a space to allow the response to be written onto the questionnaire. Other answers are coded later to produce a full list of codes for analysis (a coding frame).

'How do you usually travel to work?'

| | Code |
|---|---|
| Car | 1 |
| Train | 2 |
| Bus | 3 |
| Bicycle | 4 |
| Walk | 5 |
| Motorbike or scooter | 6 |
| Other.................................. | |

It is important that when multiple choice questions are being designed the answers are mutually exclusive. This means that there is no overlap between responses. This is important in dealing with details of age or quantities and is easy to miss.

A major petrol retailer produced a questionnaire with the following question:

'On average what mileage do you get each year?'

0–5000

5000–10 000

10 000–15 000

15 000–20 000

More than 20 000

Spot the problem?

Yes, there is overlap. The responses are not mutually exclusive.

Red faces all round.

Other issues with multiple choice responses include the number of potential responses. This may mean that the respondent cannot remember the first answers. In face-to-face interviews the responses may be put on a show card (Figure 9.1). This is not always possible in other media.

> Show card 1
>
> 0– 5000
>
> 5001–10 000
>
> 10 001 to 15 000
>
> 15 001 to 20 000
>
> More than 20 000

*Figure 9.1* Show cards

## Open-ended questions

Open-ended questions are questions in which an answer is not suggested. The respondent is free to respond in any way. Because of this, they are sometimes known as unstructured questions. It may be that a one-word answer is required or it may be that a longer response is needed. For example:

o Why did you choose to study with the CIM?
o What do you enjoy most about your course?
o What would you like to change about the course?

The problem with open questions is analysis. If there are very many categories of answers, then it may be hard to code the responses and it may reduce the effectiveness of the analysis.

Much depends on the skill of the researcher in these cases.

One way around this is to pilot the survey and produce a pre-coded list of potential responses which allows the interviewer to interpret the response and code it.

Open-ended questions can be very useful and the difficulties in managing them within a questionnaire are not huge. Their value can certainly outweigh these difficulties.

## Scaling questions

There are many types of scaling questions. They are very useful in quantifying complex and multi-dimensional concepts such as opinions, attitudes and motivation. A scale question will ask a respondent to indicate the strength of feeling about that concept. This may be done on a multi-dimensional basis, for example exploring the range of different aspects of a brand or company, or it may be done on a single dimension, for example the satisfaction with that brand or company.

The quantification allows comparison to be made.

## Graphic versus itemized scales

Scales can be itemized or graphic (Figure 9.2).

Graphical scales ask respondents to indicate the level they associate with the issue under consideration on a line:

Dissatisfied ---------------------------------------------X ---------------------------------------- Satisfied

Occasionally, a value is attached to the line whilst still allowing respondents to select any position:

Dissatisfied --------- 1 ----------2 --------- 3 ----------4---------- 5 --------- X---------- 6 -------- Satisfied

Itemized scales introduce a defined number of response choices.

Itemized scales tend to be easier for the respondent and they are easier to analyze as the graphical responses still have to be turned into value.

Indicate your opinion about CIM courses

CIM courses are
Poor value for money   1   2   3   4   5   Good value for money

*Figure 9.2* Itemized scale questions

## Comparative versus non-comparative assessments

Wilson (2003) defines comparative rating scales as scales that ask respondents to compare the organization or issues in relation to a common frame of reference. Non-comparative allows the respondents to select their own frame of reference.

The comparative approach can be used to allow companies to rate their performance relative to other companies, or in evaluating the features that a consumer values in a product.

An example from industry can be seen in train companies asking customers to rank speed of journey, the price of the journey, on-board facilities and station facilities.

## Forced versus non-forced scales

Forced scales do not allow a neutral position.

For example:

A forced scale:

Do you think that CIM courses are

| Very inexpensive | Inexpensive | Expensive | Very expensive |
|---|---|---|---|

An unforced scale:

Do you think that CIM courses are

| Very inexpensive | Inexpensive | Neither inexpensive nor expensive | Expensive | Very expensive |
|---|---|---|---|---|

Forced scales can be used when it is believed that there will be few neutral respondents. These are used also to force those who are in the neutral position to decide and can lead to spurious data being obtained.

## Balanced versus unbalanced scales

Balanced scales have a balanced number of positive and negative responses. Unbalanced may be used when piloting suggests that there will be fewer of any particular response and to explore the more common position with more sensitivity.

## Number of scale positions

There are no hard and fast rules as to the number of positions on a scale. The most common number is 5. Some researchers use 7 or 9. The idea is that there is greater sensitivity in using a higher number. The key consideration is that respondents are able to make a clear distinction between the various options.

## Labelling and pictorial representation of positions

Scales generally require at least two 'anchor' labels at each end of the scale. As we have seen earlier, it is also possible to label each position.

It is also possible to use emoticons; smiley faces or thumbs up or down can be useful in certain markets and may be useful in international markets but you need to be careful with thumbs up which has very rude meaning in some markets.

## Commonly used scales

Respondents divide certain points or other units (possibly currency) between a number of attributes.

This gives a rank order of attributes and an indication of the scale of difference between these attributes.

Train companies have used this type of research, allocating consumers a number of pounds and giving them a range of investment opportunities on which to spend them.

## Likert scales

A commonly used scale, the Likert Scale asks respondents to indicate their level of agreement with a range of statements. Responses are scored from 1 to 5 and the result is an average score for each statement indicating the level of agreement with the statement (Figure 9.3).

|  | STRONGLY DISAGREE | | | | STRONGLY AGREE |
|---|---|---|---|---|---|
| CIM courses are good value | 1 | 2 | 3 | 4 | 5 |
| CIM courses are relevant to my needs, etc. | 1 | 2 | 3 | 4 | 5 |

*Figure 9.3* Likert scales

The strength of the Likert Scale depends on the way that the statements are selected. This involves filtering and pretesting a range of statements before the final statements are selected. The initial list may be generated as a result of qualitative or exploratory research.

## Activity 9.1

Create a list of 20 statements for a Likert Scale about a product of your choice.

Test this list on a friend or colleague. How effective was your list? What have you learned from the test?

## Semantic differentials

Semantic differentials use words or statements and their opposites and measure the strength of opinion between them.

The words are generated from exploratory or qualitative research.

| Expensive | 1 | 2 | 3 | 4 | 5 | Inexpensive |
| Effective | 1 | 2 | 3 | 4 | 5 | Ineffective |
| For career women | 1 | 2 | 3 | 4 | 5 | For the housewife |
| Modern | 1 | 2 | 3 | 4 | 5 | Old-fashioned |

This can be used to rate a single brand or to compare brands.

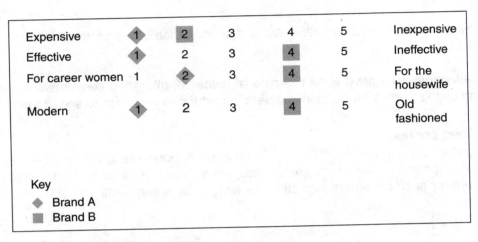

Figure 9.4 Semantic differentials

## Stapel scales

Uses a single descriptor rather than a pair and ranks opinion of this descriptor. It is rarely used in market research due to its complexity. It asks the respondents to score statements depending on how accurate they believe the statement to be; the more accurate, higher the mark, the more inaccurate, lower the score.

| | | | |
|---|---|---|---|
| +5 | +5 | +5 | +5 |
| +4 | +4 | +4 | +4 |
| +3 | +3 | +3 | +3 |
| +2 | +2 | +2 | +2 |
| +1 | +1 | +1 | +1 |
| Expensive | Effective | For career women | Modern |
| −1 | −1 | −1 | −1 |
| −2 | −2 | −2 | −2 |
| −3 | −3 | −3 | −3 |
| −4 | −4 | −4 | −4 |
| −5 | −5 | −5 | −5 |

## Purchase intent scales

These scales are used to measure the respondents' intention to buy a product or a potential product.

They look like the following example:

If this car was priced at £5999, would you:

| | |
|---|---|
| Definitely buy | 1 |
| Probably buy | 2 |
| Probably not buy | 3 |
| Definitely not buy | 4 |

## Select wording and phrasing

The next stage of the questionnaire is to word the questions. At each stage of the process, the researcher should stop and ask 'Is the question really necessary?' Each question should be carefully evaluated on its own, in relation to other questions on the questionnaire and the overall objectives of the study. If the question does not contribute to the overall purpose of the research, it should not be included in the questionnaire.

There are many rules on questionnaire wording:

*Ensure meaning is understood. For example, is dinner a meal consumed at night or at 'lunch' time. In international markets this is more important. Translation of questionnaires can cause major problems. The secret is to translate and then back translate into the original language. A question that was asked to young people 'What was the prime motivator behind your impulse purchase of confectionery countlines?' is clearly inappropriate for the audience. The language of the audience is important and this is one of the functions of qualitative research to allow the questionnaire to be constructed using appropriate terms.*

## Sexual health and the researcher

The AIDS virus has meant that an understanding of the sexual behaviour of the population is important for health budgeting and provision. Market research has been used to find out this very sensitive and important information.

A questionnaire was designed to present a range of behaviours in language that all respondents could understand.

Qualitative research via focus groups informed the language of the questionnaire.

Whilst the terms cannot be repeated here, it meant that the quantitative phase of the study was far more successful.

Use clear and simple language. Use words of one or two syllables. Use simple English:

- o Instead of 'observe', use 'look'
- o Instead of 'construct', use 'build'
- o Instead of 'regarding', use 'about'
- o Instead of 'at this moment in time', use 'now'.

Use what is known as demotic language or the language of the people. It is very easy to produce stiff and inaccessible written words. Remember, very often the questionnaire will be read out loud. It is good practice to speak the question.

- Avoid ambiguity:
  'Do you buy a newspaper regularly?'
  What does regular mean? Every day? Once a month? Once a year?

- Avoid two questions in one:
  'What do you think of our prices and product quality?'
  This is impossible to be answered accurately.

- Avoid leading or loaded questions:
  'Should the council spend money regenerating the poor environment in Brookmill ward?'
  It is hard for anyone to disagree with this question.
  'Most people think that our membership of the European Union is a good thing, Do you?'
  is a classic leading question.
  The aim has to be to reduce the potential to lead respondents.

- Avoid assumptions:
  'When driving, do you listen to your CD player?'
  This makes a number of assumptions about the respondent: That he drives, that his car has a CD player, even that he is not hearing impaired!!

- Avoid generalization:
  'How much do you usually spend on beer in a week?'
  There are much better observational or panel methodologies to ensure accuracy here. If the respondent is spending more than a few pounds, the chances are that he will not remember in any case!

- Avoid negative questions:
  'You don't think that drink-driving should be more strictly regulated, do you?' is confusing and leads to problems.

- Avoid hypothetical questions:
  'If West Ham were relegated, would you still buy a season ticket?'
  Speculation and guesswork is an outcome of this type of question.

# A poor questionnaire. But why?

○ Are you single?
(A sensitive question; ask the respondent to state what their marital status is.)

○ What is your average weekly disposable income?
(A sensitive question and hard for respondents to work out.)

○ How regularly do you come here?
(Ambiguous. Once a year or once a week.)

○ Do you buy green vegetables?
(Cabbage, fair trade or organics?)

○ Do you by are frozen and canned foods?
(Spelling is poor, and two questions in one.)

○ What about our chilled and ambient ready meals?
(Two questions in one, and what are ambient ready meals? Will the respondent understand the question?)

○ How much did you spend on food last year?
(Can you remember this?)

○ Most people say our new store layout is really good. What do you think?
(A leading and loaded question.)

○ Does your husband come with you?
(Assumption about marital status, an unnecessary question given the opening question.)

○ When do you leave the car?
(Assumption and 'when' does the researcher mean? - Overnight? When we go on holiday?)

○ Are you against drug abuse?
(A leading question, this would not produce a varied response.)

○ You don't think council tax is too high, do you?
(Use of negative and a leading question.)

○ If we moved to the high street would you come more often?
(A hypothetical question.)

○ How old are your children?

  – 0–3
  – 3–5
  – 5–10
  – 10–15
  – 15+ (Overlapping categories and what about parents of grown-up children?)

A better approach.

This is an extract from a questionnaire evaluating a new news agent.

○ What is your postcode? . . . . . . . . . . . . . . . . . . . . . . . . . . . . . . . . .

○ How did you get from home to this store?

    – Car          O

    – Motorcycle  O

    – Bus         O

    – Train       O

    – Foot        O

    – Cycle      O

    – Other

    – Please state: . . . . . . . . . . . . . . . . . . . . . . . . . . . . .

○ Did you buy any of the following today (SHOW CARD):

    – Newspapers and Magazines  O

    – Sandwiches  O

    – Other snacks  O

    – Drinks  O

    – Confectionery  O

    – Other

    – Please state       . . . . . . . . . . . . . . . . . . . . . . . . . . .

○ On a scale of 1–5, how would you rate the following aspects of this store, where 1 is very poor and 5 is very good.

|  | 1 | 2 | 3 | 4 | 5 |
|---|---|---|---|---|---|
| Cleanliness of the store | O | O | O | O | O |
| Product selection | O | O | O | O | O |
| Helpfulness of staff | O | O | O | O | O |
| Speed through the checkout | O | O | O | O | O |

Thank you for your help.

## Sequencing

Wilson suggests that the questionnaires should be funnel-sequenced, that is going from the broad to the narrow. The interviewer asks the most general questions about the subject and moves to narrower and more focused questions.

For example:

○ How do you rate the quality of management education in the United Kingdom?
○ How do you rate the quality of business education in the marketing research sector?
○ How do you rate the MRS diploma?

It is useful to start the questionnaire with some fairly straightforward questions to get the interview going. Questions about identity, occupation, family and marital status, and educational level might be included here.

Classification questions may have to be asked early to ensure that intended responder profile.

This questionnaire about marketing includes classification questions as t₁

Section 1: We need to know a few things about you:

1. Title: Mr/Mrs/Ms/Miss/Dr/Professor/Other (please state): _____
2. First name: _____
3. Last name: _____
4. Job title:_____
5. Company: _____
6. Number of employees working in your company: _____
7. Number of employees working in marketing:_____
8. What are your key areas of responsibility (please tick all those that apply)?

❑ Public Relations          ❑ Planning              ❑ Intranet
❑ Advertising               ❑ Internet              ❑ Events
❑ Exhibitions               ❑ Research
❑ Sales Force Management    ❑ Brand Management
❑ Database Management       ❑ E-Commerce
❑ Product Management        ❑ Data Analysis
❑ Campaign Management       ❑ Call Centre Management
❑ Media Buying              ❑ Sales promotion
❑ Other (please state):_____

9. Which of the following marketing publications do you read?

| | Every week | From time to time |
| --- | --- | --- |
| Marketing | ❑ | ❑ |
| Marketing Week | ❑ | ❑ |
| Admap | ❑ | ❑ |
| Campaign | ❑ | ❑ |
| Creative Review | ❑ | ❑ |
| Precision Marketing | ❑ | ❑ |
| Direct Marketing Week | ❑ | ❑ |
| Revolution | ❑ | ❑ |
| New Media Age | ❑ | ❑ |
| DM Business | ❑ | ❑ |
| Media Week | ❑ | ❑ |
| Customer Relationship Management | ❑ | ❑ |
| Marketing Direct | ❑ | ❑ |
| Direct response | ❑ | ❑ |
| Other | ❑ | ❑ |

Please give title(s):_____

Other sensitive questions, for example on age or income, might be better left to the end of the questionnaire to ensure that a rapport has been established.

## Design, layout and appearance

The physical appearance of the questionnaire will determine levels of response even if the questionnaire is interview-administered.

- o It needs to be spaced effectively, not squashed onto one page - it may save money but will reduce response.
- o It needs to be set in a serif typeface. The serifs are the feet on the letters of a serif typeface that keep the eye on the line, they are known to increase comprehension.
- o If it is to be used outside, a book format might protect the questionnaire better.
- o It needs to be set in at least 10-point font so that people can read the questionnaire.
- o It needs to be produced to a high quality with no literals and printed on high-quality paper.
- o It should look interesting. Colour can help.
- o A range of question types can help make the questionnaire more engaging.
- o Coding and interviewer instructions must be clearly distinguished from the questions.
- o Use skip and filter questions and routing instructions to help the interviewer or respondent work through the questionnaire.

## A self-completion questionnaire

College Leavers' Survey – 2006

Please take some time to complete this questionnaire as the results will help us improve the experience of students at the college.

When you have completed all the questions, please return the questionnaire to the reception.

1. Please indicate if you are:

   ❑ Male    ❑ Female

2. How old were you on 1 September 2006?

3. During your course, have you been able to learn in ways that suit you?

   ❑ Always    ❑ Mostly    ❑ Sometimes    ❑ Never

4. Has your course stretched you in your studies?

   ❑ Very much    ❑ Quite    ❑ Not very much    ❑ Not at all

5. Are you satisfied in your own efforts to attend regularly?

   ❑ Very much    ❑ Quite    ❑ Not very much    ❑ Not at all

6. Are you satisfied in your efforts to complete your work within agreed deadlines?

   ❑ Very much  ❑ Quite  ❑ Not very much  ❑ Not at all

7. How would you rate your overall progress on the course?

   ❑ Much better than you expected  ❑ Better than you expected

   ❑ Worse than you expected  ❑ Much worse than you expected

8. Have you been encouraged to update your Record of Achievement?

   ❑ Yes  ❑ No

9. Have you had the opportunity to produce a current CV?

   ❑ Yes  ❑ No

10. How many times during your course have you individually reviewed your overall progress with a tutor?

   ❑ More than once a term  ❑ Once a term

   ❑ Once a year  ❑ Never

11. If you have been given advice about your career, has this been helpful?

   ❑ Extremely helpful  ❑ Helpful

   ❑ Very helpful  ❑ Not helpful

   ❑ I have not been given any advice

12. If you have used the library, have you found this useful?

   ❑ Extremely useful  ❑ Very useful

   ❑ Useful  ❑ Not useful

   ❑ I have not used the library

13. If you have used the information in the Careers section of the library, have you found this useful?

   ❑ Extremely useful  ❑ Very useful

   ❑ Useful  ❑ Not useful

   ❑ I have not used careers information

14. If you have used the Open Access IT facility in the library, have you found this useful?

  ❑ Extremely useful   ❑ Very useful

  ❑ Useful   ❑ Not useful

  ❑ I have not used Open Access IT

15. If you have used the Learning Support Workshop in the library, have you found this useful?

  ❑ Extremely useful   ❑ Very useful

  ❑ Useful   ❑ Not useful

  ❑ I have not used the Learning Support Workshop

16. Please add any comments you wish to make on the Library, Open Access IT, Careers Advice and Learning Support facilities:

  _____

  _____

  _____

  _____

17. If you have had any personal or financial difficulties during your course, what have you done?

  (Please tick as many boxes as appropriate)

  ❑ Discussed it with friends   ❑ Discussed it with your personal tutor

  ❑ Discussed it with another lecturer   ❑ Discussed it with the Student Adviser

  ❑ Kept it to yourself   ❑ Discussed it with someone else in college

  ❑ Discussed it with parents   ❑ I have not had any personal difficulties

  ❑ Other (please state)_____

  _____

  _____

18. If you discussed a personal/financial difficulty with the Student Adviser, was this helpful?

  ❑ Extremely helpful   ❑ Helpful

  ❑ Very helpful   ❑ Not helpful

  ❑ I have not been given any advice

19. If you discussed a personal/financial difficulty with your personal tutor or lecturer, was this helpful?

    ❑ Extremely helpful    ❑ Helpful

    ❑ Very helpful    ❑ Not helpful

    ❑ I have not had any such discussions

20. How often have you met INDIVIDUALLY with your personal tutor?

    ❑ Weekly    ❑ Monthly

    ❑ Termly    ❑ Never, if never go to Q. 22

21. Have you found your INDIVIDUAL meetings with your personal tutor helpful?

    ❑ Extremely helpful    ❑ Helpful

    ❑ Very helpful    ❑ Not helpful

22. How often have you met as a GROUP with your personal tutor?

    ❑ Weekly    ❑ Monthly

    ❑ Termly    ❑ Never, if never go to Q. 24

23. Have you found your GROUP meetings with your personal tutor helpful?

    ❑ Extremely helpful    ❑ Helpful

    ❑ Very helpful    ❑ Not helpful

24. Please add any comments you wish to make about your personal tutorial sessions:

    _____

    _____

    _____

    _____

25. How long, in total, have you spent on work experience during your course?

    ❑ 1–10 days    ❑ 11–20 days    ❑ 21–30 days

    ❑ More than 30 days    ❑ I have not had any work experience

    If you have not had any work experience, please go to Q. 29; if you have had work experience please answer the following questions:

26. How many work experience placements have you had during your course?

   ❑ 1     ❑ 2 or 3     ❑ More than 3

27. Was your work experience helpful?

   ❑ Extremely helpful     ❑ Helpful

   ❑ Very helpful     ❑ Not helpful

28. Please add any comments you have on work experience:

   _____

   _____

   _____

   _____

29. What have you particularly liked about your course?

   _____

   _____

30. What have you disliked about your course?

   _____

   _____

31. Would you recommend your course to other people?

   ❑ Yes     ❑ No

32. What have you particularly liked about the College?

   _____

   _____

   _____

   _____

   _____

33. What have you disliked about the College?

_____

_____

_____

_____

_____

34. Would you recommend the College to other people?

❑ Yes    ❑ No

Thank you for your help, please return this questionnaire to the reception.

## Pilot

Piloting or testing the questionnaire is crucial. It:

- o Allows problems to be corrected
- o Helps with the coding process
- o Improves question sequencing
- o Improves wording of questions.

Piloting can be done with a small sample but it must be done. If many changes are made, the revised questionnaire should also be piloted. Piloting should be carried out by the staff who will administer the questionnaire, in a comparable environment and with respondents who share the characteristics of the sample.

The debriefing method means the respondents should be asked after completing the questionnaire what their thought processes were as they completed the questionnaires. The protocol method allows the respondent to talk through the process of completing the questionnaire.

## Questionnaire checklist

- o Are the objectives right?
- o Will the data specified meet the objectives?
- o Will the questions listed collect all the data required?
- o Is every question essential?
- o Will the right type of data be collected for:

  - fact?
  - opinion?
  - motive?

- o   Will all the identification data required be collected?
- o   Will all the classification data required be collected?
- o   Is the question sequence logical?
- o   Are the types of question being used appropriate:

  - –   dichotomous?
  - –   multiple-choice?
  - –   open-ended?
  - –   rating scales?

- o   Is the question wording:

  - –   simple to understand?
  - –   unambiguous?
  - –   clear?

- o   Have cushion statements been used when necessary?
- o   Is it reasonable to expect the respondent to answer every question?
- o   Will the answers be easy to record?
- o   Will the answers be easy to process?
- o   Does the questionnaire look good?
- o   Will it, and any show material, be easy for the interviewers to use?
- o   Has the questionnaire been piloted?
- o   Is the right type of questionnaire being used:

  - –   personal?
  - –   postal?
  - –   telephone?
  - –   online?

*Source*: Crouch and Housden (2003).

## Summary

In this unit we looked at the process of designing a questionnaire.

The questionnaire has four main purposes. It is designed to

- o   Collect relevant data
- o   Remove bias
- o   Make data comparable
- o   Motivate the respondent.

We looked at a process for questionnaire development:

1. Develop question topics
2. Select question and response formats
3. Determine sequence

4. Design layout and appearance
5. Pilot test
6. Undertake the survey.

We looked at the process of developing question topics.

We explored in depth the types of questions that can be asked which included closed dichotomous questions, closed multiple choice questions, open questions and scale questions. We looked in detail at each of these:

- Likert scales
- Stapel scales
- Semantic differential
- Intention to buy scales
- Forced and unforced scales.

We explored the wording of questions and their sequencing. We saw that there were a number of rules of right wording and phrasing of questionnaires.

- Use clear and simple language
- Avoid ambiguity
- Avoid two questions in one
- Avoid leading or loaded questions
- Avoid assumptions
- Avoid generalization
- Avoid negative questions
- Avoid hypothetical questions.

We looked at the design and appearance of the completed questionnaire and the various ways of improving this aspect of questionnaire design. We saw that:

- It should be laid out effectively in a clear font.
- It should be set in a practical format.
- It should be produced to a high quality with no literals and printed on high-quality paper.
- It should look interesting with a range of question types.
- Coding and interviewer instructions must be clearly distinguished from the questions.

Finally, we looked at the importance of the pilot test, a small-scale test of the completed questionnaire and a checklist was provided to help judge the quality of the questionnaire.

# Further study

## Question 9.1

(a) Why is questionnaire design so important in the research process?

(b) What is the role of piloting in the questionnaire design process?

## Question 9.2

CIM Professional Series Stage Two: Marketing Research and Information.

### Donaldson Builders Merchants

Donaldson Builders Merchants is a small chain of builders merchants located in the central belt of Scotland. The company has four outlets located around the edge of the major conurbations of Edinburgh and Glasgow. These supply small builders, plumbers, roofers and similar tradesmen as well as some members of the public (i.e. those more skilled in major do-it-yourself renovations and house improvements). Customers may collect items direct from the trade counter at the warehouse or have the items delivered direct to the building site or house by the company's fleet of 14 lorries. The lorries are equipped with hoists for handling the larger items.

Donaldson supplies:

o Timber and timber products
o Bricks and paving
o Sand and aggregates
o Roofing materials
o Plumbing and heating supplies
o A small range of hand tools

The company provides credit to the majority of its trade customers. As a result it has a computerized database with details on most of its trade customers relating to name, address, trading address, telephone number, type of business and purchasing patterns. There are approximately 1100 customers on the database, which probably represents 85 per cent of the company's customers. For the other 15 per cent of customers (the public and trade customers who do not have a credit account), the database holds no record, with the exception of a delivery address if a delivery is required.

The market in which Donaldson operates is becoming more competitive, with the company losing share to national chains such as Jewson and a number of recently opened B&Q trade depots. Tom Donaldson, the Managing Director, feels that the company's personal service and flexibility is far superior to these competitors, and is therefore keen to build on this and find ways in which to compete other than on price. The company has never undertaken research before but is keen to find out more from its customers about:

o Their existing and future purchasing behaviour.
o Their attitudes towards Donaldson Builders Merchants (such as product range, service, flexibility of delivery etc.).
o Their suggestions about improvements required in Donaldson's offering.

They are willing to spend up to £50 000 on the research project.

## Part B – answer Two questions only

## Question 9.3

Design a questionnaire to meet the research objectives of the project set out in Question 1. At this stage the layout of the questionnaire is not important but the questionnaire should clearly demonstrate your knowledge of sequencing, question wording and question/response format.

**(25 marks)**

*Note*: The above material has been based on a fictitious company for assessment purposes

## Question 9.4

Discuss the issue of falling response rates in marketing research, highlighting any actions that can be taken to improve the level of response.

**(25 marks)**

## Question 9.5

### SeaLux Cruises

SeaLux Cruises is a new cruise operator consisting of two ships sailing out of the port of Southampton in Southern England. It has been established for just over one year and provides cruise-based vacations using its 1400 berth ship, Med Blue, around the Mediterranean, and cruises around Scandinavia and the Baltic States on its 1250 berth ship, Northern Blue. The focus is on offering relaxing vacations with an emphasis on 'luxurious discovery' through a wide range of dining, entertainment and excursion choices. A 12-day Mediterranean cruise on the Med Blue with stops in Venice, Barcelona, Rome and five other cities, starts at around £2000.

Although the first year has gone well with very satisfied passengers and no technical problems, the cruises have been running at below optimum capacity. The level of bookings for the 16 cruises scheduled for the next 12 months is also around 35 per cent below target. This is causing the company some concern, particularly when industry sources and the performance of competitors clearly suggest that the UK cruise market is going through a period of tremendous growth. There is a view among the senior management of the company that the product offering is correct for the target market but the promotion and sales activity is failing to raise awareness and attract or convert potential passengers. Unlike other cruise lines that use travel agents to sell their cruises, SeaLux undertakes direct advertising in national newspapers and magazines leading to customers booking direct with SeaLux through their Internet site or telephone hotline. The senior management is now concerned that low sales may reflect an unwillingness of the target market (the over 40 age group) to book cruises on a direct basis, as they may require the advice and reassurance of a travel agent. Alternatively, the poor sales may simply reflect a low awareness of the advertising and the company's offerings.

SeaLux is therefore keen to undertake a programme of research to examine the effectiveness of the advertising and the attitudes of the target market towards the preferred methods and channels for the booking of cruise-based holidays. The company is willing to spend up to £70 000 on the research project.

The above data has been based on a fictitious situation drawing on a variety of events and does not reflect the management practices of any particular organization.

## PART B – Question Four

At the end of each cruise, passengers are asked to complete a customer satisfaction survey using a variety of attitude scales. There has always been disagreement between senior executives within the company regarding the scaling approaches and procedures adopted.

You have been asked as a new recruit to the Marketing Department to produce a report which sets out:

(a)   the different elements that need to be considered in designing scales for measuring attitudes

**(13 marks)**

(b)   the relative advantages and disadvantages of Likert, Semantic Differential and Stapel scales.

**(12 marks)**
**(Total 25 marks)**

Go to www.CIM.co.uk for specimen answers to this question

## Hints and tips

Go to the MRS website and download the document Questionnaire Design Guidelines. Read this and add it to your study resource pack.

## Bibliography

Wilson, A. (2003) *Marketing Research: An Integrated Approach*, FT Prentice Hall.

# unit 10 sampling

## Learning objectives

After completing this unit you will be able to

- ° Define sampling

- ° Understand how to construct a sample for a survey

- ° Understand and identify the sampling process

- ° Understand and apply the statistical basis of sampling

- ° Understand and evaluate different sampling methods

- ° Understand the concepts of population, census and sample

- ° Understand how the sampling frame is constructed

- ° Complete syllabus elements 4.6 and 5.1.

---

Design a questionnaire and topic guide

Interpret quantitative and qualitative data, and present coherent and appropriate recommendations that lead to effective marketing and business decisions

4.6 Design a questionnaire and discussion guide to meet a project's research objectives

5.1 Demonstrate an ability to use techniques for analysing qualitative and quantitative data

---

## Key definitions

**Sample** – A part or subset of a population taken to be representative of the population as a whole.

**Sampling frame** – A list of the population of interest that is used to draw the sample in a survey.

**Population** – A population is the total number of people in any defined group of interest.

**Census** – A survey of the entire population.

**Sample element** – An individual member of the sample frame.

**Confidence level** – The probability that the true population value will fall within a known range.

**Probability sampling** – A sampling method that uses objective sample selection so that every member of a population has a known probability of being selected.

**Cluster sampling** – A procedure in which clusters of population units are selected at random and then all or some of the units in the chosen clusters are studied.

**Non-probability sampling** – Non-probability sampling involves a subjective selection of respondents. Therefore, the probability of selecting respondents is unknown. This means that because the sample is not chosen objectively it is not possible to state results with any degree of statistical certainty.

**Quota sampling** – A sampling method that selects a sub-sample based on known proportions in the population.

**Convenience sampling** – Based on the convenience of the researcher. It may be that the section is made in the street, in the office or from a database. As long as the sample fits with the population as a whole, it is legitimate.

**Judgement or purposive sampling** – The researcher consciously selects a sample considered appropriate for the study.

**Sample error** – The error in a survey caused by using a sample to estimate the value of a parameter in the population.

**Simple random sampling** – A probability sampling method in which respondents are selected using random numbers.

**Systematic sampling** – A probability sampling method in which respondents are selected using a 1 in 'n' approach.

**Stratified random sampling** – A probability sampling method in which the sample is forced to contain respondents from each of the key segments of a population.

**Standard deviation** – A measurement of dispersion that calculates the average distance of the values in a data set from the mean value.

**Snowball sampling** – A type of non-probability sampling where initial respondents are selected at random and subsequent respondents are then selected by referrals or information from the earlier respondents.

## Study Guide

This unit of the coursebook will take you 3 hours to complete. You should add time to complete the exercises.

## Introduction

This unit is concerned with the process of deciding which individuals will be asked to provide information. It is very unusual for an entire population to be surveyed. A population refers to the total number of people in a group of interest. One of the few examples of this is the 10-year census in the United Kingdom. Rather as a chef tastes his food in order to determine the taste of the entire dish, so the market researcher seeks the views of a sample of the population under consideration. However, the market researcher must also ensure that all the ingredients have been used and that the ingredients have been correctly mixed.

Key to the accuracy of this is the determination of the characteristics of the sample. Wilson (2003) highlights five key questions that inform the sampling process:

1. We need to understand the nature of the people we wish to survey.
2. We need to know where they are.
3. We need to know how we select them.
4. We need to know the number of people we wish to survey.
5. We need to understand how representative this sample is of the population as a whole.

This unit outlines the sampling process.

## What is a sample?

Crouch and Housden (2003) define a sample as 'A sample is a small number taken from a large group for testing and analysis, on the assumption that the sample is representative of the population as a whole.'

The MRS (2003) defines a sample as 'A part or subset of a population taken to be representative of the population as a whole for the investigative purposes of research.'

Sampling is used to make an estimate of the characteristics of the population as a whole. Sampling overcomes the impossibility in almost every market of asking all members of a population their opinion:

o It is efficient.
o It is easier to manage.
o It is cheap.
o It is subject to statistical verification.
o It allows for a high degree of precision.

## The sampling process

Wilson (2003) outlines a six-stage sampling process (Figure 10.1).

| Step 1 | Define the population of interest |
| Step 2 | Determine whether to sample or census |
| Step 3 | Select the sampling frame |
| Step 4 | Choose a sampling method |
| Step 5 | Determine the sample size |
| Step 6 | Implement the sampling procedure |

*Figure 10.1* The sampling process

## Define the population of interest

Samples are selected from populations. The population is the total number of individuals in the group in which we are interested. This may be established at any level. We may be interested in all car dealers, we may be interested in Renault dealers, or we may be interested in Renault dealers in London and the south-east.

The definition of the population of interest is of vital importance. It is possible that the definition will produce a very low number of people in the sample. This has implications that we will explore below.

The key thing is that the definition of the population informs the whole research process. It will determine the methodology, the nature of questions asked and the interview process. The interviewer will be given screening criteria on which to select and deselect potential respondents.

For example, 'Women living in Essex who are working, and who have applied for child tax relief in the last three months'.

Some people in the defined population will be deselected by virtue of other characteristics. They work in market research and are employed by the benefits agency or Inland Revenue.

## Sample or census?

Remember the difference? A census covers the entire population; a sample is a part of that population. It is unusual for a census to take place unless the population is small. This may take place in certain b2b markets – for example, regional distributors of industrial machinery. Here the population is small and a census is appropriate. However, it is more usual that the population may include thousands or millions of individuals – for example, supermarket shoppers, voters or council tax payers.

## Selecting the sample frame

The ESOMAR (2003) defines the sampling frame as 'A list of the population of interest that is used to draw the sample in a survey, for example a telephone directory or a list of members of a profession.'

Sample frames are used to select the individual who will be interviewed. It is important that the sample frame reflects the characteristics of the population and a number of lists may need to be combined to ensure this. Wilson (2003) points out that a telephone directory may not include all elements of a population, for example those who are ex-directory, those who use a mobile phone or those with no telephone. This is known as sample frame error.

If there is no suitable list, a list of the general population may be used and classification questions used to select respondents who fit the population of interest.

## Activity 10.1

You have been commissioned to conduct research into marketing directors of companies involved in food and drinks production in the United Kingdom. What lists may be available to help you develop a sample frame?

## Choosing a sampling method

There are two broad sampling methods.

### Probability sampling
The key characteristic is that every member of the population of interest has a known chance of being selected, independent of any subjective selection by the researcher. For example, each member of a sample frame is given a number, and respondents are randomly selected until the required sample is selected.

Advantages are that the results can be projected onto the population as a whole subject to a known sampling error. This means that we can identify the limits of error for any particular result. For example, a research report might state that results are correct at the 95 per cent confidence level ±3 per cent.

What does this mean?

First that the sample has a 1 in 20 chance of being wrong, and secondly that a result of say 45 per cent actually will fall between 48 and 42 per cent, that is 45 + 3 or 45 − 3.

It should be clear that when a small sample is used to reflect the views of a population this calculation can only be approximate. The larger the sample, the greater confidence we can have that the sample will reflect accurately the population as a whole and the closer the views of the sample will be to the population as a whole. We will look at this in detail later.

Of course the way that respondents are selected adds to the cost of the survey.

### Non-probability sampling

Non-probability sampling involves a subjective selection of respondents. Therefore, the probability of selecting respondents is unknown. This means that because the sample is not chosen objectively it is not possible to state results with any degree of statistical certainty.

Non-probability sampling has advantages and disadvantages.

#### Advantages:

- o Lower cost
- o Faster
- o Smaller sample sizes
- o Important respondents can be targeted.

#### Disadvantages:

- o Results are purely indicative.
- o Sampling error cannot be computed.
- o The degree of representativeness of the sample to the population is not known.
- o Assumptions need to be made about the groupings with the population of interest.

## Probability sampling

There are four commonly used methods of probability sampling:

- (a) Simple random sampling
- (b) Systematic sampling
- (c) Stratified random sampling
- (d) Cluster sampling.

### Simple random sampling

Each member of the population has an equal chance of being selected for the survey. Members are randomly selected by a computerized random number generator or tables until the required sample size is filled.

Probability of selection is worked out as population size/sample size.

**Activity 10.2**

> What is the probability of selection for a sample of 500 from a population of 20 000?

## Systematic sampling

This is easier than random sampling as it does not use random number generation. In the previous activity, we looked at a sample size of 500 from a population of 20 000. In systematic random sampling, the figure of 40 would be used as what is known as a skip interval and every 40th name would be selected from the list.

## Stratified random sampling

This method divides the population into two or more mutually exclusive groups – for example, men or women, users or non-users of a product – and takes random samples from within them using either of the methods above.

This can be done *proportionately* where potential respondents or units are selected in proportion to the total number in each subset or *disproportionately* which takes more units from the subset with fewer respondents, that is where there is greater variation.

Whilst the disproportionate method is efficient and reliable, the proportionate method is more commonly used as the researcher may not know in advance the level of diversity within each subset.

## Cluster sampling

Cluster sampling is described by Wilson (2003) as 'A procedure in which clusters of population units are selected at random and then all or some of the units in the chosen clusters are studied.'

The technique works by identifying clusters within a population and selecting randomly from these clusters. The technique works when a population can easily be divided into representative clusters, for example in membership directories.

Disadvantages include the difficulty of forming a mini version of the population which maintains the characteristics of the population as a whole. Rather like Dr Evil and Mini Me, the characteristics may change and may be hard to control!!

Wilson (2003) identifies three approaches to cluster sampling:

1. *One stage* – Clusters are selected randomly and data is gathered from all people in the clusters.
2. *Two stage* – Clusters are selected randomly and data is gathered for a random sample of people in the selected clusters.
3. *Area sampling* – Geographical clusters are created and a random sample of individuals is selected.

## Multi-stage sampling
This is a method which has several advantages. The chief is to concentrate a dispersed sample into convenient locations.

For example in surveying UK households, a random selection of constituencies might be made, this would be followed by a random selection of wards, then polling districts and finally a selection of streets and then individuals.

Advantages include the fact that the creation of the sample frame is easier and the final interviews end up being geographically clustered reducing cost of face-to-face interviews.

## Limitations of random sampling
- It is expensive.
- Respondents selected must be interviewed to ensure the integrity of the process. This means that up to three call backs to individuals may be made before classifying a non-response.
- The cost of pulling together a large sample frame may be prohibitive.
- The random selection of a sample means that all members of a national population would have the same chance of being selected. This means that interviewers may have to cover Lands End to John O' Groats.

## Non-probability sampling

There are four types of non-probability sampling. These are listed below.

### Convenience sampling
It is based on the convenience for the researcher. It may be that the section is made in the street, in the office or from a database. As long as the sample fits with the population as a whole, it is legitimate.

### Judgement or purposive sampling
The researcher consciously selects a sample considered appropriate for the study. This may be based on certain companies representing a sector – for example, a researcher in the cutlery market might include all major department stores in the sample as well as a random selection of other outlets. This is designed to reflect the relative importance of department stores in the retail market.

### Quota sampling
It is defined by ESOMAR (2005) as 'A type of non-probability sample where the required number of units with particular characteristics are specified.' This is based on the idea that if known characteristics of the population are reproduced in the same proportion in the sample, it is representative of that population; for example, age, sex and social class can be used to select quotas.

A researcher may be required to interview equal split of men and women and a certain number of men of a certain age. The researcher selects respondents that comply with the quota laid down (Figure 10.2).

|  | Required | Achieved | Total |
|---|---|---|---|
| Male | 100 | | |
| **Age** | | | |
| 16–34 | 40 | | |
| 35–54 | 40 | | |
| 55+ ages | 20 | | |
| **Class** | | | |
| ABC1 | 40 | | |
| C2 | 35 | | |
| DE | 25 | | |

*Figure 10.2* Quota sheets

Advantages include

- ○ Speed and cost.
- ○ Allows sampling to take place where a sample frame may not be available but key characteristics of the population are known – for example, in overseas b2b research.
- ○ Interviewers do not have to interview named individuals; they are screened in or out via a small number of classification questions.
- ○ The data, when compared to random methods which are perhaps double the cost, has been proved to be acceptable provided that the research is managed effectively.
- ○ Cost savings may be used to improve the quality of research through increasing sample sizes or using a different method in support of the survey.
- ○ Its popularity shows that it works!

Disadvantages include

- ○ Whilst known characteristics may be distributed in correct proportions, unknown characteristics that may be relevant to the survey may not be. Hidden bias may exist that is not discovered.
- ○ Researchers may be biased as to the type of respondents they choose to interview or the location where they choose to carry out the interviews. A quota for young people may be filled at one youth club but will not be truly representative of the population as a whole.

## Snowball sampling

It is defined by ESOMAR (2005) as 'A type of non-probability sampling where initial respondents are selected at random and subsequent respondents are then selected by referrals or information from the earlier respondents.'

This is very useful in markets where there is low incidence of the population – in b2b markets, where buyers of competitive intelligence or where unusual behaviour is under consideration.

## Online issues

The same methods can be used in online research but the problem is that sample frames are less available. A range of panels have been set up to counter this, for example Nielsen net ratings.

## Determining the sample size

There is no necessary relationship between the size of the population and the sample. Whilst the larger the sample size the more accurate the results, this has to be traded off against the cost of producing this effect and the complexity, and therefore cost of managing the collection and processing of large amounts of data.

The cost of producing more response is normally proportional, that is the percentage increase in the cost of producing a percentage increase in sample size will be the same. However, the increase in accuracy is not proportional. As Wilson (2003) points out, sampling error tends to decrease at a rate equal to the square root of the relative increase in sample size. A sample increased by 100 per cent will improve accuracy by 10 per cent.

Sample size is often determined by past experience. Previous studies will indicate

- *The degree of variability in the population* – the more the variability, the larger the sample size will need to be.
- *The likely response rates* – if these are believed to be low, the sample will need to be larger.
- *The incident rate of the characteristic being researched* – if this is common, the sample may be smaller.
- *The number of subgroups within the data* – the smaller groups will have larger sampling errors and a larger sample might be needed to ensure that subgroups can be effectively analysed.

Other factors play a key role in determining sample size. These include

- *Budget* – always a factor in marketing decisions; the higher the sample size, the greater the cost.
- *Timings* – the larger the sample size, the longer it takes to gather data and complete the analysis.
- *The risk attached to any decision* – the greater the risk, the higher the level of accuracy required.
- The nature of the research may indicate complex analysis of sub-samples, for example women as opposed to men buying a certain product; if this is the case the sub-samples need to be large enough to ensure statistical reliability.

### Statistical techniques for determining sample size
For probability samples, statistical methods are used to establish sample sizes.

We need three pieces of information to work this out.

1. Variance and the degree of variability of the population, known as standard deviation
2. The required limit of accuracy or sampling error
3. The required level of confidence that the results will fall within a certain range.

Variance is a measure of how spread out a data set is. We work it out by looking at the average squared deviation of each number from its mean.

There are different formulae for working out variance but the one most commonly used in market research takes into account the potential bias in a sample.

The formula is

$$S^2 = \sum_{i=1}^{n} \frac{(X_i - \overline{X})^2}{n-1}$$

$X$ is the individual value in an array of data
$\overline{X}$ overline {X} is the mean of the array
$n$ is the number of values in an array.
For example, for the numbers 1, 3, 6, 4 and 1, the number of values is 5, and the variance is 4.5.

| Value | Mean | Deviation | Deviation squared |
|-------|------|-----------|-------------------|
| 1     | 3    | −2        | 4                 |
| 3     | 3    | 0         | 0                 |
| 6     | 3    | 3         | 9                 |
| 4     | 3    | 1         | 1                 |
| 1     | 3    | −2        | 4                 |
| Total |      |           | 18                |

Sum of squared differences divided by number of observations less 1 is 18/(5 − 1) = 4.5.

This is the variance.

Standard deviation is used to compare the spread of data sets. The more spread a set of values, the higher the standard deviation.

Standard deviation is the square root of the variance which we calculated above. You can see that the formula within the square root symbol is the formula we used to calculate variance.

$$SD = \sqrt{\frac{\sum (X_i - \overline{X})^2}{n-1}}$$

$X_i$ = the value of each data point
$\overline{X}$ = the average of all the data points
$\Sigma$ = the Greek letter sigma, meaning 'sum of'
$n$ = the total number of data points.

| Value | Mean | Deviation | Deviation squared |
|-------|------|-----------|-------------------|
| 1     | 3    | −2        | 4                 |
| 3     | 3    | 0         | 0                 |
| 6     | 3    | 3         | 9                 |
| 4     | 3    | 1         | 1                 |
| 1     | 3    | −2        | 4                 |
| Total | 3    |           | 18                |

Sum of squared differences divided by number of observations less 1 is $18/(5 - 1) = 4.5$.

This is the variance.

The standard deviation is the square root of the variance or 2.12

## Activity 10.3

Ok, now it is your turn, work out variance and standard deviation for the following figures

| Value | Mean | Deviation | Deviation squared |
|-------|------|-----------|-------------------|
| 200 | | | |
| 150 | | | |
| 50 | | | |
| 80 | | | |
| 150 | | | |
| 100 | | | |
| 100 | | | |
| 90 | | | |
| 170 | | | |
| 80 | | | |
| 110 | | | |

Sum of squared differences divided by number of observations less 1 is

This is the variance.

Standard deviation is the square root of the variance which is

Your mission – should you choose to accept it is – to fill in the gaps. Good luck!

### For studies involving averages or means
The formula to work out sample size is

$$N = \frac{Z^2 \sigma^2}{E^2}$$

Where, $Z$ is the confidence level
$\sigma$ is the population standard deviation
$E$ is the acceptable level of precision.

### Specify the level of precision
The level of precision is worked out by clients and researchers and reflects the budget available and the acceptable margin of error or degree of risk attached to the outcome of the research. If there is a need for accurate data, the sample size may be larger and the level of precision would be tighter.

## Determine the acceptable confidence interval

As we have seen above, the standard level of confidence is 95 per cent. Remember, this means that at the 95 per cent confidence interval there is a 1 in 20 chance of the sample being wrong. If the level of risk was high, then we could work at the 99 per cent confidence level, here there is a 1 in a 100 chance of the sample being wrong.

## Estimate the standard deviation

It is impossible to know this before carrying out the survey, so an estimate is required. This can be based upon:

- o Previous studies
- o Secondary research
- o The result of pilot surveys
- o Judgement.

Once the study is completed, the sample mean and standard deviation can be calculated, and the exact confidence level and limits of error can be worked out.

## Activity 10.4

Wilson presents an example in which the Z value is 1.96. Standard deviation is 40.8 and the limit of error is 5. What happens if we wish to increase the confidence limit to 99 per cent?

## Studies involving proportions

Studies measuring the proportion of a population having a certain characteristic are often required in marketing and in surveys, for example the proportion responding to a promotion or the number of voters against university top-up fees. To determine sample size here a different formula is needed.

$$N = \frac{Z^2[P(1 - P)]}{E^2}$$

Remember $Z$ is our confidence level; let us use the standard marketing confidence level – so $Z$ is 1.96 or the 95 per cent confidence level.

$E$ is the limit of error. In this case we need the results to be correct to within let us say ±3 per cent, written as a decimal ±0.03.

$P$ is the estimated percentage of the population who have the characteristic. In this case we will look at the number of people who may respond to a test mailing and we estimate that 15 per cent may respond. This again is written as a decimal –0.15.

So, let us work this through:

$$N = \frac{1.96 \times 1.96[0.15(1 - 0.15)]}{0.03^2}$$

$$N = \frac{3.84 \times (0.15 \times 0.85)}{0.0009}$$

$$N = \frac{0.4896}{0.0009}$$

$$N = 544$$

We would therefore need a sample of 544 to be 95 per cent confident of our 15 per cent response rate on roll out of the campaign.

If we reduced the limits of error to ±1 per cent the sample size would increase.

$$N = \frac{0.4896}{0.0001}$$

$$N = 4896$$

If the estimated response was 2 per cent we can see the sample size would decrease.

$$N = \frac{3.84 \times 0.0196}{0.0001}$$

$$N = \frac{0.075}{0.0001}$$

$$N = 750$$

The figure reduces because the difference in the proportion of the population is higher.

If the estimated response rate went to 20 per cent, then the sample required would be 6144.

### Adjustment for larger samples
We have said that there is no direct relationship between population and sample size to estimate a characteristic with a level of error and confidence.

The assumption is that sample elements are drawn independent of one another. This cannot be assumed when the sample is higher than 10 per cent of the population. If this is the case, an adjustment is made, called the finite population correction factor.

The calculation reduces the required sample:

$$N_1 = \frac{nN}{N + n - 1}$$

$N_1$ is the revised sample size
$n$ is the original sample size
$N$ is the population size.

For example, if the population has 2000 elements and the original sample size is 400, then,

$$N = \frac{400 \times 2000}{2000 - 400 - 1}$$
$$N_1 = 333$$

Other rules-of-thumb factors to consider in setting sample sizes:

- ○ Trade of cost against reliability and accuracy.
- ○ Minimum subgroup sizes should be more than 100 respondents. It is difficult to be confident in figures lower than this.
- ○ The average sample size in national surveys in the United Kingdom is around 1500–2000 respondents. Minimum sample sizes in the FMCG markets are 300–500 respondents.

## Implementing a sampling procedure

Once the sample size is worked out, the researcher can start to gather data. We have already discussed the fact that a sample will always vary in some way from the population. There are a number of reasons for this.

### Sampling error

'Sampling error is the error in a survey caused by using a sample to estimate the value of a parameter in the population' (ESOMAR, 2003).

'Sampling error is the difference between the sample value and the true value of a phenomenon for the population being surveyed' (Wilson, 2003).

Sampling error is inherent in the process of sampling and is reflected in the accuracy of estimates about the total population that can be made from the data.

Sampling errors can be estimated using statistics but other errors can occur. These are called non-sampling errors.

### Non-sampling error

*Sampling frame error* – This is the error that occurs due to the fact that the sampling frame is different from the entire population. This can be reduced by combining lists to reinforce the frame.

*Non-response error* – This may be due to refusal or the non-availability of respondents. Refusals can be reduced by incentivizing the process and through using trained, experienced interviewers and well-designed questionnaires.

*Data error* – This may be through respondent error; responders give the wrong information deliberately or unintentionally. This can be reduced through careful analysis of inconsistency in the responses, through the use of well-designed questionnaires and the use of skilled interviewers.

*Interviewer errors* – These occur as a result of the interviewer making mistakes in asking questions or recording answers. These can be reduced through careful training and back checking to ensure that the interview was carried out, that the respondent matched the required profile, that all questions were asked and that the code of conduct of the MRS was adhered to. The IQCS ensure minimum standards for back checking.

*Data analysis error* – These can be caused by keystroke or software problems. They can be reduced by checking for consistency and manually profiling hard data against that held in the computer.

## Weightings
Weightings are used to correct problems due to sampling error. Responses from subgroups are given a statistical weight reflecting the importance of the subgroup in the population of interest.

The weighting is most often used to bring the sample into line with known proportions in the population, for example age or gender.

## Summary

In this unit, we explored the process of sampling and looked in detail at the stages involved in the process.

They cover:

o The definition of the population
o The decision to sample or census
o The creation of the sampling frame
o The sampling method.

We looked in detail at probability and non-probability sampling and the various approaches under each. Probability sampling includes random sampling, systematic sampling, stratified random sampling, cluster sampling and area sampling. Non-probability techniques include convenience sampling, judgement sampling, quota sampling and snowball sampling. We looked at the constraints on the choice of sampling method.

The sample size was then discussed. Sample size is determined by financial, managerial and statistical considerations. We looked in detail at the statistical basis of establishing sample size.

Finally, we looked at the error involved in sampling and suggested ways of managing error and the process of weighting.

# Further study

## Question 10.1

You have been appointed as marketing manager to an online retailer of intimate apparel (underwear). They have succeeded in difficult times to grow their business but have appointed you to look at the marketing research function within the business. Your first piece of research is based on a quota sample. The MD of the business is sceptical.

Produce a report for the MD outlining what quota sampling is.

What benefits does it have? What are its disadvantages and how can these be overcome?

What other sampling techniques may have been considered and why would they have been rejected?

## Question 10.2
## Question 5

Discuss the proposition that the determination of sample size is simply a matter of guesswork.

**(Total 25 Marks)**

# Hints and tips

Go to the MRS website and look at the guidelines for qualitative research. Add this to your study pack.

# Bibliography

Crouch, S., Housden, M. (2003) *Marketing Research for Managers*, Butterworth-Heinemann.

ESOMAR (2005) www.esomar.nl.

MRS (2005) www.mrs.org.uk.

Wilson, A. (2003) *Marketing Research: An Integrated Approach*, FT Prentice Hall.

# unit 11 quantitative data analysis

| | |
|---|---|
| Design a questionnaire and topic guide | 4.6 Design a questionnaire and discussion guide to meet a project's research objectives |
| Interpret quantitative and qualitative data, and present coherent and appropriate recommendations that lead to effective marketing and business decisions | 5.1 Demonstrate an ability to use techniques for analysing qualitative and quantitative data |

## Key definitions

**Coding** – The process that allocates a number to each answer and it is this that allows analysis to take place.

**Editing** – The process of computer or manual checking of the data to look for respondent or interview errors.

**Frequency distributions** – Counts of the numbers of respondents who gave each possible answer to a particular question.

**Nominal data** – Numbers assigned to objects or phenomena as labels or identification numbers that name or classify but that have no true numeric meaning (Wilson, 2003).

**Ordinal data** – Numbers with the labelling characteristics of nominal data but which also have the ability to communicate the rank order of the data. They do not indicate absolute quantities and do not imply that the intervals between the numbers are equal (Wilson, 2003).

**Interval data** – Similar to ordinal data but with the added dimension that intervals between the values on a scale are equal (Wilson, 2003).

**Ratio data** – Actual or real numbers that have a meaningful or absolute zero (Wilson, 2003).

**Descriptive statistics** – Statistical devices that help to summarize data. These include measures of central tendency, mode, mean, median and measures of dispersion range, inter-quartile range and standard deviation.

**Factor analysis** – Studies the relationships between variables to simplify data into a smaller set of composite variables or factors.

**Correlation** – Examines the strength of the relationship between variables using an index.

**Cross tabulations** – Table setting out responses to one question relative to others.

**Coefficient of determination** – Measure of the strength of linear relationship between a dependent and an independent variable.

**Conjoint analysis** – Analysis that asks respondents to make decisions between various attributes measuring their relative importance.

**Chi square** – A test measuring the goodness of fit between the observed sample values and the expected distribution of those values.

**Z test** – A hypothesis test about a single mean where the sample is greater than 30.

**T Test** – A hypothesis test about a single mean where the sample is less than 30.

**Spearman's rank-order correlation** – Correlation for ordinal data.

**Pearson's product moment correlation** – A correlation technique for interval and ratio data.

**Null hypothesis** – The hypothesis that is tested.

**Alternative hypothesis** – A hypothesis competing with the null hypothesis.

**Least squares** – A regression method that produces a line of best fit for a data set involving a dependent and independent variable.

**Independent variable** – A variable that has influence on the value of the dependent variable.

**Dependent variable** – The response measure studied.

**Regression** – Examines the relationship between 2 variables.

## Study Guide

The unit should take around 3 hours to complete. You will need another 3 hours to ensure that you complete and understand the exercises. You will need to refer to other course texts throughout this unit and should have access to Alan Wilson's text.

## Introduction

The analysis of data is a key skill of the marketing manager. Very often people find the introduction of statistics a little daunting. However, an ability to understand basic methods of data analysis is very important. This unit will take you through the process of preparing data and analysing that data to inform marketing decisions. For the less numerate, it will try to show you what the various techniques do to data, and how and why they are used. Many people find that describing what the techniques do in words makes the whole task more manageable and accessible.

Data analysis can be done easily now using computer packages such as Excel and SPSS. However, the lack of understanding of the techniques remains. The statistical packages are of no use at all unless you understand what you are trying to do to the data and which technique is most appropriate. You also need to be able to interpret the results. This is what we will try to do here. If you are taking the continuous assessment route through the course, then this area will be important to you to help you present research data effectively.

## Editing and coding

Before data is processed, it is assessed for completeness and coherence. The editing process involves computer or manual checking of the data to look for respondent or interview errors or inconsistencies. If errors are identified, the respondent may be called back and if the questionnaire cannot be rescued, then it may be rejected.

Coding is the process that allocates a number to each answer and it is this that allows analysis to take place. As discussed earlier, the coding process may take place as the questionnaire is administered either manually by the interviewer ringing a number on the questionnaire or it may be managed through computer-assisted methods.

After this process is completed the data will look like this:

|  | Question 1 | Question 2 | Question 3 | Question 4 | Etc. |
|---|---|---|---|---|---|
| Record 1 | 1 | 3 | 1 | 10 | |
| Record 2 | 1 | 4 | 5 | 15 | |
| Record 3 | 2 | 2 | 3 | 12 | |
| Etc . . . 4 | | | | | |

The questionnaire might have looked like this:

| Question 1 | Code |
|---|---|
| Sex M | 1 |
| F | 2 |

| Question 2 | Code |
|---|---|
| What is your age? | |
| 18–25 | 1 |
| 26–35 | 2 |
| 36–45 | 3 |
| 46–55 | 4 |
| 55+ | 5 |

And so on.

Coding open questions involves using a sample of the completed questionnaires and developing a coding frame or a list of codes for all possible responses to an open question. This process may categorize and group certain diverse responses into a manageable number. This process must be handled carefully to reduce the processing error that might occur. The key thing is to learn from the piloting of the questionnaire and to analyse all possible responses. However, in certain questions the number of coded responses may need to be limited to ensure efficient operation of the survey; in this case, the coder or interviewer needs to be confident in allocating a certain response to a broader coded category (Figure 11.1).

Question one

What did you enjoy during the purchase of your car?

| | |
|---|---|
| Salespeople | 1 |
| Dealership facilities | 2 |
| Test drive | 3 |
| Negotiations over price | 4 |
| Follow up calls | 5 |
| Information pack | 6 |
| Other Code | 7 |

*Figure 11.1* Example of a coding frame for an open question

## Data entry

Data entry may be carried out automatically through CAPI, CAWI and CATI systems or scanned into the computer using optical character recognitions software or they may be entered by hand. After this process, the data will be once again checked or cleaned for keystroke or character recognition problems.

Once this is complete, the data can be analysed.

## Tabulation and statistical analysis

There are four types of data that can be analysed.

These are:

(a) Nominal data
(b) Ordinal data
(c) Interval data
(d) Ratio data.

### Nominal data

These refer to values that are given to objects that in themselves have no intrinsic numerical value. For example, we assigned a value to gender: 1 for men and 2 for women.

We can count them and create percentages.

Statistics based on frequency counts can be used with this type of data. These include mode, that is, most frequently occurring value and chi-square tests, that is, a test that shows whether or not the results taken from small sample are statistically significant from the expected results in the population as a whole.

The mode is the most frequently occurring figure in a set of data. For example, this may be used to say that Brand X was the most frequently mentioned brand.

Chi square tests measure the significance between cross tabulated data. For example, we may have data that shows that men buy more beer than women. Whilst we might assume that this is the case, we will have a range of values in each cell. The problem is to determine if the difference in the values is real or a result of using a sample of the population, rather than asking the whole population.

If you are struggling with these concepts, do not worry; we will explore them in more detail later in this unit.

### Ordinal data

These data represent rank order data. They do not imply that there is an equal gap between items ranked and there is no other meaning to them other than rank order.

Examples include asking consumers to rank a number of products 1–5 around a certain attribute.

For example:

Rank the following online banks 1–5 in order of their reputation for service where 1 is the bank which offers the best service and 5 is the bank that offers the worst service.

- Smile
- Cahoot
- First direct
- Egg
- Intelligent finance.

We can use mode and median analysis with this data.

The median is the middle value when responses are arranged in order.

## Interval data

It is rank order data in which the intervals between the data are equal. These are also known as interval scales. Interval scales rank elements relative to each other but not from any observable origin. This means that the data has its meaning only by virtue of the comparison between elements selected. This means that ratio analysis between values is not possible.

Rank the following online banks 1–5 in order of their reputation for service, where 1 is the bank which offers the best service and 5 is the bank that offers worst service.

| | | | | | |
|---|---|---|---|---|---|
| o Smile | 1 | 2 | 3 | 4 | 5 |
| o Cahoot | 1 | 2 | 3 | 4 | 5 |
| o First direct | 1 | 2 | 3 | 4 | 5 |
| o Egg | 1 | 2 | 3 | 4 | 5 |
| o Intelligent finance | 1 | 2 | 3 | 4 | 5 |

This data allows means and standard deviations to take place and a range of other statistical tests can be carried out.

The mean is the average of the results.

Standard deviation is a measure that looks at the distribution of results around the average value of the results.

## Ratio data

Ratio data has an absolute zero or observable origin, for example shoe size, products bought or age.

This means all analyses are possible.

## Tabulations, hole counts and frequency

Tables give researchers a feel for data. Frequency distributions are simply counts of the numbers of respondents who gave each possible answer to a particular question. They are used to help the researcher form the next stage of analysis.

## Cross tabulations (cross tabs)

These tables 'cross' the answers to one question with the answers to another, for example age of respondent and products purchased (Figure 11.2).

Q. 15 When do you plan to buy a new car?

Base: All those who intend to replace their car

| | Total | Age | |
|---|---|---|---|
| | | **21–44** | **45+** |
| Base | 127 (100%) | 63 (100%) | 64 (100%) |
| Within a month | 12 (9%) | 2 (3%) | 10 (15%) |
| Within 6 months | 45 (35%) | 25 (40%) | 20 (31%) |
| Within the year | 55 (43%) | 30 (48%) | 25 (39%) |
| Longer | 15 (12%) | 10 (16%) | 5 (8%) |

These tables can be presented graphically.

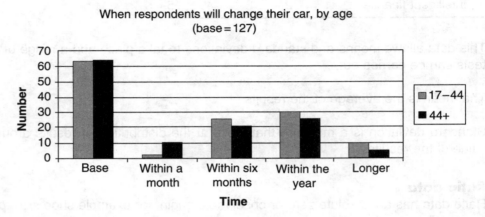

*Figure 11.2* Cross tabulations

It is easy to generate cross tabs using computers. The skill is to decide which analyses are relevant and significant.

## Descriptive statistics

These data are used to give the researcher a view of the location of the data and its spread. These are known as measures of central tendency and measures of dispersion or variability.

Measures of central tendency indicate typical values for data sets. These are the mean, median and mode.

The mean is the arithmetic average. To calculate the mean, divide the total values by the number of cases.

The median is the value of the middle case in a series of numbers put in ascending or descending order.

The mode is the value in a set of data that appears most frequently. A data set may have more than one mode – a number of categories may be equal and share the highest frequency.

For example, shoe sizes bought in one hour:

| | | | | |
|---|---|---|---|---|
| 5 | 6 | 6 | 7 | 8 |
| 9 | 8 | 8 | 8 | 8 |
| 9 | 9 | 9 | 8 | 8 |
| 11 | 10 | 10 | 9 | 9 |
| 11 | 12 | 12 | 13 | 5 |

Mode = 8    Median = 9    Mean = 8.72

## Measures of dispersion

These indicate how spread out or dispersed a data set is. We looked at these in Unit 10 and you should revisit this unit as required. Remember they include the range, variance and standard deviation.

The range is the interval from the highest to the lowest value in a data set. In the example above, the range is 13–5 = 8.

The shoe example is straightforward. However, if the size 13 man had bought 5 pairs of shoes, then the sample would be skewed towards the higher range. This is managed by using what is called the inter-quartile range; this removes any values that fall outside the 75th and 25th percentile and then calculates the range.

Remember, variance is a measure of how spread out a data set is, and we work it out by looking at the average squared deviation of each number from its mean.

Let us look at the formula once again.

$$S^2 = \sum_{i=1}^{n} \frac{(X_i - \overline{X})^2}{n - 1}$$

$X$ is the individual value in an array of data
$\overline{X}$ is the mean of the array
$n$ is the number of values in an array.

Standard deviation is the square root of the variance. Let us look once again at the formula

$$SD = \sqrt{\frac{\sum(X_i - \overline{X})^2}{n - 1}}$$

where

$X_i$ = the value of each data point
$\overline{X}$ = the average of all the data points
$\sum$ = the Greek letter sigma, meaning 'sum of'
$n$ = the total number of data points.

## Statistical significance

There are advantages to using samples rather than collecting data from the whole population under review. However, the data from a sample will always be subject to error. We cannot be sure that the difference between two results is a real change in those values or simply a result of the sampling error.

Clearly, there may be a mathematical difference between two values but if the difference is large enough not to have occurred through chance or error, then the difference is defined as statistically significant.

### Hypothesis testing

A hypothesis is defined by Wilson as an assumption about a characteristic in the population. Research will allow the researcher to conclude something about the population.

For example, in a survey of 500 customers the average number of times a customer purchased from a store was found to be 4 times per month or 52 times per year. Managers believed the actual frequency to be 60 times. Is the sample consistent with our marketing managers' beliefs? The sample has a standard deviation of 10.

The testing of hypothesis follows a simple structure. First, establish the hypothesis.

There are two forms of hypotheses:

1. The Null hypothesis or $H_0$ is the one that will be tested, that is, the existing situation where no difference is expected.
2. The Alternative hypothesis or $H_1$ is the one in which a difference is expected.

For example, our recall problem could be expressed as:

The Null hypothesis or $H_0$ Mean purchase frequency is 60 times per year.

The Alternative hypothesis or $H_1$ Mean purchase frequency is not 60 times per year.

If we use the 95 per cent confidence level we can work this out.

Standard error is

$$\frac{10}{\sqrt{500}} = 0.44.$$

The sample mean is 8 lower than the hypothesized mean $8/0.44 = 18.18$ standard errors below the mean.

At 95 per cent confidence we would expect the sample mean to be within 1.96 standard errors of our null hypothesis. Because it is not, we cannot reject the null hypothesis.

The hypotheses will either be accepted or rejected depending on the outcome of the results.

There are a range of significance tests available and the most frequently used tests are:

- o Chi-square test
- o Z test
- o T Test.

Significance tests measure whether the difference between two percentages is significant or not, or whether the difference between two means from different samples is significant. In order to carry out these tests three concepts must be considered.

## Degrees of freedom

Degrees of freedom are defined as the number of observations minus 1. A sample $n$ has $n-1$ degrees of freedom. Degrees of freedom are used to reflect potential bias in a sample.

## Independent versus related samples

Selection of the appropriate test technique may involve considering whether samples are independent or related. In related samples, the measurement of the variable of interest in one sample might affect the measurement of the variable of interest in another.

## Errors in hypothesis testing

Two types of error are known – type one and type two. A concept called the alpha level defines the probability of committing such an error and is commonly set at 0.05 or a 5 per cent chance of the error occurring.

Type one errors happen when the null hypothesis is rejected when it is true. Type two errors mean accepting the null hypothesis when it is false.

Reducing the alpha level increases the chance of a type one error occurring.

## The Chi square test

This measures whether the differences in cross tabulated data sets are significant. This is also known as 'goodness of fit' between observed distribution and expected distribution of the variable. It compares one or more sets of data to indicate if there is a real difference.

 ## Activity 11.1

A test mailing plan produced the following responses:

Pack A 5909

Pack B 5810

Pack C 6350

Using the Chi-square formula, work out if there is a variation between the packs.

$\sum$ = sum of
$f_0$ = observed
$f_e$ = expected (mean)

$$x^2 = \sum \frac{(f_0 - f_e)^2}{f_e}$$

Before proceeding look at the debrief to this activity.

Chi-square test of two or more variables can be used to test, for example, the difference between male and female respondents to the mailing.

## Hypotheses about means

Where sample data produces a mean or a proportion, researchers can use a $Z$ or a $T$ test to test hypotheses relating to them.

$Z$ tests are used if the researcher is aware of the population's mean and variance. This may be the real mean or variance, or assumed figures. The sample must be higher than 30. $T$ tests are used if the mean and variance are unknown or if a sample is less than 30. $T$ tests are more frequently used by researchers. They allow the researcher to work out if the difference between the two averages is real or significant, or simply due to the fact that the figures are derived from a sample. For example, if a customer-satisfaction survey ranks your brand higher than average, is this a real difference or due to sampling error?

In a sample of 1500 people on a scale of 1–5 your customer satisfaction was 4.5, the average of your competitors was 3.8. The sample standard deviation was 1.6.

The formula for a $Z$ test is as follows:

$$Z = \frac{\text{sample mean} - \text{population}}{\text{estimated standard error}}$$

Standard error = standard deviation/the square root of the sample size

$$\text{Standard error} = \frac{1.6}{\sqrt{1500}} = 0.04$$

$$Z = 4.5 - 3.8/0.04 = 17.5$$

This is larger than the $Z$ value of 1.64 at 0.05 level of significance and we can say that at 95 per cent confidence the results are correct.

Try changing some of these figures, the standard deviation for example. You will see that if the results were more dispersed, $Z$ score would reduce.

$T$ tests are generally used to determine the results from smaller surveys with a sample size of under 30.

The formula for $T$ tests involving a mean and one sample is:

$$T = \frac{\text{sample mean} - \text{mean under null hypothesis}}{\text{estimated standard error of the mean}}$$

For comparing the mean in two samples the following formula is used:

$$T = \frac{\text{mean from sample 1} - \text{mean from sample 2}}{\sqrt{[(\text{standard error for sample 1})^2 - (\text{standard error for sample 2})^2]}}$$

## Measuring relationships

### Correlation and regression

These techniques measure the degree of association between two variables such as income and number of foreign holidays or customer satisfaction and product repurchase, or advertising spend and sales.

Bivariate techniques measure the relationship between two variables. This does not prove that one variable causes the other but rather indicates the degree of relationship between the variables. Often a cause-and-effect link is assumed but this is not a proven relationship. It is important to apply common sense in the interpretation of the results.

Variables are labelled dependent and independent. Independent variables are those assumed to influence the dependent variable.

There are two types of correlation analysis.

*Pearson's product movement correlation* is used with interval and ratio data. It produces a correlation coefficient which can have a maximum value of +1 and a minimum value of −1.

Perfect positive correlation between two sets of variables is indicated by +1. This means that if there is a movement of 5 per cent on one variable, it is accompanied by a movement in the same direction of 5 per cent on another variable. For example, when satisfaction increases by 5 per cent, sales rise by 5 per cent. Perfect negative correlation means the two variables have a perfect negative relationship. If for every 10 per cent increase in price the sales volume decreased by 10 per cent, then the correlation coefficient would be −1.

When changes in one variable are not associated with changes in the other variable, the correlation coefficient will be calculated as zero.

Generally, correlation coefficients above +0.7 or below −0.7 are believed to show an increasing degree of association. This might require further research to explore the association in more detail from larger samples.

When ordinal data is being considered, Spearman's rank order correlation is used. This might be used to compare ranking of companies' promotional expenditure with a ranking of their sales turnover.

It is important to note that low coefficients do not mean that there is no association. It only implies absence of a linear association. It may be that a non-linear association exists. Again think about your market and apply common sense to your work.

## Activity 11.2

Work through the examples of Pearson's product movement coefficient of correlation in your texts. What other examples of the application can you think of?

$$R = \frac{n\sum xy - (\sum x)(\sum y)}{\sqrt{[n\sum x^2 - (\sum x)^2][n\sum y^2 - (\sum y)^2]}}$$

This example looks at the relationship between restaurant capacity and sales. Work out $R$ for this example.

| Restaurant | Capacity | Turnover (£100 000) |
|---|---|---|
| 1 | 210 | 1.10 |
| 2 | 80 | 0.74 |
| 3 | 80 | 0.99 |
| 4 | 160 | 1.14 |
| 5 | 100 | 1.01 |
| 6 | 70 | 0.92 |
| 7 | 160 | 1.08 |
| 8 | 60 | 0.80 |
| 9 | 300 | 1.10 |
| 10 | 200 | 1.16 |
| 11 | 150 | 1.09 |
| 12 | 50 | 0.68 |
| 13 | 80 | 0.78 |
| 14 | 150 | 1.08 |
| 15 | 100 | 1.12 |
| 16 | 100 | 0.90 |
| 17 | 90 | 0.94 |
| 18 | 170 | 0.91 |
| 19 | 80 | 0.85 |
| 20 | 110 | 1.05 |

## Simple regression analysis

Regression analysis is concerned with dependence. For example, sales volume may be predicted based on other variables.

In the insurance industry, this is used to measure the chance of a customer not renewing a policy and explores the number of inbound calls and customer complaints.

The allocation of dependent and independent variables is more important in regression analysis.

Remember, movement in the dependent variables depends upon movement in the independent variables.

Often, correlation analysis and regression analysis are both carried out on the same data sets. If correlation analysis indicates which variables have a relevant association with, say, sales volume, regression analysis can be used to predict sales volume, given a set of decisions about marketing variables and assumptions about probable movements in external variables. Sales forecasters use regression analysis. However, it is clear that the movement in a market is caused by a number of factors and this is dealt with through multivariate techniques which we will look at later.

Least squares is the most common approach to regression. Least squares identifies a line of best fit between observations and this allows us to produce an estimated regression function that indicates the relationship. To do this we need to look at the slope of the line and the line of intercept. Simple regression analysis may be enhanced through the coefficient of determination. This measures the strength of the relationship between variables.

## Activity 11.3

Using the formula, calculate the relationship between turnover and capacity.

$$\hat{b} = \frac{\sum x_j y_j - n\bar{x}\bar{y}}{\sum x_j^2 - n(\bar{x})^2}$$

$$\hat{a} = \bar{y} - \hat{b}\bar{x}$$

| Restaurant | Capacity | Turnover (£100 000) |
|---|---|---|
| 1 | 210 | 1.10 |
| 2 | 80 | 0.74 |
| 3 | 80 | 0.99 |
| 4 | 160 | 1.14 |
| 5 | 100 | 1.01 |
| 6 | 70 | 0.92 |
| 7 | 160 | 1.08 |
| 8 | 60 | 0.80 |
| 9 | 300 | 1.10 |
| 10 | 200 | 1.16 |
| 11 | 150 | 1.09 |
| 12 | 50 | 0.68 |
| 13 | 80 | 0.78 |
| 14 | 150 | 1.08 |
| 15 | 100 | 1.12 |
| 16 | 100 | 0.90 |
| 17 | 90 | 0.94 |
| 18 | 170 | 0.91 |
| 19 | 80 | 0.85 |
| 20 | 110 | 1.05 |

This can be plotted as follows (Figure 11.3).

Figure 11.3 Turnover and capacity

## Multivariate analysis techniques

These techniques analyse two or more variables simultaneously and present a more realistic approach to marketing decision-making.

There are six key techniques:

### Multiple regression analysis

This allows the researcher to understand the relationship between three or more variables and the impact on the value of a dependent value, based on the values of two or more independent values – for example, response to mailings and the impact of re-mailing or telephone follow-up.

Wilson points out that there are three common uses:

- o The impact of marketing mix variables on sales
- o The importance of components or aspects of satisfaction on overall satisfaction
- o Determining the impact of different consumer characteristics on sales.

### Multiple discriminant analysis

This technique is used to classify individuals based on two or more independent variables, for example, readiness to buy a car based on age of car, length of time spent on the website and in bound calls.

The major discriminating factor between shoppers and non-shoppers in a particular department store was found, through discriminant analysis, to be the perceived price level within the store. Subsequent advertising of lower-priced lines resulted in an increase in the number of shoppers.

### Factor analysis

Factor analysis reduces a large number of variables to a more manageable smaller set of factors based on the interrelationships between them.

It provides insight for the groupings that emerge and allows for more efficient analysis of complex data.

It is often used for rating scales or attitude statements.

Factor analysis is a subjective process as any set of factors can be rejected and new sets created. One way of managing this is to split the sample into two groups and if the same factors are created from each group, more confidence can be placed in them.

### Cluster analysis

This technique groups objects or respondents into mutually exclusive and exhaustive groups. The technique is often used in database marketing to create segments based on behaviour across a range of variables.

### Multidimensional scaling or perceptual mapping

Consumers rate objects, often brands, by the relative strength of an attribute compared to other objects or brands. This creates a perception of a 'position' in the market and is very useful for determining brand perception and repositioning.

### Conjoint analysis

Conjoint analysis is a way of looking at customers' decisions as a trade-off between multiple attributes in products or services.

In conjoint analysis, consumers are asked to make decisions about various attributes, trading lower price for comfort, for example, in car purchases.

There are two approaches to this process:

(a)  The full-profile approach describes the full product or service – respondents may rank all possible combinations of, for example, product quality, price and after sales service.

(b)  The pairwise approach presents attributes in pairs and respondents put each in rank order. This approach is generally easier for respondents to manage and care must be taken that the list of attributes is not too long.

### Software packages

Do not despair if this unit has left you slightly boggle-eyed! There are many software packages on the market that will do most of this for you. The key thing is to understand what these packages will do to your valuable data and to produce efficient analysis which allows a focus on the research problem.

Excel is perfectly adequate for most of the key formulae outlined above but there are specialists, perhaps the best known software packages, which include:

SPSS www.spss.com

SNAP www.mercator.co.uk.

 ## Activity 11.4

Visit www.spss.com and www.mercator.co.uk, make a list of the services that are available and add these to your favourites.

## Summary

In this unit, we looked at the process of data analysis. We saw that data needs to be entered, coded, edited and cleaned before data analysis can be carried out.

We saw that there are four types of data. These are:

1.  Nominal
2.  Ordinal
3.  Interval
4.  Ratio.

The type of analysis that can be carried out is dependent on the type of data that is being analysed.

We looked at the process of tabulation. In order to obtain a first look at data, we saw examples of frequency distributions or hole counts and cross tabulation.

We went on to look at the types of analysis that can be carried out looking in detail at the following:

- Descriptive statistics
- Statistical significance and hypotheses testing
- The measurement of relationships
- Multivariate analysis.

We looked in detail at methods under each of these categories.

## Further study

### Question 11.1
What tasks have to be done before data can be analysed and after surveys have been completed?

Describe the tasks and outline their role in producing effective analysis.

## Hints and tips

There are many online tutorials that cover the area of statistical analysis. A web search on the key terms above generates some great examples and exercises.

## Bibliography

Wilson, A. (2003) Marketing Research: An Integrated Approach, FT Prentice Hall.

# unit 12
# presenting marketing research

## Learning objectives

After completing this unit you will be able to

- Identify the structure for the presentation of a research report

- Outline the key features of an oral presentation

- Know how to make the most of a presentation

- Understand the use of graphics in presentation of data

- Complete syllabus elements 5.2, 5.3 and 5.4.

Interpret quantitative and qualitative data, and present coherent and appropriate recommendations that lead to effective marketing and business decisions

5.2 Write a research report aimed at supporting marketing decisions

5.3 Plan and design an oral presentation of market research reports. Critically evaluate the outcomes and quality of a research project

5.4 Plan and design an oral presentation of market research reports

## Key definitions

**Oral presentation** – A verbal presentation of research findings using a range of supporting material.

**Executive summary** – A précis of the report.

# Study Guide

This unit should take you around 1.5 hours to complete.

## Introduction

The final report to the client is perhaps the most important part of the research planning process. For the external agency, it is the moment of truth when the proposed methodology is presented to the client. For the client, it is the chance to consider the course of action based on the results. For individuals, it is the chance to impress senior colleagues and enhance their reputation. No wonder people get a little fractious and nervous as the deadline looms!

The ability to present data in the most appropriate and accessible way, whilst ensuring that the research problem is effectively dealt with, is a highly developed skill. The results are generally presented in written format and this may or may not be supported by an oral presentation supported by slides.

Wilson suggests a six-point approach to the presentation of research that focuses on the audience's needs.

1. Respect their importance
2. What do they need from the report
3. How does your report meet this need
4. Underpin the key information with evidence
5. Remind them of the key points of the report
6. Make recommendations as to action.

## The written report

The structure of a written report is standard and this helps considerably with the process of producing the document. Before producing the report, it helps to consider the objectives of the study again and the nature of the audience who will read and use the report. What are the key points that the audience is interested in? What are the key constraints on marketing decisions recommended in the report? What is the business position and what are the resource implications of decisions adequately considered? (Figure 12.1).

- o Title page
- o Contents
- o Executive summary
- o Introduction
- o Situation analysis and problem definition
- o Research methodology and limitations
- o Findings and analysis
- o Conclusions and recommendations
- o Appendices

*Figure 12.1* Research report format

## Title page

This should contain the title of the report, the name and contact details of the agency and the researcher, client details and the date of presentation.

## Contents page

This should contain full details of sections and subsections and page numbers. It should include lists of tables and figures. It should make the report navigable. If presenting on the web, the use of hyperlinks which take the browser to the relevant section can be considered.

## The executive summary

This should be a short summary of the report and its recommendations. Many say that it should be a one- or two-page summary, or a maximum of two pages. There are no hard and fast rules. The summary needs to do a job, that is, summarizing a report, and also needs to be accessible.

Production of the executive summary is a tough job. As Churchill said 'Sorry, for such a long letter. I didn't have time to write a short one.' It is hard to condense the report into a one- or two-page summary. It is also the section of the report that will be read by senior managers and so it is worth putting time and effort into its production.

The executive summary should be written after the rest of the report has been written. The executive summary should start the report. Some people feel that it should follow the contents page and some feel that it should precede it. Some companies produce a separate summary of the work and this can be useful for wider and more efficient distribution of the key findings of the report.

## Introduction

The introduction should outline the key objectives of the research, the reasons why the research has been carried out and the constraints that the researchers are working to. It may include profiles and key responsibilities of the researchers.

## Situation analysis and problem definition

This section outlines the background to the problem and reviews business and marketing objectives. It drills down into the problem's definition and the detailed objectives for the research programme, and reprises the sections of the brief and proposal.

## Research methodology and limitations

This section outlines the detailed methodology for the study. It should cover the research method, the data capture mechanism, the topic or discussion guide or questionnaire, the definition of the population of interest, the sampling approach and the method of data analysis. This section should not be too long. Details should be put into the appendices. It should cover sources of error, including sample size.

## Findings and analysis

The main body of the report should cover the findings relevant to the objectives. It should be constructed to present a solution to the problem, not on a question-by-question basis. The research data should present data to support a line of argument and the focus should be on analysis and insight. Key ideas can be supported by tables or quotes from respondents. It may include tables and graphics, and should be linked by a narrative.

## Conclusions and recommendations

This section brings the report to a close. It should present a summary of key findings and recommendations for marketing decisions and future research.

**Appendices**
Should include all supporting data. It contains material that is relevant to the research but that would be too detailed for the main report. It may include all tables, questionnaires, discussion guides and secondary data. It may be that the appendices are longer than the main report.

Example of a report contents (amended to protect client confidentiality)

1. Abstract
2. Executive summary
3. Acknowledgements
4. Introduction

   (a) Industry background – The UK Market

      (i) The 'Brand Renaissance'
      (ii) A radically changing distribution network
      (iii) Changing consumer values
      (iv) The franchised dealer

   (b) Background to organization

      (i) UK success story?
      (ii) Brand deficit
      (iii) The future

5. Research objectives
6. Research methodology

   (a) Sampling procedure and size
   (b) Research methods

      (i) In-depth interviews
      (ii) Staff focus groups
      (iii) Customer focus groups

7. Data analysis and evaluation
8. Research findings

   (a) Primary research overview
   (b) Strategic direction of the brand
   (c) Staff perception of the brand
   (d) Staff and customer value
   (e) Loyalty and interaction of staff
   (f) Effective communication
   (g) Measurement as a behavioural driver
   (h) Customer value of experience
   (i) Brand decision-making

9.  Appendices

    (a) Appendix A: In-depth interview guide
    (b) Appendix B: Staff focus group discussion guide
    (c) Appendix C: Customer focus group discussion guide
    (d) Appendix D: Participant invitation letter
    (e) Appendix E: CD Rom recording of in-depth interviews
    (f) Appendix F: Video footage of focus groups

10. Terms of reference.

The layout of the formal written report should conform to house style. Generally, companies that are producing a large number of reports will include the format of the report in their identity guidelines or will have formal guidelines elsewhere that should be followed. The font size and appearance must do justice to your work and the sequencing of the report with its headers and sub-headers should make the report more accessible. A style guide might also be used to help with language, grammar and even brand messages through the report. If you are unsure of English, then it is always best to get somebody professional to proofread your work for spelling, grammar and punctuation. Remember that proofreading is different from reading the report through. Each word and sentence needs to be considered individually as well as in connection with the rest of the report.

## The oral presentation

The process of delivering an oral presentation may be daunting, but preparation means that it does not have to be too nerve-wracking. In many cases nerves are a good sign that this matters.

The oral presentation may involve a number of people and a range of audio and visual equipment. The technology is always a problem and it is reassuring to have a back-up.

The key thing in preparing a presentation is that it is not simply a regurgitation of the report. The presentation, of course, draws on the same data and makes the same conclusions but the findings can be presented in a much livelier and, maybe, accessible and memorable way.

Wilson (2003) presents a useful structure for research presentations:

### Introduction
Thank you.

Introduce the team.

Outline the agenda of the presentation.

Set rules for questions. Will you take them at the end or through the presentation?

### Research background and objectives
An outline of the business and marketing background and the objectives of the study.

### Research methodology
Describe the methodology and data collection device along with limitations.

## Key findings

Supported by graphs and tables. Keep it simple, only present pertinent tables and graphs. Make sure that the tables and graphs are readable and clear.

## Conclusions and recommendations

Repeat key findings. Lay down your recommendations.

## Questions

A full discussion of the issues. Think about the following points at rehearsal:

1. What questions will come up? Try to pre-empt and prepare.
2. Will all presenters handle questions or will the team leader take questions and pass them on to the team's expert?
3. What will you do if you cannot answer a question?
4. Tell your audience how you want to deal with questions.

## Presentation tips

- Meet your objectives. State them early on and show throughout how your presentation contributes to their achievement. You might even ask the audience what their objectives are at the beginning of the presentation, note them on a flip chart and at the end of the presentation tick them off.
- Know your audience; what do they want to hear? How many will be present? Who are they? What positions do they hold?
- How will you dress? Is it formal or informal or will you be overdressed in a suit and a tie? What do your audience expect?
- Keep it brief and to the point, do not use too many tables and graphs. Use a balanced mixture of words and images. Keep to time.
- Be prepared for interruptions and stop presenting if your audience are distracted. Do not plough on.
- Turn off mobile phones and ask your audience to do the same. Try to manage the physical characteristics of the room, heat and lighting, and air conditioning.
- If using PowerPoint technology, make sure that it is compatible with the projection system. Make sure that your slides do not contain too much information and that tables and graphics can be read.
- During the presentation, maintain eye contact with your audience. Try to avoid having a physical barrier between you and your audience.
- Be aware of your body language, relax your shoulders, smile and try to project enthusiasm.
- Relax and use natural movements. Engage with your audience but do not invade their personal space.
- Make eye contact with all people in the room early in the presentation – get them on your side.
- Face your audience rather than the screen. If you are able to, determine where each member of the team presenting and the audience will sit.
- Never turn your back to the audience.
- Do not hide behind lecterns and A4 notes.
- Use cue cards if necessary, do not try to ad lib unless you are well rehearsed.
- Provide handouts for your audience of the slides, tables and graphs that may be hard to read.
- If working with a team of presenters, make sure that you support them. When you are not presenting, maintain a positive attitude and listen to the rest of the team. If a team member falters or technology is causing problems, act to sort out the situation. Do not sit there thinking thank goodness that is not me. You will be judged by the performance of the team as a whole.

- ° Keep to time and take responsibility for your own timings. Some audiences for competitive pitches will stop a presentation if it overruns.
- ° Use pictures, video and audio clips to enliven and add variety to the presentation, but do not make a presentation over busy.

  - Research has shown that people forget 30 per cent of what you tell them after just 3 hours and 90 per cent is forgotten after only 3 days. Visual aids can help and variety is the key. The combination of verbal and visual material has been shown to deliver 85 per cent recollection after 3 hours and up to 65 per cent after 3 days. Almost all presentations are made using PowerPoint and the lack of pacing and variety often creates a very flat atmosphere and passive audience. This is often the case as projection equipment may mean that the lights have to be dimmed and the audience sink into a soporific state. Popcorn might be a more appropriate snack than the executive biscuit selection. Liven it up by using a variety of support and dynamic pacing through the presentation.
  - Flipchart.
  - Overhead projector slides.
  - PowerPoint.
  - Story boards.
  - Video and sound clips.

- ° Practise, practise, practise, remember 'fail to prepare, prepare to fail'.

  - Make sure you carry out a 'dress' rehearsal. Practise speaking out loud.
  - Practise all aspects of the presentation including the transition between speakers and the use of supporting technology or audio-visual aids.
  - It may help to record your rehearsal and pick up your verbal tics, the 'you knows' the 'hums' and the 'yeses'. Knowing that you have these verbal tics can help control them. Practise volume and pace and the use of silence.

- ° Tell them what you will tell them, tell them and tell them what you have told them. Structure the presentation and use staging posts and summarizing slides to close sections and introduce new sections.
- ° Always start and finish on a high note.
- ° Do not be shy about saying that you want the business.

## Use of graphics

Tables and graphs will enliven reports and presentations, but with the range of technology available, overkill is possible.

## Tables

Tables should be presented with the title and a number. The tables should be labelled with base numbers, that is, the figures for the sample and sub-samples should be shown, especially when percentages are being used. Seventy-five per cent is impressive. Seventy-five per cent of 10 respondents is less so. If quantities are indicated in the table, you must specify if they are in volumes or value. If numbers are used, specify the units. If currency is used, make sure that it is included in the table description.

Tables should be structured so that data is ordered from large to small items. The layout should enable data to be read easily. If data is imported, it should always be referenced or sourced. Tables should, if appropriate, contain totals and subtotals. Numbers should be right justified. You should normally work to two decimal places (Figure 12.2).

**Beer consumption per cent volume 1998–2002 (Base = 550)**

|        | 1998 | 1999 | 2000 | 2001 | 2002 |
|--------|------|------|------|------|------|
| Bitter | 27   | 26   | 25   | 24   | 23   |
| Stout  | 15   | 15   | 15   | 16   | 16   |
| Lager  | 30   | 31   | 32   | 33   | 34   |
| Other  | 28   | 28   | 28   | 27   | 27   |

*Source*: RK Associates 2003

**Marketing spend by medium 1998–2004 (Euros '000)**

| Medium\Year  | 1998 | 1999 | 2000 | 2001 | 2002 | 2003f | 2004f |
|--------------|------|------|------|------|------|-------|-------|
| Mail         | 24   | 28   | 45   | 56   | 43   | 44    | 50    |
| Nat press    | 334  | 556  | 667  | 776  | 545  | 680   | 789   |
| TV           | 1500 | 1500 | 3456 | 3450 | 4000 | 4000  | 5700  |
| Radio        | 200  | 230  | 340  | 570  | 567  | 789   | 790   |
| Trade press  | 35   | 50   | 60   | 76   | 78   | 88    | 98    |
| Telephone    | 0    | 0    | 15   | 19   | 40   | 70    | 90    |
| **Total**    | 4091 | 4363 | 6583 | 6948 | 7275 | 5672  | 7517  |

f = forecast

*Source*: Internal marketing data

*Figure 12.2* A typical table

## Other graphics

Other graphical devices that can be used include:

- o Pie charts (Figure 12.3)

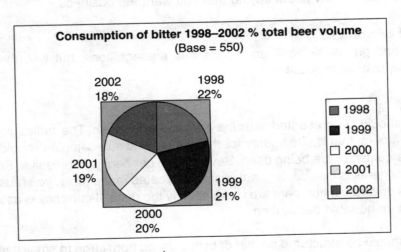

**Consumption of bitter 1998–2002 % total beer volume**
(Base = 550)

2002
18%

1998
22%

2001
19%

1999
21%

2000
20%

1998
1999
2000
2001
2002

*Figure 12.3* Graphical presentation using pie charts

○ Donuts (Figure 12.4)

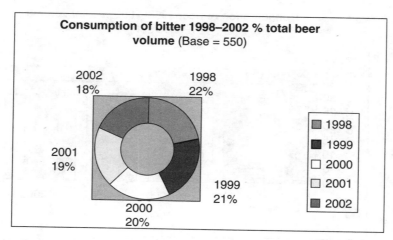

*Figure 12.4* Graphical presentation using donuts

○ Bar charts

These must present information in an accessible way, not like this (Figure 12.5):

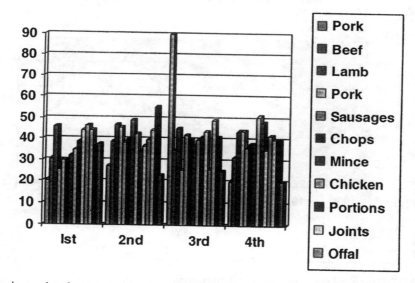

*Figure 12.5* Weak graphical presentation

This is better (Figure 12.6):

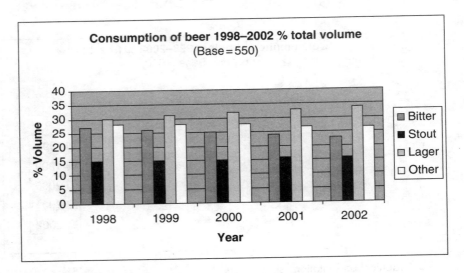

*Figure 12.6* Better graphical presentation

   o   Line graphs (Figure 12.7)

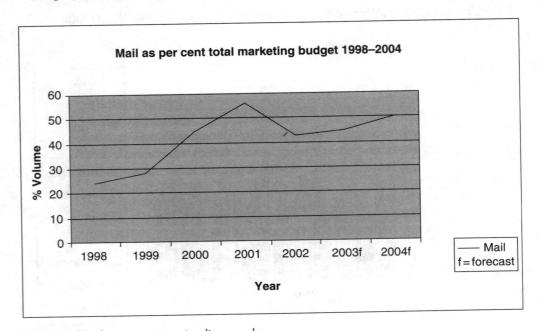

*Figure 12.7* Graphical presentation using line graphs

   o   Pictograms

These are graphics that are illustrated with pictures representing the product or object of the graphic. In the beer example above, it might be illustrated by beer glasses.

   o   PowerPoint slides

The ubiquity of PowerPoint means that often presentations can look very similar. So how will you make yours stand out? The role of a good corporate identity is important here. Equally it is tempting to overdress PowerPoint slides. Keep it simple; laying down text on 'watermarks' may reduce comprehension. Minimum font size should be 24 to ensure legibility.

## Problems in presentations

Wilson (2003) presents a list of common problems in presenting reports:

- *Assuming understanding* – there is insufficient background and interpretation given to results.
- Excessive length.
- Unrealistic recommendations which are commercially naive.
- *Spurious accuracy* – results are based on too small sample sizes.
- *Obscure statistics* – a range of obscure techniques may not be useful if the client cannot use them.
- *Over-elaborate presentation* – too many graphics and presentational devices may obscure more than it reveals.

## Summary

This unit looked at the process of delivering results from research.

It looked at the structure of a written research report and covered each of these in depth:

- Title page
- Contents
- Executive summary
- Introduction
- Situation analysis and problem definition
- Research methodology and limitations
- Findings and analysis
- Conclusions and recommendations
- Appendices.

We went on to cover the oral presentation of the results and gave tips for presentation success:

- Introduction
- Research background and objectives
- Research methodology
- Key findings
- Conclusions and recommendations
- Questions.

We then looked at the graphical presentation of the results including:

- Tables
- Bar graphs
- Pie charts and donuts
- Line graphs
- Pictograms.

Finally, we looked at common failings in presenting results.

## Further study

### Question 12.1
List the sections of a research report and briefly outline what goes into each section.

### Question 12.2
CIM Professional Series Stage Two: Marketing Research and Information.

#### Donaldson Builders Merchants

Donaldson Builders Merchants is a small chain of builders merchants located in the central belt of Scotland. The company has four outlets located around the edge of the major conurbations of Edinburgh and Glasgow. These supply small builders, plumbers, roofers and similar tradesmen as well as some members of the public (i.e. those more skilled in major do-it-yourself renovations and house improvements). Customers may collect items direct from the trade counter at the warehouse or have the items delivered direct to the building site or house by the company's fleet of 14 lorries. The lorries are equipped with hoists for handling the larger items.

Donaldson supplies:

- Timber and timber products
- Bricks and paving
- Sand and aggregates
- Roofing materials
- Plumbing and heating supplies
- A small range of hand tools

The company provides credit to the majority of its trade customers. As a result it has a computerized database with details on most of its trade customers relating to name, address, trading address, telephone number, type of business, and purchasing patterns. There are approximately 1100 customers on the database, which probably represents 85 per cent of the company's customers. For the other 15 per cent of customers (the public and trade customers who do not have a credit account), the database holds no record, with the exception of a delivery address if a delivery is required.

The market in which Donaldson operates is becoming more competitive, with the company losing share to national chains such as Jewson and a number of recently opened B&Q trade depots. Tom Donaldson, the Managing Director, feels that the company's personal service and flexibility is far superior to these competitors, and is therefore keen to build on this and find ways in which to compete other than on price. The company has never undertaken research before but is keen to find out more from its customers about their:

- Existing and future purchasing behaviour
- Attitudes towards Donaldson Builders Merchants (such as product range, service, flexibility of delivery, etc.)
- Suggestions about improvements required in Donaldson's offering

They are willing to spend up to £50 000 on the research project.

## Question 5
As one of the Directors in the agency that has been awarded the contract for doing the research for Donaldson Builders Merchants in Question 1, you are writing a memorandum to your staff to prepare them for the presentation and evaluation of information at the end of any project. The memorandum should include the following:

(a) An explanation of two approaches that can be used to analyse transcripts from a series of group discussions.

**(10 marks)**

(b) An explanation of the importance of understanding of the audience's thinking sequence to the preparation of the final report.

**(15 marks)**

## Question 12.3
You are a research executive in a research agency and have been asked to produce a guide for new staff on the communication of research results to client companies. Set out your key guidelines for:

(a) Structuring and writing marketing research reports

**(12 marks)**

(b) The design of tables for communicating data and results

**(5 marks)**

(c) The preparation of oral presentations

**(8 marks)**
**(Total 25 marks)**

## Hints and tips

The MRS code of conduct presents the duties of an agency to its clients in the research. Go to www.mrs.org.uk and review this.

## Bibliography

Wilson, A. (2003) *Marketing Research: An Integrated Approach*, FT Prentice Hall.

# appendix 1

# guidance on examination preparation

## Preparing for your examination

You are now nearing the final phase of your studies and it is time to start the hard work of exam preparation.

During your period of study you will have become used to absorbing large amounts of information. You will have tried to understand and apply aspects of knowledge that may have been very new to you, while some of the information provided may have been more familiar. You may even have undertaken many of the activities that are positioned frequently throughout your Coursebook, which will have enabled you to apply your learning in practical situations. But whatever the state of your knowledge and understanding, do not allow yourself to fall into the trap of thinking that you know enough, you understand enough, or even worse, that you can just take it as it comes on the day.

Never underestimate the pressure of the CIM examination.

The whole point of preparing this text for you is to ensure that you never take the examination for granted, and that you do not go into the exam unprepared for what might come your way for 3 hours at a time.

One thing is for sure: there is no quick fix, no easy route, no waving a magic wand and finding you know it all.

Whether you have studied alone, in a CIM study centre, or through distance learning, you now need to ensure that this final phase of your learning process is tightly managed, highly structured and objective.

As a candidate in the examination, your role will be to convince the Senior Examiner that you have credibility for this subject. You need to demonstrate to the examiner that you can be trusted to undertake a range of challenges in the context of marketing and that you are able to capitalize on opportunities and manage your way through threats.

You should prove to the Senior Examiner that you are able to apply knowledge, make decisions, respond to situations and solve problems.

Very shortly we are going to look at a range of revision and exam preparation techniques, and at time management issues, and encourage you towards developing and implementing your own revision plan, but before that, let us look at the role of the Senior Examiner.

**238**

# A bit about the Senior Examiners!

You might be quite shocked to read this, but while it might appear that the examiners are 'relentless question masters' they actually want you to be able to answer the questions and pass the exams! In fact, they would derive no satisfaction or benefits from failing candidates; quite the contrary, they develop the syllabus and exam papers in order that you can learn and then apply that learning effectively so as to pass your examinations. Many of the examiners have said in the past that it is indeed psychologically more difficult to fail students than pass them.

Many of the hints and tips you find within this Appendix have been suggested by the Senior Examiners and authors of the Coursebook series. Therefore you should consider them carefully and resolve to undertake as many of the elements suggested as possible.

The Chartered Institute of Marketing has a range of processes and systems in place within the Examinations Division to ensure that fairness and consistency prevail across the team of examiners, and that the academic and vocational standards that are set and defined are indeed maintained. In doing this, CIM ensures that those who gain the CIM Professional Certificate, Professional Diploma and Professional Postgraduate Diploma are worthy of the qualification and perceived as such in the view of employers, actual and potential.

Part of what you will need to do within the examination is be 'examiner friendly' – that means you have to make sure they get what they ask for. This will make life easier for you and for them.

Hints and tips for 'examiner friendly' actions are as follows:

o   Show them that you understand the basis of the question, by answering *precisely* the question asked, and not including just about everything you can remember about the subject area.
o   Read their needs – how many points is the question asking you to address?
o   Respond to the question appropriately. Is the question asking you to take on a role? If so, take on the role and answer the question in respect of the role. For example you could be positioned as follows:

  –   'You are working as a Marketing Assistant at Nike UK' or 'You are a Marketing Manager for an Engineering Company' or 'As Marketing Manager write a report to the Managing Partner'.

These examples of role-playing requirements are taken from questions in past papers.

o   Deliver the answer in the format requested. If the examiner asks for a memo, then provide a memo; likewise, if the examiner asks for a report, then write a report. If you do not do this, in some instances you will fail to gain the necessary marks required to pass.
o   Take a businesslike approach to your answers. This enhances your credibility. Badly ordered work, untidy work, lack of structure, headings and subheadings can be off-putting. This would be unacceptable in the work situation; likewise it will be unacceptable in the eyes of the Senior Examiners and their marking teams.
o   Ensure that the examiner has something to mark: give them substance, relevance, definitions, illustrations and demonstration of your knowledge and understanding of the subject area.
o   See the examiner as your potential employer, or ultimate consumer/customer. The whole purpose and culture of marketing is about meeting customers' needs. Try this approach – it works wonders.

- o Provide a strong sense of enthusiasm and professionalism in your answers; support it with relevant up-to-date examples and apply them where appropriate.
- o Try to do something that will make your exam paper a little bit different – make it stand out in the crowd.

All of these points might seem quite logical to you, but often in the panic of the examination they 'go out of the window'. Therefore it is beneficial to remind ourselves of the importance of the examiner. He/she is the 'ultimate customer' – and we all know customers hate to be disappointed.

As we move on, some of these points will be revisited and developed further.

# About the examination

In all examinations, with the exception of Marketing Management in Practice the paper is divided into two parts.

- o Part A – Mini-case study = 50 per cent of marks
- o Part B – Option choice questions (choice of two questions from four) = 50 per cent of the marks (each question attracting 25 per cent).

For the Marketing Management in Practice paper, the same approach is taken. However, all of the questions are directly related to the case study and in this instance the case material is more extensive.

Let us look at the basis of each element.

## Part A – The mini-case study

This is based on a mini-case or scenario with one question, possibly subdivided into between two and four points, but totalling 50 per cent of overall marks.

In essence, you, the candidate, are placed in a problem-solving role through the medium of a short scenario. On occasions, the scenario may consist of an article from a journal in relation to a well-known organization.

Alternatively, it will be based upon a fictional company, and the examiner will have prepared it in order that the right balance of knowledge, understanding, application and skills is used.

## Approaches to the mini-case study

When undertaking the mini-case study there are a number of key areas you should consider.

### Structure/content
The mini-case that you will be presented with will vary slightly from paper to paper, and of course from one examination to the next. Normally, the scenario presented will be 250–400 words long and will centre on a particular organization and its problems or may even relate to a specific industry. However, please note, for Marketing Management in Practice, the case study is more significant as all the questions are based upon the case materials.

The length of the mini-case study means that usually only a brief outline is provided of the situation, the organization and its marketing problems, and you must therefore learn to cope with analysing information and preparing your answer on the basis of a very limited amount of detail.

## Time management

There are many differing views on time management and the approaches you can take to managing your time within the examination. You must find an approach to suit your way of working, but always remember, whatever you do, you must ensure that you allow enough time to complete the examination. Unfinished exams mean lost marks.

A typical example of managing time is as follows:

Your paper is designed to assess you over a 3-hour period. With 50 per cent of the marks being allocated to the mini-case, it means that you should dedicate somewhere around 100 minutes of your time to both read and write up the answer on this mini-case, leaving a further 80 minutes for the remaining questions. Some students, however, will prefer to allocate nearly half of their time (90 minutes) on the mini-case, so that they can read and fully absorb the case and answer the questions in the context of it. This is also acceptable as long as you ensure that you work extremely 'SMART' for the remaining time in order to finish the examination.

Do not forget that while there is only one question within the mini-case, it can have a number of components. You must answer all the components in that question, which is where the balance of time comes into play.

## Knowledge/skills tested

Throughout all the CIM papers, your knowledge, skills and ability to apply those skills will be tested. However, the mini-cases are used particularly to test application, that is, your ability to take your knowledge and apply it in a structured way to a given scenario. The examiners will be looking at your decision-making ability, your analytical and communication skills and, depending on the level, your ability as a manager to solve particular marketing problems.

When the examiner is marking your paper, he/she will be looking to see how you differentiate yourself, looking at your own individual 'unique selling points'. The examiner will also want to see if you can personally apply the knowledge or whether you are only able to repeat the textbook materials.

## Format of answers

On many occasions, and within all examinations, you will most likely be given a particular communication method to use. If this is the case, you must ensure that you adhere to the requirements of the examiner. This is all part of meeting customer needs.

The likely communication tools you will be expected to use are as follows:

- Memorandum
- Memorandum/report
- Report
- Briefing notes
- Presentation
- Press release
- Advertisement
- Plan.

Make sure that you familiarize yourself with these particular communication tools and practise using them to ensure that, on the day, you will be able to respond confidently to the communication requests of the examiner.

By the same token, while communication methods are important, so is meeting the specific requirements of the question. This means you must understand what is meant by the precise instruction given. *Note the following terms carefully:*

o *Identify* – Select key issues, point out key learning points, establish clearly what the examiner expects you to identify.
o *Illustrate* – The examiner expects you to provide examples, scenarios and key concepts that illustrate your learning.
o *Compare and contrast* – Look at the range of similarities between the two situations, contexts or even organizations. Then compare them, that is, ascertain and list how activities, features and so on agree or disagree. Contrasting means highlighting the differences between the two.
o *Discuss* – Questions that have 'discuss' in them offer a tremendous opportunity for you to debate, argue and justify your approach or understanding of the subject area. *Caution*: It is not an opportunity to waffle.
o *Briefly explain* – This means being succinct, structured and concise in your explanation, within the answer. Make your points clear, transparent and relevant.
o *State* – Present in a clear, brief format.
o *Interpret* – Expound the meaning of, make clear and explicit what it is you see and understand within the data provided.
o *Outline* – Provide the examiner with the main concepts and features being asked for and avoid minor technical details. Structure will be critical here, or else you could find it difficult to contain your answer.
o *Relate* – Show how different aspects of the syllabus connect together.
o *Evaluate* – Review and reflect upon an area of the syllabus, a particular practice, an article and so on, and consider its overall worth in respect of its use as a tool or a model and its overall effectiveness in the role it plays.

*Source*: Worsam, M., *How to Pass Marketing*, Croner, 1989.

## Your approach to mini-cases

There is no one right way to approach and tackle a mini-case study, indeed it will be down to each individual to use their own creativity in tackling the tasks presented. You will have to use your initiative and discretion about how best to approach the mini-case. Having said this, however, there are some basic steps you can take.

o Ensure that you read through the case study at least twice before making any judgements, starting to analyse the information provided, or indeed writing the answers.
o On the third occasion, read through the mini-case and, using a highlighter, start marking the essential and relevant information critical to the content and context. Then turn your attention to the question again, this time reading slowly and carefully to assess what it is you are expected to do. Note any instructions that the examiner gives you, and then start to plan how you might answer the question. Whatever the question, ensure the answer has a structure: a beginning, a structured central part and, finally, always a conclusion.
o Keep the context of the question continually in mind: that is, the specifics of the case and the role which you might be performing.
o Because there is limited material available, you will sometimes need to make assumptions. Do not be afraid to do this, it will show initiative on your part. Assumptions are an

important part of dealing with case studies and can help you to be quite creative with your answer. However, do explain the basis of your assumptions within your answer so that the examiner understands the nature of them, and why you have arrived at your particular outcome. *Always ensure that your assumptions are realistic.*

o   Only now you are approaching the stage where it is time to start writing your answer to the question, tackling the problems, making decisions and recommendations on the case scenario set before you. As mentioned previously, your points will often be best set out in a report or memo-type format, particularly if the examiner does not specify a communication method.

o   Ensure that your writing is succinct, avoids waffle and responds directly to the questions asked.

## Part B – Option choice questions

Part B at the certificate level is comprised of four traditional questions, each worth 25 per cent. You will be expected to choose two of those questions, to make up the remaining 50 per cent of available marks. (Again, please note that the structure is the same for Marketing Management in Practice, but that all questions are applied to the case study.)

Realistically, the same principles apply for these questions as in the case study. Communication formats, reading through the questions, structure, role-play, context and so on – everything is the same.

Part B will cover a number of broader issues from within the syllabus and will be taken from any element of it. The examiner makes the choice, and no prior direction is given to students or tutors on what that might be.

As regards time management in this area, if you have used about 100 minutes for the mini-case you should have around 80 minutes left. This provides you with around 40 minutes to plan and write a question, to write, review and revise your answers. Keep practising – use a cooker timer, alarm clock or mobile phone alarm as your timer and work hard at answering questions within the time frame given.

## Specimen examination papers and answers

To help you prepare and understand the nature of the paper, go to www.cim.co.uk/learningzone.com to access Specimen Answers and Senior Examiner's advice for these exam questions. During your study, the author of your Coursebook may have, on occasions, asked you to refer to these papers and answer the questions. You should undertake these exercises and utilize every opportunity to practise meeting examination requirements.

Each of the Certificate Professional Diploma Coursebooks have, at the end of them, some examination questions and guidance provided by the authors and senior examiners, where appropriate, to provide you with some insight into the types of questions asked.

The specimen answers are vital learning tools. They are not always perfect, as they are answers written by students and annotated by the Senior Examiners, but they will give you a good indication of the approaches you could take, and the examiners' annotations suggest how these answers might be improved. Please use them.

Other sources of information are available at www.cim.co.uk/learningzone. This gives links to many useful case studies which will help you put your learning into context when you are revising.

# Key elements of preparation

There are three important elements to think about when preparing for your examination:

- Learning
- Memory
- Revision.

Let us look at each point in turn.

## Learning

Quite often students find it difficult to learn properly. You can passively read books, look at some of the materials, perhaps revise a little and regurgitate it all in the examination. In the main, however, this is rather an unsatisfactory method of learning. It is meaningless, shallow and ultimately of little use in practice.

For learning to be truly effective it must be active and applied. You must involve yourself in the learning process by thinking about what you have read, testing it against your experience by reflecting on how you use particular aspects of marketing, and how you could perhaps improve your own performance by implementing particular aspects of your learning into your everyday life. You should adopt the old adage of 'learning by doing'. If you do, you will find that passive learning has no place in your study life.

Below are some suggestions that have been prepared to assist you with the learning pathway throughout your revision.

- Always make your own notes, in words you understand, and ensure that you combine all the sources of information and activities within them.
- Always try to relate your learning back to your own organization.
- Make sure you define key terms concisely, wherever possible.
- Do not try to memorize your ideas, but work on the basis of understanding and, most important, applying them.
- Think about the relevant and topical questions that might be set – use the questions and answers in your Coursebooks to identify typical questions that might be asked in the future.
- Attempt all of the questions within each of your Coursebooks since these are vital tests of your active learning and understanding.

## Memory

If you are prepared to undertake an active learning programme, then your knowledge will be considerably enhanced, as understanding and application of knowledge does tend to stay in your 'long-term' memory. It is likely that passive learning will only stay in your 'short-term' memory.

Do not try to memorize in parrot fashion; it is not helpful and, even more important, examiners are experienced in identifying various memorizing techniques and therefore will spot them as such.

Having said this, it is quite useful to memorize various acronyms such as SWOT, PEST, PESTEL, STEEPLE, or indeed various models such as Ansoff, GE Matrix, Shell Directional

Policy Matrix and so on, as in some of the questions you may be required to use illustrations of these to assist your answer.

## Revision

The third and final stage to consider is 'revision', which is what we will concentrate on in detail below. Here, just a few key tips are offered.

Revision should be an ongoing process rather than a panic measure that you decide to undertake just before the examination. You should be preparing notes *throughout* your course, with the view to using them as part of your revision process. Therefore, ensure that your notes are sufficiently comprehensive that you can reuse them successfully.

For each concept you learn about, you should identify, through your reading and your own personal experience, at least two or three examples that you could use; this then gives you some scope to broaden your perspective during the examination. It will, of course, help you gain some points for initiative with the examiners.

Knowledge is not something you will gain overnight – as we saw earlier, it is not a quick fix; it involves a process of learning that enables you to lay solid foundations upon which to build your long-term understanding and application. This will benefit you significantly in the future, not just in the examination.

In essence, you should ensure that you do the following in the period before the real intensive revision process begins:

o   Keep your study file well-organized, updated and full of newspaper and journal cuttings that may help you formulate examples in your mind for use during the examination.
o   Practise defining key terms and acronyms from memory.
o   Prepare topic outlines and essay answer plans.
o   When you start your intensive revision, ensure it is planned and structured in the way described below. And then, finally, read your concentrated notes the night before the examination.

## Revision planning

You are now on a critical path – although hopefully not too critical at this time – with somewhere in the region of between 4 and 6 weeks to go to the examination. The following hints and tips will help you plan out your revision study:

o   You will, as already explained, need to be very organized. Therefore, before doing anything else, put your files, examples, reading material and so on in good order, so that you are able to work with them in the future and, of course, make sense of them.
o   Ensure that you have a quiet area within which to work. It is very easy to get distracted when preparing for an examination.
o   Take out your file along with your syllabus, and make a list of key topic areas that you have studied and which you now need to revise. You could use the basis of this book to do that, by taking each unit a step at a time.
o   Plan the use of your time carefully. Ideally you should start your revision at least 6 weeks prior to the exam, so work out how many spare hours you could give to the revision process and then start to allocate time in your diary, and do not double-book with anything else.

o Give up your social life for a short period of time. As the saying goes 'no pain – no gain'.
o Looking at each of the subject areas in turn, identify which are your strengths and which are your weaknesses. Which areas have you grasped and understood, and which are the areas that you have really struggled with? Split your page into two and make a list on each side. For example:

| Planning and control | |
| --- | --- |
| **Strengths** | **Weaknesses** |
| Audit – PEST, SWOT, models | Ratio analysis |
| Portfolio analysis | Market sensing |
| | Productivity analysis |
| | Trend extrapolation |
| | Forecasting |

o Break down your list again and divide the points of weakness, giving priority in the first instance to your weakest areas and even prioritizing them by giving each of them a number. This will enable you to master the more difficult areas. Up to 60 per cent of your remaining revision time should be given over to that, as you may find you have to undertake a range of additional reading and also perhaps seeking tutor support, if you are studying at a CIM Accredited Study Centre.
o The rest of the time should be spent reinforcing your knowledge and understanding of the stronger areas, spending time testing yourself on how much you really know.
o Should you be taking two examinations or more at any one time, then the breakdown and managing of your time will be critical.
o Taking a subject at a time, work through your notes and start breaking them down into subsections of learning, and ultimately into key learning points, items that you can refer to time and time again, that are meaningful and that your mind will absorb. You yourself will know how best you remember key points. Some people try to develop acronyms, flowcharts or matrices, mind maps, fishbone diagrams and so on, or various connection diagrams that help them recall certain aspects of models. You could also develop processes that enable you to remember approaches to various options. (But do remember what we said earlier about regurgitating stuff, parrot fashion.)

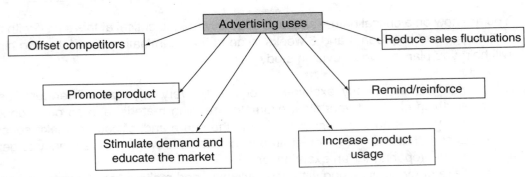

*Figure A1.1* Use of a diagram to summarize key components of a concept
*Source*: Adapted from Dibb, Simkin, Pride and Ferrell, Marketing Concepts and Strategies, 4th edition, Houghton Mifflin (2001)

Figure A1.1 is just a brief example of how you could use a 'bomb-burst' diagram (which, in this case, highlights the uses of advertising) as a very helpful approach to memorizing key elements of learning.

o Eventually you should reduce your key learning to bullet points. For example: imagine you were looking at the concept of Time Management – you could eventually reduce your key learning to a bullet list containing the following points in relation to 'Effective Prioritization'.

– Organize
– Take time
– Delegate
– Review.

Each of these headings would then remind you of the elements you need to discuss associated with the subject area.

o Avoid getting involved in reading too many textbooks at this stage, as you may start to find that you are getting confused overall.
o Look at examination questions on previous papers, and start to observe closely the various roles and tasks they expect you to undertake, and importantly, the context in which they are set.
o *Use the specimen exam papers and specimen answers* to support your learning and see how you could actually improve upon them.
o Without exception, find an associated examination question for the areas that you have studied and revised, and undertake it (more than once if necessary).
o Without referring to notes or books, try to draft an answer plan with the key concepts, knowledge, models and information that are needed to successfully complete the answer. Then refer to the specimen answer to see how close you are to the actual outline presented. Planning your answer, and ensuring that key components are included and that the question has a meaningful structure, is one of the most beneficial activities that you can undertake.
o Now write out the answer in full, time-constrained and written by hand, not with the use of IT. (At this stage, you are still expected to be the scribe for the examination and present handwritten work. Many of us find this increasingly difficult as we spend more and more time using our computers to present information. Do your best to be neat. Difficult-to-read handwriting is often off-putting to the examiner.)
o When writing answers as part of your revision process, also be sure to practise the following essential examinations techniques:

– *Identify and use the communication method* requested by the examiner.
– *Always have three key parts to the answer.* An introduction, a middle section that develops your answer in full, and a conclusion. Where appropriate, ensure that you have an introduction, main section, summary/conclusion and, if requested or help-ful, recommendations.
– *Always answer the question in the context or role set.*
– *Always comply with the nature and terms of the question.*
– *Leave white space.* Do not overcrowd your page; leave space between paragraphs, and make sure your sentences do not merge into one blur. (Do not worry – there is always plenty of paper available to use in the examination.)
– *Count* how many actions the question asks you to undertake and double-check at the end that you have met the full range of demands of the question.
– *Use examples* to demonstrate your knowledge and understanding of the particular syllabus area. These can be from journals, the Internet, the press, or your own experience.

  - *Display your vigour and enthusiasm for marketing.* Remember to think of the Senior Examiner as your Customer, or future employer, and do your best to deliver what is wanted to satisfy their needs. Impress them and show them how you are a 'cut above the rest'.

  o Review all your practice answers critically, with the above points in mind.

## Practical actions

The critical path is becoming even more critical now as the examination looms. The following are vital points:

  o Have you registered with CIM?
  o Do you know where you are taking your examination? CIM should let you know approximately one month in advance.
  o Do you know where your examination centre is? If not find out, take a drive, time it – whatever it is, do not be late!
  o Make sure you have all the tools of the examination ready. A dictionary, calculator, pens, pencils, ruler and so on. Try not to use multiple shades of pens, but at the same time make your work look professional. *Avoid using red and green as these are the colours that will be used for marking.*

## Summary

Above all, you must remember that you personally have invested a tremendous amount of time, effort and money in studying for this programme and it is therefore imperative that you consider the suggestions given here, as they will help to maximize the return on your investment.

Many of the hints and tips offered here are generic and will work across most of the CIM courses. We have tried to select those that will help you most in taking a sensible, planned approach to your study and revision. The key to your success is being prepared to put in the time and effort required, planning your revision, and, equally important, planning and answering your questions in a way that will ensure that you pass your examination on the day.

The advice offered here aims to guide you from a practical perspective. Guidance on syllabus content and developments associated with your learning will become clear to you as you work through this Coursebook. The authors of each Coursebook have given subject-specific guidance on the approach to the examination and on how to ensure that you meet the content requirements of the kind of question you will face. These considerations are in addition to the structuring issues we have been discussing throughout this Appendix.

Each of the authors and Senior Examiners will guide you on their preferred approach to questions and answers as they go. Therefore where you are presented with an opportunity to be involved in some activity or undertake an examination question either during or at the end of your study units, do take it. It not only prepares you for the examination, but also helps you learn in the applied way we discussed above.

Here, then, is a last reminder:

- Ensure you make the most of your learning process throughout
- Keep structured and orderly notes from which to revise
- Plan your revision – do not let it just happen
- Provide examples to enhance your answers
- Practise your writing skills in order that you present your work well and your writing is readable
- Take as many opportunities as possible to test your knowledge and measure your progress
- Plan and structure your answers
- Always do as the question asks you, especially with regard to context and communication method
- Do not leave it until the last minute!

The writers would like to take this opportunity to wish you every success in your endeavours to study, to revise and to pass your examinations.

*Karen Beamish*
*Academic Development Advisor*

# appendix 2

## assignment-based assessment

### Introduction – the basis to the assignments and the integrative project

Within the CIM qualifications at Professional Certificate and Professional Diploma levels, there are several assessment options available. These are detailed in the outline of modules in Figure A2.1. The purpose of an assignment is to provide another format to complete each module for students who want to apply the syllabus concepts from a module to their own or a selected organization. For either qualification, there are three modules providing assessment via an assignment and one module assessed via an integrative work-based project. The module assessed via the integrative project is the summative module for each qualification.

| | Entry modules | Research & analysis | Planning | Implementation | Management of Marketing |
|---|---|---|---|---|---|
| **Professional Postgraduate Diploma** | Entry module–Professional Postgraduate Diploma | Analysis & Evaluation | Strategic Marketing Decisions | Managing Marketing Performance | |
| **Professional Diploma** | Entry module–Professional Diploma | Marketing Research & Information | Marketing Planning | Marketing Communications | Marketing Management in Practice |
| **Professional Certificate** | | Marketing Environment | Marketing Fundamentals | Customer Communications | Marketing in Practice |
| **Introductory Certificate** | | Supporting marketing processes (research & analysis, planning & implementation) | | | |

*Figure A2.1* Outline of CIM 'standard' syllabus (© The Chartered Institute of Marketing, September 2003)

The use of assignments does not mean that this route is easier than an examination. Both formats are carefully evaluated to ensure that a grade B in the assessment/integrative project route is the same as a grade B in an examination. However, the use of assignments does allow a student to complete the assessment for a module over a longer period of time than a 3-hour examination. This will inevitably mean work being undertaken over the time span of a module. For those used to cramming for exams, writing an assignment over several weeks which comprises a total of four separate questions will be a very different approach.

Each module within the qualification contains a different assignment written specifically for the module. These are designed to test understanding and provide the opportunity for you to demonstrate your abilities through the application of theory to practice. The format and structure of each module's assignment is identical, although the questions asked will differ and the exact type of assignment varies. The questions within an assignment will relate directly to the syllabus for that particular module, thereby giving the opportunity to demonstrate understanding and application.

# The assignment structure

The assignment for each module is broken down into a range of questions. These consist of a core question, and a selection of optional questions. The core question will always relate to the main aspects of each module's syllabus. Coupled with this are a range of four optional questions which will each be drawn from a different part of the syllabus. Students are requested to select two optional questions from the four available. In addition, a reflective statement requires a student to evaluate his/her learning from the module. When put together, these form the assessment for the entire module. The overall pass mark for the module is the same as through an examination route, which is set at 50 per cent. In addition, the grade band structure is also identical to that of an examination.

## Core question

This is the longest and therefore the most important section of your assignment. Covering the major components of the syllabus, the core question is designed to provide a challenging assignment which both tests the theoretical element and also permits application to a selected organization or situation. The rubric on the front of the assignment will provide you with clear guidance on the word counts, word limits and appendices; therefore please adhere to them. However, please note that the appendices should be kept to a minimum. Advice here is that they should be no longer than five pages of additional pertinent information.

## Optional questions

There are a total of four questions provided for Professional Certificate and Professional Diploma of the syllabus from which a student is asked to select two. Each answer is expected to provide a challenge, although the actual task required varies. The rubric on the front of the assignment will provide you with clear guidance in respect of word limits; therefore pay close attention to them and the overall requirements of CIM in relation to the use of appendices.

These are designed to test areas of the syllabus not covered by the core question. As such it is possible to base all of your questions on the same organization although there is significant benefit in using more than one organization as a basis for your assignment. Some of the questions specifically require a different organization to be selected from the one used for the core question. This only occurs where the questions are requiring similar areas to be investigated and will be specified clearly on the question itself.

Within the assignment, there are several types of questions that may be asked, including:

- *A report* – The question requires a formal report to be completed, detailing an answer to the specific question set. This will often be reporting on a specific issue to an individual.
- *A briefing paper or notes* – Preparing a briefing paper or a series of notes which may be used for a presentation.
- *A presentation* – You may be required to either prepare the presentation only or deliver the presentation in addition to its preparation. The audience for the presentation should be considered carefully and ICT used where possible.
- *A discussion paper* – The question requires an academic discussion paper to be prepared. You should show a range of sources and concepts within the paper. You may also be required to present the discussion paper as part of a question.
- *A project plan or action plan* – Some questions ask for planning techniques to be demonstrated. As such, the plan must be for the timescale given and costs shown where applicable. The use of ICT is recommended here in order to create the plan diagrammatically.
- *Planning a research project* – Whilst market research may be required, questions have often asked for simply a research plan in a given situation. This would normally include timescales, the type(s) of research to be gathered, sampling, planned data collection and analysis.
- *Conducting research* – Following on from a research plan, a question can require student(s) to undertake a research gathering exercise. A research question can be either an individual or a group activity depending upon the question. This will usually result in a report of the findings of the exercise plus any recommendations arising from your findings.
- *Gathering of information and reporting* – Within many questions, information will need gathering. The request for information can form part or all of a question. This may be a background to the organization, the activities contained in the question or external market and environmental information. It is advisable to detail the types of information utilized, their sources and report on any findings. Such a question will often ask for recommendations for the organization – these should be drawn from the data and not simply personal opinion.
- *An advisory document* – A question here will require students to evaluate a situation and present advice and recommendations drawn from findings and theory. Again, any advice should be backed up with evidence and not a personal perspective only.
- *An exercise, either planning and/or delivering the exercise* – At both Professional certificate and Professional Diploma, exercises are offered as optional questions. These provide students with the opportunity to devise an exercise and may also require the delivery of this exercise. Such an activity should be evidenced where possible.
- *A role-play with associated documentation* – Several questions have asked students to undertake role-plays in exercises such as team building. These are usually videoed, and documentation demonstrating the objectives of the exercise provided.

Each of these questions is related directly towards specific issues to be investigated, evaluated and answered. In addition, some of the questions asked present situations to be considered. These provide opportunities for specific answers relating directly to the question asked.

In order to aid students completing the assignment, each question is provided with an outline of marking guidance. This relates to the different categories by which each question is marked. The marker of your assignment will be provided with a detailed marking scheme constructed around the same marking guidance provided to students.

For both the core and optional questions, it is important to use referencing where sources have been utilized. This has been a weakness in the past and continues to be an issue. There have been cases of plagiarism identified during marking and moderation, together with a distinct lack of references and bibliography. This becomes more important at Professional Diploma where the nature of the syllabus lends itself to a more academic approach. It is highly recommended that a bibliography be included with each question and sources are cited within the text itself. The type of referencing method used is not important, only that sources are referred to.

## Integrative project structure

The integrative project is designed to provide an in-company approach to assessment rather than having specified assignments. Utilized within the summative module element of each level's syllabus, this offers a student the chance to produce a piece of work which tackles a specific issue. The integrative project can only be completed after undertaking other modules as it will rely on information in each of these as guidance. The integrative project is approximately 5000 words in length and was introduced from September 2002 at Professional Certificate. It was introduced in September 2003 at Professional Diploma with the commencement of the new syllabus. The integrative project is marked by CIM assessors and not your own tutors.

# Professional Diploma assignments – Marketing Research and Information

This module covers five different elements all relating to the subject area of marketing information. This covers the use of ICT and databases, together with the entire marketing research process. The result is a range of opportunities for questions relating to the module and its element to be asked. Questions can cover the role of ICT in an organization, together with planning market research or the use of market research data.

## Element 1 – Information and research for decision-making

This element forms the foundation for all other aspects within the module by setting the role and purpose of marketing information into context. The purpose of information is covered within the element together with issues of marketing information requirements and support systems. This leads towards questions which centre on the need for information and how it may be used:

> *Your manager has asked you to prepare a presentation on the use and value of marketing information. This will form part of an all-day set of workshops and presentations used within the in-company programme 'Run-around'. This aims to give employees throughout the organization an insight into other job roles and activities. The presentation is to last approximately 30 minutes together with associated handout(s).*

The first aspect of this question is the setting. The organization's employees could come from any area or job role. As such, the presentation will need to assume no knowledge whatsoever, aiming to build up an understanding and appreciation of the subject. Elements contained within an answer to this question include

- ○ Setting the scene; the organization itself together with a picture of the typical roles and activities of the employees. This can be part of the introductory setting within the presentation or a separate component of the answer.
- ○ An introduction to marketing information and its purpose, together with the setting of marketing information within marketing and market research. This is required due to the audience comprising employees from every part of the organization.

**253**

- o The need for information and knowledge management will require explaining as part of the presentation.
- o The application of information to different issues needs to be covered. Incorporating examples from a range of organizational areas would be beneficial here.
- o Finally, within the presentation the use of support systems is required.
- o The presentation should be supplied on disk together with a paper copy. In addition, there needs to be a handout containing the presentation plus notes at a level appropriate to the non-marketer. A good handout will cover more than simply the presentation – it will often come in a typed format, with suitable examples to illustrate the points made in the presentation.

## Element 2 – Customer databases

The second element of the module addresses aspects of the role of databases together with database management. This draws into consideration aspects of the role of databases, customer profiling and the use of databases within market research. Questions drawn from this element will use databases as their foundation, building in other aspects of the syllabus in order to cover the element.

Taking an organization of your choice, investigate the current customer database in operation and its use for Customer Relationship Management. Make appropriate recommendations for the potential use of the database together with a consideration of how this data can be used for improved marketing performance.

Element 2 covers the use of databases in detail. Therefore an answer to a question will require an in-depth analysis of issues deriving from the element. With this element comprising only 15 per cent of the module syllabus, it is unlikely that an entire core question would be drawn from this element. An answer needs to include the following:

- o A background to the organization selected for the question, their use of information and current approach to Customer Relationship Management.
- o The second component of an answer would cover the use of information within the organization. This includes how customer records are kept and accessed.
- o An answer would examine how information is utilized and the process of gathering market research from customer data. Where this is not undertaken, later recommendations would cover the process of establishing a data collection and analysis mechanism.
- o Recommendations made would centre around improved use of data and customer information. They should incorporate both a theoretical and practical perspective, relating theory to practice.
- o The format of a response to the question should be laid out as a report, directly relating to the organization type selected in the answer.

## Element 3 – Marketing research in context

This element forms the foundation of study regarding market research. It identifies the role which market research has to play, together with the market research process, issues regarding research and a market research proposal. This will provide several opportunities to ask questions regarding the basis for market research and the process itself.

Your class has been approached to develop the proposal for a market research activity investigating issues of stakeholder perceptions of the CIM centre/an organization of your choice. The supplier's brief for the proposal includes the following elements:

- A research brief
- A specification of the research proposed
- Types of secondary/primary data to be used
- Sampling
- Any social/ethical issues arising from the proposed research.

Individually, develop a research proposal and presentation covering all the aspects.

The brief provides little information regarding the type of research required. Therefore, there exists considerable scope to provide an answer aimed at a situation selected by the student. The answer would need to cover the components of element 3. In addition, part of element 4 is drawn into the question as an answer requires a consideration of both primary and secondary data plus the sampling approach. An answer would consist of:

- A description of the situation given. This needs to cover the issue selected and a description of the stakeholders involved. For example a college would have a range of stakeholders including the students, employees, local and national government, suppliers, businesses together with the local and wider population.
- The market research process needs explaining, plus the components of a marketing plan. This draws the theoretical perspective and combines theory with a practical situation.
- The types of information required by the client can be defined next within an answer plus a decision as to whether primary or secondary data is appropriate in each circumstance.
- It would be beneficial to propose a sampling methodology as part of the research plan and incorporate this into the proposal report given to the client.
- The final stage would be to prepare a presentation for the client outlining the research approach. The question does not ask for the presentation to be made, only that this is prepared. A presentation needs to be provided on disk in addition to paper format.

## Element 4 – Research methodologies

The fourth component of the module is aimed at the specifics of data-gathering methodologies. These cover both quantitative and qualitative mechanisms, including primary and secondary data. In addition, the element includes sampling and the roles of each data type. Questions which arise from this module include:

> *Your line manager wishes to gather data to answer a specific research problem. Evaluate the types of data available, both primary and secondary. Compare and contrast each type of research mechanism to meet data-gathering requirements, together with a discussion of the value and methods of sampling.*

An answer to this question could cover a wide range of aspects. As this element is the most likely to form a core question, an answer will be quite detailed. The information needed here will range from an organizational setting to the evaluation of appropriate research methods to solve an identified problem.

- The setting of an answer is the first component here. This will require both an organization plus a specific research problem.
- The second element is to consider the available research, in order to identify potential sources of primary and/or secondary data.

- o Each of the sources should be identified, drawing on the components of element 4. This needs to include an evaluation of the benefits and limitations of both primary and secondary data, together with the respective types of research. In addition, the use of qualitative and quantitative data should also be evaluated.
- o An answer needs to incorporate issues of sampling and types of sampling, in order for the research to be appropriate and valid.
- o Finally, the format of an answer to the question is not given. An appropriate choice would be a report, identifying the research problem and organization, leading into a discussion of the available sources of data. The answer would then lead onto an evaluation of potential data sources and recommendations made.

## Element 5 – Presenting and evaluating information to develop business advantage

The final element in the Market Research and Information module covers the use of data that has already been gathered. Building on all other aspects of the module, the element covers issues such as data analysis, presentation of data and the development of recommendations built on findings. As such, this element leads to two types of questions. The first type of question draws in element 4 (research methodologies) and would require a research project to be conducted, analysed and presented with recommendations made. The second type of question takes already gathered data and presents findings. Two example questions are shown below:

*A regional charity has a declining base of donors, and little use of customer information. As their advisor, you have been asked to give a presentation on their chances for success in gaining funding. However, the data available shows that there is little opportunity for sources of funding from current donors. Therefore, you should incorporate a discussion on potential research and sources of information that will highlight both donor data and other data sources.*

or

*As part of the management of your CIM course, the college is intending to identify a range of perceptions regarding the quality of the college and your course, in particular, with the aim of using customer data for improved CRM. Identify a range of potential sources of information which would enable accurate and detailed data to be gathered. Evaluate these sources, preparing a research proposal which details the planned research methodology. Conduct the research and analyse the data. Prepare a presentation and report demonstrating your findings with suitable recommendations drawn from the data.*

Both of these relate to the presentation of data, which is element 5. They draw in components from other elements, with the charity question considering customer (donor) data and the CIM centre question drawing in sections of elements 3 and 4. The second question would also act as a stand-alone core question due to the volume of research and analysis required. Covering the presentation aspect, a typical answer would include:

- o A background to the situation and the available research. This would set the scene for either question.
- o The data should be shown visually in both PowerPoint and word-processed format. Where possible, statistics need to be given to back up any points made.
- o Recommendations should be drawn from the data. A recommendation is best related directly back to the data, emphasizing the point(s) made.
- o A presentation would normally include a handout containing the notes, with the answer being submitted in both paper format and electronically on disk or CD-ROM.

# Assignment regulations

There have been a number of changes to the assignment structure compared with previous years, timed with the introduction of the new syllabus. These have been designed to provide consistency in approach for a student whether they are completing the assessment for a module by examination, assignment or integrative project. The more significant changes include

○ For the current academic year, tutors at CIM centres will mark assignments. These are then moderated by CIM assessors. An integrative project is marked by CIM assessors only.

○ No resubmission of assignments, as per an examination. In previous years a range of assignments were being submitted. Where a student does not achieve the 50 per cent pass mark, he/she is requested to retake the assessment for the module through examination or assignment/integrative project.

○ Whichever assessment route is selected, it is fixed rather than having the option to change at the last minute. Past history has shown that students sometimes begin on an assignment route, change to an examination at the last minute due to not meeting a deadline and then score badly in the examination. The paths to an assignment and to an examination are different and therefore it is unadvisable to switch, which is the reason for the change of rule.

○ In the 2002–3 academic year, word limits for questions and assignments were introduced. This was introduced due to assignments being submitted which were of a wide variety of lengths. These ranged from under 2000 words to over 25 000 words. Where a student is completing four modules by assignment this would equal over 100 000 words – the equivalent of a medium-sized textbook or novel. As such it became impossible for two assignments to be considered together. Therefore the word-limit guidance was introduced in order to provide equality for all students undertaking assessment by assignment.

○ Two sets of assignments per year as with the examination route. With this change, students are required to complete the assignment aimed at the nearest examination session. Previously students had between 3 months and 9 months to complete an assignment depending upon whether it was given out in September for a June deadline or March for the June deadline. Therefore a decision was made to follow the examination route with the intention of giving all students equal time to complete an assignment.

These summarize the key changes which have occurred due to the introduction of new syllabuses with the assignment/integrative project route in order that there is parity of assessment at all levels and using all formats. Some of these changes have been significant, others minor. However, all the changes have been considered thoughtfully and with the best intentions for the student in mind.

# Use of case studies

For anyone who is not working or has difficulty in access to information on their or another organization, there are a number of case studies available which allow the completion of a module using a case-based approach rather than basing it upon an organization identified by the student. These case studies are provided on a request-only basis through your accredited CIM centre and should only be used as a last resort. Using a case study as the basis for your assignment will not mean an easier approach to the assignment. However, they do provide an opportunity to undertake assignments when no other alternative exists. Each case study comes with a certain amount of information which can be used specifically for the completion of a question. Additional information may need to be assumed or researched in order to create a comprehensive assignment.

# Submission of assignments/integrative project

The following information will aid both yourself and your tutor who marks your work and also the CIM assessor who will be moderating your work and the integrative project. In addition, the flow diagram (Figure A2.2) represents the process of an assignment/integrative project from start to final mark.

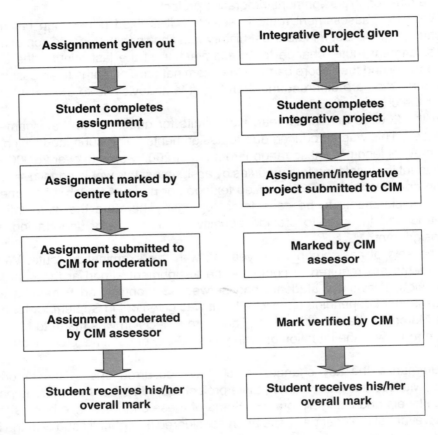

*Figure A2.2*

When completing and submitting assignments or the integrative project, refer to the following for guidance:

o Read through each question before starting out. Particularly with the core question, there will be a considerable amount of work to undertake. Choose your optional questions wisely.
o Answer the question set and use the mark guidance given regarding the marking scheme.
o Reference each question within the assignment and use a bibliography.
o Complete all documentation thoroughly. This is designed to aid both the CIM and yourself.

- Ensure that the assignment is bound as per instructions given. Currently, assignments are requested not to be submitted in plastic wallets or folders as work can become detached or lost. Following the submission instructions provided aids both the CIM administrators and the CIM assessor who will be marking (integrative project) or moderating (assignments) your work.
- Complete the candidate declaration sheet showing that you have undertaken this work yourself. *Please note that if you wish the information contained in your assignment to remain confidential you must state this on the front of the assignment.* Whilst CIM assessors will not use any information pertaining to your or another organization, CIM may wish to use the answer to a question as an example.

An assignment will be marked by a tutor at your CIM centre followed by moderation by a CIM assessor. The integrative project will be marked by a CIM assessor as per an examination with moderation by the CIM. To ensure objectivity by CIM assessors, there exists a mark-in meeting prior to any marking in order that standardization can occur. The senior assessor for each subject also undertakes further verification of both examinations and assessments to ensure parity between each type of assessment.

*Based on the appendix written by David C. Lane,*
*Former Senior Moderator (Advanced Certificate),*
*February 2003*

# appendix 3
## answers and debriefings

## Unit 2

### Debriefing Activity 2.1

You may have come up with the following which are both in the CIM website:

Marketing is the management process responsible for identifying, anticipating and satisfying customer requirements profitably (CIM, 2005).

OR

Marketing is both a concept dedicated to meeting customer requirements and a range of techniques which enables the company to determine those requirements and ensure they are met (CIM, 2003).

You may have come up with the American Marketing Association's definition:

Marketing is the process of planning and executing the conception, pricing, promotion and distribution of ideas, goods and services to create exchanges that satisfy individual and organizational objectives (Bennett, 1995).

You may have paraphrased these definitions and have a range of points which may include:

- o Customer focus
- o Profits
- o Customer needs
- o Process
- o Management
- o Satisfaction
- o Products.

Don't worry if you can't remember the definition precisely at the moment; however, it may be useful to remember at least one of these definitions. Breaking down definitions into their parts can be useful in that it can unlock a lot of thinking and by expanding on the elements of a definition you can learn a great deal.

## Debriefing Activity 2.2

You probably have a long list which might include the following:

- ○ I am thirsty.
- ○ I am hot.
- ○ I am concerned about the chemical contents of tap water.
- ○ I care for my family.
- ○ I want a healthy lifestyle.
- ○ I am buying packaged water for convenience.
- ○ I am going to the gym and need to rehydrate.
- ○ I like sparkling water with my meal.
- ○ Buying this water says that I am sophisticated.
- ○ I like the taste of this brand.
- ○ I like the new packaging.
- ○ It is cheaper than cola.
- ○ I make a better margin on this brand of water.
- ○ My staff enjoy discussing business around the water cooler.

You can see that there are a range of needs that are being satisfied. They depend on the type of person, their financial background, their age, their household composition, their life style, whether they are buying for a business or to resell.

Remember Maslow's hierarchy of needs?

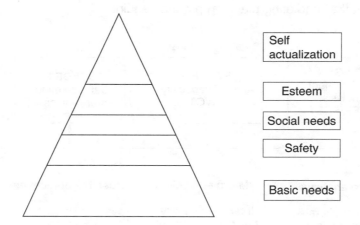

*Figure A3.1 Maslow's hierarchy of needs*

The basic need, that is 'I'm thirsty', is the simplest to understand. The more complex needs emerge from a greater understanding of the way a product or service is consumed. This is the role of research and information.

## Debriefing Activity 2.3

You may have covered some or all of the following:

- ○ Employee knowledge and competencies, for example the sales force, call centre staff and so on
- ○ Experiential knowledge at individual and group level, for example work with other companies on other projects
- ○ Informal shared knowledge, the internal beliefs and values that sustain a business

- ○ Task-based knowledge, as a result of certain functional specialisms or activity
- ○ Knowledge from the MkIS and other databases, for example accounts, operations, logistics and so on
- ○ Knowledge from internal structures, for example Intranets, the relationship between departments and internal suppliers
- ○ Knowledge from external structures, for example Extranets, supplier and intermediary relationships
- ○ Knowledge of customers through all touch points, for example research, Internet analysis, customer databases, CRM systems, sales force, contact centres and so on.

## Debriefing Activity 2.4

The four characteristics are:

1. Generates information to aid marketing decision-making
2. Involves the collection of information
3. Involves the analysis of information
4. Involves the communications and dissemination of information.

We will look at each of these areas in detail as we work through the text.

## Debriefing Activity 2.5

Let's look at the marketing planning process again.

*Figure A3.2* The marketing planning process

First of all, research and the database can work also at the corporate level. Rese\ determine the nature and scope of the organization, and may be used in developing \ and values of an organization.

Research and the database will be used significantly in the PEST and SWOT analysis. will help us understand the current attitudes and opinions of our customers. They will \ ⌐ip define our distinctive competence relative to competitive companies. They will help determine future strategies for the business by looking at markets and customers and our brands, products and services. As we drive-in to tactics, research and the database inform the configuration of the marketing mix and help us evaluate its effectiveness. Chisnall talks about this in his book (Chisnall, 2001).

He shows that research works at each of four areas of the marketers' responsibilities. These are:

1. Analysis – Identify market trends, competitors' activities, customer preferences in existing and potential markets.
2. Planning – Decide on a range of products and services likely to satisfy identified needs present and emergent.
3. Control – Check that standards of performance are maintained.
4. Implementation – Organize development production and distribution of specific products and services.

Of course, the database also works at all these levels.

Wilson (2003) suggests three key information areas. Organizations need:

1. Information on customers
2. Information on other organizations
3. Information on the marketing environment.

This list is useful but not exhaustive. A more comprehensive list is provided in Sunny Crouch's book on Market Research and this is outlined below (Crouch and Housden, 2003):

Information is used in corporate planning in order to make decisions about what goals the organization, as a whole, should have in both the short and long term:

o Forecasting the size of future demand and trends for the organization's products
o Identifying markets to be served
o Assessing the strengths and weaknesses of the organization both absolutely and relative to its competitors
o Measuring dissatisfaction and needs in relevant market segments
o Industry/market structure and composition
o Competitor, market share and profitability analysis
o Highlighting significant marketing problems
o Stimulating research for new or exploitation of existing products and markets by planned policies
o Evaluating corporate identity and image
o Selecting companies for acquisition or divestment.

**Market planning**

Research and the database are used in market planning to keep the firm in touch with its markets and customers:

o Identifying, measuring and describing key market segments' behaviour and attitudes
o Assessing relative profitability of markets over time
o Analysis and interpretation of general market data
o Placing individual customer transactions, perhaps recorded on a database, in the broader market context
o Analysing business potential of new market areas
o Identifying and evaluating markets for products and new products for markets
o Measuring consumer preferences
o Identifying changes in competitive activity
o Sales forecasting.

**Product planning (including packaging and service levels)**

Research and the database may be used in making and adapting products to fulfil customer wants more accurately and profitably:

o Generating and screening new product ideas and modifications
o Concept testing
o Product testing and re-testing for acceptance and improvement
o Testing formulation and presentation preferences
o Packaging tests
o Product name tests
o Test marketing
o Comparative testing against competitive products
o Product elimination or product line simplification
o Evaluating perceived service quality.

**Promotional planning**

Research and the database may be concerned with the selection and effectiveness of persuasive communications. Two main areas are identified below:

*Communications planning*

o Developing sustainable brand positioning
o Message design and content
o Development of the creative proposition
o Developing effective multimedia communications strategies
o Pre-testing ads
o Post-testing ads, for example awareness, comprehension, recall, attitude shifts, brand switching effects
o Advertising weight-of-expenditure tests
o Media planning: evaluation, selection and scheduling
o Advertising effectiveness
o Public relations and publicity effects on awareness/attitude
o Sponsorship effectiveness
o Exhibition effectiveness research
o Direct marketing effectiveness research
o Assessing the impact of integration
o Developing the optimum communications mix.

*Sales force planning*

- ○ Determining sales areas
- ○ Testing alternative selling techniques and messages
- ○ Setting sales targets
- ○ Evaluating sales performance
- ○ Evaluating sales compensation system
- ○ Making selling operations more productive.

## Distribution planning

Research and the database may be concerned with the formulation and effectiveness of distribution policy:

- ○ Channel selection
- ○ Distribution cost analysis
- ○ Wholesaler/retailer margin
- ○ Incentive policy
- ○ Dealer sales levels
- ○ Distribution achievement
- ○ Penetration levels
- ○ Stock checks
- ○ Inventory policy.

## Price planning

Research and the database may help as one of the inputs to price selection.

# Unit 3

## Debriefing Activity 3.1

You probably have a few points of similarity and they may include the following:

- ○ The database may be manual or computerized, but, almost always, today it will be computerized.
- ○ It is a source of accurate up-to-date information or data about our past, present and current customers.
- ○ It is relevant to the organization's goals.
- ○ Data is collected systematically.
- ○ Data is maintained and monitored.
- ○ It is used to formulate strategy.
- ○ It supports the formulation of marketing objectives of the enterprise.

## Debriefing Activity 3.2

So, what do you have? Below are some of the data elements you might have written down. We'll start with consumer markets:

What data should be collected?

Consumer identification data

- Customer reference number
- First name
- Last name
- Title – Mr, Mrs, Dr and so on
- Suffixes, for example B.A., M.A., Ph.D., M.CIM. and so on
- Date of birth
- Address
- Postcode
- Telephone
- E-mail
- Sales area
- Media sales area
- Fax
- Account number.

Demographic data

- Gender
- Age
- Occupation
- Employment status
- Marital status
- How many children?
- What age are the children?

Financial

- Job title
- Income
- What is their credit history and rating?
- Are they a homeowner?
- What is the value of their home?
- Do they own a car?
- Share ownership
- Do they have a credit card?
- What insurance products do they have?

Lifestyle

- Life stage – student, retired and so on
- Number of holidays per year
- Where do they holiday?
- What leisure interests do they have?
- Media reading
- TV viewing.

Shopping behaviour

- When did they last buy? – Recency
- How often do they buy? – Frequency
- What is the value of their purchases? – Value
- What profit does the customer generate for the business over time? – Lifetime value
- Loyalty scheme member.

Other

- Length of time at current address
- Have they responded before?
- To what campaign?
- Customer service history
- Complaints
- Are they a VIP?
- Data protection issues
- Have they opted out of or into communications?
- Are they a shareholder?

Let's look at business data:

Business identification data

- Company name
- Trading name
- Trading status
- Credit rating
- Contact name or names in the decision-making unit
- Job title
- Areas of responsibility
- Address
- Website address
- Postcode
- Account number
- VAT number
- Region
- Territory
- Salesperson.

Business details

- Size of business
- Turnover
- Employees
- Number of offices
- Head office
- Budget
- Financial year end.

Transaction data

- o Account number
- o Purchase history
- o Recency, frequency and value
- o Order size
- o Service·history
- o Response
- o Method of acquisition.

Sector

- o Standard Industrial Classification code (SIC)
- o Type of business.

Key contact

- o Contact name
- o Job
- o Telephone
- o Fax
- o E-mail.

The differences are immediate. Then so are the similarities. There are standard elements and these are generally the 'golden' fields, which should be completed and maintained for good database marketing. Clearly these include identification data and the fields that cover customers' behaviour. Generally the most important categories here are recency, frequency, amount and product category. The key fields for any database will be different from the next due to the different business contexts and objectives the data supports.

## Debriefing Activity 3.3

Data is obtained from a range of sources. Some of these are planned and managed and some are as a result of the day-to-day operation of the business.

Data that comes as a result of the day-to-day activity of the business may include:

- o Accounts records
- o Sales force reports
- o Service records
- o Reports from intermediaries
- o Customer enquiries or complaints
- o Responses to marketing communications
- o Guarantee cards.

Any contact with a customer of prospect is an opportunity of data capture. The data strategy must be established in order to ensure that these opportunities are appraised effectively and that relevant data is captured consistently and constantly.

Information that is generated from planned activity includes:

- o Bought lists
- o Industry sector reports
- o Primary marketing research
- o Competitor analyses
- o Responses to exhibitions and public relations events.

# Unit 4

## Debriefing Activity 4.1

Quite a few things to consider are not there. Amongst others you may have:

- o Is there a market for whisky-based drinks?
- o What is the market worth?
- o Who is the target market?
- o What are their characteristics?
- o What is the reaction of the retail and catering trade?
- o How will the competition react?
- o What brand strategy should we pursue?
- o What shall we call the product?
- o How much will it cost to produce?
- o What price should we charge?
- o How should we promote the product? and so on. The list is endless.

## Debriefing Activity 4.2

Exploratory Research is intended to develop initial ideas or insights and to provide direction for further research.

Conclusive research covers all other research that is aimed at evaluating alternative courses of action or measuring and monitoring the organization's performance.

Conclusive descriptive research provides answers to the who, what, where, when and how of marketing research. It explains what is happening, not why it is happening.

Descriptive research may be cross-sectional, that is involving data collection at a single point of time. Or, it may be longitudinal involving data collection over time to examine trends.

Conclusive causal research tells us if one variable is related to another. That is, if one variable causes or determines the value of another. For example, drinks and ice cream companies look at the influence of temperature on product sales. A simpler more common approach would be to look at the effect of different creative executions on response rates. This latter example is an example of experimental research or the changing of one variable to observe the effect on another whilst other extraneous variables are kept constant.

## Debriefing Activity 4.3

What you came up with on your list might have included the following:

- Advice from colleagues
- Past experience
- Seen their work in the trade press
- Seen a credentials publication
- Size of the business
- Reputation
- Sector-specific skills
- Industry award winners
- Response to marketing activity
- Web searches
- They are local to us
- Recommendation from consultants or business advisors, for example business link
- Trade body research.

Trade body research is very useful. As a follow-up to this exercise visit the MRS and ESOMAR websites and try their online research buyer's guide.

www.mrs.org.uk

www.esomar.org

They are both excellent at identifying potential agencies and their relevant skills base. The Research Buyer's guide of the MRS lists the following for all its members:

- Address and telephone number
- Turnover (Bands)
- Services (all and specialities)
- Key executives/All full members
- Brief description
- MRQSA/BMRA memberships
- Date formed
- Ownership.

# Unit 5

## Debriefing Activity 5.1

The key point is that the information has generally been gathered to serve some other purpose. It is not directly related to the research problem under consideration. Crouch and Housden point out that it has been gathered at a different time. It may be out of date. In today's fast-moving technological market this may be a major factor limiting the use of external data. Wilson's definition also outlines its key strengths. It maybe cheap or free of charge.

# Debriefing Activity 5.2

This is the type of information that you might have found – pretty useful for those contemplating setting up an e-commerce operation.

E-commerce Inquiry to Business 2000

E-commerce could have a huge impact on the way businesses operate. It has the potential to lead to growth in trade, increase markets, improve efficiency and effectiveness, and transform business processes.

Author: Magdalen Williams

Economic Trends, no. 572

ISSN: 0013 0400

Download (Pdf file, 39 Kb)

Abstract

E-commerce could have a huge impact on the way businesses operate. It has the potential to lead to growth in trade, increase markets, improve efficiency and effectiveness, and transform business processes. In response, the ONS has developed a package of measures which will help monitor the United Kingdom's use of e-commerce.

One strand of the strategy is the e-commerce Inquiry, a new annual survey of UK business which asks about the use of, and attitude to, the Internet and e-commerce. The ONS launched it in January 2001 as part of a European Union (EU) initiative which will provide EU-comparable data on e-commerce later this year.

The UK element was a survey of 9000 businesses randomly sampled from the Interdepartmental Business Register, stratified by employment size. The sampling methodology ensured wide coverage of the UK economy and the estimates produced cover all sectors except agriculture, fishing, mining, construction and the public sector, and all businesses with employment of 10 or more. The first results were published on 15 May 2001 and indicated that in 2000 there were nearly £57 billion of sales made over the Internet: 2 per cent of total sales by the sectors surveyed.

Published on 1 August 2002 (National Statistics, 2003).

Other e-commerce publications include

**E-commerce and related activities**

**Measuring web business and Internet access**

Access e-commerce survey of business data, articles and reference material available from the Office for National Statistics (ONS).

Guide to e-commerce and Internet

A short introduction to e-commerce

International e-commerce Benchmarking – Experimental Statistics

ONS is working, with the DTI and OeE, to develop a comparison of e-commerce readiness, usage and impact across nine major economies – Australia, Canada, France, Germany, Italy, Japan, Sweden, the United Kingdom and United States.

ONS e-commerce Database

Latest data – Experimental Statistics

The 2002 e-commerce Survey of Business has been reclassified as 'experimental statistics'.

This new survey is still under development and the results are subject to quality improvements involving user consultation. Data validation continues to be difficult and is compounded by changing technologies and ICT definitions. Methodological aspects are also still under consideration at an international level involving both Eurostat and the Organization for Economic Co-operation and Development (OECD).

Data published in respect of the previous 2 years has also been reclassified as experimental.

2002 e-commerce survey of business: value of e-trading (experimental)

2002 e-commerce survey of business (experimental)

**Archive data – Experimental Statistics**

**2001 e-commerce survey of business**

2001 e-commerce survey: Online trading by UK business by sector

2001 online trading by UK business

2001 e-commerce survey of business

2001 e-commerce: a regional analysis

**2000 e-commerce survey of business**

First e-commerce survey of business

E-Commerce Inquiry to Business 2000

E-Commerce Inquiry 2000 – Further analysis

**Articles and associated material**

Cross-border electronic commerce and international trade statistics

Measuring international e-commerce

Measuring e-commerce in the United Kingdom

Measuring e-commerce: Developments in the United Kingdom

Measuring e-commerce – the ONS Approach

Electronic Commerce and Business Change

E-commerce survey does the business

**Related activities**

**Internet**

Guide to e-commerce and Internet

Latest on Internet

Internet Connectivity

Internet access – First Release

New Socio-economic Classification user manual on the Internet

**Information and Communications Technology**

Use of ICT by UK businesses in 2001; sectoral and regional analyses

ICT: Deflation and Growth: A sensitivity Analysis

New economy

Official Statistics and the New Economy; Report of the 2002 IAOS conference

Measuring the new economy, ET January 2003

Where, and how, to look for the New Economy

Measuring the new economy, ET March 2002

The output is similarly comprehensive in every other category and these cover:

- o Agriculture, Fishing and Forestry
- o Commerce, Energy and Industry
- o Crime and Justice
- o Economy
- o Education and Training
- o Health and Care
- o Labour Market
- o Natural and Built Environment
- o Population and Migration
- o Public Sector and Other
- o Social and Welfare
- o Transport, Travel and Tourism.

## Debriefing Activity 5.3

What is TGI?

The Target Group Index (TGI) is a continuous survey where data collection runs throughout the year so that seasonality does not skew results. TGI yields information on the usage of over 4000 brands in 500 product areas for those aged 15+. It is updated four times a year on a rolling quarterly basis.

What is the sample size?

The survey is based on a sample size of c.25 000 interviews per annum. Results are weighted to match known demographic profiles and re-weighted to the National Readership Survey.

How is data captured?

A self-completion questionnaire is placed with selected respondents at the end of BMRB's Access Omnibus survey.

What are the implications for my business?

TGI data is used to assist the understanding of target markets to aid marketing and advertising decisions. The data helps the users of TGI to optimize their marketing and advertising receipts/expenditures. *Source*: TGI

## Debriefing Activity 5.4

As you can see there are significant differences. It pays to use a range of search engines.

# Unit 6

## Debriefing Activity 6.1

ACNielsen's services include:

Retail Measurement Services (provides) data on product movement, market share, distribution, price and other market-sensitive information.

Using in-store scanning of product codes and store visits by professional auditors, ACNielsen offers a complete portfolio of sample and census information across the food, household, health and beauty, durables, confectionery and beverage products industries.

Retail Measurement Services help to gauge product penetration, overall product performance, distribution, promotion effectiveness and price sensitivity. Whether long-term strategic planning or tactical decision-making, ACNielsen measures and tracks sales volume, selling price, observed promotion and merchandising execution, encompassing an organization's own brands as well as competitive brands.

*Source*: www.acnielsen.com.

Taylor Nelson Sofres' services include:

Taylor Nelson Sofres Superpanel is GB's leading continuous consumer panel and provides purchasing information on all main grocery markets. The panel was launched in 1991 and now consists of 15 000 households which are demographically and regionally balanced to offer a representative picture of the GB marketplace. Data is collected twice weekly via electronic terminals in the home, with purchases being recorded via home-scanning technology. This is how TN Sofres capture their data.

- All household members are asked to record details of purchases they make and bring into the home. This is done by using a palm computer equipped with a laser scanner to scan the barcodes on products they buy plus some details from a codebook.
- Panel members enter information on products bought through a sequence of questions asked by the kit.
- 'Purchaser identity' (scanned from codebook).
- 'Shop name' (scanned from codebook).
- 'Total amount spent' (entered manually from till roll receipt).
- 'Product' (bar-code scanned).
- Details for non-barcoded fresh food products are collected by answering specific on-screen questions displayed on the palm kit.
- The terminal is also programmed to recognize random weight bar-codes which appear on packs that come in a range of different weights. These are common among markets such as cheese and meat. In these cases the weight of the item is collected on-screen.
- Panel members are also asked to return their till receipts. These are scanned and put through an optical character recognition process which extracts the price paid for each item bought. This price information is then linked back to the details of the same shopping trip scanned in by that panel member. In this way, the workload on panel members is reduced to a minimum, and their recruitment and retention made easier.
- The terminal software automatically records the date and time when each shopping trip is recorded, and which barcodes were keyed in rather than scanned due to poor print quality on difficult pack designs. This information is used for quality control purposes.
- When not being used for scanning the kit is normally kept in a modem, directly linked to the power supply and a telephone socket. This allows data capture (or polling) to take place overnight twice weekly without disturbing panel members.

*Source*: www.tnsofres.com/superpanel.

## Debriefing Activity 6.2

1. Postar.
2. Nielsen Net ratings US/UK, Netvalue, France, Hitwise (Australia).
3. The NRS is a non-profit-making but commercial organization, which sets out to provide estimates of the number and nature of the people who read UK newspapers and consumer magazines. Currently, the survey publishes data covering some 270 different publications.
4. The Audit Bureau of Circulations provides an independent verification of a circulation, attendance or electronic media delivery claim. All titles in ABC membership are audited at least once a year.

## Debriefing Activity 6.3

You may have some or all of the following:

- o To improve customer service
- o To improve store layout
- o To improve staffing levels to ensure reduced waiting time at call centres or at service points
- o To generate information to inform reward and recognition schemes
- o To monitor time spent on any activity, for example TV consumption
- o To measure the amount of product consumed
- o To look at product combinations
- o To explore alternative product uses
- o To explore product interaction.

# Unit 7

## Debriefing Activity 7.1

Customer Focus Group Discussion Guide

Below is an outline discussion guide. Each of the sections could have more detail but the framework is correct. A skilled researcher could use this to carry out discussion in the group.

Introduction

   Objectives

   Rules of the road for focus group research

   Introductions: Introduce the person next to you.

5 mins

Customer service generally

   Experiences of really good service – why?

   Experience of a really bad service – why?

10 mins

The dealership

   What was the experience like in the dealership pre-purchase?

10 mins

   During the negotiation

10 mins

 After sales

10 mins

 People

10 mins

 Facilities

10 mins

 Marketing Collateral

5 mins

 Projective technique Dealership CV

10 mins

 Summary

 Other issues

 Key elements

 Thank you and gift

5 mins

## Debriefing Activity 7.2

Volvo is interesting; despite the millions spent in advertising Volvo as an exciting car to drive, non-Volvo drivers will invariably describe the Volvo as:

- Male
- Middle class
- Married with children (2. 5)
- Two black Labradors and a pair of green wellies; while Volvo owners may present a different view. Try this and see what results you get.

## Debriefing Activity 7.3

Exploratory research to define problems

Motivational research to define areas for quantitative research

Attitudes and motivation research

Segmentation studies

Positioning studies

Creative concept testing

Product development and line extensions

Brand and name development

Brand perception studies.

# Unit 8

## Debriefing Activity 8.1

### Sex

The majority are women. At the risk of being sexist, there are several reasons for this: Part-time work, interview work is flexible and fits around child-care responsibilities. Women tend to have better listening skills and find it easier to elicit information from respondents.

### Age

The ideal age requirements for entry to consumer interviewing is between 25 and 45 years. In B2B markets, older, more experienced interviewers may be required.

### Social background

It is useful if the interviewer is not obviously from any social class. It helps if the interviewer has the ability to be 'chameleon-like' so as to be able to fit-in with the respondent. Politically, interviewers should be aware but not activists. It is usual, when interviewers are recruited, for them to be screened for political activity if they are likely to be employed in asking political questions.

### Education

Interviewers should be numerate and literate. Interviewers should have at least GCSE level English and Maths. In certain B2B projects it may be useful to have some business education.

### Experience

Some experience of dealing with people and b2b interviewing experience in the sector under review may be desirable. Training in research interviewing is not vital but those who are not trained will require to be trained under the terms of the MRS's IQCS scheme. MRS training is available via the Accredited Interviewer Training Scheme. Information can be found at www.mrs.org.uk/training/aits.htm.

### Personality

The ideal researcher is gregarious and outgoing, but not overbearing, and a good listener capable of empathy. They should be capable of multitasking, that is listening and recording data simultaneously.

## Debriefing Activity 8.2

You may have written down some or all of the following points:

- ○ Prescreening – Calls can be made to respondents prior to sending the questionnaire. This could confirm details and create a sense of expectation and commitment to the process.
- ○ Reminder calls or letters to encourage the respondent to reply – These may take place at a specified time after the questionnaire has been sent. Some agencies will send duplicate copies of the research questionnaires.
- ○ The covering letter is crucial to introduce the research and the organization carrying out the research. It may contain letter of reference or professional membership symbols.

Wilson (2003) suggests that the covering letter should contain:

- ○ The purpose of the research
- ○ Assurances of confidentiality
- ○ Reasons why they should respond
- ○ The time needed to complete the research
- ○ A number and name for enquiries
- ○ Time scales and manner of return
- ○ Thanks
- ○ The research may be incentivized. In consumer markets, coupons or vouchers can be used; in b2b markets access to an executive summary of the final report may be offered as an incentive.
- ○ Personalize the survey. Postal research response rates tend to be higher when the research is part of an existing relationship. Data collection methods need to reflect the nature of the population under consideration.

# Unit 10

## Debriefing Activity 10.1

You may have several:

The members' list of the CIM, MRS or IDM

Members of the institute of directors

Companies' house

Subscriber lists to the marketing press

Business directory services such as Kompass

Business-to-business profiling companies like Dunn and Bradstreer

Trade Association in the food and drinks sector

You may have others . . .

## Debriefing Activity 10.2

Probability of selection = 20 000/500.

Probability of selection is 40.

## Debriefing Activity 10.3

| Value | Mean | Deviation | Deviation squared |
|---|---|---|---|
| 200 | 116.36 | 83.64 | 6995.65 |
| 150 | 116.36 | 33.64 | 1131.65 |
| 50 | 116.36 | −66.36 | 4403.65 |
| 80 | 116.36 | −36.36 | 1322.05 |
| 150 | 116.36 | 33.64 | 1131.65 |
| 100 | 116.36 | −16.36 | 267.6496 |
| 100 | 116.36 | −16.36 | 267.6496 |
| 90 | 116.36 | −26.36 | 694.8496 |
| 170 | 116.36 | 53.64 | 2877.25 |
| 80 | 116.36 | −36.36 | 1322.05 |
| 110 | 116.36 | −6.36 | 40.4496 |
| Total | | | 20,454.55 |

Sum of squared differences divided by number of observations less 1 is $20\,454.55/(11 - 1) = 2045.46$

This is the variance.

Standard deviation is the square root of the variance which is 45.23.

Standard deviation is a measure of how widely values are dispersed from the average value (the mean). The higher the standard deviation, the more widely the values are spread. This allows us to use standard deviation to compare data sets.

In order to apply this to the determination of sample size, we need to understand another concept. That is normal distribution.

Normal distribution is an important concept. What it implies is that the distribution of values within any data set will be similar, for example shoe size, height or income, and will follow the pattern shown below – known as a bell-shaped curve.

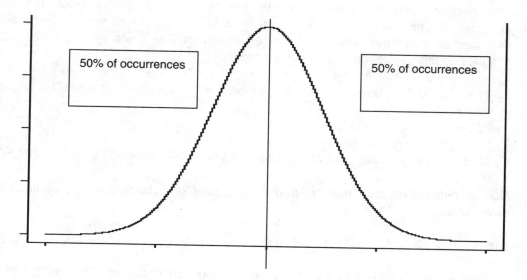

*Figure A3.3* Normal distribution, the bell-shaped curve

So what does this mean?

The area under the curve represents all occurrences. The line through the centre of the curve is the mean value.

Normal distribution has another key characteristic.

Sixty-eight per cent of all occurrences fall within one standard deviation of the mean.

For the example we have worked out above it means that if 68 per cent of values fall within one standard deviation the mean is 116.36 and the standard deviation is 45.23. Therefore for the population as a whole 68 per cent of the occurrences fall between 71.13 and 161.59.

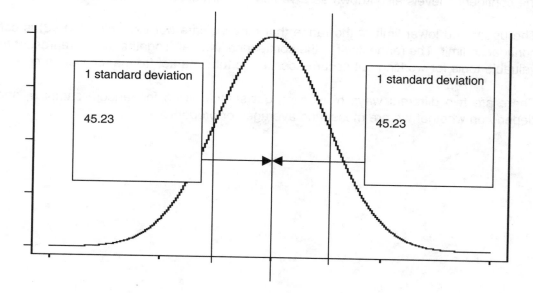

Normal distribution also tells us that 95 per cent of occurrences would fall between 1.96 standard deviations. This is very important as for the most part market researchers work at this level of certainty. What it means effectively is that there is a 1 in 20 chance of an occurrence falling outside this predicted range.

So again using the above example 95 per cent of the occurrences would fall between:

$116.36 = \pm1.96 \times 45$ or 88.2

Or in other words 95 per cent of occurrences would fall between 28.16 and 204.56.

Normal distribution also tells us that 99 per cent of occurrences fall within 2.58 standard deviations:

$116.36 = \pm2.58 \times 45$ or 116.1

Or in other words 99 per cent of occurrences would fall between 0.26 and 232.46.

The key point is that for any normal distribution, for any data set, the distribution of values is the same.

To repeat:

- o   68 per cent of values fall within 1 standard deviation.
- o   95 per cent fall within 1.96 standard deviations.
- o   99 per cent fall within 2.58 standard deviations.

These percentages (68, 95 and 99 per cent) are known as confidence levels and are the same for all data sets that conform to a normal distribution. There are other types of distribution but you need not go further into this for the course. For our purpose, marketers generally use 95 or 99 per cent confidence limits. These relate to 1.96 and 2.58 standard deviations and these are the confidence levels also known as Z values that are used.

The upper and lower limit of the range that they indicate (for example $= \pm1.96$) is called the confidence limit. The range itself is the confidence interval. Together these represent the most valuable tools for working out occurrences in the total market from a smaller sample.

There are two different ways of working out sample sizes for random samples, and these depend on whether we are measuring averages or proportions.

## Debriefing Activity 10.4

Remember the formula, and work through the example

$$N = \frac{Z^2 \sigma^2}{E^2}$$

$$N = \frac{(2.58 \times 2.58) \times (40.8 \times 40.8)}{5 \times 5}$$

$$N = \frac{6.6564 \times 1664.64}{25}$$

$$N = \frac{11076.514}{25}$$

The sample required is 443.

Play around with the formula. Change the required level of precision and look at the impact on the sample size required.

# Unit 11

## Debriefing Activity 11.1

Determine the hypotheses:

$H_0$ The number of responses to each mailing is equal.

$H_1$ There is a significant difference between the responses to the mailings.

5909 5810 6350 = observed values

6023 = expected value

2.16 7.53 17.75 = observed values – expected values/expected values

27.44 = chi value

Because we are comparing 3 packs we use two degrees of freedom (n – 1). If we were comparing two packs we would work at one degree of freedom.

Chi-squared distribution

| Dof F | 0.995 | 0.99 | 0.975 | 0.95 | 0.9 | 0.75 | 0.5 | 0. 25 | 0. 1 | 0.05 | 0.025 | 0.01 | 0.005 |
|---|---|---|---|---|---|---|---|---|---|---|---|---|---|
| 1 | 0.000 | 0.000 | 0.001 | 0.004 | 0.016 | 0.102 | 0.455 | 1.323 | 2.706 | 3.841 | 5.024 | 6.635 | 7.879 |
| 2 | 0.010 | 0.020 | 0.051 | 0.103 | 0.211 | 0.575 | 1.386 | 2.773 | 4.605 | 5.991 | 7.378 | 9.210 | 10.597 |
| 3 | 0.072 | 0.115 | 0.216 | 0.352 | 0.584 | 1.213 | 2.366 | 4.108 | 6.251 | 7.815 | 9.348 | 11.345 | 12.838 |
| 4 | 0.207 | 0.297 | 0.484 | 0.711 | 1.064 | 1.923 | 3.357 | 5.385 | 7.779 | 9.488 | 11.143 | 13.277 | 14.860 |
| 5 | 0.412 | 0.554 | 0.831 | 1.145 | 1.610 | 2.675 | 4.351 | 6.626 | 9.236 | 11.071 | 12.833 | 15.086 | 16.750 |
| 6 | 0.676 | 0.872 | 1.237 | 1.635 | 2.204 | 3.455 | 5.348 | 7.841 | 10.645 | 12.592 | 14.449 | 16.812 | 18.548 |
| 7 | 0.989 | 1.239 | 1.690 | 2.167 | 2.833 | 4.255 | 6.346 | 9.037 | 12.017 | 14.067 | 16.013 | 18.475 | 20.278 |
| 8 | 1.344 | 1.647 | 2.180 | 2.733 | 3.490 | 5.071 | 7.344 | 10.219 | 13.362 | 15.507 | 17.535 | 20.090 | 21.955 |
| 9 | 1.735 | 2.088 | 2.700 | 3.325 | 4.168 | 5.899 | 8.343 | 11.389 | 14.684 | 16.919 | 19.023 | 21.666 | 23.589 |
| 10 | 2.156 | 2.558 | 3.247 | 3.940 | 4.865 | 6.737 | 9.342 | 12.549 | 15.987 | 18.307 | 20.483 | 23.209 | 25.188 |
| 11 | 2.603 | 3.053 | 3.816 | 4.575 | 5.578 | 7.584 | 10.341 | 13.701 | 17.275 | 19.675 | 21.920 | 24.725 | 26.757 |
| 12 | 3.074 | 3.571 | 4.404 | 5.226 | 6.304 | 8.438 | 11.340 | 14.845 | 18.549 | 21.026 | 23.337 | 26.217 | 28.300 |
| 13 | 3.565 | 4.107 | 5.009 | 5.892 | 7.042 | 9.299 | 12.340 | 15.984 | 19.812 | 22.362 | 24.736 | 27.688 | 29.819 |
| 14 | 4.075 | 4.660 | 5.629 | 6.571 | 7.790 | 10.165 | 13.339 | 17.117 | 21.064 | 23.685 | 26.119 | 29.141 | 31.319 |
| 15 | 4.601 | 5.229 | 6.262 | 7.261 | 8.547 | 11.037 | 14.339 | 18.245 | 22.307 | 24.996 | 27.488 | 30.578 | 32.801 |
| 16 | 5.142 | 5.812 | 6.908 | 7.962 | 9.312 | 11.912 | 15.339 | 19.369 | 23.542 | 26.296 | 28.845 | 32.000 | 34.267 |
| 17 | 5.697 | 6.408 | 7.564 | 8.672 | 10.085 | 12.792 | 16.338 | 20.489 | 24.769 | 27.587 | 30.191 | 33.409 | 35.718 |
| 18 | 6.265 | 7.015 | 8.231 | 9.390 | 10.865 | 13.675 | 17.338 | 21.605 | 25.989 | 28.869 | 31.526 | 34.805 | 37.156 |

| 19 | 6.844 | 7.633 | 8.907 | 10.117 | 11.651 | 14.562 | 18.338 | 22.718 | 27.204 | 30.144 | 32.852 | 36.191 | 38.582 |
| 20 | 7.434 | 8.260 | 9.591 | 10.851 | 12.443 | 15.452 | 19.337 | 23.828 | 28.412 | 31.410 | 34.170 | 37.566 | 39.997 |
| 21 | 8.034 | 8.897 | 10.283 | 11.591 | 13.240 | 16.344 | 20.337 | 24.935 | 29.615 | 32.671 | 35.479 | 38.932 | 41.401 |
| 22 | 8.643 | 9.542 | 10.982 | 12.338 | 14.041 | 17.240 | 21.337 | 26.039 | 30.813 | 33.924 | 36.781 | 40.289 | 42.796 |
| 23 | 9.260 | 10.196 | 11.689 | 13.091 | 14.848 | 18.137 | 22.337 | 27.141 | 32.007 | 35.172 | 38.076 | 41.638 | 44.181 |
| 24 | 9.886 | 10.856 | 12.401 | 13.848 | 15.659 | 19.037 | 23.337 | 28.241 | 33.196 | 36.415 | 39.364 | 42.980 | 45.559 |
| 25 | 10.520 | 11.524 | 13.120 | 14.611 | 16.473 | 19.939 | 24.337 | 29.339 | 34.382 | 37.652 | 40.646 | 44.314 | 46.928 |
| 26 | 11.160 | 12.198 | 13.844 | 15.379 | 17.292 | 20.843 | 25.336 | 30.435 | 35.563 | 38.885 | 41.923 | 45.642 | 48.290 |
| 27 | 11.808 | 12.879 | 14.573 | 16.151 | 18.114 | 21.749 | 26.336 | 31.528 | 36.741 | 40.113 | 43.195 | 46.963 | 49.645 |
| 28 | 12.461 | 13.565 | 15.308 | 16.928 | 18.939 | 22.657 | 27.336 | 32.620 | 37.916 | 41.337 | 44.461 | 48.278 | 50.993 |
| 29 | 13.121 | 14.256 | 16.047 | 17.708 | 19.768 | 23.567 | 28.336 | 33.711 | 39.087 | 42.557 | 45.722 | 49.588 | 52.336 |
| 30 | 13.787 | 14.953 | 16.791 | 18.493 | 20.599 | 24.478 | 29.336 | 34.800 | 40.256 | 43.773 | 46.979 | 50.892 | 53.672 |

*Figure A3.4* Example of a coding frame for an open question

At 2 degrees of freedom, alpha value = 5.99.

Chi-value is higher, therefore we can be 95 per cent confident that there is a difference and the null hypothesis should be rejected.

## Debriefing Activity 11.2

There are many but you may have come up with some of the following:

Sales volume and variables such as price, level of advertising expenditure, competitive activity, and various consumer variables such as purchase behaviour, income, attitude and so on.

| Restaurant | Capacity $X$ | Turnover (£100 000) $Y$ | $x^2$ | $y^2$ | $xy$ |
|---|---|---|---|---|---|
| 1 | 210 | 1.10 | 44 100 | 1.199025 | 229.95 |
| 2 | 80 | 0.74 | 6 400 | 0.540225 | 58.80 |
| 3 | 80 | 0.99 | 6 400 | 0.97515625 | 79.00 |
| 4 | 160 | 1.14 | 25 600 | 1.29390625 | 182.00 |
| 5 | 100 | 1.01 | 10 000 | 1.010025 | 100.50 |
| 6 | 70 | 0.92 | 4 900 | 0.837225 | 64.05 |
| 7 | 160 | 1.08 | 25 600 | 1.1664 | 172.80 |
| 8 | 60 | 0.80 | 3 600 | 0.63600625 | 47.85 |
| 9 | 300 | 1.10 | 90 000 | 1.199025 | 328.50 |
| 10 | 200 | 1.16 | 40 000 | 1.334025 | 231.00 |
| 11 | 150 | 1.09 | 22 500 | 1.18265625 | 163.13 |
| 12 | 50 | 0.68 | 2 500 | 0.45900625 | 33.88 |
| 13 | 80 | 0.78 | 6 400 | 0.60450625 | 62.20 |
| 14 | 150 | 1.08 | 22 500 | 1.16100625 | 161.63 |
| 15 | 100 | 1.12 | 10 000 | 1.243225 | 111.50 |
| 16 | 100 | 0.90 | 10 000 | 0.80550625 | 89.75 |
| 17 | 90 | 0.94 | 8 100 | 0.874225 | 84.15 |
| 18 | 170 | 0.91 | 28 900 | 0.819025 | 153.85 |
| 19 | 80 | 0.85 | 6 400 | 0.7225 | 68.00 |
| 20 | 110 | 1.05 | 12 100 | 1.1025 | 115.50 |
| Sum | 2500 | 19.375 | 386 000 | 19.165175 | 2538.03 |
| Mean | 125 | 0.97 | | | |

$R = 0.68112$

The value of R in this example indicates some association and given that capacity should be a strong indicator of sales in the restaurants, further work may be required.

# Debriefing Activity 11.3

What is the impact of increasing capacity on turnover?

| Restaurant | Capacity X | Turnover (£100 000) Y | $x^2$ | $y^2$ | xy |
|---|---|---|---|---|---|
| 1 | 210 | £1.10 | 44 100 | 1.199025 | 229.95 |
| 2 | 80 | £0.74 | 6 400 | 0.540225 | 58.80 |
| 3 | 80 | 0.99 | 6 400 | 0.97515625 | 79.00 |
| 4 | 160 | 1.14 | 25 600 | 1.29390625 | 182.00 |
| 5 | 100 | 1.01 | 10 000 | 1.010025 | 100.50 |
| 6 | 70 | 0.92 | 4 900 | 0.837225 | 64.05 |
| 7 | 160 | 1.08 | 25 600 | 1.1664 | 172.80 |
| 8 | 60 | 0.80 | 3 600 | 0.63600625 | 47.85 |
| 9 | 300 | 1.10 | 90 000 | 1.199025 | 328.50 |
| 10 | 200 | 1.16 | 40 000 | 1.334025 | 231.00 |
| 11 | 150 | 1.09 | 22 500 | 1.18265625 | 163.13 |
| 12 | 50 | 0.68 | 2 500 | 0.45900625 | 33.88 |
| 13 | 80 | 0.78 | 6 400 | 0.60450625 | 62.20 |
| 14 | 150 | 1.08 | 22 500 | 1.16100625 | 161.63 |
| 15 | 100 | 1.12 | 10 000 | 1.243225 | 111.50 |
| 16 | 100 | 0.90 | 10 000 | 0.80550625 | 89.75 |
| 17 | 90 | 0.94 | 8 100 | 0.874225 | 84.15 |
| 18 | 170 | 0.91 | 28 900 | 0.819025 | 153.85 |
| 19 | 80 | 0.85 | 6 400 | 0.7225 | 68.00 |
| 20 | 110 | 1.05 | 12 100 | 1.1025 | 115.50 |
| Sum | 2500 | 19.375 | 386 000 | 19.165175 | 2538.03 |
| Mean | 125 | 0.97 | | | |

To calculate the slope

$$B = \frac{2538.03 - 20 \times 125 \times 0.97}{386000 - 20 \times 125^2}$$

$$B = \frac{113.03}{73500}$$

$$B = 0.0015$$

To calculate the intercept

$a = 0.97 - 0.0015 \times 125$

$a = 0.7825$

Therefore, for every increase in capacity of 7.8, sales should increase by 0.015 hundred thousand pounds or £1500 per year.

# appendix 4

# sample exam questions and answers

## Learning objectives

After completing this unit you will be familiar with the type of questions that may be asked in the exam.

You will be able to identify the structure to answer these questions. These should be read in conjunction with the CIM exam questions that are included throughout the text.

## Question 2.1

You are the marketing manager for a major supplier of computer hardware, mainly to the consumer market. The company has a database of 350 000 active customers. The company wishes to enter the small office/home office sector. You have been given the job of researching and contributing to the development of the marketing plan for this new venture. The board feels that their investment on the database should be adequate to inform the development process.

Write a report to the board outlining the following:

- o How the database and marketing research will work together to help the marketing planning process?
- o In order to convince the board, illustrate your report with examples from other industries.

This question is fairly straightforward.

### Answer

#### Introduction
How information works to produce better decisions in companies? What decisions will the company need to make and how can research and the database facilitate these decisions?

How information is managed? Cover the MkIS briefly.

Define your terms.

What is marketing? What is marketing research? What is database marketing?

288

**Main body**
Outline the marketing planning process. You may use one of a number of different frameworks:

- o Analysis
- o Objectives
- o Strategy
- o Tactics
- o Control.

Under each of these headings, show how research and the database can contribute to decision-making.

Make all points relevant to the business context.

Make sure that you include examples. These can be built in at each stage of your answer or can be included as a separate section at the end.

Try to cover a range of examples, may be online or B2B examples. Use your file of examples to inform this section.

**Conclusion**
Why companies need information.

Constraints on the use of data – Ethics and legislation.

Future – Where will we be in Five years?

# Question 2.2

## Splash Ltd

The Spanish-based cosmetics company Splash Ltd has built an international retail chain that is in a strong expansion phase. Its fresh, handmade soaps and cosmetics are available in 240 stores worldwide. The emphasis is on making and selling products without animal ingredients, made from only fresh fruit and vegetables, finest essential oils and safe synthetics. It controls the whole process of getting its products to the consumer, including design, manufacturing and retail.

The retail stores look like a cross between a cheese shop and a market stall, with slabs of soap and other fresh products stacked ready for cutting and bagging. The retail environment is dominated by an aroma of soaps and perfumes. The company is now planning to open its first UK store in the centre of London.

Prior to designing the outlet, determining the product range and potential promotions, the company is keen to undertake a programme of market research with potential customers, to examine the buying behaviour and attitudes of British consumers of high-quality soap and cosmetic products.

The company hopes that answers to such questions will help in the successful launch of their first UK store.

The company is willing to spend up to £50 000 on the research project.

*Note*: The above data has been based on a fictitious situation drawing on a variety of events and does not reflect the management practices of any particular organization.

**PART B** – Answer **TWO** questions only

## Question 2

As a recent graduate recruited to the marketing department of Splash Ltd, you have received an enquiry from the marketing director asking for a report which addresses the following:

(a) The descriptive, comparative, diagnostic and predictive roles that marketing information can provide.

**(8 marks)**

(b) Why are some marketing research departments in large organizations widening their remit beyond marketing research?

**(10 marks)**

(c) What ethical issues are raised by such a change being made?

**(7 marks)**
**(Total 25 marks)**

## Answer

### Part B Question 2.a

To: Marketing Director – Splash Ltd

From: Arwi Cleenyet

Date: 7/6/05

Subject: The roles, future and issues associated with market research and its related concepts.

Marketing information is vital to any business wishing to remain viable. It is data from the internal and external environment of the company which have been gathered, evaluated, sorted and analysed in order to assist the marketing managers in their role of planning, implementing and controlling.

Market Information can have one of four roles:

### Descriptive
- This information generally describes the who, where, how and when.
- The information can give us a profile of people most likely to or who most often buy a product or use a service. EPOS is very useful for such things.
- EPOS is also useful to find out when they are most likely to buy the product and in what region a number of outlets are available.
- Customer databases and contact/transaction records are also useful for this purpose.
- Satisfaction forms and surveys can be helpful too.

## Comparative

- This information allows the company to compare itself to others in the same market.
- Some areas to be compared could be impact of advertising vs. the competitors, price, promotions, market share.
- Market information can also be used to compare sales in one area vs. another; sales of one product vs a similar competitor's product; effectiveness of sales campaign and effectiveness of sales force with regard to orders taken, sales made, achievement vs. target and territories.

## Diagnostic

- This information tells us what is bought or identification of what the market is doing.
- Using diagnostic methods we can assess potential of a target market by looking at current market growth and previous growth and what is currently in fashion/desirable.
- Predictive roles
- Allows/helps a company to foretell what will happen in the market
- Need to forecast events
- Can use previous sales history to forecast trends
- Competitor information, that is new product may have negative impact on your sales or potential problems may have positive impact.
- Supply problems
- Raw material sourcing problems
- Latest technology
- All can help analyse what may happen in the markets.

## Question 2.b

As the industry grows and changes there is a trend towards going beyond market research and into database research. The aim of developing a database is to better assist the marketing managers in their decision-making. A database comprises of a marketing information system as outlined below and allows collection, evaluation, analysis and distribution of pertinent, timely and accurate data in order to assist marketing decisions.

A good database is accessible by all, easily integrated into the current resources and allows more accurate analysis of data, forecasting of markets, segmentation of customers and forecasting of trends.

All of this has the ultimate aim of not only increasing sales or market share, achieving penetration or keeping competitors out but it also incorporates the fundamentals of customer relationship management.

CRM aims to improve loyalty and improve customer relationship and add value and service by means of five key elements:

1. Tangibles
2. Responsiveness
3. Empathy
4. Reliability
5. Assurance

Thus, the customer feels 'cared for' and appreciated. They are made to feel an important and almost integral part of the company. It also allows for their loyalty to be rewarded, for example Loyalty card points.

A database can be implemented using the following process:

1. Business review: Where we are, what we have, where we want to be.
2. Data audit: What data we have now and how we use it.
3. Data strategy and segmentation: What do we need, how will it be segmented.
4. Data verification: Is the data correct, completely up to date, not duplicated.
5. Hardware and software: Can it be integrated into what we have; cost involved.
6. Management: Who will manage it in-house/external.
7. Application: What will all the info be used for.
8. Review: Assess benefits of the database.

Since Splash is moving into a new market, the introduction of a database could prove to be very beneficial in segmenting, targeting and identifying new opportunities.

## Question 2.c

One problem with database research is the question of ethics. Although Splash is an ethical company in all of its undertakings we must continue to be so in this area also.

The search for information is governed by many codes of conduct and participants need to be made aware of the nature of the research, who will use it, what it will be used for and anonymity.

We need to be ethical in order to create goodwill, trust, professionalism and confidentiality.

Storage of data is subject to the Data Protection Act 1998 and the EU Data Protection Directive. We must also take into account the Human Rights Act 2005 and the rules in place now that protect a consumer's rights to have their names withdrawn from a database or to be taken off a register.

Research is covered by ESOMAR and MRS protecting the client and research company. Data storage is subject to scrutiny and the respondent has the right to request any incorrect data be destroyed. Data cannot be passed on unless the respondent has given permission. It must be securely stored and cannot be held for an unreasonable amount of time.

However, if Splash continues to be as transparent and ethical in this respect as it is in all other business transactions, I see no reason as to why we should encounter untoward problems with incorporating a database research system as well as our marketing research objectives.

## Comments

Very good answer. In section A, good definitions of the different types of information. Good understanding of the changes happening in section B, a few more marks would have been awarded for a greater use of examples of customer information sources (loyalty cards etc.). Demonstrates understanding of the ethical issues in section C.

# Question 3.1

You have been appointed as marketing manager for the Drama Factory, a small regional arts and entertainments venue. You want to develop a marketing database to facilitate the marketing of the centre, but need to convince the trustees of the centre of its value in order to receive funding.

Write a report for the trustees outlining the process involved in establishing a database for marketing.

How will external suppliers help this process?

What applications will the database facilitate?

## Outline answer

Define the marketing database and outline its role in marketing decision-making. Outline the process of setting up the database. Under each heading, discuss the requirements for good practice:

- Business review
- Data audit
- Data strategy, specification and verification
- Data verification
- Hardware/software
- Data capture, maintenance and enhancement
- Management issues – should the database be run in-house/out-of-house
- Applications
- Review.

Discuss the advantages and disadvantages of in-house operation.

### Disadvantages
- Cost of hardware and consultancy may be significant.
- Speed of development can be slow.
- Service standards may be lower than those from an out-of-house provider.
- Skills in IT and strategy may be weak.
- Specialist processing skills may not be readily available.

### Advantages
- Strategic orientation of the business should be assured.
- Integration and access are manageable.
- Greater control and ownership.
- Cost may be lower.

Finally, outline the advantages of data bureaux.

## Database bureaux have the following advantages

- Skills and systems are developed and tested.
- No fixed costs. You pay for what you get.
- Speed. Resources can be allocated to ensure prompt delivery and penalty clauses can be built in.
- Performance guarantees can be built into the contract.

Often, there is migration from the bureau into the organization. This means that learning can take place at lower risk. The usual approach is outlined below:

- Set up the bureau
- Sort out data issues
- Set up updates and enhancements

- o Develop internally
- o Run the two in parallel
- o Import.

Conclude by focusing on the need to establish a business case for a database and establishing the most cost-effective solution.

Applications can be structured around the marketing planning process. This includes analysis, objective setting, segmentation, the development of strategies, campaigns and controls, or as the text identifies find, acquire, develop, keep and reactivate. You should give examples relevant to the context of the question.

## Question 3.2

CIM Professional Series Stage Two: Marketing Research and Information

### Jack Ltd

Jack Ltd is a leading international speciality retailer offering clothing, accessories and personal care products for men, women, children and babies under the Jack brand name. In the United Kingdom, Jack Ltd operates more than 150 stores nationwide. Each of the stores employs sales associates and other store personnel that are trained to answer customers' questions about fabric, fit and fashion and to help them select merchandise that's perfect for them. However, even with this training, around 85 per cent of all potential customers that enter a Jack store (measured using electronic counters in the doorways of each store) leave without buying anything. Senior management are keen to reduce this percentage, however, they are unclear as to the reasons why people leave their stores empty-handed. It may be due to the product range, store layout, service quality, pricing or any range of factors. Marketing research is therefore needed to explore the reasons why such a large percentage of potential customers fail to make a purchase.

The company hopes that answers to such questions will help to identify ways to increase sales amongst these customers.

The company is willing to spend up to £40 000 on the research project.

**PART B** – Answer **TWO** Questions Only

### Question 2

As a recent graduate recruited to the marketing department of Jack Ltd, you have received an enquiry from the marketing director asking for a report which sets out:

(a)  The differences between a marketing decision support system and a customer database
**(8 marks)**

(b)  The issues involved in using the respondent details from the marketing research project to create a customer database.
**(8 marks)**

(c)  The benefits of building a customer database through the creation of a loyalty card scheme.
**(9 marks)**
**(Total 25 marks)**

# Answer (Grade C)

FAO: Marketing Director/Jack Ltd

From: Miss Jones, Marketing Graduate, Jack Ltd

Re: Customer database

Date: 7 Dec 2004

FAO Mr Smith

Thanks for the recent memo with re to customer database (dated 1 Dec 2004)

With specific regard to your queries:

## Question 2.a

Differences between a marketing decision support system and customer database are to my knowledge:

- o A customer database will exist to hold information about customer, for example name, address, age, job, what they are interested in, and so on.
- o A marketing decision support system will hold information and data which will help marketing manager and key management personnel make decisions. This type of system is usually supported by a MkIS – a central point of information, which features internal info, external info, primary research and has an IT system in place to add efficiency and effectiveness.
- o Typical information contained in a marketing decision support system include: information on current pricing policies, sales volume, promotional spend, distribution outlets, supplies and marketing budget allocation. This type of info will come internally from customers (majority).
- o Information being imputed into the customer database will come externally from customers themselves. Usually done via loyalty cards, data capture forms and consensual self-administration forms.
- o Both databases have different objectives:

    - Customer = understand customers better
    - Mass = helping marketers access into before making decisions

## Question 2.b

There are a number of issues which Jack Ltd need to bear in mind before going ahead and using respondents' details from recent marketing research activity:

- o All respondents taking part in marketing research have to be kept anonymous to protect their identity. This was laid out to them prior to their taking part to include them on the database which goes against this. Breaks trust between respondent and organization.
- o It is illegal to use the name record and use respondents' details as laid down by the ICC/ ESOMAR
- o If found out, this could mean that several of our marketing teams could be barred from carrying out any future marketing research.
- o Respondents may resent being approached/communicated with especially if their permission has not been sought. This may in turn put them off Jack Ltd for good. It is always best to get the customers' consent before including them on any database.

○ This could be a waste of time – many respondents/participants didn't form part of Jack Ltd audience, for example in Exit polls; many people were browsing and didn't intend to buy and have never bought anything from Jack Ltd. So including them on the database would be a waste of time and sending them out info/deals would also waste time and money.

○ I, personally, would not take part in this type of activity; this goes against my integrity and everything I was taught whilst studying marketing. We rely on respondents to help us do our jobs and to break that trust and use respondents for our own gain is unethical and may put off the particular respondent taking part in any marketing activity ever again.

## Question 2.c

Benefits of building a customer database through the creation of loyalty card scheme; my key points are listed below to this type of activity:

○ By introducing a customer loyalty scheme, customers feel direct benefits by either collective points or money off and Jack Ltd can monitor all customer transactions transparently.

○ This type of scheme would encourage customer loyalty, customer retention, customer satisfaction and repeat purchases.

○ You wouldn't have been able to miss all the news regarding Tesco's grasp of the market. Some put this down to the Tesco Clubcard which gave them in-depth knowledge in customer behaviour, allowed them to segment the market and target specific sections of the market with appropriate info/deals and at the right time. This provided them with key customer information which they have used accordingly. Aim of loyalty schemes is to focus and understand customers whilst at the same time rewarding customers.

○ A huge investment will be required from Jack Ltd but in the long term this should pay off. Marketing managers will have all the unique info at hand when making big marketing decisions; this type of information is a huge asset to the organization. 'Information is power' as Bacon once said.

A customer database built on a loyalty scheme will allow you to mine for information which in turn could help in a variety of issues. Look for correlations between type of customer and time/ day of sale. This could help store operations, layouts and procedures.

○ A customer database will allow you to profile your customer and even provide the possibility of cross-selling products.

○ Customer loyalty is extremely important nowadays especially with the level of competition we face – retaining customers is far more profitable than attracting new ones. Loyal customers are also more likely to spend more.

○ Introducing a system like this, will focus Jack Ltd to becoming committed to customer service. We don't want to go the way MTS is going by not giving the customer what they want. Knowing the customer is key to being successful and profitable, 'analyse, plan, implement and control – Kotler'. Finding out what customers want is key to our future success. I hope these points help. If you have any further questions, please do not hesitate to call me.

Kind regards
Miss Jones
Marketing Graduate, Jack Ltd

## Comments

Very good answer. In section A, good definitions of customer database and marketing decision support system. However, slightly more detail needed about the components of the marketing decision support system and how it is used. Section B needs more detail about the MRS Code of Conduct, The Data Protection Act, the responsibilities to market research respondents and transparency about the use being made of data. Section C is good, although it could focus more on how the data could be used.

## Question 3.3

CIM Professional Series Stage Two: Marketing Research and Information

### Donaldson Builders Merchants

Donaldson Builders Merchants is a small chain of builders merchants located in the central belt of Scotland. The company has four outlets located around the edge of the major conurbations of Edinburgh and Glasgow. These supply to small builders, plumbers, roofers and similar tradesmen as well as some members of the public (i.e. those more skilled in major do-it-yourself renovations and house improvements). Customers may collect items from the trade counter at the warehouse or have the items delivered direct to the building site or house by the company's fleet of 14 lorries. The lorries are equipped with hoists for handling the larger items.

Donaldson supplies:

- Timber and timber products
- Bricks and paving
- Sand and aggregates
- Roofing materials
- Plumbing and heating supplies
- A small range of hand tools.

The company provides credit to the majority of its trade customers. As a result it has a computerized database with details on most of its trade customers relating to name, address, trading address, telephone number, type of business, and purchasing patterns. There are approximately 1100 customers on the database, which probably represents 85 per cent of the company's customers. For the other 15 per cent of customers (the public and trade customers who do not have a credit account), the database holds no record, with the exception of a delivery address if a delivery is required.

The market in which Donaldson operates is becoming more competitive, with the company losing share to national chains such as Jewson and a number of recently opened B&Q trade depots. Tom Donaldson, the Managing Director, feels that the company's personal service and flexibility are far superior to these competitors, and is therefore keen to build on this and find ways in which to compete other than on price. The company has never undertaken research before but is keen to find out more from its customers about:

- Their existing and future purchasing behaviour.
- Their attitudes towards Donaldson Builders Merchants (such as product range, service, flexibility of delivery, etc.).
- Their suggestions about improvements required in Donaldson's offering.

They are willing to spend up to £50000 on the research project.

## Part B Question 2

Tom Donaldson is keen to make more use of his company's database and turn it into a customer database for marketing intelligence and customer relationship purposes. He has asked you as a newly qualified Marketing Executive within the firm to produce a report which sets out:

(a)  The benefits and weaknesses of database information to a company such as Donaldson Builders Merchants.

**(7 marks)**

(b)  The manner in which data should be stored and processed for it to be of most use in the provision of marketing intelligence and customer relationship activity.

**(9 marks)**

(c)  The need for the distinction between marketing research and the creation of databases for direct marketing purposes.

**(9 marks)**
**(25 marks in total)**

## Answer

### Debriefing Part B Question 2a

The benefits of the database should be laid out. These include:

- o  Better understanding of customers and their buying behaviour
- o  The ability to quantify loyalty and the value of customers
- o  The ability to track response to communication.

### Disadvantages include:
- o  Does not explain why customers behave in the way they do
- o  We are using past behaviour as a predictor of future behaviour
- o  Only shows the details of those customers who are on the database and does not include non- or lapsed customers.

### Debriefing Part B Question 2b

Answers should cover the capturing of data, its formatting, validation and verification of data and the deduplication of data.

### Debriefing Part B Question 2c

Central to this is the codes of conduct governing activity in the market.

Candidates should also cover the requirement for anonymity in research, the need for transparent relations with customers, the impossibility of generalization from database information to marketing research. And the need for aggregated rather than personal data in research.

# Question 3.4

Davidson Hotels operate a group of seven hotels in the United Kingdom. The hotels are all rated at the three- or four-star level, with four of them having swimming pools and leisure centres. They tend to be located close to tourist/leisure type areas of outstanding natural beauty and local heritage sites. Their customer mix has traditionally consisted of 50 per cent business travellers, 30 per cent coach parties, and 20 per cent leisure travellers/leisure breaks. However, with the growth in budget hotels offering standard rooms and limited additional services, the number of business travellers has dropped by more than 38 per cent over the past 12 months. The coach party market is relatively static, therefore the company's main opportunity for growth is seen by management as being in the leisure travel market, with the swimming pools being used to promote all-weather/all-year leisure destinations.

The company is therefore keen to understand more about the leisure travel sector, in particular:

o  The trends in the market
o  The criteria used by leisure travellers when selecting their accommodation in areas with outstanding natural beauty or heritage sites
o  The reasons why existing leisure customers use Davidson Hotels and their likelihood of returning to the same hotel or another hotel in the Davidson Hotel chain.

They are willing to spend up to £50 000 on the research project.

*Note*: The above material has been based on a fictitious company for assessment purposes.

## Part B Question 2

Tom Davidson in Question 1 is of the opinion that his hotels' management should know much more about the characteristics of their guests. This would reduce the need for research and would also be useful for future direct marketing activity, building loyalty, and obtaining repeat business. Currently, basic name and address information is stored on the hotels' reservations systems. However, this is only used for operational and billing purposes. He has asked you as a new recruit to the company to produce a report that sets out:

(a)  The types of information that could be collected on a database about hotel guests and the manner in which the information could be collected.

**(9 marks)**

(b)  The benefits that would result from holding such information.

**(7 marks)**

(c)  The issues involved in attempting to merge the information from the marketing research study with the databases.

**(9 marks)**
**(25 marks in total)**

### Answer

Go to www.cim.co.uk for specimen answers to this question.

## Question 4.1

You are the marketing manager for a company marketing china collectibles. You wish to establish an online service for your products. You wish to recruit a research agency to evaluate the potential of this market. Write a briefing document for the project. Explain how you would choose a short list of agencies to pitch for your business and how you would go about selecting the company to do the work.

## Answer

This question asks for a report-type approach. The briefing document outline provides a good structure. You should write the answer as you would lay out a brief in real life, and the use of separate pages for each section, numbered sections and even a contents page and executive summary can show an examiner that you are in control of the paper.

Remember the structure of the briefing document?

- Identification details
- Current business position
- Marketing and business objectives should be laid down and distinguished between
- Research objectives
- How the results will be used?
- Outline methodology
- Sample details
- Previous research
- Timings
- Budget
- Deliverables
- Terms and conditions
- Key personnel.

In choosing the agency, the following points should be considered:

- The agency's ability to understand the brief and translate it into a comprehensive proposal
- The compatibility of agency and client teams. Can we work with them?
- The evidence of innovation on the proposal. Has the agency added value?
- Evidence of understanding of the market and the problem facing the organization
- Sound methodology
- Meeting budget and time scales
- Relevant experience
- Professional body memberships.

The way a question like this would be assessed by the examiner is to consider the commercial sense of the content. As a delegate, you would be expected to outline methodology and sampling techniques in the brief.

# Question 4.2

CIM Professional Series Stage Two: Marketing Research and Information

## Donaldson Builders Merchants

Donaldson Builders Merchants is a small chain of builders merchants located in the central belt of Scotland. The company has four outlets located around the edge of the major conurbations of Edinburgh and Glasgow. These supply to small builders, plumbers, roofers and similar tradesmen as well as some members of the public (i.e. those more skilled in major do-it-yourself renovations and house improvements). Customers may collect items from the trade counter at the warehouse or have the items delivered direct to the building site or house by the company's fleet of 14 lorries. The lorries are equipped with hoists for handling items.

Donaldson supplies:

- o Timber and timber products
- o Bricks and paving
- o Sand and aggregates
- o Roofing materials
- o Plumbing and heating supplies
- o A small range of hand tools.

The company provides credit to the majority of its trade customers. As a result it has a computerized database with details on most of its trade customers relating to name, address, trading address, telephone number, type of business, and purchasing patterns. There are approximately 1100 customers on the database, which probably represents 85 per cent of the company's customers. For the other 15 per cent of customers (the public and trade customers who do not have a credit account), the database holds no record, with the exception of a delivery address if a delivery is required.

The market in which Donaldson operates is becoming more competitive, with the company losing share to national chains such as Jewson and a number of recently opened B&Q trade depots. Tom Donaldson, the Managing Director, feels that the company's personal service and flexibility are far superior to these competitors, and is therefore keen to build on this and find ways in which to compete other than on price. The company has never undertaken research before but is keen to find out more from its customers about:

- o Their existing and future purchasing behaviour
- o Their attitudes towards Donaldson Builders Merchants (such as product range, service, flexibility of delivery, etc.)
- o Their suggestions about improvements required in Donaldson's offering.

They are willing to spend up to £50 000 on the research project.

## Part A Question 1

You are the director of a market research agency and have been asked to:

(a) Identify any further information that you would require from Donaldson prior to writing a proposal.

**(10 marks)**

(b) Having made reasonable assumptions regarding the answers to the information required in Question 1a, produce a short three- to five-page proposal to address the needs of Tom Donaldson. (For the purpose of this question your proposal should exclude the sections relating to personal CVs, related experience and references and contract details.)

**(40 marks)**
**(50 marks in total)**

## n 4

in Question 1 has never undertaken research before, he needs guidance in the gency to undertake the research. He has received proposals from three agencies ed you as an old friend who has used agencies in the past to provide a report on:

selection criteria to use in determining the successful agency.

**(15 marks)**

ie elements of the professional codes of market and social research practice that elate to the relationships between researchers and clients.

**(10 marks)**

**(25 marks in total)**

## Answer

### Debriefing Part A Question 1a

As with any marketing question there are a range of possible answers to this question; however, you should have organized your answer around the following points.

What is the background to the research? Why does the research need to be carried out? What is the nature of the business and its customers?

What are the precise objectives for the research? What business decisions will be informed by the research?

Does Tom have any idea on the type of methodology and sample design he would like to employ? What access can the agency have to customer data? What about lapsed and non-customers? Within the company's customers what job roles should be targeted?

What report and presentation requirements are there?

What timings are required?

### Debriefing Part A Question 1b

The Proposal

The proposal should follow the standard structure as outlined in the text. Remember the headings?

- o Identification data
- o Situation analysis

    - The client, his business situation and its customers

- o Research objectives

    - Precise and more detail than in the case

- o Methodology and rationale

    - Include quantitative and qualitative

- ○ Sample

  - – Brief details on the nature of the sample

- ○ Fieldwork
- ○ Questionnaire/topic guide

  - – This can be included but will need to be in outline only

- ○ Data handling and processing

  - – Type of analysis to be carried out could be included here

- ○ Reporting

  - – When and to whom and how?

- ○ Timetable

  - – Schedule laid out for activity

- ○ Costs

  - – Some detail required here.

You were asked in the question to exclude certain elements. So do not waste time and miss marks by bothering to include them in your answer.

## Debriefing Part B Question 4a
Answers should cover the following points:

- ○ The agency's ability to understand the brief and translate it into a comprehensive proposal
- ○ The compatibility of agency and client teams. Can we work with them?
- ○ The evidence of innovation in the proposal. Has the agency added value?
- ○ Evidence of understanding of the market and the problem facing the organization
- ○ Technical capacity
- ○ Previous experience in the sector and location
- ○ Sound methodology
- ○ Meeting budget and time scales
- ○ Relevant experience
- ○ Financial stability
- ○ Reputation
- ○ Resources.

## Debriefing Part B Question 4b
Answers will draw on the ICC MRS code of conduct and will vary according to the local interpretation of these codes. However the following general areas will be covered.

- ○ Confidentiality
- ○ Subcontracting

- o Proposals and costs are property of the agency. Briefs and specifications and the data gathered is property of the client
- o The need to distinguish between findings and interpretation and recommendations
- o Contractual details.

# Question 4.3

CIM Professional Series Stage Two: Marketing Research and Information

Davidson Hotels operate a group of seven hotels in the United Kingdom. The hotels are all rated at the three- or four-star level, with four of them having swimming pools and leisure centres. They tend to be located close to tourist/leisure type areas of outstanding natural beauty and local heritage sites. Their customer mix has traditionally consisted of 50 per cent business travellers, 30 per cent coach parties and 20 per cent leisure travellers/leisure breaks. However, with the growth in budget hotels offering standard rooms and limited additional services, the number of business travellers has dropped by more than 38 per cent over the past 12 months. The coach party market is relatively static, therefore the company's main opportunity for growth is seen by management as being in the leisure travel market, with the swimming pools being used to promote all-weather/all-year leisure destinations.

The company is therefore keen to understand more about the leisure travel sector, in particular:

- o The trends in the market
- o The criteria used by leisure travellers when selecting their accommodation in areas with outstanding natural beauty or heritage sites
- o The reasons why existing leisure customers use Davidson Hotels and their likelihood of returning to the same hotel or another hotel in the Davidson Hotel chain.

They are willing to spend up to £50 000 on the research project.

*Note*: The above material has been based on a fictitious company for assessment purposes.

## PART A Question 1

You are the manager of a market research agency and have been asked to:

(a) Identify any further information that you would require from Tom Davidson, the chief executive of the company, prior to writing a marketing research proposal.

**(10 marks)**

(b) Using the information in Question 1a and making reasonable assumptions, you are required to produce a short 3- to 5-page proposal to address the needs of Tom Davidson. (For the purpose of this question, your proposal should exclude the sections relating to personal CVs, related experience and references and contract details.)

**(40 marks)**
**(50 marks in total)**

## Answer

Go to www.cim.co.uk for specimen answers to this question.

# Question 4.4

Professional Diploma in Marketing: Marketing Research and Information

## Splash Ltd

The Spanish-based cosmetics company Splash Ltd has built an international retail chain that is in a strong expansion phase. Its fresh, handmade soaps and cosmetics are available in 240 stores worldwide. The emphasis is on making and selling products without animal ingredients, made from only fresh fruit and vegetables, finest essential oils and safe synthetics. It controls the whole process of getting its products to the consumer, including design, manufacturing and retail.

The retail stores look like a cross between a cheese shop and a market stall, with slabs of soap and other fresh products stacked ready for cutting and bagging. The retail environment is dominated by an aroma of soaps and perfumes. The company is now planning to open its first UK store in the centre of London.

Prior to designing the outlet, determining the product range and potential promotions, the company is keen to undertake a programme of market research with potential customers, to examine the buying behaviour and attitudes of British consumers of high-quality soap and cosmetic products.

The company hopes that answers to such questions will help in the successful launch of their first UK store.

The company is willing to spend up to £50 000 on the research project.

*Note*: The above data has been based on a fictitious situation drawing on a variety of events and does not reflect the management practices of any particular organization.

## PART A Question 1

You are a research executive in a market research agency and have been asked to:

(a) Identify appropriate further information that you would require from the company, prior to writing a proposal.

**(10 marks)**

(b) Having made reasonable assumptions regarding the answers to the information required in part 1.a, produce a proposal to address the research needs of the company.

**(40 marks)**

For the purpose of this question, your proposal should exclude the sections relating to personal CVs, related experience and references and contract details

**(Total 50 marks)**

## Answer

### Part A Question 1.a
**Memorandum**
From: Jane Ford, Research Exec, Joe Bloggs Research Agency

To: Research Manager, Joe Bloggs Research Agency

Date: 7/6/05

Re: Research proposal for Splash Ltd.

Our agency has been approached by Splash Ltd to propose a programme of research to aid in the successful launch of their first UK store. In order to design a research plan that will best meet their needs I have identified a number of areas where further information would be useful:

- Do they have any information about the UK market for high-quality soap and cosmetics already?
- Do they have details of who their customers are in other countries, especially countries that might be considered similar to the United Kingdom?
- Do they have any information on the area where they plan to open their London store, for example average *footfall* at different times of day, types of consumers that shop there and so on?
- What is the exact price range they will be offering, and who will be their target customers?
- Is there a specific reason for the choice of a central London site?
- Are they planning to expand further into other UK cities, and if so where?
- Who do they see as their key competitors in the market?
- Are there any specific products they want to test with UK consumers?
- Will the London store be available to use as a venue for research?
- Will they have any creative concepts (e.g. advertisements, POS material, packaging) that will need to be tested?
- When will stimulus be available (e.g. products/creatives)
- When are results required by?
- How would they like results to be reported?

The answers to these questions will help us when designing a number of areas of the research:

- Sample design (to aim at target customers)
- Discussion guide/questionnaire content
- Interview length (to cover all stimulus)
- Data collection method, for example whether it needs to be face-to-face.

## Comments

A good answer. Large number of questions relating to background material, although could possibly have asked for a little more on areas relating to objectives and methodology such as: (a) For objectives – the depth of information required and asking for specific detail on what the client means by buyer behaviour (is this the decision-making process/purchasing patterns/selection of retailers or what?) and attitudes (to what specific areas). (b) For method – qualitative or quantitative; target segments that should be interviewed; geographical boundaries to the study; will clients attend group discussions and so on.

## Part A Question 1.b
### Research proposal

Prepared by: Jane Ford, Joe Bloggs Agency Background

Prepared for: Consumer insight team, Splash

Date: 7/6/05

### Background

Following a period of successful expansion worldwide, Splash Ltd is planning to move to the UK market with the launch of a central London store. The UK market presents a strong opportunity for growth, but Splash will face stiff competition and it is therefore essential for Splash to deliver a well-positioned proposition that has real value to the consumer. With the market leader in the UK mass beauty market (Boots) showing signs of decline in recent years, and the growth of price competition from the grocery multiples, Splash will have to deliver a very strong offering in order to succeed at the higher end of the market.

In order to help Splash tailor its offering to the needs of the target consumer, a research programme is planned to help Splash understand the buying behaviour and attitudes within their market.

This document sets out our agency's recommended approach to the research along with associated timescales and costs.

### Objectives

The business objective could be stated as: To ensure a profitable and sustainable move into the UK market through a detailed understanding of the target consumer.

The overall research objective is therefore: To provide a detailed understanding of the attitudes and behaviours associated with the high-quality soaps and cosmetics consumer in the United Kingdom.

This overall objective breaks down into a number of key areas:

1. Identify who is most likely to buy high quality soap and cosmetics (e.g. Are they male/ female, younger or older)
2. What motivations do consumers of these products have (e.g. Are they concerned about appearance, cruelty to animals, fair trade, cost)
3. What do they enjoy about the shopping process for these products and what do they find frustrating?
4. Which of the Splash products do they find most appealing and are there any they don't like?
5. How do they respond to the experience of the Splash store?

### Methodology

A number of different options are available in order to meet the research objectives. Assuming that Splash does not at this stage have a detailed understanding of the UK market, secondary research can be conducted to provide a general overview and to aid the design of subsequent primary research which will provide more specific understanding of Splash's target customer.

### Secondary Research

This is also known as 'desk research' as it can be conducted from the office rather than having to go out into the field. A number of different sources are available to the desk researcher, and the most appropriate should be selected based on:

- How recently it was collated
- Relevance to the objectives of the research
- Validity of the methods used
- Cost of procurement

It is recommended that the following sources are used in this case:

- Market reports (such as Mintel or Data monitor)
- Trade/Industry journals
- Financial statements of key competitors (e.g. Books/Body Shop)

This period of desk research will provide an understanding of:

- Market size and growth
- Key players
- Trends in the market
- Potential gaps in the market

It will also help when deciding on sampling and data collection for the primary research phase.

### Primary Research

Primary research is essential to help us understand the target consumer better, in particular their attitudes, and how these might shape future behaviour.

It is possible to conduct primary research by qualitative methods (this helps us understand why consumers might act in a certain way) or quantitative methods (to help us identify how many consumers are likely to act in a certain way).

In order to meet all the research objectives it is recommended that a mixed methodology be used to give Splash a full understanding of the market.

### Qualitative research

This can be conducted using either one-to-one interviews or group discussions, facilitated by a trained moderator. In this case, we would recommend group discussions for a number of reasons:

- Group discussions provide a creative environment where ideas can be explored and respondents can bounce ideas off each other
- Given the nature of the research, noone is likely to feel uncomfortable talking in a group (as they might when discussing financial services). On the contrary they are likely to enjoy the group experience and therefore their responses will be more spontaneous.
- Logistically, group discussions will be easier to administer, meaning the research can cover more people in a more cost-effective way.

### Sample

The exact sample must be reflective of the target customer; we recommend the following breakdown be applied (subject to review after the desk research)

- Eight groups of 6–8 respondents all to be non-rejectors of the products and brand.
- Predominantly held in London. However, in order to help Splash move into other UK cities, some groups could be held in other locations.
- Groups split between different ages, life stages and SEG groups, for example

   AB 18–40
   AB 40–55
   CIC2 18–40
   CIC2 40–55

- It is assumed that all respondents will be women (unless there are products specifically targeted at men, in which case two groups should be held with men only).

Discussion guide/content: It is recommended that, if possible, groups are held in the London store so that the shopping experience can be discussed in full.

Other topics covered will be the products, packaging, pricing and promotions that Splash are considering launching. General shopping habits, brand perceptions and media consumption relative to the market should also be covered, as should motivations. It is anticipated that the groups will need to last 1 1/2 hours.

### Quantitative Research

It will be best to conduct this face-to-face, as this will allow the interviewer to show the respondent different products and/or packaging options. Other options such as telephone or on-line self-completion are less likely to be effective in this context due to the nature of the products being tested, as respondents will need to be able to feel and smell them. However, telephone could be used if Splash does not want to focus on which products are likely to be best for the UK market. Interviews could be conducted on-street, however this will make it difficult for the interviewers who will need to carry the stimulus and will also limit the interview length. It is therefore recommended that interviews be conducted in a hall; this will be a central location such as a hotel conference room.

### Sample

Random sampling will not be possible in this case as no sampling frame will be available. Quota sampling will therefore be used, and it has been proved that this method is generally accurate enough for most research purposes.

Sample size must be determined by the level of confidence required from the results. The larger the sample, the smaller the confidence interval, and therefore the smaller the risk that the reported result is not representative of the population as a whole.

Sample size must also be determined by the level of homogeneity in the population. The more subgroups that must be analysed, the larger the overall sample must be (each subgroup needs to be at least 50 to be considered as robust).

Given the level of risk involved in the decisions to be made is moderate (e.g. It is important to get the product and the promotion decisions right, but the results will not be used to say yes or no to the major investment in the London store altogether) and the relative homogeneity of the target consumer (women who shop in the area and buy into the higher-end cosmetics). We recommend a sample size of 250 for the hall test. The restrictions and quotas should mirror the structure used within the qualitative research.

### Questionnaire content

The questionnaire will focus on the appeal of different products, price ranges and promotional material, allowing Splash to identify the best offerings to have in store to maximize sales. The questionnaire will also cover details about the respondents' buying behaviour, for instance how much they spend on cosmetics, how frequently they buy different products, where they tend to shop and why, and what would tempt them to try a new supplier. It will also test the appeal of different marketing messages such as 'only made from fresh fruit and vegetables'.

### Reporting

Splash will be provided with the following outputs:

- Detailed report and analysis in Word (covering all three stages)
- Debrief of results to key research personnel and debrief document in PowerPoint
- Transcripts and videos of the discussion groups
- Data tables from the quantitative survey showing key breaks (such as age) as well as overall results
- Statistical analysis of the quantitative data (e.g. Indication of confidence interval for each result, $x^2$ testing).

### Timescales

| Week | Activity |
| --- | --- |
| 1 | Commission/briefing meeting |
| 2/3 | Desk research |
| 4 | Discussion guide design |
| 5/6 | Qualitative fieldwork |
| 7 | Interim debrief |
| 8 | Questionnaire design |
| 9/10 | Quantitative fieldwork |
| 11/12/13 | Analysis |
| 14 | Report and debrief |

### Costs

Desk research               £5000

(Exec time and report costs)

Qualitative research      £25 000 (including expenses and incentives for respondents)

Quantitative research     £20 000 (including hall test venue)

## Comments

Very good background/rationale section. The objectives are probably the weakest part of this answer as they simply list a series of questions. They could be laid out better with more detail being given in the form of objectives and information targets. The methodology section is good in as much as it sets out the scale of the research and attempts to justify the different approaches. Possibly the quantitative research could be better explained and laid out. The reporting, timescales and costs are very good and appropriate to the study.

# Question 4.5

Professional Diploma in Marketing: Marketing Research and Information

## Jack Ltd

Jack Ltd is a leading international speciality retailer offering clothing, accessories and personal care products for men, women, children and babies under the Jack brand name. In the United Kingdom, Jack Ltd operates more than 150 stores nationwide. Each of the stores employs sales associates and other store personnel that are trained to answer customers' questions about fabric, fit and fashion and to help them select merchandise that's perfect for them. However, even with this training, around 85 per cent of all potential customers that enter a Jack store (measured using electronic counters in the doorways of each store) leave without buying anything. Senior management are keen to reduce this percentage; however, they are unclear as to the reasons why people leave their stores empty-handed. It may be due to the product range, store layout, service quality, pricing or any range of factors. Marketing research is therefore needed to explore the reasons why such a large percentage of potential customers fail to make a purchase.

The company hopes that answers to such questions will help to identify ways to increase sales amongst these customers.

The company is willing to spend up to £40 000 on the research project.

## PART A Question 1

You are a research executive in a market research agency and have been asked to:

(a) Identify any further information that you would require from the company, prior to writing a proposal.

**(10 marks)**

(b) Having made reasonable assumptions regarding the answers to the information required in Part 1.a, produce a proposal to address the research needs of the company. (For the purpose of this question, your proposal should exclude the sections relating to personal CVs, related experience and references and contract details).

**(40 marks)**
**(Total 50 Marks)**

## Answer

### PART A Question 1.a (Grade C)
**Additional Information**

We would require the following information prior to writing the proposal

1. Situation Analysis

   o If it is an international retailer, in which other countries they operate
   o What type of clothing, accessories and personal care products they sell?(smart clothes, sporty ones, bags, etc.)
   o Which is their target market? (age, class, . . . . . )
   o Exact location of the 150 stores in the United Kingdom
   o Also we would need to know their profitability and turnover, also mission and vision
   o Finally, we will need to know their main competitors and if they have any environmental pressures.

2. Objectives

   o What do they mean with 'ways to increase sales'?
   o These ways to increase sales will be for next year, next 6 months or is it a long-term objective?

3. Methodology

   o Do they have any database or MkIS that we can use (existing customers, former customers, competitor's customers)?
   o Does the company have strong views on contacting unhappy customers, ex-customers or competitor customers? Main contact in company.

4. Report and presentation

   o When the research should be submitted?
   o When the report should be presented?
   o How and where?
   o PowerPoint presentation
   o How many hardbound copies they need?
   o Detailed structure analysis needed?

5. Timebound and fees

   o As well as the budget given (£40 000), is there any other budget for implementing the recommendations?
   o Does the company have a specific deadline that we should know?

## Comments

Very good answer. Could possibly have asked for a little more on areas relating to methodology such as:

- The possibilities of undertaking interviews in-store or at the entrance to the stores
- The possibilities of using video observation within stores
- If only a sample of stores is to be used, any suggestions as to the basis on which stores could be selected (i.e. geography, turnover, square footage, type of store (out of town shopping centre vs high street outlet))
- Having made reasonable assumptions regarding the answers to the information required in Part 1.a, produce a proposal to address the research needs of the company. (For the purpose of this question, your proposal should exclude the sections relating to personal CVs, related experience and references and contract details.)

### PART A Question 1.b (Grade C)
**Proposal**

*Identification Data*

To: Research Director

From: Research Executive

Date: 7 December 2004

Subject: Ways to Increase Sales

*Situation Analysis*

Jack Ltd is a leading international retailer which sells clothing, accessories and personal care products for men, women, children and babies in 15 different countries.

In the UK they operate mainly in the South East but they have quite a few shops all over the country.

Their target market are people from 0 to 45 years old, middle-upper class.

Each employee is being trained about fabric, fit and fashion to keep and understand customer's requirements.

Their main problem is that around 85 per cent of all potential customers leave the shop without buying anything.

To discuss the reason 'why' of this fact they require a marketing research project.

*Objectives*

1. Discuss reason why people have left their stores empty-handed in the last 12 months

   - Product range
   - Store layout (old-fashioned)
   - Service quality (poor?)
   - Pricing (too high? too low?)
   - Range of the below factors.

2. Identify ways to increase sales amongst existing customers for the next 21 months

   o How they can retain customers?
   o How they can decrease the leave rate?

3. Provide ways to increase sales in potential customers by the end of 2006

   o Gaining competitor's customers
   o More training needed
   o Change pricing
   o Offering a wide range of products.

*Methodology*

For the first objective we will require any previous research they may have and also we will use their database and MkIS to extract a sample and do around 200 questionnaires (self-administered, postal, £5 each). We will also purchase secondary data to update about trends and consumption patterns in the last 12 weeks (Mintel, Enviromentor). Also, we will use a convenience sample in the store to undertake the same face-to-face questionnaires (200, £30 each) and ask questions about product range, store layout, service quality, pricing, etc.)

For the second database we would use the database they already have to organize 5 focus groups (£2000 each) from our main customers (women between 15 and 35 years old, middle-upper class). With this qualitative data we will have some suggestions from them about which improvements we can do.

Also we can use desk research and internal records such as sales reports, advertising spending, complaints and satisfaction records and so on. Finally we can do mystery shopping (as an observing method).

Finally for the third objective, we will create questionnaires and we will organize telephone surveys (around 150, £15 each) with really tailored questions. Also, we will select another 5 focus groups (£2000 each) of competitor's customers to know the strengths and weaknesses about competitor customers and how we can improve our range of products, services and store layout.

For the focus group and face-to-face interviews we will use well-trained professionals. The moderator for the focus group will be qualified and experienced in research as well as in psychology and marketing and business aware, a strong communicator and a good listener, quick thinker, innovative, and anonymous in region and social class.

We will use incentives for both questionnaires and focus groups such as 20 per cent off with the next purchase and our employees will follow the MRS code of practice.

For the sequence/wording and format of questionnaires we will avoid ambiguous questions as well as negative questions, two questions in one generalization, assumptions or any hypothetical questions. We will use funnelling (from broad to narrow questions) and classification questions at the beginning and sensitive questions at the end.

About samples, we will use convenience samples in the store, samples extracted from the company database and simple random sampling for the potential customers.

About handling and processing we will use CATI system for the telephone interviews, laptops or PDA's for the face-to-face surveys and spider diagrams and cut and paste for organizing the data from the focus groups.

Report and presentation – hardbound copies will be given as well as in a CD. If any additional information will be required we will send by e-mail or in a disk. In the presentation we will keep a gap for questions, recommendation or explanation of any detailed statistical analysis misunderstood.

*Time bound and Fees*

Once the proposal is accepted we would start the field work in the next two weeks, that will take around four weeks. We will be ready to present in the next two weeks after the field work is finished and one week later we will send the final report. So the completed project will take about nine weeks.

Our project will be £35 000 and the amount is all-inclusive. Once the company has accepted, this will be payable in three months' time.

So agencies, hire, refreshments, data handling, fieldwork, hard copies of the report, and so on are included in this price. We will attach a detailed bill to the final report.

## Comments

Good background/rationale section although the section should be retitled 'Background' rather than 'Situation Analysis.' Although the objectives are laid out correctly, only objective one is a research objective, the other two are recommendations and inappropriate for a proposal. The information targets of objective one could be expanded upon and broken out into two or three separate objectives. The methodology section is good in as much as it sets out the scale of the research and attempts to justify the different approaches. However, more detail is needed with regard to the sampling process and the numbers of different types of customers to be included. With regard to the chosen method, postal surveys are unlikely to be appropriate as it will be difficult to obtain address details for potential customers who leave the store without purchasing anything. Fees shouldn't appear in the methodology section. Slightly more detail is needed on presentation, fees and timing – setting out what is likely to be the format of the report/presentation, the timing and fees for each of the parts of the research.

# Question 5.1

You are working for a small Midlands-based manufacturer of components for the motor industry. Your sales manager has identified a potential new market in the Czech Republic. The company cannot afford to carry out marketing research without establishing the nature of the demand for the product.

You have been asked to produce a preliminary market report from secondary data. There is no syndicated study available. What are the advantages and disadvantages of this approach? How can the disadvantages be overcome?

## Answer

### Introduction
Define secondary research. Discuss the range of strengths and weaknesses using the following framework:

### Strengths

- It is cheap or free of charge.
- It may provide an answer to the problem; this will save enormous time and effort.
- It can guide or provide direction for primary work.
- It can suggest methodologies for data collection.
- It can indicate problems with particular methodologies.
- It can provide historic or comparative data to enable longitudinal studies.

### Weaknesses

- It is not related to the research question and the temptation may be to force the data to fit the question.
- It may not be directly comparable.
- Data may be incomplete.
- It may not be available.

In evaluating secondary data, the following points should be explored:

- The data may have been gathered for a particular purpose.
- Who published the study? Was it a national government? Was it a trade association? What is the nature of the organization? Is the publisher of the data the same as the organization that collected the data?
- For what purpose? Is the study designed to sell a service? Is it designed to counter negative publicity? Is it designed to generate publicity?
- When were the data gathered? Is it relevant?
- How were the data collected? Was the data capture mechanism reliable? Was it a self-selecting sample?
- Who collected the data? Are they independent? Are they trained? Are they members of a professional body? What sample was used?
- How reliable are the data?
- Are raw data presented?
- Can I replicate the study? Is the methodology included? Can I test the data for accuracy?
- Are the data comparable?

You may identify other organizations that can help – for example trade partners, the DTI and the Chambers of Commerce. The use of embassy staff and trade associations may also be mentioned.

## Question 6.1

You work as a marketing manager for a major car dealership. The dealership has 150 sites throughout the United Kingdom. Your Customer Satisfaction Scores have been falling recently. You have been to an MRS training course on Mystery Shopping and feel that this technique might help identify the causes for the fall in satisfaction.

Write a report to your director outlining why you feel that this might help.

Discuss the role of mystery shopping in delivering service quality.

What are the benefits and limitations of this technique?

Your report should outline what other research techniques might help uncover the cause of the problem.

## Answer

### Introduction
Define mystery shopping.

Mystery shopping is defined as 'The use of individuals trained to observe, experience and measure the customer service process, by acting as a prospective customer and undertaking a series of pre-determined tasks' (MRS, 1997).

### Discuss this definition
Why is mystery shopping used? The following points form the basis of paragraphs in an essay or sections in a report:

- To act as a diagnostic tool identifying failings and weak points in service delivery
- To encourage and reward staff
- To assess competitors.

Conditions for the delivery of good research should be discussed.

- Mystery shoppers should present facts rather than opinions.
- These should include the shopping environment as well as interactions between the researcher and the staff. The potential for bias must be recognized in all markets.
- There needs to be careful recruitment of mystery shoppers.
- Age, gender and appearance of shoppers may affect the experience.
- Training is very important.
- Data capture and recording need to be carefully considered.
- Mechanical recording may be desirable.

You should discuss data protection issues.

Other techniques that may help include:

- Focus groups or group discussions with customers
- Group discussions and depth interviews with staff
- Quantitative studies by telephone to customers representing all dealerships to identify if the problem is based in certain areas
- Groups with competitors' customers to identify key success factors in their dealerships.

# Question 6.2

Davidson Hotels operate a group of seven hotels in the United Kingdom. The hotels are all rated at the three- or four-star level, with four of them having swimming pools and leisure centres. They tend to be located close to tourist/leisure-type areas of outstanding natural beauty and local heritage sites. Their customer mix has traditionally consisted of 50 per cent business travellers, 30 per cent coach parties and 20 per cent leisure travellers/leisure breaks. However, with the growth in budget hotels offering standard rooms and limited additional services, the number of business travellers has dropped by more than 38 per cent over the past 12 months. The coach party market is relatively static, therefore the company's main opportunity for growth is seen by the management as being in the leisure travel market, with the swimming pools being used to promote all-weather/all-year leisure destinations.

The company is therefore keen to understand more about the leisure travel sector, in particular:

- o The trends in the market
- o The criteria used by leisure travellers when selecting their accommodation in areas with outstanding natural beauty or heritage sites
- o The reasons why existing leisure customers use Davidson Hotels and their likelihood of returning to the same hotel or another hotel in the Davidson Hotel chain.

They are willing to spend up to £50 000 on the research project.

*Note*: The above material has been based on a fictitious company for assessment purposes.

**PART B** – Answer **TWO** questions only

### Question 4

Tom Davidson in Question 1 has heard about other hotels using mystery shopping techniques to monitor the quality of their services. He has asked you to produce a report explaining:

(a) The advantages and disadvantages of using mystery shopping

**(10 marks)**

(b) The issues to consider when establishing and implementing a mystery shopping programme.

**(15 marks)**
**(25 marks in total)**

### Answer

Go to www.cim.co.uk for specimen answers to this question.

## Question 6.3

Professional Diploma in Marketing: Marketing Research and Information

### Jack Ltd

Jack Ltd is a leading international speciality retailer offering clothing, accessories and personal care products for men, women, children and babies under the Jack brand name. In the United Kingdom, Jack Ltd operates more than 150 stores nationwide. Each of the stores employs sales associates and other store personnel that are trained to answer customers' questions about fabric, fit and fashion and to help them select merchandise that's perfect for them. However, even with this training, around 85 per cent of all potential customers that enter a Jack store (measured using electronic counters in the doorways of each store) leave without buying anything. Senior management are keen to reduce this percentage; however, they are unclear as to the reasons why people leave their stores empty-handed. It may be due to the product range, store layout, service quality, pricing or any range of factors. Marketing research is therefore needed to explore the reasons why such a large percentage of potential customers fail to make a purchase.

The company hopes that answers to such questions will help to identify ways to increase sales amongst these customers.

### PART A Question 4

The senior executives of Jack Ltd have been examining their long-term marketing research requirements. In order to better understand customer and staff behaviour, they would like to make more use of observation techniques. However, their knowledge of these techniques is limited and they have asked you to write a paper clarifying:

(a) The approaches available for observing customer behaviour in a retail environment and the issues involved in using them

**(15 marks)**

(b) The nature of mystery shopping and the issues involved in running an effective mystery shopping programme.

**(10 marks)**
**(Total 25 Marks)**

## Answer (Grade C)

### Question 4.a

To: Senior Executives, Jack, Ltd

From: Bob Smith, Research manager, Jack Ltd

Date: 7/12/2004

Re: Observation in a retail environment

There are a number of approaches available for observing customer behaviour in a retail environment.

Observation can be made:

- o People watching people
- o People watching events
- o Machines watching people
- o Machines watching events

In observing customer behaviour in a retail environment we could also observe covertly and overtly. Covert is more favourable as customer behaviour would not be affected by our observations as they would not know they were being observed. This could involve the use of one-way mirrors to watch customers, video cameras or people in store pretending to be customers but actually observing the customers. Overt observation could involve staff openly watching customers perhaps with a clipboard taking notes. This is too intrusive however, and is highly likely to affect customers' behaviour.

In order for observation to be valid and informative it needs to be in the most natural setting possible. There are also ethical issues associated with observing people – especially when they do not know you are doing so. If customers are to be filmed or taped in any way, we may need to inform them of this. As we do not want to affect their behaviour we could tell them as they leave the store and if they object we could destroy the tape.

Observation could focus as a number of things:

- o How the customers move around the store. Do they follow a pattern or the aisles or choose direction?
- o How the customers interact with staff. Do they ask for help. Who do they ask for help?
- o How the customers interact with the product. Do they pick things up and look at them? Do they avoid certain products?

**319**

> o How the customers read and interact with other customers. Do they speak to each other? Do they make suggestions such as the best skis to buy?

For the retail environment such as a specialist sports shoe it is key to understand how the customer interacts with products – whether they try things out and how they behave once in the store. We know that customers are entering our stores but 85 per cent do not make a purchase, so we need to find out why this is so.

## Question 4.b
### *Mystery Shopping*

*Definition*

Mystery shopping involves someone external to a company observing and trying out the service of that company or its competitors. It aims to measure service quality and record observations in an objective manner.

*Why use mystery shopping?*

Mystery shopping can provide insight into the customer experience. It can offer information which is not available from speaking with customers alone. Mystery shopping can inform training needs, help to improve staffing levels or shop layout. It can highlight areas where service is tailing and suggest improvements. It can also show where staff are doing well and offer incentives and encouragement.

*The nature of mystery shopping*

Mystery shopping can involve a number of approaches. It can be:

> o Via the telephone – For example someone calling a store to find out about a product and measuring the service quality
> o Via the internet – Someone making an online booking or enquiry or measuring the ease of navigation
> o Quick purchase
> o Scenario set-up – For example trying to return faulty goods and assessing the service
> o Full mystery shop – The mystery shopper experiences the whole process as a customer might.

Issue involved in running an effective mystery shopping programme

*Mystery Shopper training* – It is essential that the mystery shopper is properly trained and can objectively feed back on the service. The mystery shopper should have a predefined set of objectives and measures and must use rating scales and justify observations. This will ensure that the observation is objective.

*Fit the correct profile* – The mystery shopper should fit the company's customer profile such as age, gender, social class. He/she should also be able to appear as a customer and not give away their identity.

*Timings and number of visits* – It must be noted that a mystery shop visit is only measuring or observing at one particular time and place. Service experience may vary according to the time of day, who is working, how busy the store is and so on. A number of visits should therefore be completed to cover different times and different geographical locations at stores. With more visits, more information can be collected and this will be more representative.

*Ethics* – In some instances mystery shopping can be seen as intrusive to staff. It may be preferable to warn staff of a time period when they may be observed – possibly one week.

*Competitors* – It may be necessary to conduct mystery shopping on one's own company and on competitors. This provides comparison and something to benchmark your own company against.

An effective mystery shopping programme should consider all these points. It should be conducted by a trained mystery shopper from a reputable agency. The mystery shopping should be made as objective as possible and be conducted over a number of stores, geographical areas and times.

By its nature, mystery shopping can become highly subjective as it relies on individuals' observations. However, this can be overcome with training, good briefing and clear objectives and justifications for observations.

## Comments

Part 4.a – Slightly more detail needed on the limitations of observation. The ethical issues are incorrectly explained and also subjects should be informed on entering a store not when they are leaving

Part 4.b – Very good coverage of mystery shopping and the issues involved in running an effective mystery shopping programme

# Question 7.1

As the marketing research executive of a leading confectionery company, you have been asked to commission qualitative research into the positioning of your leading brand in the market place. You have to select a moderator to facilitate the groups.

What is the role of the moderator in managing focus groups?

Describe the key skills required by a moderator of focus groups.

How would you make your final decision?

## Answer

### Introduction
Define focus groups and the moderator.

Focus groups: A number of respondents gathered together to generate ideas through the discussion of, and reaction to, specific stimuli. Under the steerage of a moderator, focus groups are often used in exploratory work or when the subject matter involves social activities, habits and status (MRS, 2003).

Moderator: An individual who facilitates but does not influence a group discussion.

The moderator will control the group, keeping the discussion on track and probing for further information when needed.

The moderator will introduce other tasks that may occur within the group.

The main aim of the group is to ensure that the group members discuss the topic amongst themselves; the moderator's touch should be as light as possible.

The moderator will use a range of techniques to control the input of particularly vociferous members and to encourage quieter members of the group to make their contribution.

The moderator manages the timing of the group and ensures that the group is kept to reasonable time limits – normally between 45 minutes and 2 hours.

The moderator will capture information on tape or digitally.

The moderator may take instruction from remote observers of the group.

The moderator may administer the group, recruiting respondents and inviting them to attend. They may also give the respondents refreshments and payment or an incentive.

The moderator may analyse the results of the groups and should therefore understand the context of the research.

You should identify the fact that moderators may be employed by the agency, may be independent or be employed by a fieldwork agency.

Your decision should be based around the fact that moderators should have the following characteristics:

o Highly qualified and experienced in research and, possibly, psychology
o Business and marketing aware. They need to be able to translate respondents' feelings into business advantage for their clients
o Strong communicators – able to relate to a range of people
o Hard to place regionally in terms of socio-economic class
o Socially able, relaxed and friendly, but strong enough to control a room of animated, or conversely, disinterested respondents
o Flexible and quick thinking, with the ability to respond to the unexpected.

# Question 7.2

Davidson Hotels operate a group of seven hotels in the United Kingdom. The hotels are all rated at the three- or four-star level, with four of them having swimming pools and leisure centres. They tend to be located close to tourist/leisure type areas of outstanding natural beauty and local heritage sites. Their customer mix has traditionally consisted of 50 per cent business travellers, 30 per cent coach parties, and 20 per cent leisure travellers/leisure breaks. However, with the growth in budget hotels offering standard rooms and limited additional services, the number of business travellers has dropped by more than 38 per cent over the past 12 months. The coach party market is relatively static, therefore the company's main opportunity for growth is seen by management as being in the leisure travel market, with the swimming pools being used to promote all-weather/all-year leisure destinations.

The company is therefore keen to understand more about the leisure travel sector, in particular:

- ○ The trends in the market
- ○ The criteria used by leisure travellers when selecting their accommodation in areas with outstanding natural beauty or heritage sites
- ○ The reasons why existing leisure customers use Davidson Hotels and their likelihood of returning to the same hotel or another hotel in the Davidson Hotel chain.

They are willing to spend up to £50 000 on the research project.

*Note*: The above material has been based on a fictitious company for assessment purposes.

## PART B – answer TWO questions only

### Question 3
Assuming that qualitative research could be used to meet some of the research objectives of the project set out in Question 1, design a discussion guide involving appropriate projective techniques to address these specific objectives.

**(25 marks)**

### Answer
Go to www.cim.co.uk for specimen answers to this question.

# Question 7.3

Professional Diploma in Marketing: Marketing Research and Information

## Splash Ltd

The Spanish-based cosmetics company Splash Ltd has built an international retail chain, that is, in a strong expansion phase. Its fresh, handmade soaps and cosmetics are available in 240 stores worldwide. The emphasis is on making and selling products without animal ingredients, made from only fresh fruit and vegetables, finest essential oils and safe synthetics. It controls the whole process of getting its products to the consumer, including design, manufacturing and retail.

The retail stores look like a cross between a cheese shop and a market stall, with slabs of soap and other fresh products stacked ready for cutting and bagging. The retail environment is dominated by an aroma of soaps and perfumes.

The company is now planning to open its first UK store in the centre of London.

Prior to designing the outlet, determining the product range and potential promotions, the company is keen to undertake a programme of market research with potential customers, to examine the buying behaviour and attitudes of British consumers of high-quality soap and cosmetic products.

The company hopes that answers to such questions will help in the successful launch of their first UK store.

The company is willing to spend up to £50 000 on the research project.

*Note*: The above data has been based on a fictitious situation drawing on a variety of events and does not reflect the management practices of any particular organization.

## PART A Question 3

Design a discussion guide and appropriate projective techniques, for use in a series of group discussions, to address the research objectives of the mini-case set out in Question 1.

**(25 Marks)**

## Answer

Although focus group sessions are a qualitative research observational method and therefore are relatively unstructured in nature, it is necessary to design a discussion guide with relevant topics that need to be addressed during the session in order for that session to have any relevance and value for the client. This is where a discussion guide comes in as it provides a guideline for the moderator – a 'checklist' as well as appropriate timings.

Projective techniques are used in discussions firstly as a means of getting everyone involved. It can be quite intimidating being within a group of people you don't know and asked to give your opinions and personal attitudes on a product or subject. Projective techniques can be things such as word association tasks which are quite fun and easy to do and provide a good introduction. An example of this would be to say the first word you think of when I say 'Chocolate'. Answers could range from Cadbury's, milky, guilty, diet, sugar and so on. Another projective technique is to start a sentence and get everyone in the discussion group to think of an ending. For example 'People who eat Pot Noodle are . . .' Answers could be 'lazy', 'on the run', 'hungry', 'students' and so on. Another projective technique is to have two peoples' faces, one with a speech bubble saying a statement, for example 'I fly with Easyjet'. The other face has a thought bubble and the focus group must fill in what the person is really thinking, for example 'I like a good deal', 'I don't have much money to spend', 'I booked it last minute'. Projective techniques are less intrusive to people than asking outright of them 'Why do you fly with Easyjet?' and let them put themselves in 'someone else's shoes'. It lets them project their own feelings and sometimes even say things they didn't realize they felt.

Discussion guide for focus group examining buying behaviour and attitudes of British consumers of high-quality soap and cosmetic products:

Introduction – 10 minutes

- o Welcome and thank the participants for coming
- o Run through the agenda. Put the participants at ease, tell them what the focus group is about and what is required of them
- o Get everyone to introduce themselves (e.g. name, age, occupation)

Discussion – 90 minutes

- o Start with some projective techniques. This will ensure that everyone gets the chance to say something; it's quite fun to do and introduces the topics.

Projective Technique 1

Have some of the Splash Ltd. product range, for example some soaps and some products from their cosmetic range like moisturizers and lip gloss. Ask participants to end the following sentences:

- People who buy this product are . . .
- The cost of this product is . . .
- This product smells of . . .
- The main benefit of this product is . . .
- The main drawback of this product is . . .

Projective Technique 2

Ask participants to fill in the thought bubbles of the following statements to find out attitudes towards different 'classes' of stores, for example

Insert picture here?

I shop at Harrods for my soap and cosmetics.

I shop at Boots for my soaps and cosmetics.

The discussion continues with topics to cover including: (for moderator's use)

- Preferred product range
- Concerns/non-concerns over ingredients used in soaps and cosmetics
- Definitions of value for money
- Identify stores that sell soaps and cosmetics
- Identify numbers of high-quality soaps and cosmetic products that participants currently own and likely to purchase as a regular consumer
- Identify differences, if any, between consumers of high-quality soaps and cosmetics.

Conclusion

- To include any last thoughts from participants
- A summary from moderator
- Thank you from the moderator
- Monetary payment given.

## Comments

Very good answer with good sequencing, topics and appropriate but not excessive projective techniques. The topics could be slightly more detailed.

# Question 7.4

## Jack Ltd

Jack Ltd is a leading international speciality retailer offering clothing, accessories and personal care products for men, women, children and babies under the Jack brand name. In the United Kingdom, Jack Ltd operates more than 150 stores nationwide. Each of the stores employs sales associates and other store personnel that are trained to answer customers' questions about fabric, fit and fashion and to help them select merchandise that's perfect for them. However, even with this training, around 85 per cent of all potential customers that enter a Jack store (measured using electronic counters in the doorways of each store) leave without buying anything. Senior management are keen to reduce this percentage; however, they are unclear as to the reasons why people leave their stores empty-handed. It may be due to the product range, store layout, service quality, pricing or any range of factors. Marketing research is therefore needed to explore the reasons why such a large percentage of potential customers fail to make a purchase.

The company hopes that answers to such questions will help to identify ways to increase sales amongst these customers.

The company is willing to spend up to £40 000 on the research project.

## PART B Question 3

Design a discussion guide involving appropriate projective techniques for use in a series of group discussions to address the research objectives of the project set out in Question 1.

**(Total 25 Marks)**

## Answer (Grade C)

### Discussion guide for Jack Ltd

This discussion guide is for use by the moderator(s) of six focus groups to be held regionally in town halls close to chosen Jack Ltd store sites.

1. Introduction (10 mins)

   o Introduce self as moderator and welcome group
   o Position the reason for gathering and the objectives of the discussion
   o Advise of length (1.5 hrs) and position as being a necessary stage of research to be informative but fun
   o Relax the respondents with some introductory questions, such as
   o How they travelled to the venue
   o What they do for a living, and so on.

2. Discussion Phase 1 (25 mins)

   o Establish who has bought from the company and who has visited but not purchased (split should be 70/30 in favour of not buying).
   o Identify their perception of the products offered

      – Range too wide and confusing
      – Not tailored to UK market

   o Identify perception of customer service

      – Is it meeting requirements
      – Are there enough staff
      – Identify opinions on the store location and layout
      – Arranged conveniently?
      – Could they find what they were looking for?

   o Identify competitors used and reason for non-purchase

3. Discussion Phase 2 (20 mins)

   o Brand image + style
   o Ask some projective questions, that is 'If Jack Ltd was a car, what sort of car would it be?'; 'If you were a famous film star would you stop at Jack Ltd'
   o Some pictures of branding can be used as stimulus
   o Also word association techniques, that is What do you think of when I say 'quality', 'value for money', 'customer service'?

4. Brand Mapping (20 mins)

   o This can be used to ascertain more clarity around service and pricing comparables, that is

      - Price vs. service
      - Price vs. product
      - Price vs. availability + access
      - Service vs. product

   o These can be represented on a chart and respondents asked to 'map' where they think Jack Ltd belongs.

5. Summary (15 mins)

   o Thank all for coming, advise on information + assure them that all data 'is subject to ethical rules + regulations and that personal data will not be used unless consented to. Give incentives to all respondents in the form of £10 Jack Ltd voucher.

## Comments

Very good answer with good sequencing, topics and appropriate but not excessive projective techniques. The topics could be slightly more detailed.

# Question 8.1

As an executive of a leading research agency, you are pitching to persuade a client to extend the qualitative work they have carried out on their brands to include quantitative work, using face-to-face interviews.

Write a report to the client outlining the advantages and disadvantages of quantitative research.

What are the advantages and disadvantages of face-to-face interviewing?

How can the disadvantages be countered?

## Answer

You should start the report by defining quantitative research as 'research that is undertaken using a structured research approach with a sample of the population to produce quantifiable insights into behaviour motivations and attitudes'.

You can identify the five key characteristics of quantitative data:

1. Data gathering is more structured.
2. Research involves larger samples than qualitative research.
3. The data gathered can provide answers that will quantify the incidence of particular behaviour motivations and attitudes in the population under consideration.
4. Studies can be more easily replicated and direct comparisons can be made between studies.
5. Analysis is statistical in nature and will usually be done with the help of computer software.

The answer should then place the idea of face-to-face interviewing in context and define the term. The alternatives of self-completion could be outlined and other methods of interview-assisted survey could be identified and discussed.

The advantages of face-to-face contact methods are many:

o There is greater acceptance of the validity of the research if an interviewer can introduce the reasons for the research and show professional membership cards.
o The interview process is more efficient as non-eligible respondents can be screened out more effectively.
o They improve response rates as the interviewer can answer questions or help with any difficulty in completing the questionnaire.
o Personal contact creates a sense of obligation and this can be useful with long surveys. This can reduce the incidence of incomplete or unfinished interviews.
o Complexity can be introduced into the survey – for example the use of show cards or other stimuli material is more easily managed.
o Empathy and encouragement can enable deeper consideration of the questions and ensure accuracy of some claims – for example gender and age.

There are some disadvantages:

o Costs, particularly in B2B research, may be high, but this must be offset against a higher response rate.
o It can take a considerable amount of time to complete a survey.
o Interviewers may be demotivated and may take shortcuts to ensure that their quota of completed surveys is made.
o Interview bias is a problem. Bias may affect.

   – Who is interviewed? – interviewers may select those people who want to be interviewed. An Australian researcher used to do all his interviews on the beach at Bondi.
   – The way questions are asked. With a negative inflection or a preceding ad-libbed comment 'I know this sounds stupid but . . .
   – The way an interviewer responds verbally and visually to an answer. A raised eyebrow or expression of shock is not required!
   – The way an answer is recorded; the interpretation of a response may be biased.

- ○ Safety of interviewing staff may be an issue in some areas.
- ○ The training and control of field staff is important and adds to costs.
- ○ A geographically dispersed sample, for example regional store managers, is clearly difficult to administer in this way, and other data collection methods might need to be considered.

Ways to overcome the potential problems are as follows:

- ○ Good briefing
- ○ Training
- ○ Motivation
- ○ Ensuring that the research design is sound
- ○ Making sure that questionnaires are easy to use
- ○ Careful management of the field force
- ○ Using the IQCS
- ○ Using a reputable field force agency
- ○ Back checking completed surveys
- ○ Careful editing
- ○ Ensuring that the data is consistent and complete.

The use of face-to-face methods is dependent on the nature of the research problem and the resources of the business.

# Question 8.2

Professional Diploma in Marketing: Marketing Research and Information

## Splash Ltd

The Spanish-based cosmetics company Splash Ltd has built an international retail chain that is in a strong expansion phase. Its fresh, handmade soaps and cosmetics are available in 240 stores worldwide. The emphasis is on making and selling products without animal ingredients, made from only fresh fruit and vegetables, finest essential oils and safe synthetics. It controls the whole process of getting its products to the consumer, including design, manufacturing and retail.

The retail stores look like a cross between a cheese shop and a market stall, with slabs of soap and other fresh products stacked ready for cutting and bagging. The retail environment is dominated by an aroma of soaps and perfumes.

The company is now planning to open its first UK store in the centre of London.

Prior to designing the outlet, determining the product range and potential promotions, the company is keen to undertake a programme of market research with potential customers, to examine the buying behaviour and attitudes of British consumers of high-quality soap and cosmetic products.

The company hopes that answers to such questions will help in the successful launch of their first UK store.

The company is willing to spend up to £50 000 on the research project.

*Note*: The above data has been based on a fictitious situation drawing on a variety of events and does not reflect the management practices of any particular organization.

## PART B Question 4

The senior executives of Splash Ltd have been examining their future marketing research requirements for testing new products. However, their knowledge of product testing techniques is limited and they have asked you to write a paper that:

(a) Describes the workings of hall tests and placement tests in the context of cosmetics and soaps.

**(15 marks)**

(b) The circumstances when one of these techniques should be used in preference to the other.

**(10 marks)**
**(Total 25 marks)**

## Answer

### PART B Question 4.a
*Report*

Prepared by: Jane Ford, Joe Bloggs Agency

Prepared for: Senior exec. team, Splash Ltd

Date: 6/6/05

Subject: Product testing techniques

Introduction

Before a product is launched it is beneficial to test the appeal of the product with consumers for a number of reasons:

o To identify which products are most likely to succeed in the market (for instance if a number of different products have been developed but not all can be launched)
o To explore the most appropriate pricing and communication strategy
o To identify areas of weakness that can be improved on before launch.

There are two main techniques used in market research for testing products before they are launched to the market:

o Hall tests
o In home placement tests

This paper explains how each of these techniques is used, and provides guidance as to the circumstances they should be used in.

*Hall Tests*

Hall tests involve respondents being pre-recruited (usually on the street) and taken to a central location (often a hotel conference room) to participate in an interview. For this reason, hall tests are usually conducted in busy areas such as town centres or shopping malls, to ensure enough people will be passing. Respondents are normally offered a small 'thank you' gift as an incentive to take part (e.g. a pen, or a product sample).

Once in the hall the respondent will take part in an interview conducted by a specialist interviewer using either a paper questionnaire or an electronic data capture tool (such as PDA or laptop). The respondent will be asked to look at/sample a number of different products and will be asked a series of questions about each such as:

- o Appeal of the product
- o Likelihood to buy
- o Price expectations
- o Likes and dislikes
- o Rating of specific attributes (e.g. smell, texture)

The order in which respondents are shown products must be rotated in order to reduce bias (e.g. A respondent may respond more favourably to the first product they see).

This type of interview is known as sequential monadic and will provide a score for each product (which can be weighted according to the importance placed on each attribute such as weight, size, appearance etc). In order to provide a measure of the relative performance of each product against others in the range (or competitive set) a ranking exercise (e.g. Top 3/bottom 3 or first to last) is often conducted. More complex conjoint techniques can also be used to identify how appealing each product is and how much new innovations might cannibalize existing products instead of winning share from competitors.

*Placement Tests*

This is where a product will be left with a respondent for a period of time to allow them to use it in their home. Before the placement starts a questionnaire will be completed to capture their initial expectations from the product. At the end of the test a more detailed questionnaire will be completed exploring how they experienced the product, for example:

- o Ease of use
- o Effectiveness
- o Durability/how long it lasted
- o Likelihood to buy/recommend

Respondents for a placement test can be recruited for one specific test, or alternatively might be recruited to a panel and asked to test a number of items over a period of time. The benefit of this is that it is more cost-effective and also provides the opportunity to compare different product innovations with the same person. The drawback is that their responses may become biased due to exposure to other products or simply through continued exposure to the research process. Company staff are often used for initial placement tests before/instead of consumers.

## PART B Question 4.b
Circumstances for use

Hall tests might be more appropriately used when:

- o There are a lot of different concepts to test, or comparison is necessary with existing products or the competitive set.
- o There is no working model of the product available (e.g. For Splash this may mean the colour/texture and smell of the product is right but the product composition has not been finalized. In hall tests the respondent would be asked to look at and smell the product and would be given an explanation of what to do.

- o If product innovations are too valuable/sensitive to loan out. In hall tests, Splash will have more control over who sees the new products and can be sure that a new formula does not fall into competitors' hands.
- o When the appearance and/or packaging of a product is the only thing that needs to be tested (e.g. To explore whether UK consumers would prefer their solid shampoo bar cut from a block or sold separately in a tin).

Placement tests should be used in the following circumstances:

- o Where continued use will be important (e.g. To test a moisturizer that claims to reduce wrinkles in 14 days).
- o Where there is a need to test usability (e.g. Whether a new soap bar disintegrates after two or three uses).
- o Where repeat purchase and recommendation are vital.
- o To provide statistics for PR and/or advertising (e.g. '90 per cent say our moisturizer makes their skin firmer').
- o To help staff understand the products and therefore sell more effectively.

## Comments

Section 4.a – Very good description of hall tests and placement tests. Could possibly have done more to apply the answer to the cosmetic and soap markets.

Section 4.b – Very good discussion of the circumstances when each of the techniques should be used.

# Question 9.1

(a) Why is questionnaire design so important in the research process?
(b) What is the role of piloting in the questionnaire design process?

## Answer

Questionnaires collect data. The quality of data depends on their professional design. It is designed to:

- o Collect relevant data
- o Remove bias
- o Make data comparable
- o Motivate the respondent.

They must be developed in consideration of the research question, the data that is to be gathered, the respondents who will be answering the questions and the method of administering the questionnaire.

Classification questions will ensure that the respondent is part of our sample.

The questionnaire needs to reflect the objectives of the research programme.

The questionnaire must minimize bias through careful wording and phrasing of questions.

A good questionnaire will motivate interviewers and respondents.

The questionnaire and interview time are expensive. It should be efficiently produced to save time and money in the interview process.

Equally, it must be easy to code, edit and analyse.

A questionnaire should be tested in a pilot survey before it is rolled out.

The next stage of the questionnaire is to word the questions. At each stage of the process, the researcher should stop and ask 'is the question really necessary?' Each question should be carefully evaluated on its own, in relation to other questions on the questionnaire and in relation to the overall objectives of the study. If the question does not contribute to the overall purpose of the research, it should not be included in the questionnaire.

Piloting or testing the questionnaire is crucial:

- o It allows problems to be corrected.
- o It helps with the coding process.
- o It improves question sequencing.
- o It improves wording of questions.

Piloting should be carried out by the staff who will administer the questionnaire, in a comparable environment and with respondents who share the characteristics of the sample.

There are two methods:

1. The debriefing method means the respondents should be asked after completing the questionnaire what their thought processes were as they completed the questionnaires.
2. The protocol method allows the respondent to talk through the process of completing the questionnaire.

# Question 9.2

CIM Professional Series Stage Two: Marketing Research and Information

## Donaldson Builders Merchants

Donaldson Builders Merchants is a small chain of builders merchants located in the central belt of Scotland. The company has four outlets located around the edge of the major conurbations of Edinburgh and Glasgow. These supply small builders, plumbers, roofers and similar trades-men as well as some members of the public (i.e. those more skilled in major do-it-yourself renovations and house improvements). Customers may collect items from the trade counter at the warehouse or have the items delivered direct to the building site or house by the company's fleet of 14 lorries. The lorries are equipped with hoists for handling the larger items.

Donaldson supplies:

- o Timber and timber products
- o Bricks and paving

- o Sand and aggregates
- o Roofing materials
- o Plumbing and heating supplies
- o A small range of hand tools.

The company provides credit to the majority of its trade customers. As a result it has a computerized database with details on most of its trade customers relating to name, address, trading address, telephone number, type of business, and purchasing patterns. There are approximately 1100 customers on the database, which probably represents 85 per cent of the company's customers. For the other 15 per cent of customers (the public and trade customers who do not have a credit account), the database holds no record, with the exception of a delivery address if a delivery is required.

The market in which Donaldson operates is becoming more competitive, with the company losing share to national chains such as Jewson and a number of recently opened B&Q trade depots. Tom Donaldson, the Managing Director, feels that the company's personal service and flexibility are far superior to these competitors, and is therefore keen to build on this and find ways in which to compete other than on price. The company has never undertaken research before but is keen to find out more from its customers about:

- o Their existing and future purchasing behaviour
- o Their attitudes towards Donaldson Builders Merchants (such as product range, service, flexibility of delivery etc.).
- o Their suggestions about improvements required in Donaldson's offering.

They are willing to spend up to £50 000 on the research project.

## Part B Question 3

Design a questionnaire to meet the research objectives of the project set out in the Question. At this stage the layout of the questionnaire is not important but the questionnaire should clearly demonstrate your knowledge of sequencing, question wording and question/response format.

**(25 marks)**

## Answer

### PART B Question 3

The question is simple but care needs to be taken in determining why the questionnaire is being developed and the objectives of the research. It may be worth restating this and identifying the type of respondent.

The questionnaire should focus on structure including funnelling and the use of screening identification, skip questions and routing instructions.

Format choice must demonstrate a range of format choices including:

- o Closed dichotomous questions
- o Closed multiple-choice questions
- o Open questions and
- o Scale questions.

Wording will also be important and the following should be considered:

- Use clear and simple language
- Avoid ambiguity
- Avoid two questions in one
- Avoid leading or loaded questions
- Avoid assumptions
- Avoid generalization
- Avoid negative questions
- Avoid hypothetical questions.

# Question 9.3

Davidson Hotels operate a group of seven hotels in the United Kingdom. The hotels are all rated at the three- or four-star level, with four of them having swimming pools and leisure centres. They tend to be located close to tourist/leisure type areas of outstanding natural beauty and local heritage sites. Their customer mix has traditionally consisted of 50 per cent business travellers, 30 per cent coach parties and 20 per cent leisure travellers/leisure breaks. However, with the growth in budget hotels offering standard rooms and limited additional services, the number of business travellers has dropped by more than 38 per cent over the past 12 months. The coach party market is relatively static, therefore the company's main opportunity for growth is seen by management as being in the leisure travel market, with the swimming pools being used to promote all-weather/all-year leisure destinations.

The company is therefore keen to understand more about the leisure travel sector, in particular:

- The trends in the market
- The criteria used by leisure travellers when selecting their accommodation in areas with outstanding natural beauty or heritage sites
- The reasons why existing leisure customers use Davidson Hotels and their likelihood of returning to the same hotel or another hotel in the Davison Hotel chain.

They are willing to spend up to £50 000 on the research project.

*Note*: The above material has been based on a fictitious company for assessment purposes.

## Answer

Go to www.cim.co.uk for specimen answers to this question.

# Question 9.4

Discuss the issue of falling response rates in marketing research, highlighting any actions that can be taken to improve the level of response.

**(25 marks)**

# Question 10.1

You have been appointed as marketing manager to an online retailer of intimate apparel (underwear). They have succeeded in difficult times to grow their business but have appointed you to look at the marketing research function within the business. Your first piece of research is based on a quota sample. The MD of the business is sceptical.

Produce a report for the MD outlining what quota sampling is.

What benefits does it have? What are its disadvantages and how can these be overcome?

What other sampling techniques may have been considered and why would they have been rejected?

## Answer

Define quota sampling:

'A type of non-probability sample where the required number of units with particular characteristics is specified.'

Known characteristics of the population are reproduced in the same proportions as in the sample. Therefore, it is representative of that population. For example age, sex and social class can be used to select quotas.

Advantages of quota sampling include:

- Its speed and cost
- It allows sampling to take place where a sample frame may not be available but key characteristics of the population are known
- Interviewers do not have to interview named individuals – they are screened in or out via a small number of classification questions.
- The data when compared to random methods, which are perhaps double the cost, has been proved to be acceptable, provided that the research is managed effectively.
- Cost savings may be used to improve the quality of research through increasing sample sizes or using a different method in support of the survey.
- Its popularity shows that it works!

Disadvantages include:

- Whilst known characteristics may be distributed in correct proportions, unknown characteristics that may be relevant to the survey may not. Hidden bias may exist that is not discovered.
- Researchers may be biased as to the type of respondents they choose to interview or the location where they choose to carry out the interviews.

Other sampling techniques include:

- Probability sampling
- Simple random sampling
- Systematic sampling
- Stratified random sampling
- Cluster sampling.

Disadvantages:

- ○ It is expensive.
- ○ Respondents selected must be interviewed to ensure the integrity of the process. This means that up to three call backs to individuals may be made before classifying a non-response.
- ○ The cost of putting together a large sample frame may be prohibitive.
- ○ The random selection of a sample means that all members of a national population would have the same chance of being selected.

Non-probability sampling includes:

- ○ Convenience sampling
- ○ Judgement or purposive sampling
- ○ Snowball sampling.

These may have been rejected as less reliable than quota sampling or inappropriate to the research programme under consideration.

# Question 10.2

## December 2004 Question Five

Discuss the proposition that the determination of sample size is simply a matter of guesswork.

**(Total 25 Marks)**

## Answer (Grade C)

When carrying out surveys that are analysed through quantitative data analysis techniques, an effective sample size needs to be established relevant to your research requirements. A sample can be defined as a group of people selected to be representative of a population of interest. Sample size is very important and cannot be left to guess work, otherwise errors will occur and the validity of your research will be significantly reduced.

A sample is chosen to represent the population of interest. Although the selection of respondents is also of vital importance, the sample size cannot be neglected. Generally speaking, the larger your sample size, the more accurate your results are, which means that your results are more likely to represent the characteristics of interest in the population. However, accuracy does not increase in proportion to the sample size, for example if you increase a sample of 100 people by 10 per cent, accuracy will be increased by 1 per cent, that is accuracy is increased by the square root of the increase in sample size. This has to be offset against the cost of increasing the sample size. Generally the increase in sample size is proportionate to the increase in cost.

A number of factors have to be considered when selecting a sample size:

- ○ Timescale – How long do you have to carry out the research, if you don't have much time, sample size will have to be smaller.
- ○ Cost – What is your budget. Again, if budget is tight, the sample size will be smaller.
- ○ Risk involved with the decision-making. If there is a high risk involved, a higher level of accuracy is generally required and sample size should be increased.

Other factors have to be considered when looking at who you are surveying. Previous research carried out will give you an indication of the following:

- Non-response – Are you looking at a group that is likely to have little response, will incentives be required or follow-up calls (which adds to the cost).
- Subgroups – How many subgroups are there within the sample and are the subgroups adequately represented?
- Availability – If there is a small population you may find it difficult to get a big enough sample and may have to look at the whole population rather than a sample. It may also increase the cost in searching for respondents.
- Is the sample you are looking at representative of the whole population? Errors in this can be reduced by selecting your sample from multiple lists.

There are a number of methods that can be employed to determine the sample size. They can be worked out mathematically or estimated based on data you already have.

The general formula for working out sample size is:

$$N = \frac{Z^2 \sigma^2}{E^2}$$

Z = Confidence limit

$\sigma$ = Standard deviation (worked out by formula or estimated given previous data)

$$\sigma = \sqrt{\frac{\sum (X_1 - \overline{X})^2}{n - 1}}$$

$E^2$ = Degree of accuracy required

N = Sample size

A different formula is used to identify the sample size if a percentage of respondents are expected to respond and for very large samples, again another formula is used.

In conclusion, the determination of sample size cannot simply be left to guesswork. There are other important issues such as selection methods of the respondents for your survey but sample size is equally important. A number of factors outlined above must be considered and applied to the situation you are in and what the survey aims to achieve. These are outlined above but the main issues concerning decision-makers in marketing are the accuracy required for the research project and the cost that will be incurred when deciding how big the sample size may be.

There are a number of statistical methods that can be employed to determine sample size based on the required accuracy and standard deviation of a sample. It must be noted however, that these methods are based on the assumptions of a normal distribution of respondents. The determination of sample size must consider the above-mentioned factors in order to assure validity of results and make informed decision-making in marketing.

## Comments

Good answer, although some inaccuracies exist regarding the impact of sample size on accuracy. Answer could also be slightly more balanced emphasizing that selecting the sample size does require some level of subjective judgement.

## Question 11.1

What tasks have to be done before data can be analysed and after surveys have been completed?

Describe the tasks and outline their role in producing effective analysis.

### Answer

Data need to be:

- ○ Entered
- ○ Coded
- ○ Edited
- ○ Cleaned

Before data analysis can be carried out.

### Editing and coding

Before data is processed, it is assessed for completeness and coherence. The editing process involves computer or manual checking of the data to look for respondent or interview errors or inconsistencies. If errors are identified the respondent may be called back. If the questionnaire cannot be rescued then it may be rejected.

**Coding** is the process that allocates a number to each answer and it is this that allows analysis to take place. As discussed earlier, the coding process may take place as the questionnaire is administered either manually by the interviewer ringing a number on the questionnaire, or it may be managed through the computer-assisted methods.

Coding open questions involves using a sample of the completed questionnaires and developing a coding frame or a list of codes for all possible responses to an open question. This process may categorize and group certain diverse responses into a manageable number. This process must be handled carefully to reduce the processing error that might occur.

### Data entry

Data entry may be carried out automatically through CAPI, CAWI and CATI systems or may be scanned into the computer using optical character-recognition software or they may be entered by hand. After this process, the data will be once again checked or cleaned for keystroke or character-recognition problems.

Data tabulations may also be carried out.

Once this is complete, the data can be analysed.

# Question 12.1

List the sections of a research report and briefly outline what goes into each section.

## Answer

### Title page
This should contain the title of the report. The name and contact details of the agency and the researcher, client details and the date of presentation.

### Contents page
This should contain full details of sections, subsections and page numbers. It should include lists of tables and figures. It should make the report navigable. If presenting on the web, the use of hyperlinks which take the browser to the relevant section can be considered.

### The executive summary
This should be a short summary of the report and its recommendations. Many say that it should be a one- or two-page summary or it should be a maximum of two pages. There are no hard and fast rules. The summary needs to do a job, that is, summarizing a report, and it also needs to be accessible.

### Introduction
The introduction should outline the key objectives of the research, the reasons why the research has been carried out and the constraints that the researchers are working to. It may include profiles and key responsibilities of the researchers.

### Situation analysis and problem definition
This section outlines the background to the problem, and reviews business and marketing objectives. It drills down into the problem's definition and the detailed objectives for the research programme, and reprises the sections of the brief and proposal.

### Research methodology and limitations
This section outlines the detailed methodology for the study. It should cover the research method, the data capture mechanism, the topic or discussion guide or questionnaire, the definition of the population of interest, the sampling approach and the method of data analysis. This section should not be too long. Details should be put into the appendices. It should cover sources of error, including sample size.

### Findings and analysis
The main body of the report should cover the findings relevant to the objectives. It should be constructed to present a solution to the problem, not on a question-by-question basis. The research data should present data to support a line of arguments, and the focus should be on analysis and insight. Key ideas can be supported by tables or quotes from responders. It may include tables and graphics, and it should be linked by a narrative.

### Conclusions and recommendations
This section brings the report to a close. It should present a summary of key findings and recommendations for marketing decisions and future research.

**Appendices**

This should include all supporting data. It contains material that is relevant to the research but that would be too detailed for the main report. It may include all tables, questionnaires, discussion guides and secondary data. It may be that the appendices are longer than the main report.

## Question 12.2

CIM Professional Series Stage Two: Marketing Research and Information

### Donaldson Builders Merchants

Donaldson Builders Merchants is a small chain of builders merchants located in the central belt of Scotland. The company has four outlets located around the edge of the major conurbations of Edinburgh and Glasgow. These supply small builders, plumbers, roofers and similar tradesmen as well as some members of the public (i.e. those more skilled in major do-it-yourself renovations and house improvements). Customers may collect items from the trade counter at the warehouse or have the items delivered direct to the building site or house by the company's fleet of 14 lorries. The lorries are equipped with hoists for handling the larger items.

Donaldson supplies:

- o Timber and timber products
- o Bricks and paving
- o Sand and aggregates
- o Roofing materials
- o Plumbing and heating supplies
- o A small range of hand tools

The company provides credit to the majority of its trade customers. As a result it has a computerized database with details on most of its trade customers relating to name, address, trading address, telephone number, type of business, and purchasing patterns. There are approximately 1100 customers on the database, which probably represents 85 per cent of the company's customers. For the other 15 per cent of customers (the public and trade customers who do not have a credit account), the database holds no record, with the exception of a delivery address if a delivery is required.

The market in which Donaldson operates is becoming more competitive, with the company losing share to national chains such as Jewson and a number of recently opened B&Q trade depots. Tom Donaldson, the Managing Director, feels that the company's personal service and flexibility are far superior to these competitors, and is therefore keen to build on this and find ways in which to compete other than on price. The company has never undertaken research before but is keen to find out more from its customers about:

- o Their existing and future purchasing behaviour
- o Their attitudes towards Donaldson Builders Merchants (such as product range, service, flexibility of delivery, etc.)
- o Their suggestions about improvements required in Donaldson's offering

They are willing to spend up to £50 000 on the research project.

### Part B Question 5

As one of the Directors in the agency that has been awarded the contract for doing the research for Donaldson Builders Merchants in Question 1, you are writing a memorandum to your staff to prepare them for the presentation and evaluation of information at the end of any project. The memorandum should include the following:

(a) An explanation of two approaches that can be used to analyse transcripts from a series of group discussions.

**(10 marks)**

(b) An explanation of the importance of understanding of the audience's thinking sequence to the preparation of the final report.

**(15 marks)**
**(25 marks in total)**

### Answer

### Debriefing Part B Question 5a
You should write in memorandum format and cover two of the following techniques:

- Tabular method
- Cut and paste
- Spidergrams
- Annotation method
- Content analysis software including Nvivo
- Text analysis software

### Debriefing Part B Question 5b
The question relates directly to Wilson's points and you should in memorandum format cover the following audience needs:

- Respect their importance
- What do they need from the report?
- How does your report meet this need?
- Underpin the key information with evidence
- Remind them of the key points of the report
- Make recommendations as to action.

## Question 12.3

June 2005

You are a research executive in a research agency and have been asked to produce a guide for new staff on the communication of research results to client companies. Set out your key guidelines for:

(a) Structuring and writing marketing research reports

**(12 marks)**

(b) The design of tables for communicating data and results

**(5 marks)**

(c) The preparation of oral presentations

**(8 marks)**
**(Total 25 marks)**

# Answer

## PART B Question 5a
*BM Research*

Giles Smith, Research Executive

Guide to communicating research results to clients

June 2005-08-15

Structuring and writing marketing research reports

A first thought is Wilson (2002) audience thinking sequence – think what your audience wants or needs as the basis of what you deliver. Wilson says the audience thinks:

- *Respect me* – provide the right level of details for their knowledge, consider their seniority in the company and the pressures on their time
- *Consider my needs* – what level of detail do they require, why are they here?
- *Tell me how this information will help me* – remind them of their objectives and how this research report can help them
- *Give me the detail that underpins this* – provide the research findings, analysis and conclusions
- *Remind me what you have told me* – summarize what has come before
- *Tell me what I should do next* – provide some recommendations for the next stage and actions required.

With this sequence in mind the report should take the following format:

1. *Title page* – research title, data, contributions and so on
2. *Introduction* – summarize the objectives of the research and what was undertaken
3. *Executive summary* – provide a summary of the findings and conclusions. This section is meant for the busy executive who hasn't the time to read the full report. From reading the introduction and the executive summary he can have an understanding of the whole research project.
4. *Research findings* – The results of the research, the table of qualitative research results, spider diagrams, pie charts, graphs and so on. The analysis of the data
5. *Conclusion and recommendations* – The outcome of the research, the answer to the client's question, fulfilled objectives and recommendation of the next step
6. *Index* – A long report may require an index to enable information to be found easily
7. *Appendices* – Any additional information that may have been referred to in the report, copies of the questionnaires, samples from in-depth interviews and so on.

Reports should be checked for spelling and grammar errors and be provided in the standard company font with blue binding and standard cover and rear sheet.

## PART B Question 5b
Tables should be clear and easy to understand with neat straight lines creating the table (preferably produced in Word or Excel). Areas to consider are:

- Does the table convey the message and results you want to?
- Is it easy to read? In most cases it is best to read down the table rather than across.

- o Does it fit on the document page?
- o Is it clearly labelled, with each column and row labelled too?
- o Is a table the best or the only way to present this data? Is a pie chart or graph better?

Carefully plan what you want the table to convey and then try various layouts/designs until you get it right.

## PART B Question 5c

Oral presentations should still follow Wilson's audience thinking sequence as a basis, but the presentation should be kept short and succinct to ensure the audience doesn't fall asleep! There are also additional considerations with oral presentations:

1. The room – where are you giving this oral presentation? Consider seating, lighting, temperature.
2. The audience – who are they, their level of knowledge, why are they there (compulsory, voluntary)?
3. Presentation tools – overheard projector, flip chart, laptop and projector. Make sure they are present in the room and they work.
4. The presentation itself – the format should be a mini-version of the written report. My advice is to tell the audience what you are going to tell them, tell them, and then remind them what you have told them:

   - o Agenda, presentation content
   - o Introduction
   - o Key findings
   - o Conclusions
   - o Next stage/actions
   - o Questions.

   PowerPoint presentations are fairly standard these days but be sure to keep it simple and the slides clear and easy to read.
5. Questions – Allow time for questions but prepare possible questions and your proposed answers so you are not easily caught out or tripped up.
6. Personal appearance – Make sure you look tidy and comfortable, make eye-contact with the audience and smile. With regards to nerves, everyone is nervous about making a presentation, but make sure you have prepared thoroughly and practised your presentation (in front of a mirror) and then keep calm, breath slowly and deeply and you will be fine!

## Comments

Section 5a – Good answer, using audience thinking sequence and an appropriate report structure. Could possibly have expanded on other areas similar to: assuming understanding, excessive length, unrealistic recommendations, spurious accuracy, obscure statistics, too much gloss, use of tables/graphs.

Section 5b – Could include further information about bases, sources/footnotes etc

Section 5c – Very good answer – could possibly have said a little bit more about the structure of the presentation.

# appendix 5

# past examination papers and examiners' reports

The Chartered
Institute of Marketing

## Professional Diploma
## in Marketing

**42 – Marketing Research and Information**

**Time:**    **09:30 – 12:30**
**Date:**    **6th December 2005**

**3 Hours Duration**

This examination is in **TWO** sections.

**PART A** - Is compulsory and worth **50%** of total marks

**PART B** - Has **FOUR** questions; select **TWO**. Each answer will be worth **25%** of the total marks

**DO NOT** repeat the question in your answer, but show clearly the number of the questions attempted on the appropriate pages of the answer book.

Rough work and notes must be written into the answer book or on supplementary sheets and must be clearly identified.

## Professional Diploma in Marketing

## 42 - Marketing Research and Information

## PART A

Parfumerie de France, which manufactures and sells a range of women's fragrances worldwide, wishes to develop a new style of packaging for its *Aujourdhui* brand. Innovative packaging is a critical differentiating factor in the perfume market, and this may explain Aujourdhui's fall in market share, as it has been using the same pink bulb-shaped bottle for over eight years. Designers have now come up with three new design concepts, but before proceeding with any of these designs, the company requires a programme of marketing research to a) determine market awareness and attitudes towards the Aujourdhui brand and the existing packaging, and b) determine customer and potential customer attitudes and preferences with regard to the new design concepts. Research should initially focus on the European market.

The company hopes that answers to such questions will help in the successful re-launch of the brand.

The company is willing to spend up to £120,000 (approximately US$210,000) on the research project.

*The above data has been based on a real-life organisation, but details have been changed for assessment purposes and do not reflect current management practices.*

## PART A - Compulsory

## Question One

You are a research executive in a market research agency and have been asked to do the following:

a.      identify appropriate further information that you would require from the company, prior to writing a proposal.

*(10 marks)*

b.      having made reasonable assumptions regarding the answers to the information required in Question 1a, produce a proposal to address the research needs of the company. (For the purpose of this question, your proposal should exclude the sections relating to personal CVs, related experience, references and contract details).

*(40 marks)*

*(Total 50 marks)*

## PART B - Answer TWO Questions Only

## Question Two

As a recent graduate recruited to the marketing department of Parfumerie de France, you have received a request from the Marketing Director for a report which addresses the following:

a.      the benefits of developing a database of customers for each of their branded products.

*(9 marks)*

b.      the logistics of collecting the data, in terms of the type of information and the method of collection.

*(9 marks)*

c.      the ethical issues involved in using the customers and information on the database for future marketing research activity.

*(7 marks)*

*(Total 25 marks)*

## Question Three

Design a discussion guide and appropriate projective techniques for use in a series of group discussions to address the research objectives of the project set out in Question1.

*(Total 25 marks)*

## Question Four

The senior executives of Parfumerie de France have asked for your assistance in understanding the concept of sampling in marketing research studies. In particular, they have asked you to write a paper that:

a.      explains how sample size is determined

*(10 marks)*

b.      explains the differences between sampling error and non-sampling error, as well as the manner in which such errors can be reduced.

*(15 marks)*

*(Total 25 marks)*

## Question Five

Discuss the proposition that establishing panels of respondents for marketing research is the only way to overcome falling response rates. Answers should highlight the benefits and drawbacks of this approach over other potential actions aimed at addressing this issue.

*(Total 25 marks)*

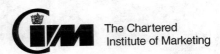

The Chartered
Institute of Marketing

Moor Hall, Cookham
Maidenhead
Berkshire, SL6 9QH, UK
Telephone: 01628 427120
Facsimile: 01628 427158
**www.cim.co.uk**

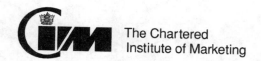

The Chartered
Institute of Marketing

# Professional Diploma in Marketing

## Marketing Research and Information

Time:     09.30 – 12.30

Date:     5th June 2006

3 Hours Duration

This examination is in **TWO** sections.

**PART A** – Is compulsory and worth **50%** of total marks

**PART B** – Has **FOUR** questions; select **TWO**. Each answer will be worth **25%** of the total marks

**DO NOT** repeat the question in your answer, but show clearly the number of the questions attempted on the appropriate pages of the answer book.

Rough work and notes must be written into the answer book or on supplementary sheets and must be clearly identified.

© The Chartered Institute of Marketing 2006

## Professional Diploma in Marketing

## Marketing Research and Information

## PART A

### SeaLux Cruises

SeaLux Cruises is a new cruise operator consisting of two ships sailing out of the port of Southampton in Southern England. It has been established for just over one year and provides cruise-based vacations using its 1,400 berth ship, Med Blue, around the Mediterranean, and cruises around Scandinavia and the Baltic States on its 1,250 berth ship, Northern Blue. The focus is on offering relaxing vacations with an emphasis on 'luxurious discovery' through a wide range of dining, entertainment and excursion choices. A 12-day Mediterranean cruise on the Med Blue with stops in Venice, Barcelona, Rome and five other cities, starts at around £2,000.

Although the first year has gone well with very satisfied passengers and no technical problems, the cruises have been running at below optimum capacity. The level of bookings for the sixteen cruises scheduled for the next 12 months is also around 35% below target. This is causing the company some concern, particularly when industry sources and the performance of competitors clearly suggest that the UK cruise market is going through a period of tremendous growth. There is a view among the senior management of the company that the product offering is correct for the target market but the promotion and sales activity is failing to raise awareness and attract or convert potential passengers.

Unlike other cruise lines that use travel agents to sell their cruises, SeaLux undertakes direct advertising in national newspapers and magazines leading to customers booking direct with SeaLux through their internet site or telephone hotline. The senior management is now concerned that low sales may reflect an unwillingness of the target market (the over 40 age group) to book cruises on a direct basis, as they may require the advice and reassurance of a travel agent. Alternatively, the poor sales may simply reflect a low awareness of the advertising and the company's offerings. SeaLux is therefore keen to undertake a programme of research to examine the effectiveness of the advertising and the attitudes of the target market towards the preferred methods and channels for the booking of cruise-based holidays. The company is willing to spend up to £70,000 on the research project.

*The above data has been based on a fictitious situation drawing on a variety of events and does not reflect the management practices of any particular organisation.*

## PART A – Compulsory

## Question One

You are a Research Executive in a market research agency and have been asked to:

a.    identify appropriate further information that you would require from SeaLux, prior to writing a proposal

**(10 marks)**

Having made reasonable assumptions regarding the answers to the information required in part 1a, produce a proposal[1] to:

b.    address the research needs of the company.

**(40 marks)**

**(Total 50 marks)**

[1] *For the purpose of this question, your proposal should exclude the sections relating to personal CVs, related experience and references and contract details*

## PART B – Answer **TWO** questions only

## Question Two

The senior management of SeaLux is of the opinion that the company should know much more about the characteristics of their passengers. This would be useful in customer profiling, building loyalty and obtaining repeat business. Currently, basic name, address and billing information are stored on the company's computers. You have been asked as a new recruit to the Marketing Department to produce a report which sets out:

a.   the types of information that could be collected on a database about passengers and the approaches that could be adopted to collect such information

**(9 marks)**

b.   the potential benefits that would result from holding such information

**(7 marks)**

c.   the issues involved in attempting to merge the information from the database with the customer satisfaction surveys undertaken at the end of each cruise.

**(9 marks)**

**(Total 25 marks)**

## Question Three

a.   Design a discussion guide for use in a series of group discussions to address the research objectives of the project set out in answer to Question 1.

**(15 marks)**

b.   Provide a detailed description of **TWO** projective techniques that could also be used within the group discussions, alongside the discussion guide, to help address the research objectives.

**(10 marks)**

**(Total 25 marks)**

## Question Four

At the end of each cruise, passengers are asked to complete a customer satisfaction survey using a variety of attitude scales. There has always been disagreement between senior executives within the company regarding the scaling approaches and procedures adopted. You have been asked as a new recruit to the Marketing Department to produce a report which sets out:

a.  the different elements that need to be considered in designing scales for measuring attitudes

**(13 marks)**

b.  the relative advantages and disadvantages of Likert, Semantic Differential and Stapel scales.

**(12 marks)**

**(Total 25 marks)**

## Question Five

"Postal surveys take too long and response rates are typically low. Therefore, it is not usually a worthwhile approach".

a.  Is there any future for marketing research using postal surveys? Give reasons for your viewpoint.

**(8 marks)**

b.  Suggest ways in which you might overcome the disadvantages usually associated with postal surveys. Illustrate your answer with examples.

**(9 marks)**

c.  What advantages and disadvantages would e-mail based surveys offer in comparison with postal surveys?

**(8 marks)**

**(Total 25 marks)**

The Chartered
Institute of Marketing

Moor Hall, Cookham
Maidenhead
Berkshire, SL6 9QH, UK
Telephone: 01628 427120
Facsimile:  01628 427158
**www.cim.co.uk**

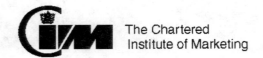

The Chartered
Institute of Marketing

# Professional Diploma in Marketing

## Marketing Research & Information

**SENIOR EXAMINER'S REPORT FOR STUDENTS AND TUTORS**
**JUNE 2006**

**SENIOR EXAMINER'S REPORT**
**FOR STUDENTS AND TUTORS**

MODULE NAME:     MARKETING RESEARCH AND INFORMATION

AWARD NAME:      PROFESSIONAL DIPLOMA IN MARKETING

DATE:            AUGUST 2006

## 1. General Strengths and Weaknesses of Candidates

Some centres clearly demonstrated evidence of good tutoring with cohorts of candidates that understood what was required of them and performed well. In particular, improvements are evident in student's handling of Question 1. However, there are still some groups of candidates who seem to be totally unaware of what is expected of them. By this stage in a subject where the exams have a common format, candidates and their tutors should be aware of the structure and the format of what is required. The vast majority of the candidates avoided doing the more technical question (question 4) relating to attitude scales. In addition, evidence from the proposal question, suggests that knowledge of sampling is still weak.

In the main, there weren't too many borderline fails, the majority of candidates who failed, performed very poorly. There were more A grade answers than previously, although the majority of the passing papers tended to receive an overall grades in the C category.

The poorer candidates had a very superficial knowledge of the subject and tended to only partially address the questions set. Weaker candidates were also unable to apply their knowledge and provided very superficial content to their proposals and questions.

The proposal is worth a large number of marks as it covers a broad sweep of the syllabus. By this stage, candidates should be aware of the structure and key points, however, the scripts suggest that many still need more guidance on tying the selected methodology to the objectives and arguing logically for their recommended approach. If significant marks are lost on Question 1, it is generally difficult for candidates to make up sufficient marks in section (b) to compensate.

## 2. Strengths and Weaknesses by Question

### Question 1.
Most candidates achieved an answer broadly in line with the Marketing Proposal outlined in the marking scheme.

### Part 1a.
There was a significant improvement in the answers to this question. However, some candidates are simply listing a wide range of information that would be relevant for the creation of the background section of the proposal.

It was good to see that more candidates recognised the importance of questions aimed at clarifying the objectives and determining the potential method. Good questions on objectives and methodology included: asking about the role of the research in the company's decision making; clarifying what was meant by advertising effectiveness ; asking whether the client wished to attend any group discussions, determining if the customer database could be used for sampling purposes etc.

**Part 1b.**
In most cases the structure was well handled and matched the format set out in the core textbook. The main weaknesses related to: a very short/ superficial background and rationale section; candidates who simply repeated the objectives from the brief without any further elaboration or clarification; candidates listing all possible methods (including techniques such as mystery shopping which has only very limited relevance to the scenario) rather than selecting a preferred approach; candidates giving no details of the numbers of interviews or the sample being used. In particular, weaker candidates produced a proposal with had very superficial objectives and methodology. In a small number of cases, marketing objectives rather than research objectives were listed. Also some candidates included the full contents of a fully designed questionnaire and/ or discussion guide in the method section with little else. These should not appear in the proposal.

Candidates should remember that the objectives and the method are the most critical parts of a proposal and are therefore awarded the largest proportion of the marks.

**Question 2**
A popular question which was generally handled well. Weaker candidates simply produced bullet-point type answers with no explanation or demonstration of understanding. In part 2a) good candidates used a table with the headings: Type of Information and Collection Methods, this was an efficient and thorough way to summarise the information. Candidates should also attempt to apply their answers to the scenario in the case. Some candidates used the structure of volunteered/ attributed data to classify different types of information, and although this was not wrong, the relevance to the scenario was not always made clear. Part 2b) was generally well handled. In part 2c), candidates needed to demonstrate an understanding of ethics and legislation. Some failed to include the Data Protection Act or the MRS / ESOMAR codes of conduct and their impact on the problem of merging data.

**Question 3**
Another popular question. There seems to be a better global understanding of discussion guides than in previous exams. The content of the discussion guide should match the stated objectives, this wasn't always the case and marks were therefore lost unnecessarily. There were essentially four approaches (i): Topic Guide with 2 Projective Techniques named and applied to the case (with any description or commentary in a margin or in brackets); (ii): Topic Guide with no Projective Techniques (no part b); (iii): Topic Guide with a list of Projective Techniques without application; (iv): Topic Guide with a list of Projective Techniques and a generic description, without application. Only the first was correct although (iv) did achieve passes when well written. In a minority of cases, numerous projective techniques were listed, described and applied. In these cases only the first two were graded by the examiners.

Overall poor answers had no structure or content and were almost certainly less than three sides. A significant number of candidates structured their discussion guide as Introduction – Projective Techniques – Summary – with no discussion topics in the middle part of the discussion guide. Discussion topics need to be identified for the middle of the discussion guide as that is the main part of the group discussion. A few candidates continue to adopt the approach of debating what goes into a focus group rather than creating the research instrument itself – this was not what was asked for.

**Question 4**

This was not a popular question. The small number of candidates who did attempt the question did reasonably well. In part 4(a) candidates were expected to give an account of design considerations that mention Uni- v multi-dimensional scales; Graphic v itemised rating; Non- versus comparative scales; Forced versus non-forced; Unbalanced versus balanced scales; the number of scale positions; whether labels or pictures are used. Some candidates picked up on these aspects, others simply wrote with little structure. In part 4(b) where an explanation of three scales was required candidates generally performed well.

**Question 5**

Poor answers failed to plan and organise answers in a logical and systematic way. Candidates needed to develop a discussion / argument for part 5(a) rather than simply producing bullet point lists of advantages and disadvantages. Better scripts did this . Parts 5(b) and 5(c) were generally well handled with some of the better answers being formulated into a table with columns setting out the disadvantages and suggested courses of action.

**3. Future Themes**

Although the topics and the research scenario will change in future papers, the general format will remain unchanged with a core section relating to a proposal and an elective section of 4 questions linked to the theme of the core section. Concerns about candidate knowledge of sampling and attitude measurement may mean that these will be targeted further in future exams.

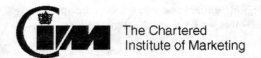

The Chartered
Institute of Marketing

# Professional Diploma
# in Marketing

## Marketing Research and Information

**SENIOR EXAMINER'S REPORT FOR STUDENTS AND TUTORS**

**DECEMBER 2005**

© The Chartered Institute of Marketing, 2006

**SENIOR EXAMINER'S REPORT**

**FOR STUDENTS AND TUTORS**

**MODULE NAME:**    **Marketing Research and Information**

**AWARD NAME:**    **Professional Diploma in Marketing**

---

## 1. General Strengths and Weaknesses of Candidates

Students who were well prepared and had covered the material and practised on past papers performed well. Some centres clearly demonstrated evidence of good tutoring with cohorts of students that understood what was required of them and performed well. Other groups of students seemed to be totally unaware of what was expected of them. By this stage in a subject where the exams have a common format, candidates and their tutors should be aware of the structure and the format of what is required.

Improvements (since June 2005) are evident in students' understanding of what is in a discussion guide, but in a small number of centres, it is evident that the candidates have still been given little guidance at all particularly on Part A. Knowledge of sampling also seems to be weak and the majority of candidates avoided the sampling question.

In the main, there weren't too many borderline fails, the majority of students who failed, performed very poorly. There were also few outstanding papers, with most of the passing candidates receiving C grades.

The poorer candidates had a very superficial knowledge of the subject and tended to only partially address the questions set. Weaker candidates were also unable to apply their knowledge; some students wrote answers that were more suitable for the papers set in June 2005, suggesting that they had learnt previous answers by rote.

The proposal is worth a large number of marks as it covers a broad sweep of the syllabus. By this stage, candidates should be aware of the structure and key points, however, the scripts suggest that many still need more guidance on thinking through possible methodologies. Candidates were still listing a large number of methodologies rather than focusing on the one or two appropriate to the situation in the question. It is the appropriate application of techniques (and the appropriate numbers of interviews/groups etc) rather than the number of mentions of different techniques that is rewarded. If significant marks are lost on Question 1, it is generally difficult for students to make up sufficient marks in Part B to compensate.

## 2. Strengths and Weaknesses by Question

### Question 1

Most candidates achieved an answer broadly in line with the Marketing Proposal outlined in the marking scheme.

### Part 1a

The main weakness in part a) was that candidates simply listed a wide range of information that would be relevant for the creation of the background section of the proposal. Very few considered the information required for clarifying the objectives (an important area) and determining the potential method. Questions do need to be asked to help plan the research approach, such as, can the company database be used for research or the geographic limits of the study? Overall, few candidates scored more than 5 or 6 out of the available 10 marks.

### Part 1b

In most cases, the structure was well handled and matched the format set out in the core textbook. The main weaknesses related to: candidates who simply repeated the objectives from the brief without any further elaboration or clarification; candidates listing all possible methods (including techniques such as mystery shopping, which has no relevance to the scenario at all) rather than selecting a preferred approach; candidates giving no details of the numbers of interviews or the sample being used. In particular, many candidates produced a proposal with very superficial objectives and methodology. These are the most critical parts of a proposal and are awarded the largest proportion of the marks. Poor answers tended to involve regurgitation of generic subject matter from past papers with the hope that it may be relevant to this particular proposal. However, better candidates did demonstrate understanding of methods such as hall tests and sampling than was the case in the past

### Question 2

A popular question. Candidates tended to answer part a) well with better answers identifying numerous examples to support the points. In part b), good candidates provided a range of types on information and collection methods. Some even used a table with the headings Type of Information and Collection Methods, this was an efficient and thorough way to summarise the information. Poorer answers were very short and superficial with some students simply going through different marketing research methods rather than thinking of other ways of gathering customer information. In part c), some candidates demonstrated a clear understanding of data protection and marketing research code of conduct issues, others had only a limited and superficial knowledge of data protection

## Question 3

Another popular question. The content of the discussion guide should match the stated objectives, this wasn't always the case and marks were therefore lost unnecessarily. A number of candidates listed a whole range of projective techniques, (sometimes as many as 8-9), combined with a very superficial discussion guide. The better performing candidates produced a well structured and relevant discussion guide with two or three well explained and relevant projective techniques. The projective techniques should be relevant to the topics being asked rather than simply regurgitating techniques that had been used in past papers. A significant number of candidates structured their discussion guide as: Introduction, Projective Techniques and Summary, with no discussion topics in the middle part of the discussion guide. Discussion topics need to be identified for the middle of the discussion guide as that is the main part of the group discussion, and projective techniques alone are unlikely to provide all the information that is required. A few candidates adopted the approach of debating what goes into a focus group rather than creating the research instrument itself – this was not what was asked for.

## Question 4

This was not a popular question and there were few very good answers. Better candidates tackled each part of the question reasonably well. Weaker candidates generally failed to write anything meaningful or simply listed every sampling technique they could think of (which had no relevance to the question). There were very few candidates in between these extremes. Part b), in particular, was generally handled poorly.

## Question 5

Some candidates produced well argued answers to this question. Others produced poorly structured answers that frequently failed to address the question. A worrying number of candidates confused a panel with a focus group, and talked about focus groups throughout their answer.

### 3. Future Themes

Although the topics and the research scenario will change in future papers, the general format will remain unchanged with a core section relating to a proposal and an elective section of 4 questions linked to the theme of the core section. The low awareness of panels and sampling suggests that these areas will need to be explored further in future papers.

# appendix 6
# curriculum information and reading list

## Aim

The Marketing Research and Information unit covers the management of customer information and research projects as part of the marketing process. It provides students with both the knowledge and skills to manage marketing information and the more specialist knowledge and skills required to plan, undertake and present results from market research.

This unit is a joint syllabus, shared with the Marketing Research Society.

## Related statements of practice

Ac.1   Identify information requirements and manage research projects and the MkIS.
Ac.2   Evaluate and present information for business advantage.
Bc.1   Contribute information and ideas to the strategy process.

## Learning outcomes

Students will be able to

8.41.1   Identify appropriate marketing information and marketing research requirements for business decision-making.
8.41.2   Plan for and manage the acquisition, storage, retrieval and reporting of information on the organization's market and customers.
8.41.3   Explain the process involved in purchasing market research and the development of effective client–supplier relationships.
8.41.4   Write a research brief to meet the requirements of an organization to support a specific plan or business decision.
8.41.5   Develop a research proposal to fulfil a given research brief.
8.41.6   Evaluate the appropriateness of different qualitative and quantitative research methodologies to meet different research situations.
8.41.7   Design and plan a research programme.
8.41.8   Design a questionnaire and discussion guide.

8.41.9 Interpret quantitative and qualitative data and present coherent and appropriate recommendations that lead to effective marketing and business decisions.
8.41.10 Critically evaluate the outcomes and quality of a research project.
8.41.11 Explain the legal, regulatory, ethical and social responsibilities of organizations involved in gathering, holding and using information.

# Knowledge and skill requirements

Element 1: Information and research for decision-making (15 per cent)

1.1 Demonstrate a broad appreciation of the need for information in marketing management and its role in the overall marketing process.
1.2 Explain the concept of knowledge management and its importance in a knowledge-based economy.
1.3 Explain how organizations determine their marketing information requirements and the key elements of user specifications for information.
1.4 Demonstrate an understanding of marketing management support systems and their different formats and components.

Element 2: Customer databases (15 per cent)

2.1 Demonstrate an understanding of the application, the role in customer relationship management (CRM) and the benefits of customer databases.
2.2 Describe the process for setting up a database.
2.3 Explain how organizations profile customers and prospects.
2.4 Explain the principles of data warehouses, data marts and data mining.
2.5 Explain the relationship between database marketing and marketing research.

Element 3: Marketing research in context (25 per cent)

3.1 Describe the nature and structure of the market research industry.
3.2 Explain the stages of the market research process.
3.3 Describe the procedures for selecting a market research supplier.
3.4 Identify information requirements to support a specific business decision in an organization and develop a research brief to meet the requirements.
3.5 Develop a research proposal to fulfil a given research brief.
3.6 Explain the ethical and social responsibilities inherent in the market research task.

Element 4: Research methodologies (30 per cent)

4.1 Explain the uses, benefits and limitations of secondary data.
4.2 Recognize the key sources of primary and secondary data.
4.3 Describe and compare the various procedures for observing behaviour.
4.4 Describe and compare the various methods for collecting qualitative and quantitative data.
4.5 Design a questionnaire and discussion guide to meet a project's research objectives.
4.6 Explain the theory and processes involved in sampling.

Element 5: Presenting and evaluating information to develop business advantage (15 per cent)

5.1 Demonstrate an ability to use techniques for analysing qualitative and quantitative data.
5.2 Write a research report aimed at supporting marketing decisions.
5.3 Plan and design an oral presentation of market research results.
5.4 Use research and data to produce actionable recommendations for a marketing plan or to support a business decision.

## Related key skills

| Key skill | Relevance to unit knowledge and skills |
| --- | --- |
| Communication | Develop a research brief<br>Develop a research proposal or plan<br>Present research results to decision-makers |
| Application of number | Determine information requirements for a business or marketing decision<br>Plan a research project<br>Use quantitative research methods, analysis and calculations |
| Information technology | Use IT tools for research planning<br>Use IT tools to acquire, store, retrieve and communicate research data |
| Working with others | |
| Improving own learning and performance | Review current capabilities. Identify opportunities and set realistic targets for development and learning<br>Plan how these targets will be met (methods, timescales, resources)<br>Use a variety of methods for learning<br>Seek feedback, monitor performance and modify approach<br>Assess effectiveness of learning and development approach |
| Problem solving | Use research to establish the critical features of a business or marketing problem |

## Assessment

CIM will normally offer two forms of assessment for this unit from which study centres may choose: written examination and an assignment. CIM may also recognize, or make joint awards for, units at an equivalent level undertaken with other professional marketing bodies and educational institutions.

## Recommended support materials

### Core texts

Wilson, A. (2002) *Marketing Research: An integrated approach*, London: FT Prentice Hall.

## Workbooks

Housden, M. (2006) *Marketing Research and Information*, Oxford: Butterworth-Heinemann.

BPP (2006) *Marketing Research and Information Study Text*. London: BPP Publishing.

## Supplementary readings

Birn, R.J. (2002) *Handbook of International Market Research Techniques*, London: Kogan Page.

BPP (2006) *Marketing Research and Information: Practice and Revision Kit*. London: BPP Publishing.

Brace, I (2004) *Questionnaire Design: How to Plan, Structure and Write Survey Material for Effective Market Research*. London: Kogan Page.

Butterworth-Heinemann (2006) *CIM Revision Cards: Marketing Research and Information*. Oxford: Butterworth-Heinemann.

Christopher, M., Payne, A. and Ballantyne, D. (2002) *Relationship Marketing: Creating Shareholder Value*, 3rd edition, Oxford: Butterworth-Heinemann.

Gordon, W. (1999) *Goodthinking: A Guide to Qualitative Research*, Henley on Thames: Admap.

Tapp, A. (2005) *Principles of Direct and Database Marketing*, 3rd edition. Harlow: FT Prentice Hall.

## Marketing journals

Students can keep abreast of developments in the academic field of marketing by reference to the main marketing journals, a selection of which is listed in the Appendix to this document.

## Press

Students will be expected to have access to current examples of marketing campaigns and so should be sure to keep up to date with the appropriate marketing and quality daily press. A selection of marketing press titles is given in the Appendix to this document.

## Websites

A list of websites that tutors and students may find useful is shown in the Appendix at the end of this document.

# Overview and rationale

## Approach

This unit aims to provide students with both the knowledge and skills to manage customer information and the more specialist knowledge and skills required to plan, undertake and present results from market research. This is a joint CIM and MRS unit reflecting the importance of effective gathering, managing and using of customer information to members of both professional bodies.

This unit's focus on customer information and market research builds on the Marketing Environment unit of the CIM's Professional Certificate syllabus, which examines the broader elements involved in analysing an organization's marketing environment. Students are expected to be familiar with the contents of the Marketing Environment unit before starting on this unit.

The unit addresses all of the activities involved in managing a market research project from the initial brief through to the completion of the final written report. It integrates the management of this process with the management of an organization's customer databases.

## Syllabus content

The balance of weighting allocated to each of the five elements of the syllabus reflect the importance of the area to the achievement of learning and performance outcomes, and the depth and breadth of material to be covered. Although each area may be regarded as a discrete element, there are clear progressions and overlaps in the knowledge and skills base considered, which has important implications for the delivery of the unit.

### Element 1: Information and research for decision-making (15 per cent)
This element focuses on the importance of information and particularly customer information to marketing planning and management decisions. It is important that students understand how research and information integrate with the overall marketing process. Within this, the concept of knowledge management and marketing management support systems should be explored.

### Element 2: Customer databases (15 per cent)
Organizations may hold large amounts of information about customers and their behaviour in customer databases. This element looks at the tasks involved in managing and using the information stored in customer databases. It introduces the concepts of data warehouses, data marts and data mining. It also examines the boundaries between database marketing and marketing research. The role of customer databases within CRM should also be explored.

### Element 3: Marketing research in context (25 per cent)
This element provides an overview of the market research industry and how it operates as well as its ethical and social responsibilities. It also introduces the various stages of the marketing research process. The material places particular focus on the initial planning of the research and the agency selection process. As such, emphasis should be placed on developing practical skills in writing research briefs and research proposals.

### Element 4: Research methodologies (30 per cent)
This element focuses on the methods used in secondary and primary (qualitative and quantitative) data collection. Students should be able to compare different approaches as well as design a questionnaire and discussion guide. Probability and non-probability sampling theory and processes should also be fully understood.

## Element 5: Presenting and evaluating information to develop business advantage (15 per cent)

This element focuses on the evaluation of information (qualitative and quantitative) as well as the communication of information (both verbally and in writing) to assist marketing decision-making. Although students will not be tested on their ability to undertake statistical analysis, they are expected to show an understanding of various statistical techniques and their outputs. Knowledge and understanding of the communication of results is important in this element; however, there is also a large amount of skill development required.

### Delivery approach

Although it is expected that learning outcomes should be achieved as discrete goals of attainment, it is also expected that tutors recognize and impart an understanding of the integrated nature of the syllabus content. To achieve this, the continuous assessment could involve the students undertaking a research project or assessing a case involving a total research project. Practical exercises, such as the development of research briefs, proposals, questionnaires, topic guides and sampling plans, are critical to the development of skills required within this unit. It is important that the projects or case studies illustrate the integration of research and information with the marketing process as a whole.

## Additional resources (Syllabus – Professional Diploma in Marketing)

### Introduction

Texts to support the individual units are listed in the syllabus for each unit. This Appendix shows a list of marketing journals, press and websites that tutors and students may find useful in supporting their studies at Professional Diploma.

### Marketing journals

Students can keep abreast of developments in the academic field of marketing by reference to the main marketing journals.

- Corporate Reputation Review – Henry Stewart
- *European Journal of Marketing* – Emerald
- *Harvard Business Review* – Harvard
- *International Journal of Advertising* – WARC
- *International Journal of Corporate Communications* – Emerald
- *International Journal of Market Research* – NTC Pubs
- *International Journal of Market Research* – WARC
- *Journal of the Academy of Marketing Science* – Sage Publications
- *Journal of Consumer Behaviour An International Review* – Henry Stewart
- *Journal of Marketing* – American Marketing Assoc. Pubs Group
- *Journal of Marketing Communications* – Routledge
- *Journal of Marketing Management* – Westburn Pubs Ltd
- *Journal of Product and Brand Management* – Emerald
- *Journal of Services Marketing* – Emerald
- *Marketing Review* – Westburn Pubs Ltd.

## Press

Students will be expected to have access to current examples of marketing campaigns and so should be sure to keep up to date with the appropriate marketing and quality daily press, including:

- *Campaign* – Haymarket
- *Internet Business* – Haymarket
- *Marketing* – Haymarket
- *Marketing Business* – Chartered Institute of Marketing
- *Marketing Week* – Centaur
- *Revolution* – Haymarket.

## Websites

| | |
|---|---|
| *The Chartered Institute of Marketing* | |
| www.cim.co.uk | The CIM site with information and access to learning support for students |
| www.cim.co.uk/learningzone | Full details of all that's new in CIM's educational offer including specimen answers and Hot Topics |
| *Publications on-line* | |
| www.revolution.haynet.com | Revolution magazine |
| www.FT.com | A wealth of information for cases (now charging) |
| www.IPA.co.uk | Need to register – communication resources |
| www.booksites.net | Financial Times/Prentice Hall Text websites |
| *Sources of useful information* | |
| www.acnielsen.co.uk | AC Nielsen – excellent for research |
| www.elsevierbooks.com | |
| http://advertising.utexas.edu/world/ | Resources for advertising and marketing professionals, students and tutors |
| www.bized.com | Case studies |
| www.corporateinformation.com | Worldwide sources listed by country |
| www.esomar.org. | European Body representing Research Organizations – useful for guidelines on research ethics and approaches |
| www.dma.org.uk | The Direct Marketing Association |
| www.eiu.com | The Economist Intelligence Unit |
| www.euromonitor.com | Euromonitor consumer markets |
| www.europa.eu.int | The European Commission's extensive range of statistics and reports relating to EU and member countries. |
| www.managementhelp.org/research/research.htm | Part of the 'Free Management Library' – explaining research methods |
| www.marketresearch.org.uk | The MRS site with information and access to learning support for students – useful links on ethics and code of conduct |
| www.mmc.gov.uk | Summaries of Competition Commission reports |
| www.oecd.org | OECD statistics and other information relating to member nations including main economic indicators |
| www.quirks.com | An American source of information on marketing research issues and projects. |
| www.statistics.gov.uk | UK Government statistics |
| www.un.org | United Nations publish statistics on member nations |

www.worldbank.org

World bank economic, social and natural resource indicators for over 200 countries. Includes over 600 indicators covering GNP per capita, growth, economic statistics and so on.

*Case sites*
www.bluelagoon.co.uk
www.ebay.com
www.glenfiddich.com
www.interflora.co.uk
www.moorcroft.co.uk
www.ribena.co.uk

Case – SME website address
Online auction – buyer behaviour
Interesting site for case and branding
E-commerce direct ordering
Good for relationship marketing
Excellent targeting and history of comms

© CIM 2007

# Index